40,000 SELECTED WORDS

Organized by Letter Sound and Syllable

Valeda D. Blockcolsky, M.S., CCC-SLP
Joan M. Frazer, M.S., CCC-SLP
Douglas H. Frazer, B.A., J.D.

Communication Skill Builders ®
a division of
The Psychological Corporation
555 Academic Court
San Antonio, Texas 78204-2498
1-800-228-0752

Preface

40,000 Selected Words is a sourcebook of words sorted by consonant sounds in the English language. It has been prepared for Communication Disorder Specialists, teachers in Special Education and ESL, regular classroom teachers, students, parents, and professionals dedicated to the task of improving communication skills. The lists are comprehensive and varied enough to be used with children or adults.

Professionals who teach speech sounds to students use materials that facilitate teaching consonant sounds and blends. When professionals control each level of complexity, student success rate should be enhanced. The variables that control these levels may be the length of a word, the phonetic environment of the sound, the position of the sound in a word, and the combination of blends or clusters within a word. This book extends the range of materials available by offering a large selection of words organized according to these variables.

These alphabetical word lists are arranged with each consonant sound in initial, medial, and final positions. The blends or sound clusters for each consonant follow in family groupings (for example, /br/ initial, /br/ medial, /rb/ medial, /rb/ final). Consonant blends are listed under each consonant in the blend (the /br/ blend will be found in the /b/ section as well as in the /r/ section).

The first letters of each heading represent the sounds of words in the list. They do not always match the spellings of the words in the list. Phonetic symbols of the International Phonetic Alphabet (IPA) are shown between slashes / / after the letter representation.

Each group of words representing a consonant blend, in a specific position, is organized by number of syllables. Words of 1 to 6 syllables may be listed.

Contents

viii • Contents

B

Pronounced: /b/
Spelled: b, bb

B /b/ Initial—one syllable

baa	barn	beech
babe	barred	beef
Babs	base	been
back	bask	beet
bad	basked	beg
bade	bass	begged
badge	baste	bell
bag	bat	belle
bail	bath	Belle
bailed	bathe	belt
bait	bathed	bench
bake	bawl	benched
baked	bawled	bend
bald	bay	bent
bale	be	Bert
ball	Bea	berth
balm	beach	best
ban	beached	bet
band	bead	Beth
bang	beak	bib
banged	beam	bid
bank	beamed	bide
banned	bean	bier
bar	bear	bike
barb	beard	biked
Barb	beast	bile
bare	beat	bilge
bared	beau	bilk
bark	bed	bilked
barked	bee	bill

[1]

Bill	boon	built
billed	boot	bulb
bills	booth	bulge
bin	bore	bulk
bind	bored	bump
Bip	born	bun
birch	borne	bunch
bird	boss	bunk
birth	botch	bunt
bit	both	burl
bite	bought	Burl
boar	bounce	burn
board	bound	Burns
boast	bout	burnt
boat	bow	burr
bob	bowed	Burr
Bob	bowl	burst
bobbed	bowled	bus
bog	box	bush
bogged	boxed	bussed
boil	boy	but
boiled	Boyd	Butch
bold	Bub	buy
bolt	buck	buzz
bond	Bucks	by
bone	bud	bye
boo	Bud	Byrd
book	budge	byte
booked	buff	_____
boom	bug	_____
boomed	build	_____

B /b/ Initial—two syllables

baba	backache	backing
babble	backfire	backlash
babbled	backfired	backlog
babies	background	backstop
baboon	backhand	backup
baby	backhouse	backwoods

bacon	barter	bedside
badger	bartered	bedspread
badgered	baseball	bedtime
baffle	baseboard	beehive
baffled	basement	beeline
baggage	bashful	beeswax
bagpipe	basic	before
balance	basket	began
balanced	baton	Bella
ballad	batter	Belmont
ballet	battle	bender
balloon	battled	Berlin
ballot	Bayley	Bernard
balsa	Baylor	Bernice
balsam	bayou	berry
Bambi	beach ball	Berry
bamboo	beach boy	Bertha
bandage	beachhead	Beryl
bandaged	beacon	Bessie
bandit	beagle	Bethel
bandstand	beaker	Bethune
Bangor	bean-bag	betroth
banjo	beanie	betrothed
banker	bearing	Betsy
banking	beating	Betty
banner	beaver	bias
banter	because	biased
bantered	beckon	Bible
barber	beckoned	biceps
bareback	Becky	bidder
barely	becloud	Big Bird
bargain	become	bigot
bargained	bedbug	big top
barley	bedding	bike path
baron	bedlam	biking
barracks	bed rest	billboard
barrage	bedrock	billfold
barraged	bedroll	billiards
barrel	bedroom	billion

billow
billowed
Billy
binder
binding
biped
birdbath
birdhouse
birdseed
birthday
birthstone
biscuit
bishop
bison
bitter
bizarre
boa
boardwalk
boasted
boastful
Bobbi
bobbin
Bobby
bobcat
bobsled
bobtail
bodice
body
bogus
boiler
Boise
bolster
bombard
Bombay
bonbon
bonfire
bongo
Bonnie
bonus

boohoo
bookcase
bookend
bookmark
bookshelf
bookworm
booster
booting
border
bordered
boric
borrow
borrowed
bossy
Boston
bother
bothered
bottle
bottled
bottling
bottom
bouillon
boulder
Boulder
bounty
bouquet
bowstring
boxcar
boxer
boxing
boycott
boyish
Boy Scouts
bubble
bubbled
bucket
buckle
buckled
buckskin

Buddha
buddy
Buddy
budget
buffer
buffered
buffet
buffoon
buggy
builder
building
build-up
bulky
bulldog
bulldoze
bullfrog
bullied
bully
bumper
bumpy
bundle
bundled
bungle
bungled
bunk bed
bunny
Bunyan
buoy
burden
burdened
burgher
buried
burlap
Burma
Burmese
burned-out
burner
burrow
burrowed

Burton	butter	byline
bury	buttered	byname
bushel	button	bypass
bushy	buttoned	bypassed
business	buzzard	byway
busy	buzzer	_____
butcher	buzzing	_____
butchered	bygone	_____
butler	bylaw	_____

B /b/ Initial—three syllables

Babinski	basketball	Benita
babushka	bassinet	Benjamin
baby doll	Baton Rouge	Bermuda
Babylon	battalion	Bernadine
babysat	battery	Bethlehem
babysit	battleship	betrothal
bachelor	bayberry	beverage
backgammon	Bay City	Beverly
backhanded	bay window	bewilder
badminton	beachcomber	bewildered
bakery	beanshooter	bicuspid
Balboa	Beatrice	bicycle
balcony	becoming	bifocal
ballistics	bedridden	big-hearted
baloney	beforehand	bike safety
Baltimore	befuddle	bilingual
banana	befuddled	billionaire
bandana	beginner	bimonthly
bandmaster	beginning	bird watcher
bandwagon	begonia	bittersweet
banister	behavior	biweekly
bankruptcy	beholden	boardinghouse
baritone	belated	bobby socks
barnacle	belittle	bobolink
barricade	belittled	bobsledding
barrier	belongings	bodily
barrister	beloved	bodyguard
baseball park	benefit	boisterous

bologna
bonanza
bon voyage
bookkeeper
boomerang
bootery
borderline
botany
boulevard
bountiful
bowlegged
bubble bath
bubble gum
buccaneer

bucketful
Buckingham
buckle-up
buffalo
buffaloed
bulldozer
bulletin
bumblebee
bungalow
Bunker Hill
buoyancy
bushmaster
businesslike
businessman

bus safety
bus station
buttercup
butterfly
buttermilk
butternut
butterscotch
buttonhole
bypassing
by-product
_____
_____
_____
_____

B /b/ Initial—four syllables

baby buggy
baby carriage
bacteria
baking powder
baking soda
barometer
Bavarian
belligerent
benediction
benefactor
beneficial

Beverly Hills
bicarbonate
bilateral
biography
biologist
biology
biophysics
boating safety
Bohemian
boilermaker
bone conduction

boogie-woogie
Bostonian
botanical
Boulder Canyon
Boulder City
business woman
butterfly net
buying power
_____
_____
_____

B /b/ Medial—two syllables

Abby
Abel
abide
aboard
abound
about
above
abyss
Babar
Babbitt

babies
baboon
baby
backbone
bareback
bedbug
bobber
Bobbi
bobbin
bobbing

Bobby
bobcat
booby
cabby
cabin
caboose
chubby
clobber
cobweb
cowbell

cowboy	labored	rubbing
Cuba	Libby	ruby
cubic	lobby	Ruby
cupboard	logbook	scrubbing
debate	lubber	Seabee
Debbie	Lubbock	shabby
debug	Mabel	Sibyl
debut	Mabelle	skyborne
dobbin	mailbox	slobber
dubbing	maybe	sober
Eben	mobile	soybean
fibber	neighbor	subject
fibbing	obey	subway
fiber	obeyed	tabby
gabby	oboe	Tabby
Gaby	Phoebe	taboo
Gibby	rabbit	tea bag
go-by	rabid	throbbing
good-bye	Rayburn	Toby
grabbing	Reba	toyboat
grubby	rebate	tubby
habit	rebel	tuber
Hibbing	rebid	tubing
high beam	rebind	tugboat
high boy	rebirth	two-bits
Hobbit	reborn	Wabash
hobble	rebound	webbing
hobby	rebuild	whalebone
hubbub	rebus	Yuba
hubby	rebut	_____
hubcap	Reuben	_____
jabber	ribbon	_____
jabbered	Robbie	_____
jabot	Robbin	_____
jay bird	Robert	_____
keyboard	robin	_____
kickball	robot	_____
knobby	Robyn	_____
labor	rubber	_____

B /b/ Medial—three syllables

abdomen
Abigail
abolish
abounding
about face
aboveboard
above ground
abutment
acrobat
adobe
aerobics
alphabet
Annabelle
Audobon
autobahn
babushka
babydoll
baby grand
Babylon
baby-sit
baby step
baby talk
baby tears
baby tooth
basketball
bayberry
blackberry
blueberry
Bobbielee
bobby pin
bobbysocks
bobolink
bugaboo
cabinet
candy bar
cheeseburger
chili beans
cowboy boots

cowboy hat
cubbyhole
data base
day labor
debated
debating
debonair
Deborah
dewberry
dubious
ebony
fabulous
fiberglass
foam rubber
gaberdine
gadabout
gazebo
gibberish
Gila Bend
good-neighbor
habitat
halibut
hawberry
hibernate
hobby-horse
honeybee
inhabit
jubilant
Labor Day
laborer
labor force
labyrinth
ladybug
liberal
liberate
liberty
lima beans
lobbying

log cabin
Nairobi
navy beans
neighborhood
nobody
obelisk
obeying
obsessive
October
peek-a-boo
phobia
pinto beans
Rebecca
rebounder
rebounding
rebozo
rebuilding
rebuttal
Rock-a-Bye
rubber band
rubber stamp
rubbery
sabotage
safety belt
shabbier
shabbiest
shrubbery
somebody
stabilize
storybook
strawberry
subsequent
tubercle
tuberous
vagabond
volleyball
wallaby

B /b/ Medial—four syllables

abalone	baby carriage	obedient
abolition	chinaberry	observation
absolution	debility	protuberant
Alabama	deliberate	tubercular
anybody	inhabited	Winnebago
baboonery	neighborhood watch	_____
baby buggy	nobility	_____

B /b/ Medial—five syllables

abomination	inability	subterranean
aborigine	obituary	_____
Babylonian	observatory	_____
disability	submarine captain	_____

B /b/ Final—one syllable

Abe	drab	lab
babe	drub	lob
bib	dub	lobe
blab	ebb	lube
blob	fib	mob
bob	flab	nab
Bob	flub	nub
bribe	fob	probe
Bub	gab	pub
cab	Gabe	rib
chub	gibe	rob
club	glib	Rob
cob	globe	robe
Cobb	gob	rub
crab	grab	Rube
crib	grub	SAAB
cub	hob	scab
cube	hub	scribe
dab	jab	scrub
daub	jibe	shrub
deb	job	Sib
Deb	Job	slab
dib	knob	slob

snob	swab	tube
snub	tab	web
sob	Tab	_____
strobe	throb	_____
stub	tribe	_____
sub	tub	_____

B /b/ Final—two syllables

ad-lib	fan club	press club
ascribe	flashcube	Punjab
backrub	girls club	rehab
ball club	glass tube	sand crab
bathrobe	glee club	sand dab
bathtub	golf club	sea crab
bike tube	health club	ski club
book club	hobnob	Skylab
boys club	hubbub	smack-dab
Calab	ice cube	snow job
carob	imbibe	sparerib
Cherub	inscribe	subscribe
cobweb	Jacob	test tube
confab	Joab	tire tube
corncob	kabob	transcribe
corn crib	Kaibab	tree crab
Danube	king crab	wardrobe
Deneb	Moab	wolf cub
describe	mole crab	yacht club
doll crib	nabob	_____
doorknob	prefab	_____
ear lobe	prescribe	_____

B /b/ Final—three syllables

astrolabe	flying club	kennel club
beef kabob	Four-H Club	lion cub
Blue Danube	garden club	Lion's Club
bouillon cube	giant crab	Mr. Webb
Christmas club	health spa club	oyster crab
cotton swab	inner tube	pedicab
country club	jockey club	photo lab

picture tube
Piper Cub
reading lab
rub-a-dub
running club

service club
shish kebab
soft-shell crab
spider web
tanning club

taxicab
ticket stub
women's club
writing lab

_____

BL /bl/ Initial—one syllable

blab
blabbed
black
blade
Blaine
Blake
blame
blamed
blanch
Blanche
bland
blank
blare
blared
blast
blaze
blazed
bleach
bleached
bleak
blear
bleat
bled

bleed
blench
blend
bless
blessed
blest
blew
blight
blimp
blind
blink
blinked
blintz
blip
bliss
blithe
blitz
bloat
blob
bloc
block
blocked
blocks

blond
blood
bloom
bloomed
blot
blotch
blotched
blouse
blow
blown
blue
blues
bluff
bluffed
blunt
blur
blurb
blurred
blurt
blush
blushed
Blythe

_____

BL /bl/ Initial—two syllables

blackball
blackballed
black bear
black belt
blackbird
blackboard
blacken

Blackett
black eye
black flag
Blackfoot
blackhead
blacking
blacklist

blackmail
blackmailed
blackout
Black Sea
black sheep
blacksmith
blackthorn

blacktop
black whale
blameless
blanket
blarney
blasé
blaspheme
blasphemed
blast off
blatant
blazer
blazon
blazoned
bleachers
bleary
blemish
blemished
blcsscd
blessing
blinder
blinders
blindfold
blinding
blinker
blinkers
blissful
blister

blistered
blithesome
blizzard
blockade
blocker
blockhead
blockhouse
bloodhound
bloodline
bloodstream
blood test
blossom
blossomed
blotchy
blotter
blower
blowgun
blowout
blowpipe
blowtorch
blubber
blubbered
bluebell
blue belt
bluebird
blue cheese
blue fish

bluegill
bluegrass
blue jay
blue jeans
blue moon
blueprint
bluer
Blue Ridge
blue shark
blue sky
bluest
bluets
blue whale
bluffer
bluffing
bluing
bluish
blunder
blundered
bluster
blustered
Blytheville
_____
_____
_____
_____
_____

BL /bl/ Initial—three syllables

black and blue
blackberry
black market
black widow
blamelessly
blameworthy
blandishing
blandishment
blasphemy
bleeding heart

blindman's bluff
blockbuster
bloodmobile
blood pressure
Blue Angels
blueberry
bluebonnet
bluebottle
blue color
bluejacket

blue marlin
Blue Moutains
blue ribbon
blustery
_____
_____
_____
_____
_____
_____

BL /bl/ Medial—two syllables

ablaze
abloom
babbling
bubbling
bubbly
cobbler
dabbling
doublet
doubly
dribbling
emblaze
emblem
gambling
giblet
glibly
gobbler
gobbling
goblet

goblin
grabbler
hobbling
mumbling
nibbling
nimbly
nosebleed
oblate
oblige
oblique
oblong
problem
public
publish
pueblo
Pueblo
rambler
Red Bluff

sandblast
sand-blind
semblance
sibling
squabbling
sublease
sublet
sublime
tableau
tablet
trembling
troubling
tumbler
tumbling
warbler
warbling
wobbly
_____

BL /bl/ Medial—three syllables

ablation
ablution
cable car
emblazing
emblazon
emblem book
emblements
establish
established
Navy blue

night blindness
notably
obligate
obliging
obligor
public school
publisher
publishing
red-blooded
republic

resemblance
San Pablo
shoulder blade
sublimate
unpublished
_____
_____
_____
_____

BL /bl/ Medial—four syllables

ablactating
ablepsia
army blanket
baby-blue eyes
disestablish
emblazonment

establishment
obligation
obligato
oblique angle
obliterate
publication

public domain
publicity
publishing house
reestablish
republican
subliminal

BL /bl/ Final—two syllables

Abel	gobble	scribble
able	grumble	squabble
amble	hobble	stable
babble	humble	stubble
Bible	jumble	stumble
brabble	label	Sybil
bramble	libel	table
bubble	marble	thimble
bumble	mumble	treble
cable	nibble	tremble
crumble	nimble	tribal
cymbal	noble	trouble
dabble	pebble	tumble
double	quibble	verbal
drabble	ramble	wabble
dribble	rebel	waddle
fable	rubble	warble
feeble	ruble	wobble
fumble	rumble	_____
gable	sable	_____
gamble	scramble	_____
global	scribal	_____

BL /bl/ Final—three syllables

affable	legible	soluble
assemble	liable	suitable
audible	livable	syllable
cannibal	lovable	terrible
capable	notable	timetable
constable	portable	unable
decibel	possible	usable
disable	preamble	_____
durable	probable	_____
edible	quotable	_____
flammable	resemble	_____
flexible	sellable	_____
gullible	sensible	_____
horrible	sociable	_____

BL /bl/ Final—four syllables

acceptable
advisable
agreeable
answerable
available
comfortable
convertible
dependable
desirable
eligible
enjoyable
favorable
formidable
habitable
handleable
honorable
Honorable
hospitable

illegible
impossible
incredible
inedible
inflammable
invisible
miserable
perishable
practicable
preferable
presentable
profitable
questionable
reasonable
reassemble
receivable
reliable
remarkable

respectable
responsible
separable
tolerable
unchangeable
unmatchable
unprintable
unquenchable
unspeakable
unsuitable
unthinkable
valuable
variable
vegetable
veritable
vulnerable
_____
_____

BL /bl/ Final—five syllables

dishonorable
indivisible
inevitable
inhospitable
innumerable
inoperable
irresistible
recoverable

unalterable
unapproachable
unavoidable
unbelievable
undesirable
unmistakable
unprofitable
unquestionable

unreasonable
unreliable
unutterable
unwarrantable
_____
_____
_____
_____

LB /lb/ Medial—two syllables

Albert
album
ball bat
ball boy
bellbird
bell book
bell boy
billboard

callboard
call box
coalbin
Delbert
Elbe
Elbert
Elbie
elbow

file box
Galbraith
Gilbert
Holbrook
mailbag
mailbox
Melba
Melbourne

Milbank	sailboat	steel box
millboard	school band	tool box
Millburn	school board	wallboard
nail bag	schoolbooks	whalebone
Olbers	school bus	Wilbanks
pillbox	skull bone	Wilbur
roll bar	spellbound	_____

LB /lb/ Medial—three syllables

Albany	bell buoy	Gilberta
albatross	doll buggy	melba toast
Alberta	Elberta	mulberry
albino	Elberton	Mulberry
ball bearings	elbow grease	nail-biting
bell-bottoms	elbowroom	wheelbarrow

LB /lb/ Final—one syllable

alb	Kalb	_____
bulb	Kolb	_____

LB /lb/ Final—two syllables

DeKalb	light bulb	_____
flashbulb	wet bulb	_____

BR /br/ Initial—one syllable

brace	branch	bread
braced	brand	breadth
brad	Brant	break
Brad	brash	breath
brag	brass	breathe
bragged	brat	bred
braid	brave	breech
braille	brawl	breed
brain	brawn	breeze
braise	bray	Brent
braised	brayed	Bret
brake	braze	brew
brakes	breach	brewed
bran	breached	bribe

bribed
Brice
brick
bricked
bride
bridge
brief
briefed
brig
bright
brim
brimmed
brine
bring
brink
brisk
broach

broached
broad
brogue
broil
broiled
broke
Bronx
bronze
bronzed
brooch
brood
brook
Brooks
broom
broth
brought
brow

brown
browse
browsed
Bruce
bruise
bruised
brunch
brunt
brush
brushed
brusque
brute
Bryce

_____

_____

_____

_____

BR /br/ Initial—two syllables

bracelet
bracer
braces
bracing
bracken
bracket
brackish
Bradford
Bradley
braggart
Brahma
brainless
brainstorm
brainwash
brain wave
brainy
brakeage
brake drum
brake dye
brakeman

brake shoe
bramble
brandish
brandished
brand-new
brass band
brassy
bravo
brazen
brazier
Brazil
breadfruit
breakage
breakdown
breaker
breakfast
breakneck
breakup
breastbone
breastplate

breaststroke
breathing
breathless
breeches
breeder
breeding
breezy
Brenda
brethren
brewer
Brian
briar
brickbat
brickwork
brickyard
bridal
bridegroom
bridesmaid
bridge house
bridge lamp

Bridgeport	brisket	brooder
bridge sign	bristle	brooding
Bridget	bristled	brooklet
Bridgeton	Britain	Brooklyn
Bridge View	British	broomstick
Bridgeville	brittle	brother
bridgework	broadcast	browbeat
bridging	broadcloth	brownie
bridle	broaden	Brownie
bridled	broadened	brownish
bridling	broad jump	brown rice
briefcase	broadloom	bruin
briefing	broadside	Bruins
briefly	Broadway	brunette
briefness	brocade	brush fire
brier	brochure	brush work
brigade	brogan	Brussels
Brigham	broiler	Brutus
brighten	broken	Bryan
brightened	broker	Bryant
brilliance	bromide	_____
brilliant	bromine	_____
brimful	bronchi	_____
brimstone	bronco	_____
brindle	Bronze Age	_____
briny	brooded	_____
		_____

BR /br/ Initial—three syllables

bravado	brigadier	brokerage
bravery	brilliancy	bronchial
Brazil nut	bringing-up	bronchitis
breakable	British Isles	Brooklyn Bridge
breakwater	Britisher	brotherhood
breathtaking	broadcaster	brotherly
brevity	broadcasting	brouhaha
bribery	broad jumper	Brussels sprouts
bric-a-brac	broad-minded	_____
bricklayer	broccoli	_____
bridle path	broken down	_____

BR /br/ Medial—two syllables

abrade	drawbridge	purebred
Abram	embrace	rye bread
abreast	eyebrow	sagebrush
abridge	fabric	sea breeze
abridged	fibrous	shoebrush
abroad	float bridge	sweetbread
abrupt	Gambrel	toll bridge
cambric	hairbrush	toothbrush
Cambridge	Hebrew	vibrant
clothes brush	hybrid	vibrate
cobra	inbred	whisk broom
cornbread	Libra	white bread
daybreak	membrane	windbreak
Debra	nail brush	zebra
debrief	outbreak	_____
debris	paint brush	_____

BR /br/ Medial—three syllables

Abraham	Labrador	umbrella
abrasive	library	unabridged
abridgment	London Bridge	unbroken
algebra	lubricate	underbrush
Brooklyn Bridge	Nebraska	upbringing
celebrate	paint brushes	vertebra
embracement	pawnbroker	vertebral
embracer	Rainbow Bridge	vertebrate
embrasure	rebroadcast	vibration
embroider	scatterbrain	whole wheat bread
Gabriel	sombrero	_____
gingerbread	thoroughbred	_____

BR /br/ Medial—four syllables

abbreviate	celebrity	librarian
abranchial	embraceable	lubrication
abreaction	embracery	Natural Bridge
candelabra	embroidery	_____
celebrated	Golden Gate Bridge	_____
celebration	invertebrate	_____

RB /rb/ Medial—two syllables

air base	derby	orbit
airborne	disturbed	sherbet
air bus	doorbell	turban
arbor	Fairbanks	turbid
barbed wire	forbear	turbine
barbells	forbid	turbot
barber	forborne	urban
bareback	garbage	verbal
Burbank	gerbil	verbose
carbon	harbor	warble
choirboy	Herbert	warbler
Corbet	marble	yearbook
Corbin	morbid	_____
Corby	nearby	_____

RB /rb/ Medial—three syllables

Ann Arbor	harboring	urbanite
Barbara	orbital	urbanize
barbaric	overbear	verbalize
barbecue	tetherball	verbally
barber chair	turbulence	verbatim
barber shop	turbulent	_____
fur bearer	undisturbed	_____

RB /rb/ Medial—four syllables

barbecue sauce	orbicular	urbanity
carbon paper	overbearing	verbosity
carburetor	roller derby	_____

RB /rb/ Final—one syllable

barb	curb	Herb
Barb	garb	verb
blurb	herb	_____

RB /rb/ Final—two syllables

absorb	exurb	rhubarb
adverb	potherb	suburb
disturb	proverb	superb

BER /bɚ/ Medial—three syllables

cheeseburger	liberty	rubber band
fiberglass	limburger	rubber stamp
gabardine	lumbering	shrubbery
hamburger	lumberjack	slumberer
harboring	lumberyard	tubercle
hibernate	membership	tuberous
Kimberly	neighborhood	_____
liberal	numbering	_____
liberate	number line	_____

BER /bɚ/ Medial—four syllables

deliberate	tubercular	_____
remembering	_____	_____

BER /bɚ/ Final—two syllables

barber	labor	slobber
blubber	neighbor	sober
clobber	rubber	tuber
fiber	saber	_____

BER /bɚ/ Final—three syllables

belabor	October	_____
foam rubber	_____	_____

MB /mb/ Medial—two syllables

amber	embank	limber
Amber	embark	Limberg
Bambi	embed	limbo
bamboo	ember	Lombard
Bombay	emboss	lumbar
chamber	gambit	lumber
chambers	game bag	mambo
combine	game bird	member
combined	gumbo	nameboard
combo	imbibe	number
combust	imbibed	numbered
comeback	Lambert	Romberg
Dumbo	Lemberg	rumba

samba	tambour	_____
slumber	timber	_____
slumbered	trombone	_____
somber	umber	_____

MB /mb/ Medial—three syllables

ambition	gamboling	outnumber
bambino	hamburger	rambunctious
bamboo shoots	Kimberly	reimburse
bamboozle	Limburger	remember
Columbus	lumbering	remembered
combustion	lumberjack	September
cucumber	lumbermill	sombrero
cumbersome	lumberyard	somebody
December	membership	tambourine
embankment	November	unnumbered
embargo	numbering	Zambezi
embarrass	numberline	Zambia
embassy	ombudsman	_____

MB /mb/ Medial—four syllables

ambassador	Columbia	mumbo jumbo
ambiguous	combination	_____
Cambodia	combustible	_____

MBER /mbɚ/ Final—two syllables

amber	lumber	timber
Amber	member	umber
chamber	number	_____
ember	slumber	_____
limber	somber	_____

MBER /mbɚ/ Final—three syllables

cucumber	November	remember
December	outnumber	September

BY /bj/ Medial—three syllables

ambulance	tabulate	_____
ambulate	tubular	_____

BY /bj/ Medial—four syllables

contributor	tabulator
distributor	tribulation
tabulated	tributary

BZ /bz/ Final—one syllable

babes	garbs	rubs
bibs	gobs	sobs
cabs	grubs	stubs
clubs	hobs	subs
cobs	hubs	swabs
crabs	jibes	tabs
cribs	jobs	throbs
cubes	knobs	tribes
cubs	labs	tubes
dabs	lobes	tubs
debs	mobs	webs
dubs	nabs	
fibs	probes	
fobs	ribs	
gabs	robes	

BZ /bz/ Final—two syllables

bathrobes	earlobes	sea crabs
bathtubs	flashcubes	spareribs
bear cubs	girls' clubs	wolf cubs
book clubs	golf clubs	
boys' clubs	health clubs	
cobwebs	ice cubes	
doorknobs	sand crabs	

CH

Pronounced: /tʃ/
Spelled: ch, tch, te, ti, tu

CH /tʃ/ Initial—one syllable

Chad
chafe
chaff
chain
chair
chalk
champ
chance
change
changed
chant
chap
chapped
chaps
char
chard
charge
charged
Charles
charm
charms
chart
chase
chaste
chat

chaw
cheap
cheat
check
cheek
cheep
cheer
cheered
cheers
cheese
chess
chest
Chet
chew
chick
chide
chief
child
chill
chime
chin
chink
chintz
chip
chipped

chips
chirp
chit
chive
choice
choke
choose
chop
chopped
chops
chore
chose
chow
chub
chuck
Chuck
chug
chum
chummed
chump
chunk
church
churl
churn

CH /tʃ/ Initial—two syllables

cello
Chadwick
chairman

chalice
challenge
challenged

chamber
Chandler
changing

[24]

channel	cheesecloth	chipmunk
chapel	cheetah	chirrup
chaplain	Cheney	chisel
chapter	cherish	chitchat
charcoal	cherry	Choctaw
charge card	cherub	choker
Charleston	chessboard	choosy
Charlestown	chessman	chopper
Charlie	Chester	chopping
charming	chestnut	choppy
charter	chicken	chopsticks
chartered	chickweed	chortle
chastise	Chico	chosen
chattel	chilblain	chow chow
chatter	childbirth	chowder
cheaper	childhood	chow mein
checkbook	childish	chubby
checker	childlike	chuck full
checkers	children	chuckhole
check mark	Chile	chuckle
checkmate	chili	chumming
checkroom	chilly	chummy
checkup	chimney	Churchill
cheekbone	china	churchyard
cheerful	China	chutney
cheery	Chinese	_____
cheese cake	chipper	_____

CH /tʃ/ Initial—three syllables

Challenger	charwoman	Cherryville
challenges	chatterbox	Chesapeake
challenging	checkerboard	chewing gum
champion	cheddar cheese	chickadee
chancellor	cheerleaders	Chickasaw
changeable	cheerily	chicken coop
chain letter	Cherokee	chicken pox
chariot	cherry bomb	chicory
charity	cherry pie	chief of staff
charley horse	Cherryvale	Chihuahua

chili sauce
Chilkoot Pass
chimpanzee
China Sea
Chinatown
chinchilla

Chippewa
chokecherry
chocolate
chop suey
chuck-a-luck
chuck wagon

chuckwalla
churchgoer

_____
_____
_____
_____

CH /tʃ/ Initial—four syllables

challengingly
chancellery
chancellorship
Chancellor's List
charioteer

charitable
Chattanooga
cherry pepper
chicken chow mein
chili pepper

chili powder
chinaberry
Chinese checkers
chocolate chip

_____

CH /tʃ/ Medial—two syllables

achieve
armchair
beachball
beachcomb
beachhead
bechance
benches
bleacher
blotchy
blue cheese
branching
broaches
bunches
butcher
capture
catcher
catching
catch-up
chitchat
chow chow
cincture
clincher
coaches
coachman

corn chips
creature
crouching
crunchy
crutches
culture
denture
discharge
ditches
duchess
enchain
enchant
etching
exchange
feature
fetches
fetching
fire chief
fixture
flincher
fracture
franchise
future
gesture

godchild
grandchild
Gretchen
hat check
hatchet
hatching
henchman
high chair
hitchhike
hitching
hope chest
hunchback
ice chips
inches
itching
ketchup
key chain
kitchen
latches
launcher
launching
launch pad
lecture
lunch box

luncheon
lunches
lunchroom
lunchtime
matches
mischief
mixture
moisture
moocher
nachos
Natchez
nature
notches
notchy
Pancho
pasture
patches
patchwork
peaches
peach tree
peachy
picture
pinch-hit
pitch-black
pitcher
pitches
pitchfork
pitching
poacher

posture
preacher
punchball
punch bowl
punch card
puncher
punch line
puncture
question
Rachel
rancher
ranchman
rancho
rapture
reaching
recharge
Richard
richer
richest
Richie
righteous
roaches
rupture
satchel
scratch pad
scripture
sculpture
sea chest
sketchy

statue
stature
statute
stepchild
stitches
structure
switching
teacher
teaching
texture
Thatcher
tincture
touchdown
touches
touching
trenchant
venture
voucher
vulture
watchdog
watcher
watchful
watching
watchman
witchcraft
witchy
_____
_____
_____

CH /tʃ/ Medial—three syllables

actual
adventure
amateur
anchovy
Apache
beachcomber
bedchamber
bewitching

bird watcher
chinchilla
chokecherry
combustion
congestion
conjecture
cow catcher
cowpuncher

cultural
curvature
detachment
digestion
disenchant
dispatcher
dog catcher
enchanted

encroachment	matchable	situate
exchequer	matchmaker	statuesque
factual	mutual	structural
fistula	natural	structuring
fluctuate	night watchman	taco chips
flycatcher	overture	tactual
forfeiture	picturesque	teachable
furniture	police chief	titular
futureless	premature	teacher's aide
hatchery	punching bag	treacherous
hitchhiker	punctuate	venturesome
immature	ritual	venturous
impeachment	rupturing	watchtower
kitchenette	sandwiches	witchery
launching pad	scratchable	_____
ligature	signature	_____

CH /tʃ/ Medial—four syllables

agriculture	Indian chief	perpetuate
approachable	legislature	potato chips
barbecue chips	literature	reproachable
caricature	manufacture	sanctuary
chocolate chips	maturation	situation
contractual	miniature	spiritual
detachable	Natural Bridge	temperature
effectual	natural gas	tortilla chips
estuary	naturalist	unnatural
eventual	naturalize	_____
habitual	naturally	_____
hickory chips	perpetual	_____

CH /tʃ/ Medial—five syllables

ineffectual	intellectual	unapproachable
infatuation	obituary	_____

CH /tʃ/ Final—one syllable

batch	blanch	blotch
beach	Blanche	botch
bench	bleach	branch

breach	itch	scratch
breech	latch	screech
broach	leach	scrunch
brooch	leech	sketch
brunch	lunch	slouch
bunch	match	snatch
Butch	Mitch	snitch
catch	much	speech
clench	munch	splotch
clutch	niche	stench
cinch	notch	stitch
coach	ouch	stretch
couch	patch	such
crouch	peach	swatch
crunch	pitch	switch
crutch	poach	teach
ditch	pooch	thatch
drench	pouch	touch
Dutch	preach	trench
each	punch	twitch
etch	quench	vetch
fetch	ranch	watch
French	reach	which
grouch	retch	witch
hatch	rich	wrench
hitch	Rich	wretch
hunch	roach	_____
hutch	scotch	_____

CH /tʃ/ Final—two syllables

approach	door latch	mismatch
attach	dude ranch	night watch
beseech	enrich	nonesuch
bewitch	hemstitch	nuthatch
cockroach	homestretch	ostrich
crosspatch	hopscotch	outmatch
cross stitch	impeach	outreach
detach	key punch	outstretch
dispatch	Long Beach	pipe wrench

rematch	ski coach	track coach
reproach	South Beach	unlatch
retouch	swim coach	wrist watch
sandwich	topnotch	_____

CH /tʃ/ Final—three syllables

avalanche	honeybunch	P.E. coach
baseball coach	lettuce patch	pocket watch
butterscotch	Mission Beach	pony ranch
briar patch	mix and match	rabbit hutch
cattle ranch	monkey wrench	Union Beach
crescent wrench	Myrtle Beach	West Palm Beach
feather stitch	Newport Beach	wrestling coach
football coach	overreach	wrestling match
hockey coach	overstretch	_____

CHER /tʃɚ/ Medial—three syllables

archery	futurism	_____
cultural	futurist	_____
futureless	rupturing	_____

CHER /tʃɚ/ Medial—four syllables

naturalist	_____	_____
naturally	_____	_____

CHER /tʃɚ/ Final—two syllables

archer	future	posture
bleacher	gesture	preacher
butcher	launcher	puncture
capture	leacher	rancher
catcher	lecture	richer
clincher	luncher	rupture
creature	lurcher	rupture
culture	mixture	stature
facture	moisture	teacher
feature	nature	Thatcher
fixture	pasture	venture
flincher	picture	voucher
fracture	pitcher	watcher

CHER /tʃɚ/ Final—three syllables

adventure	dogcatcher	ligature
back scratcher	flycatcher	overture
bird watcher	furniture	signature
departure	indenture	_____

CHER /tʃɚ/ Final—four syllables

agriculture	manufacture	_____
legislature	miniature	_____
literature	temperature	_____

RCH /rtʃ/ Medial—two syllables

archduke	lurching	porches
archer	marches	purchase
Archie	marching	purchased
arching	merchant	researched
archway	nurture	scorching
birch bark	nurtured	searchlight
churches	orchard	starchy
Churchill	parchment	surcharge
fortune	perchance	torchlight
kerchief	perches	virtue
lurcher	perching	_____

RCH /rtʃ/ Medial—three syllables

archbishop	departure	nurturing
archdeacon	fortunate	orange orchard
archduchess	handkerchief	overcharge
archduchy	interchange	pear orchard
archerfish	marching band	purchaser
archery	March of Dimes	purchasing
Archibald	merchandise	sea urchin
arch support	misfortune	starchiest
cheddar cheese	neckerchief	virtual

RCH /rtʃ/ Medial—four syllables

apple orchard	fortunately	fortuneteller
archery set	fortune cookie	fortunetelling
birch bark basket	fortune hunter	grapefruit orchard

merchant marine	purchase order	_____
mortuary	torchlight parade	_____
purchasable	unfortunate	_____

RCH /rtʃ/ Final—one syllable

arch	March	search
birch	parch	smirch
church	perch	starch
lurch	porch	torch
march	scorch	_____

RCH /rtʃ/ Final—two syllables

| blowtorch | out march | white birch |
| cornstarch | research | _____ |

RCHT /rtʃt/ Final—one syllable

arched	perched	starched
marched	scorched	_____
parched	searched	_____

D

Pronounced: /d/
Spelled: d, dd, ed

D /d/ Initial—one syllable

dab	dense	dole
dad	dent	doll
Dale	depth	dome
dam	desk	Don
damp	deuce	done
Dan	dew	don't
dance	dice	door
dare	Dick	dorm
dark	did	dot
dart	dig	Dot
dash	dike	dots
date	dill	doubt
dawn	dim	Doug
day	dime	dough
deaf	din	douse
deal	dine	dove
Dean	dip	down
dear	Dirk	Doyle
Deb	dirt	dub
debt	dish	duck
deck	disk	duct
Dee	ditch	dud
deed	dive	dude
deem	do	due
deep	dock	dues
deer	dodge	dug
deft	Dodge	duke
dell	doe	Duke
delve	does	dull
den	dog	dump

dune	dust	dyed
dunk	Dutch	_____
dusk	dye	_____

D /d/ Initial—two syllables

dabble	deadline	Delhi
Dagan	dealer	delight
dagger	Dean's List	Della
daily	Dearborn	delta
dainty	debate	Delta
dairy	Debbie	deluxe
daisy	debit	demand
Daisy	debris	demise
Dallas	decade	demure
damage	decal	Dena
damask	decamp	denim
dampen	decay	Denise
damper	decayed	Denmark
Dana	deceit	Dennis
dancer	deceive	denounce
dandruff	decent	dentist
dandy	decide	Denton
danger	decode	Denver
Daniel	decor	deny
Danish	decoy	depart
Danny	decrease	depend
Danube	deep freeze	depict
Darlene	Deep South	deplane
dartboard	default	deploy
data	defeat	deport
daughter	defend	depose
David	defense	depot
Davy	deflate	depress
Dawson	defrost	derby
daydream	degree	derive
daylight	Deland	descend
Dayton	delay	desert
deacon	Delbert	design
dead end	delete	desire

Des Moines	distinct	doorway
dessert	divan	Dora
detail	diver	Doran
detour	diverge	Doreen
Detroit	divide	Doris
device	divine	dory
devil	divorce	dosage
devote	Dixie	Dottie
devour	Dixon	double
devout	dizzy	doubtful
Dewey	doctor	doubtless
DeWitt	doctrine	doughnut
Dexter	dodger	Douglas
dial	Dodgers	downbeat
diesel	dogcart	downcast
diet	doghouse	down draft
digit	dog sled	downfall
dimple	dog tag	downfield
Dina	dogwood	downgrade
Dinah	doily	downhill
dinky	doing	Downing
dinner	doleful	downpour
dipper	dollar	downstairs
discount	doll house	downtime
discus	dolly	downtown
discuss	Dolly	downwind
disdain	dolphin	dozen
disease	Donald	dozer
disgrace	donate	dual
disguise	donkey	dubbing
dish cloth	Donna	Dublin
dish pan	donor	duchess
diskette	doorbell	duckling
dismiss	doorknob	dude ranch
dismount	doorman	Dudley
dispatch	doormat	duel
display	door prize	duet
dispute	doorstep	dugout
distance	doorstop	dullish

Duluth	during	duststorm
dumbbells	dusky	dusty
Dumbo	dust cloth	Dutchman
dumpling	duster	Dutch treat
dump truck	dusting	duty
dumpy	dust mop	dyeing
dungeon	dustpan	_____
duplex	dust proof	_____

D /d/ Initial—three syllables

daffodil	delinquent	dialing
dangerous	Delores	dialogue
daredevil	demagogue	diamond
data base	demanding	Diana
data disk	demeanor	diary
Deanna	demolish	dictator
Deborah	demonstrate	difference
dcbutantc	Denali	different
decanter	denial	difficult
decibel	department	digestion
decided	deposit	digression
decimal	deprecate	dilated
decipher	deputy	dilemma
decision	derelict	diligence
declaring	derisive	dimension
declining	description	diminish
decoder	designate	dinosaur
decoding	desperate	diploma
decorate	destitute	diplomat
dedicate	destroyer	disconnect
deduction	detective	discretion
deep freezer	deterrent	disfigure
deep fryer	detonate	dishtowel
defiance	devastate	dishwasher
deficit	deviled eggs	disk jockey
definite	devotee	dislocate
Delaware	dewberry	disorder
delegate	diagram	dissipate
delicate	dialect	distinguish

distribute
diversion
diving board
diving boat
diving suit
division
document
dogberry
dogcatcher
dog collar
dog paddle

dog sledding
doll buggy
domestic
dominate
domineer
Dominic
dominion
Dorothy
double take
double talk
double time

down-to-earth
duffel bag
dungaree
duplicate
duration
dust devil
Dutch Harbor
dynamic
dynamite
_____
_____

D /d/ Initial—four syllables

dandelion
debilitate
declaration
deferential
definition
degenerate
delegation
deliberate
delineate
delirious
democracy
democratic
demolition
designation
desirable
despotism
destination
dexterity
diabetic
diagnosis

diagonal
diameter
dictionary
difficulty
dignitary
directory
dirigible
disadvantage
disarmament
disconcerting
disconsolate
discontinue
discourteous
discovery
discriminate
disinfectant
disintegrate
dispensation
disposition
disseminate

Dominion Day
dormitory
double bassoon
double boiler
double-breasted
double-decker
Dutch East Indies
dyslexia
_____
_____
_____
_____
_____
_____
_____
_____
_____
_____
_____
_____

D /d/ Initial—five syllables

depository
deteriorate
dilapidated
disability

disagreeable
disciplinary
disintegration
dissatisfaction

_____
_____
_____
_____

D /d/ Initial—six syllables

decarbonization	desalinization	disorientation
democratically	disorganization	disqualification

D /d/ Medial—two syllables

Ada	headache	rider
Adam	heading	riding
Adams	hidden	roadway
adding	hiding	rudder
beading	hoodoo	Rudolph
bedding	hot dog	Rudy
bidder	Ida	sadden
biddy	Judy	shadow
birthday	kiddie	shudder
bleeder	ladder	siding
bleeding	laddie	skydive
body	lady	soda
broaden	ladies	speeder
buddy	leader	speeding
Buddy	leading	spider
cadet	loading	strident
chowder	louder	sudden
cider	maiden	Sweden
Cody	May Day	threader
daddy	meadow	Thursday
deaden	modem	tidy
dead end	muddy	today
deadline	needed	trident
disdain	nodding	Tuesday
Eddie	odor	vandal
Eden	plodder	voodoo
Edie	powder	waded
edit	pudding	wading
Edith	radar	wedding
feeding	radish	Wednesday
Friday	raider	woody
glider	reader	Woody
guiding	reading	_____
guide dog	ready	_____

D /d/ Medial—three syllables

abdomen	editing	Mother's Day
Adeline	face powder	nobody
adenoids	Father's Day	odorous
adequate	federal	powderhorn
advocate	First Lady	powdery
anecdote	floppy disk	radio
baby doll	Florida	rodeo
Bermuda	gadabout	shadowing
Bernadine	honeydew	sky diver
bobsledding	Idaho	soda pop
Canada	idea	somebody
cheddar cheese	Kennedy	spider web
cheerleaders	Madison	tedious
chickadee	medial	tidal wave
comedy	medicine	tostada
data disk	medieval	video
Edison	moderate	_____

D /d/ Medial—four syllables

adding machine	Cambodia	scuba diver
adenoidal	Colorado	scuba diving
adenoma	deciduous	South Dakota
anybody	medicinal	video game
auditory	misadventure	video tape
avocado	North Dakota	Yankee Doodle
cadaverous	riding safety	_____

D /d/ Medial—five syllables

cock-a-doodle-do	macadamia	_____
expediency	rudimentary	_____
hydrodynamics	_____	_____

D /d/ Final—one syllable

ad	bead	bled
add	bed	bleed
aid	bid	blood
aide	bide	bode
bad	blade	bowed

Boyd	flood	mid
brad	food	mod
Brad	Fred	mode
braid	fried	mood
bread	gad	mowed
bred	glad	mud
bride	glade	Ned
broad	glide	need
brood	good	nod
bud	grad	odd
Bud	grade	ode
cad	greed	pad
Chad	grid	paid
clad	guide	plaid
Claude	had	played
clod	head	plead
cloud	heed	pled
Clyde	hid	plowed
cod	hide	pod
code	hood	pride
could	I'd	quad
creed	jade	quid
cried	Judd	raid
crude	Jude	read
dad	kid	red
dead	knead	reed
deed	lad	rid
did	laid	ride
died	lead	road
dread	led	rod
dud	lid	Rod
dude	lied	rode
dyed	load	rowed
Ed	loud	sad
fad	mad	said
fade	made	sand
fed	maid	sawed
feed	Maude	seed
fled	mead	send

shade	stayed	void
shed	Swede	vowed
shied	tad	wad
should	Tad	wade
shrewd	Ted	Wade
side	Thad	wed
skid	thread	we'd
shred	thud	weed
Sid	tide	wide
sled	toad	wood
slid	Todd	would
slide	trod	you'd
sod	trade	_____
spade	tread	_____
squad	tweed	_____
squid	tried	_____
spread	used	_____

D /d/ Final—two syllables

abide	beside	David
abroad	biped	decade
acrid	birch wood	decide
added	birdseed	decode
afraid	blockade	divide
ahead	bobsled	dog food
aided	broadside	dog sled
Alfred	brocade	download
amid	brown bread	dried food
applaud	bunk bed	elude
arcade	canned food	embed
arid	carload	Enid
aside	cascade	exceed
avid	cat food	exclude
avoid	charade	fireside
batted	cited	fireweed
beachhead	co-ed	firewood
beaded	concede	first aid
bedside	crowded	fish food
bedspread	crusade	flash flood

flood tide
gifted
hardhead
hardwood
hated
hayride
hayseed
headed
high tide
hillside
hot rod
hunted
impede
include
inlaid
inside
instead
invade
junk food
knotted
landslide
limeade
low tide
luge sled
mermaid
mislead
misread
Morse code

muted
needed
nodded
outside
padded
painted
parade
persuade
pine wood
plywood
pointed
postpaid
precede
prepaid
punted
railroad
rated
reside
rooted
rotted
rounded
routed
rye bread
salad
seafood
seaside
seaweed
seeded

sided
slotted
snow slide
spotted
spruce wood
stampede
succeed
suited
tight wad
toll road
tooted
tour guide
unpaid
upload
waded
wayside
welded
white bread
Whiz Kid
widespread
winded
woodshed
yuletide
zip code

_____
_____
_____
_____

D /d/ Final—three syllables

a la mode
accepted
alkaloid
appointed
attitude
barricade
brotherhood
Cable Guide
centigrade

centipede
certified
chicken feed
Chinese food
classified
copperhead
expected
fishing rod
foreign aid

gingerbread
hearing aid
heating pad
Hollywood
intercede
invalid
lemonade
limited
myriad

neighborhood
one-man sled
orangeade
overhead
overplayed
pony ride
pyramid
riverside
Riverside
Robin Hood

serenade
soft-hearted
sourdough bread
spirited
super slide
supersede
talented
teacher's aide
teaching aid
tossed salad

tourist guide
two-man sled
two-sided
united
visited
water bed
_____
_____
_____
_____

DER /dɚ/ Medial—three syllables

elderish
elderly
eldermost
orderly
powderhorn
powdering
powdery
spider web
tenderfoot
thunderbolt
thunderclap
thunderhead
thunderous
thunderstorm

thunderstruck
tinderbox
underbrush
underclothes
underdog
underfoot
underground
underling
undermine
underneath
underpass
undersea
undershirt
underside

understand
understood
undertake
undertook
underwear
underweight
underwent
wanderer
wandering
wanderlust
wanderoo
wilderness
wonderful
_____

DER /dɚ/ Medial—four syllables

elderberry
elder statesman
kindergarten
misunderstand
misunderstood
orderliness

powdering tub
powder monkey
thundershower
undercover
undergarment
underlying

understanding
undertaker
undertaking
underwater
_____
_____

DER /dɚ/ Final—two syllables

alder
bidder
binder

bladder
bleeder
blender

blinder
blunder
border

boulder	hinder	shudder
chowder	ladder	slander
cider	launder	slender
cinder	leader	speeder
colder	louder	spider
condor	odor	splendor
elder	order	spreader
Elder	plodder	tender
fender	plunder	threader
fielder	powder	thunder
flounder	raider	tinder
folder	reader	udder
gander	render	under
glider	rider	weeder
grinder	rudder	_____
grounder	sander	_____
herder	sender	_____

DER /dɚ/ Final—three syllables

asunder	disorder	outsider
bewilder	embroider	remainder
calendar	faultfinder	reminder
cheerleader	free-loader	ringleader
commander	insider	shareholder
consider	islander	stepladder
crusader	lavender	_____
cylinder	left-hander	_____

DER /dɚ/ Final—four syllables

Alexander	ice cream vendor	_____
ambassador	winter splendor	_____

DL /dl/ Medial—two syllables

badly	Hadley	idling
Bradley	headlight	kindling
deadline	headline	loudly
deadlock	heedless	madly
deadly	huddling	meddling
gladly	hurdler	medley

midland	sadly	twiddling
needless	seedless	wedlock
needling	seedling	widely
oddly	soundly	windlass
paddling	swindling	_____
padlock	toddler	_____
red light	toddling	_____

DL /dl/ Medial—three syllables

bridal veil	idleness	Middle East
candlestick	meddlesome	Middle West
candlewick	middle age	_____
handlebars	middle ear	_____

DL /dl/ Final—two syllables

bridal	kindle	riddle
bridle	ladle	saddle
bundle	medal	sandal
candle	meddle	scandal
caudal	middle	spindle
cradle	model	swindle
dwindle	muddle	tidal
fiddle	needle	toddle
griddle	noodle	twiddle
handle	paddle	vandal
huddle	pedal	wheedle
hurdle	peddle	yodel
idle	poodle	_____
idol	puddle	_____

LD /ld/ Medial—two syllables

Alden	childhood	cold snap
alder	childish	cold wave
Baldwin	children	Elden
boulder	cold cuts	elder
Boulder	colder	Elder
builder	coldest	eldest
building	cold front	fielded
build-up	cold pack	fielder

field goal	holding	Waldon
field trip	hold-up	welded
file disk	mildew	Welden
folder	molding	welder
folding	olden	welding
gelding	older	wildcat
golden	oldest	wildfire
goldfinch	scalding	wildlife
goldfish	scolding	wild west
gold mine	seldom	yielded
gold pan	Sheldon	yielding
gold rush	shielded	_____
gold stream	shoulder	_____
holder	smolder	_____

LD /ld/ Medial—three syllables

beholden	golden age	shipbuilder
blindfolded	goldenrod	shouldering
bulldozer	gold nugget	unfolding
bulldozing	gold panner	unwieldy
cul-de-sac	grandchildren	unyielding
deviled eggs	left fielder	upholder
elderly	old-fashioned	wilderness
Eldora	right fielder	wildflower
field glasses	shareholder	withholding
field worker	shelled pecans	World Series
folding chair	shelled walnuts	_____

LD /ld/ Final—one syllable

bald	fold	polled
billed	gild	pulled
bold	gold	rolled
build	guild	scald
called	held	scold
child	hold	shelled
cold	mild	shield
field	mold	skilled
filed	mulled	sold
filled	old	spilled

told	wield	yield
veiled	wild	_____
weld	world	_____

LD /ld/ Final—two syllables

afield	enfold	Sea World
age-old	foothold	stepchild
ahold	foretold	stronghold
airfield	Gerald	threefold
appalled	grandchild	threshold
appealed	Harold	twofold
Arnold	household	unfold
backfield	infield	unsold
beheld	infold	untold
behold	left field	upheld
billfold	marbled	uphold
blindfold	marveled	windshield
coal field	outfield	withheld
cornfield	rebuild	withhold
corralled	retold	_____
Donald	right field	_____
downfield	Ronald	_____

LD /ld/ Final—three syllables

battlefield	initialed	marigold
center field	interfold	soccer field
centerfold	landing field	_____
emerald	MacDonald	_____
football field	manifold	_____

DR /dr/ Initial—one syllable

drab	drape	dreams
draft	draped	dreamt
drag	draw	dredge
drain	drawl	dredged
drake	drawn	drench
Drake	dread	dress
dram	dream	dressed
drank	dreamed	drew

dried	drone	drudge
drift	drool	drug
drill	droop	drum
drilled	drop	drummed
drink	dropped	drunk
drip	drought	drupe
dripped	drove	dry
drive	drown	_____
droll	drowse	_____

DR /dr/ Initial—two syllables

draftsman	dreamland	droopy
drafty	dreary	dropkick
dragging	dredger	droplet
dragnet	dredging	droplight
dragon	dresser	dropping
dragoon	dressing	druggist
drag race	dribble	drugstore
drag strip	drier	druid
drainage	driest	drummer
drainpipe	drifter	drumstick
drama	drifting	dry cell
drastic	driftwood	dry clean
drawback	drilling	drydock
drawbridge	drip-dry	dryer
drawer	drive-in	dry goods
drawing	driven	dry ice
drawstring	driver	dry milk
dreadful	drive-through	dryness
dreamer	driveway	_____
dreaming	drizzle	_____

DR /dr/ Initial—three syllables

Dracula	dramatize	dreadfully
draft dodger	drapery	dreamily
dragonfly	drawing board	dressing gown
Drakensburg	drawing card	dressing room
dramatic	drawing frame	dressing up
dramatist	drawing room	dressmaker

drillmaster
drinkable
drive-in bank
driver's seat
driving range
drollery
drop kicker

dropsical
drop table
drowsiness
drudgery
drum major
drummer boy
dry cleaner

dry cleaning
dry goods store
dry measure
_____
_____
_____
_____

DR /dr/ Initial—four syllables
draconian
dramatical
dramaturgy
drastically

Dravidian
drawing table
dromedary
drosophila

dry battery
_____
_____
_____

DR /dr/ Medial—two syllables
address
adrift
Andrew
Audrey
bass drum
bed rest
bedroll
bedroom
Cedric
children
coughdrop
dandruff
daydream
dewdrop
drip-dry
eardrop
eardrops
eardrum
eye drops
fire drill
foundry
fruit drink
gumdrop
headdress

hindrance
hum-drum
hundred
hundredth
hydrant
hydrate
hydro
laundry
lime drink
line drive
Madrid
Mildred
nose drops
Pedro
quadrant
quadrille
raindrops
Sandra
scoundrel
snare drum
snowdrift
soft drink
sundress
sun-dried

sundries
sundrops
sundry
tawdry
tendril
tundra
undress
withdraw
withdrawn
withdraws
withdrew
wondrous
Woodrow
_____
_____
_____
_____
_____
_____
_____
_____
_____
_____

DR /dr/ Medial—three syllables

Adrian	hydrogen	quadruplet
Andrea	hydrophone	race driver
apple drink	hydroplane	San Pedro
bongo drums	kettle drum	screwdriver
cathedral	lemon drink	snapdragon
dehydrate	line drawing	truck driver
eye dropper	orange drink	withdrawal
Fredericksburg	overdrawn	withdrawing
grapefruit drink	overdrive	_____
hair dresser	quadrangle	_____
hair dryer	quadruped	_____
hydraulics	quadruple	_____

DR /dr/ Medial—four syllables

adrenalin	overdrawing	quadruplicate
dehydrated	Padre Island	rhododendron
driving safety	philodendron	salad dressing
hydroponics	photodrama	taxi driver
lemon-lime drink	pineapple drink	_____
melodrama	quadrennial	_____

DR /dr/ Medial—five syllables

ambulance driver	hypochondriac	_____
hydrodynamics	quadrilateral	_____
hydrophobia	_____	_____

RD /rd/ Medial—two syllables

Airedale	garden	hardware
birdhouse	guarded	hardwood
birdie	guardhouse	hardy
birdseed	guardrail	herdsman
border	hair-do	hors d'oeuvre
burden	hard-boiled	hurdle
card tricks	harden	hurdler
cardboard	hardhead	ordain
cording	Harding	ordeal
cordless	hardly	order
cordwood	hardship	ordered

pardon	Third World	yardage
sturdy	Verde	yard light
tardy	warden	yardstick
third base	warder	Zardax
third class	wardrobe	_____

RD /rd/ Medial—three syllables

bird watcher	Hoover Dam	reorder
borderline	Labor Day	rewording
cardinal	ordering	rose garden
card table	orderly	Saturday
concordance	ordinal	stamdardize
concordant	ordinance	standard time
corduroy	ordinate	stewardess
disorder	overdo	stewardship
disordered	overdone	unguarded
gabardine	overdue	wardenship
gardener	preordain	_____
Garden Grove	recorder	_____
gardening	recording	_____
Garden State	regarding	_____
guardian	regardless	_____

RD /rd/ Medial—four syllables

accordion	garden party	ordination
coordinate	guard of honor	outboard motor
disorderly	guardianship	standardizing
Garden City	inboard motor	Verde River
gardenia	ordinary	_____

RD /rd/ Medial—five syllables

| coordination | ordinal number | overburdensome |
| guardian angel | ordinarily | _____ |

RD /rd/ Final—one syllable

bard	bored	chord
beard	Byrd	cleared
bird	card	cord
board	chard	ford

Ford	moored	stirred
gird	poured	stored
gourd	roared	third
guard	scared	toward
hard	scarred	ward
heard	scored	weird
herd	shared	word
hoard	spared	yard
horde	sparred	_____
lard	stared	_____
lord	steered	_____

RD /rd/ Final—two syllables

aboard	Coast Guard	Leonard
accord	colored	leopard
afford	Concord	lifeguard
appeared	cornered	lizard
award	courtyard	Lombard
awkward	coward	mallard
backboard	cupboard	Maynard
backward	custard	measured
backyard	dashboard	mouth guard
barnyard	discard	mud guard
Bedford	eastward	mustard
Bernard	Edward	nameboard
Big Bird	flashcard	night guard
billboard	front yard	numbered
blackbird	game bird	onward
blackboard	gizzard	orchard
blizzard	graveyard	outboard
bluebird	Harvard	outward
bombard	hazard	Oxford
Buford	Howard	pampered
buzzard	inboard	password
cardboard	inward	postcard
charge card	keyboard	prepared
chessboard	kickboard	punch card
Clifford	landlord	Radford
clipboard	leeward	rear guard

record	southward	unheard
regard	Spaniard	upward
reward	splattered	vineyard
Rexford	springboard	wallboard
Richard	standard	washboard
rip cord	Stanford	watchword
Ruford	starboard	watered
safeguard	steward	wayward
scoreboard	stockyard	westward
scorecard	surfboard	Willard
seaboard	switchboard	wizard
shepherd	tagboard	_____
shipyard	tattered	_____
skateboard	thundered	_____
skyward	timecard	_____
songbird	tutored	_____

RD /rd/ Final—three syllables

aboveboard	horned lizard	Scotland Yard
afterward	hummingbird	shuffleboard
birthday card	leotard	smorgasbord
bodyguard	lumberyard	spinal cord
boulevard	mockingbird	substandard
checkerboard	outnumbered	thank-you card
Christmas card	overboard	union card
color guard	remembered	unnumbered
cribbage board	report card	unwatered
disregard	Rocky Ford	Weatherford
diving board	room and board	_____
drawing board	rose-colored	_____
early bird	rust-colored	_____
harpsichord	Rutherford	_____

ND /nd/ Medial—two syllables

Andy	Brenda	Candy
bandage	bundle	cinder
bandstand	Candace	Cindy
branding	candle	condemn
Brandon	candy	condor

dandy	jaundiced	sand crab
fender	kindly	sander
flounder	kindness	Sandy
foundry	landing	sender
gander	landlord	send-off
Gandhi	landscape	slander
Glenda	landslide	slender
Glendale	Landy	splendor
grinder	launder	Sunday
grounded	laundry	sunder
grounder	Linda	tandem
handbag	London	tender
handball	mandate	thunder
handbook	Mandy	tundra
handcuff	Monday	undamped
handful	plunder	under
handle	ponder	undone
handsaw	Randolph	undress
handshake	random	vendor
handsome	Randy	Wendy
handspring	reindeer	window
handy	render	windup
hinder	rounded	windy
Hindi	rounding	wonder
Hindu	round trip	_____
hundred	roundup	_____
indeed	sandbox	_____
indent	sandbug	_____
indulge	sandbur	_____

ND /nd/ Medial—three syllables

Amanda	conduction	Honduras
amendment	conductor	India
appendage	endurance	Indian
appendix	handicap	inundate
bandaging	handicraft	landlady
candy bar	handiwork	Laplander
condition	handwriting	laundromat
conducive	handwritten	left-handed

London Bridge
mandarin
meander
plundering
sandalwood
sandbagging
sand dollar
sandpaper
sandpiper
storm window
Sunday School
sundial
tendency
tenderfoot
thunderbolt
thunderclap
thunderhead

thunderous
thunderstorm
thunderstruck
tinderbox
underbrush
underclothes
underdog
underfoot
underground
underline
undermine
underneath
underpass
undersea
undershirt
underside
understand

understate
understood
undertake
undertook
undertow
underwear
underweight
underwent
underworld
unfounded
wanderer
wanderlust
wonderful
_____
_____
_____
_____

ND /nd/ Medial—four syllables
candelabra
Cinderella
condemnation
conditional
incandescent
indecently

indelible
indentation
independent
Indiana
indicative
indiscretion

Indonesia
kindergarten
mendaciously
mendacity
undulating
_____

ND /nd/ Medial—five syllables
appendicitis
condominium
hypochondriac
incandescently
incendiary
indefensible

independency
indeterminate
indiscriminate
industrialist
Indy 500
serendipity

underachiever
underdeveloped
underestimate
underexposure
underprivileged
understandingly

ND /nd/ Final—one syllable
and
band
bend
bind

bland
blend
blind
blond

bond
bound
brand
canned

end	land	spanned
find	lend	spend
fined	mend	stand
fond	mind	strand
found	mound	tend
fund	pond	trend
gland	pound	vend
grand	rend	wand
grind	rind	weaned
ground	round	wind
hand	sand	wound
hind	send	yawned
hound	skinned	_____
kind	sound	_____

ND /nd/ Final—two syllables

abound	dead end	intend
aground	defend	Ireland
airbound	demand	island
almond	depend	jocund
amend	descend	kickstand
ascend	diamond	left-hand
astound	England	legend
attend	errand	longhand
backbend	expand	mainland
background	extend	mankind
backhand	fairground	Midland
bandstand	farmland	misspend
behind	Finland	offend
beyond	firebrand	Portland
bloodhound	foreground	pretend
Cleveland	grassland	profound
combined	greyhound	quicksand
command	headband	Raymond
commend	highland	rebound
compound	Holland	refund
confound	homeland	remand
contend	husband	remind
dachshund	inland	respond

right-hand	snowbound	upland
Roland	spellbound	waistband
rotund	stagehand	woodland
second	thousand	wristband
shorthand	unbind	_____
side band	unwind	_____
snowblind	up-end	_____

ND /nd/ Final—three syllables

apprehend	marching band	Sugar Land
beforehand	Maryland	Sutherland
comprehend	New England	Switzerland
condescend	Newfoundland	Tamarind
contraband	New Zealand	underground
correspond	overland	underhand
countermand	recommend	understand
dividend	Rhode Island	upper hand
fairyland	rhythm band	vagabond
Gila Bend	rubber band	wonderland
integrand	savings bond	wraparound
intertwined	secondhand	_____

ND /nd/ Final—four syllables

merry-go-round	superintend	_____
misunderstand	_____	_____

DW /dw/ Initial—one syllable

Duane	dwell	Dwight
dwarf	dwelled	_____
Dwayne	dwelt	_____

DW /dw/ Initial—two syllables

dwarfish	dwindle	_____
dwelling	dwindling	_____

DZ /dz/ Final—one syllable

adds	bids	crowds
aids	codes	dads
beads	creeds	deeds

fades	nodes	sleds
fads	nods	slides
feeds	odds	spades
floods	odes	speeds
gods	pads	suds
goods	pleads	tides
grades	pods	toads
guides	raids	trades
heads	reads	wades
hides	reds	wads
kids	rides	weds
lads	rids	weeds
leads	roads	woods
lids	seeds	_____
loads	shades	_____
modes	sheds	_____
needs	sides	_____

ZD /zd/ Final—one syllable

braised	grazed	raised
brazed	hosed	seized
breezed	paused	sized
caused	phased	sneezed
closed	phrased	teased
dazed	pleased	wheezed
eased	posed	_____
gazed	praised	_____

LDZ /ldz/ Final—one syllable

builds	molds	yields
fields	scalds	_____
folds	scolds	_____
holds	worlds	_____

NDZ /dzs/ Final—one syllable

bends	glands	lands
binds	grinds	lends
ends	hands	mends
finds	kinds	minds

ponds	sends	tends
rends	sounds	winds
rinds	spends	_____
sands	stands	_____

RDZ /rdz/ Final—one syllable

bards	cords	wards
beards	gourds	words
birds	guards	yards
boards	hoards	_____
cards	lords	_____
chords	towards	_____

RDZ /rdz/ Final—two syllables

backyards	leopards	skateboards
blackbirds	lifeguards	songbirds
bluebirds	lizards	Spaniards
buzzards	orchards	surfboards
clipboards	postcards	timecards
cupboards	punch cards	vineyards
discards	rear guards	wizards
flashcards	rewards	_____
kick boards	score cards	_____
leewards	shepherds	_____

DY /dj/ Medial—two syllables

woodyard	_____	_____

DY /dj/ Medial—three syllables

Scotland Yard	trade union	_____

LVD /lvd/ Final—one syllable

delved	solved	_____
shelved	_____	_____

LVD /lvd/ Final—two syllables

absolved	involved	unsolved
dissolved	resolved	_____
evolved	revolved	_____

RVD /rvd/ Final—one syllable

carved	starved	_____
curved	swerved	_____
served		

RVD /rvd/ Final—two syllables

deserved	reserved	_____
observed	unnerved	_____
preserved	_____	_____

DTH /dθ/ Final—one syllable

breadth	_____	_____
width	_____	_____

DTH /dθ/ Final—two syllables

bandwidth	hundredth	_____
hairbreadth	thousandth	_____

DTH /dθ/ Final—three syllables

one hundredth	_____	_____
two thousandth	_____	_____

THD /ðd/ Final—one syllable

bathed	seethed	teethed
breathed	sheathed	tithed
clothed	smoothed	writhed
loathed	soothed	_____
scathed	swathed	_____

F

Pronounced: /f/
Spelled: f, ff, gh, ph

F /f/ Initial—one syllable

face	feast	find
fact	feat	fine
facts	fed	fined
fad	fee	fir
fade	feed	fire
fail	feel	firm
faint	feet	first
fair	feign	fish
faith	fell	fist
Faith	felt	fit
fake	fence	five
fall	fend	fix
falls	fern	fizz
false	fetch	foal
fame	fete	foam
fan	fib	fob
fang	fibbed	foe
fanned	field	fog
fans	fiend	foil
far	fierce	foist
farce	fifth	fold
fare	fig	folk
farm	fight	fond
farmed	file	food
fast	filed	fool
fat	fill	foot
fault	filled	for
fawn	film	force
Faye	filth	ford
fear	fin	Ford

fork	fourth	fuzz
form	fowl	phase
fort	fudge	Phil
forth	full	phone
fought	fun	phoned
foul	fund	phones
fouled	fur	_____
found	fuss	_____
four	fussed	_____

F /f/ Initial—two syllables

fable	farmyard	festive
fabric	farther	festoon
facet	fashion	fever
facial	fasten	fiber
facing	fatal	fickle
factor	father	fiction
failing	fathom	fiddle
failure	fatigue	fiddler
Fairbanks	fatten	fidget
fairground	faucet	Fifi
Fairview	faulty	figment
fairway	favor	figure
fairy	fearful	Fiji
faithful	feather	filbert
falcon	feature	file disk
falter	feeble	filing
famine	feline	filling
famish	Felix	fillings
famous	fellow	Fillmore
fan belt	felon	filter
fancy	female	final
Far East	fencing	finals
farewell	ferment	finesse
farm belt	ferry	finger
farmer	fertile	finish
farmhouse	fervid	Finland
farming	fervor	Finnish
farmland	fester	firebrick

fire drill	footnote	fumble
firefly	footprint	function
fire hat	footrest	fungus
fireman	footstep	funnel
fireplace	footstool	funny
fireproof	forage	furlough
fire sale	forbid	furnace
fireside	forebear	furnish
fire thorn	forecast	furry
firetrap	forego	further
fire truck	forehead	fusses
fireweed	foreign	fussy
firewood	foreman	phalanx
fireworks	foremost	phantom
first aid	foresee	pharoah
first base	foresight	pharynx
first class	forgave	pheasant
first name	forget	Phillip
Fisher	forgive	Phoebe
fishing	forgot	Phoenix
fishy	formal	phoneme
fitness	format	phonic
fitting	former	phonics
fittings	For Rent	phony
fizzle	For Sale	phooey
focal	Fort Knox	phosphate
focus	Fort Wayne	photo
foible	Fort Worth	Phyllis
follow	forward	physique
folly	fossil	_____
foment	foster	_____
fondant	Foster	_____
fondle	founder	_____
fondue	foundry	_____
foolish	fourscore	_____
footage	fourteen	_____
football	fuchsia	_____
foothill	fullback	_____
footlights	fuller	_____

F /f/ Initial—three syllables

Fabian
factory
factual
faculty
fairy tale
fairyland
fallacy
familiar
family
fanatic
fanciful
fantastic
fantasy
fascinate
Father's Day
favorite
Fayetteville
feasible
featherstitch
featherweight
feathery
federal
federate
feminine
feminist
Ferdinand
ferocious
Ferris wheel
fertilize

festival
fiance'
fiasco
fiddlesticks
fiery
fiesta
filament
fingernail
fingerpaint
fingerprint
finicky
fire alarm
firecracker
fire engine
fire escape
fire fighter
fire marshal
fire safety
fire station
fire tower
first lady
foliage
follicle
follower
following
follow-through
follow-up
football field
forever

forgetful
forgetting
forgiven
forgiving
formation
formula
foundation
Four-H-Club
four-wheeler
furniture
pharmacist
pharmacy
Philippi
Philippines
Philistine
Phillipsburg
phlebitis
phobia
phonetics
phonograph
photocell
photoflash
photo lab
physical
physician
_____
_____
_____
_____

F /f/ Initial—four syllables

facilitate
facility
fashionable
fastidious
fatality
favorable
federation

felicity
Felicity
fidelity
Fiji Islands
formaldehyde
formidable
fundamental

pharyngeal
phenomena
phenomenal
phenomenon
philanthropy
philharmonic
philodendron

philology   phonetician   photography

philosopher   phonography   _____

philosophy   phonology   _____

phonetical   photographer   _____

F /f/ Medial—two syllables

afar	caffeine	defer
affair	campfire	defile
affect	camphor	define
affirm	catfish	deform
affix	chiff-chaff	defunct
afford	chiffon	defy
afield	Clifford	differ
afire	clubfoot	differed
afoot	codfish	diffuse
afore	coffee	dishful
afoul	coffer	dumbfound
aphid	coiffeur	efface
aphis	comfort	effect
beefsteak	confab	effort
befall	confer	enfold
befit	confide	enforce
befog	confine	Fifi
before	confined	gaffer
blackfish	confirm	Gifford
bluefish	conform	goldfinch
boastful	confound	goldfish
boldface	crawfish	gopher
boldfaced	crayfish	graphic
bonfire	crow's-foot	guffaw
boxful	cupful	half-hour
breakfast	daffy	handful
brimful	deafen	hayfork
buffer	deface	headfirst
buffet	defame	headphone
buffing	default	heartfelt
buffoon	defect	heifer
Buford	defend	hyphen
cafe	defense	infant

infect	paleface	Sophie
infer	pan fish	sophist
infest	platform	spoon-fed
infirm	playful	spoonful
inform	prefer	state fair
jiffy	prefix	stiffen
joyful	profane	stuffer
laughing	profess	suffer
laughter	profile	suffice
leafy	profit	suffix
lifeboat	profound	syphon
lifeguard	proofread	taffy
lifelike	prophet	talkfest
lifeline	puffin	thankful
lifetime	puffing	threefold
loafer	rainfall	tiffin
loafers	refer	tinfoil
loafing	refine	toffee
lowfat	reform	toughen
mouthful	refund	traffic
muffin	roughage	trophy
muffle	roughen	two-fold
offend	roughhouse	unfold
offense	roughshod	wafer
offer	safeguard	watchful
offhand	safer	wayfare
offing	safety	whitefish
offshoot	sapphire	windfall
offshore	scaffold	wishful
offspring	seafood	wistful
often	Sioux Falls	zephyr
outfield	snowfall	_____
outfit	sofa	_____

F /f/ Medial—three syllables

about-faced	afferent	artifact
aerophone	affirmant	atrophy
affable	amorphous	awfully
affection	amplify	balefully

beautify	dictaphone	modify
bedfellow	difference	mortify
befuddle	difficult	nonfiction
benefit	diffidence	notify
bifocal	diffident	nullify
bike safety	discomfort	offensive
bona fide	disinfect	offering
buffalo	edifice	officer
bus safety	edify	official
calcify	effective	officious
cellophane	efficient	Pacific
centrifuge	effigy	pacifist
certified	elephant	pacify
certify	emphasis	paraffin
Chief of Staff	emphasize	petrify
chiffonier	emphatic	phosphorus
chloroform	euphony	preference
chlorophyll	fire safety	profession
clarify	frankfurter	professor
classify	glorify	proficient
close-fisted	gratify	purify
coffeehouse	half-and-half	qualify
comforter	horrify	ratify
conference	infamous	referee
confidante	infancy	reference
confidence	infantry	refinement
confident	infarction	Rocky Ford
confiscate	infection	safari
Confucius	infernal	safety belt
confusion	infinite	safety pin
crucifix	interfere	Santa Fe
crucify	Jefferson	satisfy
daffodil	Josephine	saxophone
decipher	laughable	seafarer
de facto	lymphocyte	signify
defection	magnify	Sophia
defiance	megaphone	Sophocles
deficient	microfilm	sophomore
deficit	microphone	soundproofing

sousaphone
specify
suffocate
telephone

terrific
terrify
unfasten
unfurnished

verify
vilify

_____

_____

F /f/ Medial—four syllables

affidavit
affiliate
affinity
affirmative
amphibian
anaphora
anaphoric
antiphonal
antiphony
artificial
beautifying
benefactor
beneficial
biographer
biographic
biography
biophysics
boating safety
cacography
cacophony
calligraphy
catastrophe
certificate
circumference
climbing safety
coefficient
confectioner

confederate
confidential
confirmation
confiscation
conformation
coniferous
defamation
defensible
deferential
deficiency
definition
defoliate
differential
diversify
driving safety
emphysema
emulsify
esophagus
flying safety
geographer
identify
indifference
ineffective
infallible
inferior
infinitive
infirmary

infirmity
information
inoffensive
insufficient
intensify
manufacture
officiate
peripheral
philosopher
photographer
preferential
profitable
radiophone
referendum
reformation
riding safety
safety glasses
safety helmet
scientific
seat belt safety
South Pacific
topographic
topography
typographic
walking safety
water safety

_____

F /f/ Medial—five syllables

affiliation
angiography
asphyxiation
bibliography

cafeteria
configuration
diophoretic
edification

encephalitis
hemophilia
hydrophobia
infatuated

informational	officiary	unforgettable
insufferable	paraphernalia	_____
modification	sophisticated	_____

F /f/ Final—one syllable

beef	gruff	ruff
biff	guff	safe
bluff	half	scoff
brief	hoof	scuff
buff	huff	sheaf
calf	if	skiff
chafe	Jeff	spoof
chaff	knife	staff
chef	laugh	stiff
chief	leaf	strife
clef	life	stuff
cliff	loaf	thief
Cliff	miff	tiff
cough	muff	tough
cuff	off	trough
deaf	pouf	waif
doff	prof	whiff
fife	proof	wife
fluff	puff	woof
gaff	quaff	_____
goof	reef	_____
graph	roof	_____
grief	rough	_____

F /f/ Final—two syllables

aloof	distaff	kerchief
behalf	dust proof	kickoff
belief	enough	layoff
blow-off	fire chief	midriff
carafe	fire proof	penknife
cast-off	giraffe	plaintiff
checkoff	housewife	play-off
cutoff	jackknife	pontiff
dandruff	Joseph	rainproof

relief	stop-off	take off
sheriff	sun proof	tariff
show-off	sun roof	_____

F /f/ Final—three syllables

autograph	homograph	spirograph
barograph	monograph	tamper-proof
carving knife	neckerchief	telegraph
Chief of Staff	paragraph	tomograph
coral reef	phonograph	unbelief
dictograph	photograph	waterproof
epitaph	pocket knife	weatherproof
half-and-half	powder puff	_____
handkerchief	spectrograph	_____

F /f/ Final—four syllabes

angiograph	choreograph	oscillograph
cardiograph	Indian chief	_____

FER /fɚ/ Medial—three syllables

afferent	inference	reference
conference	offering	referent
difference	phosphorus	suffering
different	preference	_____

FER /fɚ/ Medial—four syllables

indifference	preferable	reoffering
indifferent	preferential	_____
inferential	referable	_____
long-suffering	referential	_____

FER /fɚ/ Final—two syllables

buffer	gaffer	prefer
camphor	golfer	refer
chauffeur	gopher	roofer
confer	infer	rougher
deafer	loader	safer
defer	loafer	scoffer
differ	offer	suffer

sulphur	wafer	_____
transfer	zephyr	_____

FER /fɚ/ Final—three syllables
bus transfer   _____   _____
decipher   _____   _____

FL /fl/ Initial—one syllable

flab	fleck	floss
flagged	fled	flounce
flagged	flee	flounced
flail	fleece	flour
flair	fleet	flout
flaired	flesh	flow
flak	flew	flown
flake	flex	Floyd
flakes	flick	flu
flame	flies	flub
flamed	flight	flue
flank	flinch	fluff
flap	fling	fluffs
flapped	flint	fluke
flare	flip	flume
flared	flipped	flung
flash	flirt	flunk
flashed	flit	flush
flask	Flo	flute
flat	float	flux
flaunt	flock	fly
flaw	flood	phlegm
flax	floor	phlox
flay	flop	_____
flea	flopped	_____

FL /fl/ Initial—two syllables

flabby	flagman	flaky
flaccid	flagpole	flameproof
Flag Day	flagrant	flaming
flagging	Flagstaff	flanker

flannel	Flemish	Flora
flapjack	fleshy	floral
flapper	Fletcher	Florence
flare-up	flexion	florid
flashback	flicker	florist
flashbulb	flier	flossy
flash card	flight path	flounder
flashcube	flighty	flourish
flash flood	flimsy	flow chart
flashgun	flip-flops	flower
flashing	flipper	flowing
flashlight	flippers	fluent
flashy	flipping	flue pipe
flatbed	flitter	fluffy
flatboat	float bridge	fluid
flatcar	floater	flunky
flatfoot	floating	flurry
flatter	float plane	fluster
flattop	flocking	flutist
flautist	floodlight	flutter
flavor	floorboard	flying
flaxseed	floor lamp	flywheel
flection	floor show	_____
fledgling	floozy	_____
fleecy	floppy	_____

FL /fl/ Initial—three syllables

flabbergast	flea-bitten	flotation
flagrantly	flea market	flotilla
flamboyant	flexible	flower girl
flamenco	flight control	flowerpot
flamethrower	floating dock	fluctuate
flamingo	flood control	fluency
flammable	floodwater	fluffier
flannelette	floorwalker	fluid ounce
flashier	floppy disk	fluorine
flatiron	Florentine	flutter kick
flattery	florescent	flyable
flavoring	Florida	fly-casting

flycatcher   phlegmatic   _____

flying fish   _____   _____

FL /fl/ Initial—four syllables

floriculture	flying safety	_____
fluctuation	flying saucer	_____

FL /fl/ Medial—two syllables

afflict	firefly	muffler
aflame	flip-flops	pamphlet
afloat	horsefly	reflect
blowfly	housefly	roughly
chiefly	ice floe	snowflake
conflict	inflame	soufflé
cornflakes	inflate	stiffly
deflate	inflict	top-flight
deflect	leaflet	_____

FL /fl/ Medial—three syllables

affliction	deflower	overflow
affluence	disfluent	reflection
affluent	dragonfly	reflector
butterfly	genuflect	sunflower
camouflage	ice flowers	wallflower
cornflower	inflation	_____
deflation	inflection	_____
deflection	influence	_____

FL /fl/ Medial—four syllables

cauliflower	inflammation	influenza
conflagration	inflatable	superfluous
genuflection	inflexible	_____
inflammable	influential	_____

FL /fl/ Final—two syllables

armful	baleful	doleful
artful	careful	doubtful
awful	changeful	dreadful
baffle	cheerful	Eiffel

faithful	mournful	spiteful
fateful	mouthful	spoonful
fitful	muffle	stifle
forceful	needful	thankful
fretful	pailful	thoughtful
frightful	painful	trifle
fruitful	peaceful	tuneful
gainful	playful	useful
gleeful	raffle	waffle
graceful	restful	wakeful
grateful	rightful	wasteful
handful	rueful	watchful
harmful	ruffle	willful
healthful	sackful	wishful
heedful	scoopful	woeful
helpful	scuffle	wrathful
hopeful	shuffle	wrongful
hurtful	skillful	youthful
joyful	sniffle	_____

FL /fl/ Final—three syllables

beautiful	eventful	resourceful
bountiful	fanciful	respectful
colorful	forgetful	sorrowful
deceitful	masterful	teaspoonful
disdainful	meaningful	unlawful
disgraceful	merciful	unthankful
distasteful	pitiful	untruthful
distressful	plentiful	wonderful
distrustful	reproachful	_____
dutiful	resentful	_____

FL /fl/ Final—four syllables

tablespoonful	uneventful	unmerciful

LF /lf/ Medial—two syllables

Alfred	bullfrog	elfkin
baleful	elfin	elflock
bullfinch	elfish	golfer

golfing	self-serve	welfare
Gulf Stream	self-taught	willful
self-care	shellfish	wolf cub
self-ease	sulfa	wolfhound
self-fed	sulfate	wolfish
self-help	sulfine	wolf pack
selfish	sulfite	_____
self-pride	sulfur	_____

LF /lf/ Medial—three syllables

alfalfa	self-control	self-righteous
alphabet	self-defense	self-searching
bellflower	self-esteem	self-serving
Bellflower	self-giving	self-support
bisulphate	self-glory	skillfully
bullfiddle	self-image	skillfulness
self-addressed	self-imposed	sulfatic
self-assured	selfishly	sulfitic
self-aware	self-pity	sulfuric
self-composed	self-possessed	unselfish
self-concept	self-regard	_____
self-conscious	self-reproach	_____
self-contained	self-respect	_____

LF /lf/ Medial—four syllables

alphabetic	self-confidence	self-evident
self-appointed	self-determined	self-reliance
self-assurance	self-directed	self-sacrifice
self-awareness	self-discipline	self-sufficient

LF /lf/ Final—one syllable

elf	Ralph	wolf
golf	self	_____
gulf	shelf	_____

LF /lf/ Final—two syllables

Adolf	engulf	himself
Adolphe	gray wolf	itself
bookshelf	herself	myself

oneself	Rudolph	white wolf
ourself	thyself	yourself
Randolph	werewolf	————————

FR /fr/ Initial—one syllable

frail	freight	frog
frame	French	from
Fran	fresh	frond
franc	fret	front
France	fried	frost
Frank	friend	froth
fraud	fright	frown
fray	frill	froze
freak	fringe	fruit
Fred	frisk	fry
free	Fritz	phrase
freeze	frock	————————

FR /fr/ Initial—two syllables

fraction	freehand	freshen
fracture	free-lance	freshman
fragile	free lunch	fretful
fragment	Freeport	friar
fragrance	freestyle	friction
fragrant	free throw	Friday
framework	free time	Frieda
framing	freeway	friendly
Frances	free will	friendship
franchise	freezer	frigate
Francis	freighter	frighten
Frankfurt	Fremont	frigid
Franklin	French fries	frisky
frantic	French horn	fritter
Frazer	Frenchman	frizzy
freakish	French toast	frogman
freckle	frenum	frolic
Freda	frenzied	frontage
freedom	frenzy	frontal
freefall	frequent	fronted

frontier
front page
front room
frostbite
frosted
frosting

frosty
frozen
frugal
fruitcake
fruit cup
frustrate

fryer
frying

_____
_____
_____
_____

FR /fr/ Initial—three syllables

fractional
fragmental
frankfurter
fraternal
Frederica
Frederick
Fredricksburg
freewheeling
frequency
fresh water
fricative

frictional
friction tape
friendliness
frivolous
frizzier
frolicking
frolicsome
frontal lobe
front runner
frostbitten
frost warning

fruitfulness
fruit salad
frustrating
frustration
frying pan
phrenetic
phrenitis

_____
_____
_____
_____

FR /fr/ Initial—four syllables

fractionary
fragility
fragmentary

fraternity
fraternizing
frighteningly

phraseogram
phrenology

_____

FR /fr/ Medial—two syllables

affray
affront
afraid
A-frame
Alfred
befriend
belfry
boyfriend
breadfruit
bullfrog
carefree
cold front
confront

deep freeze
deepfry
defraud
defray
defrost
fish fry
girl friend
grapefruit
Hausfrau
Humphrey
infract
infringe
Jack Frost

Jeffrey
leapfrog
refrain
refresh
scot-free
sea front
Wilfred
Winfred

_____
_____
_____
_____

FR /fr/ Medial—three syllables

affricate	infraction	unfriendly
Africa	infrared	unfrozen
antifreeze	infrequent	unfruitful
deep freezer	infringement	waterfront
defrosted	refreshing	Winifred
defroster	refreshments	_____
defrosting	sassafras	_____
Good Friday	unafraid	_____

FR /fr/ Medial—four syllables

confrontation	refrigerate	unfrequented
infractible	San Francisco	unfriendliest
infrequently	South Africa	unfruitfulness
refreshingly	tutti frutti	_____

FR /fr/ Medial—five syllables

infrangibleness	rcfractomctcr	rcfrigcrativc
refractivity	refrigeration	refrigerator

RF /rf/ Medial—two syllables

airfield	fearful	starfish
barefaced	forfeit	surface
barefoot	Garfield	surfboard
careful	orphan	surfer
cheerful	parfait	surfing
curfew	perfect	_____
earful	perform	_____
earphone	perfume	_____

RF /rf/ Medial—three syllables

butterfat	interfere	performer
carefully	interfold	performing
carefulness	labor force	tenderfoot
colorful	orphanage	underfoot
counterfeit	perfection	waterfall
fire fighter	perfectly	_____
forfeiture	perforate	_____
interface	performance	_____

RF /rf/ Medial—four syllables

butterfinger	morphology	_____
imperfection	performing arts	_____

FS /fs/ Medial—three syllables

cough syrup	lifesaving	_____
life cycles	_____	_____

FS /fs/ Final—one syllable

beefs	fluffs	ruffs
bluffs	goofs	scoffs
briefs	huffs	scuffs
buffs	Jeff's	spoofs
chefs	muffs	staffs
chiefs	proofs	stuffs
cliffs	puffs	whiffs
coughs	reefs	_____
cuffs	roofs	_____

FS /fs/ Final—two syllables

beliefs	handcuffs	show-offs
cast offs	kerchiefs	takeoffs
cutoffs	layoffs	tariffs
giraffes	play-offs	_____

FS /fs/ Final—three syllables

photographs	telegraphs	_____
powder puffs	_____	_____

SF /sf/ Initial—one syllable

sphere	_____	_____
sphinx	_____	_____

SF /sf/ Initial—two syllables

spheric	_____	_____
spheroid	_____	_____

SF /sf/ Initial—three syllables

spherical	_____	_____

SF /sf/ Initial—four syllables
spherically _____ _____

SF /sf/ Medial—two syllables

asphalt	henceforth	transfix
blaspheme	houseful	transform
cat's fur	peaceful	transfuse
forceful	thenceforth	useful
graceful	transfer	_____

SF /sf/ Medial—three syllables

atmosphere	gas furnace	transference
blasphemer	hemisphere	transfigure
blasphemous	lithosphere	transformer
blasphemy	misfortune	transfusion
disfavor	phosphorus	usefulness
disfigure	satisfy	_____
gas fixture	stratosphere	_____

SF /sf/ Medial—four syllables

asphyxiate	satisfaction	transformation
dysphasia	transferable	transfusible

FT /ft/ Medial—two syllables

after	left hand	softball
chieftain	lifter	soft drink
Clifton	lift-off	softness
driftwood	lift truck	software
fifteen	lofty	softwood
fifteenth	nifty	thriftless
fifty	rafter	thrift store
half time	ruffed grouse	thrifty
left field	sifter	_____

FT /ft/ Medial—three syllables

afterglow	afternoon	afterworld
afterlife	aftertaste	after-years
aftermath	afterthought	hereafter
aftermost	afterwards	leftovers

shoplifter   thereafter   thriftily

soft-hearted   thriftier

soft-shell crab   thriftiest

_____

_____

FT /ft/ Final—one syllable

aft	huffed	shrift
cleft	laughed	sift
craft	left	soft
croft	lift	swift
daft	loft	Taft
deft	oft	theft
draft	raft	thrift
drift	rift	tuft
gift	roofed	waft
goofed	ruffed	weft
graft	shaft	_____
heft	shift	_____

FT /ft/ Final—two syllables

adrift	hayloft	spacecraft
aircraft	ingraft	spendthrift
airlift	life raft	uncuffed
aloft	makeshift	uplift
crankshaft	night shift	witchcraft
day shift	ski lift	woodcraft
gearshift	skin graft	_____
handcraft	snowdrift	_____

FT /ft/ Final—three syllables

birthday gift	leisure craft	water craft
Christmas gift	overdraft	_____
handicraft	pleasure craft	_____
leather craft	rubber raft	_____

G

Pronounced: /g/
Spelled: g, gg, gh, gu, gue

G /g/ Initial—one syllable

gab	ghost	gouge
gad	gift	gout
gag	gig	gown
gage	Gil	guard
Gail	gild	guess
gain	gill	guessed
gained	gilt	guest
gait	gird	guide
gale	girl	guild
Gale	girth	guilt
gall	give	guise
game	go	gulch
games	goad	gulf
gang	goal	gull
gap	goals	gulls
garb	goat	gulp
gas	gob	gum
gash	goes	Gus
gasp	gold	gush
gate	golf	gust
gauche	gone	guy
gauge	gong	Guy
gaunt	good	_____
gauze	goods	_____
gave	goof	_____
Gayle	goofed	_____
gaze	goofs	_____
gear	goose	_____
geese	gorge	_____
get	got	_____

G /g/ Initial—two syllables

gable	gaudy	goldfinch
Gaby	gavel	goldfish
gadget	Gavin	goldie
gaily	Gaylord	good-bye
gainful	gazelle	goodness
gala	gazette	gopher
gallant	Gertrude	Gordon
galley	getting	gorgeous
gallon	geyser	gosling
gallop	ghastly	gossip
gallstone	ghostly	govern
galore	ghost town	guarded
galosh	Gibby	Guernsey
gambit	Gibson	guffaw
gamble	giddy	guidance
game bag	gifted	guidebook
game bird	Gilbert	guide dog
gander	Gilda	guidepost
Gandhi	Gilford	guiding
Ganges	gimmick	guilty
gangway	girdle	guinea
garage	girlhood	gully
garden	girlish	gumbo
Garfield	given	gumdrop
garish	giving	guppy
garland	gizzard	gurgle
garlic	goal post	gusto
garment	goalie	Guthrie
garnet	goatee	_____
garnish	gobble	_____
garret	goblet	_____
garter	goblin	_____
Gary	go-cart	_____
gaseous	Godfrey	_____
gasket	goggle	_____
gaslight	going	_____
gateway	goiter	_____
gather	golden	_____

G /g/ Initial—three syllables

gadabout	gas station	gorilla
gaiety	gathering	government
Galena	Gaza Strip	governor
Galilee	gazebo	guarantee
gallery	getaway	guardian
galvanize	Gettysburg	Guiana
Galveston	Gideon	guinea fowl
game tokens	goal keeper	guinea hen
gardener	godfather	guinea pig
garden hose	golden age	gurgitate
gardenia	goldenrod	_____
gardening	golden years	_____
gasoline	gooseberry	_____

G /g/ Medial—two syllables

again	biggest	dogear
against	bighead	dogfight
agape	bighorn	dogfish
agate	bigot	dogged
agaze	bogus	doggy
aghast	braggart	dogie
Agnes	bragging	dogma
auger	brigade	dog sled
August	buggy	dog tag
bagful	bygone	dragging
baggage	chigger	dragnet
bagman	chugging	dragon
bagpipe	cognate	dragoon
began	cognize	drugstore
beget	cougar	dugout
beggar	Dagan	eager
begging	dagger	Edgar
begin	digger	eggnog
begone	digging	eggplant
begot	disgorge	eggshell
beguile	disguise	ego
begun	disgust	engage
bigger	dogcart	engulf

figure	logo	rugger
flagman	log on	saga
flagship	luggage	sea gull
flagstone	lugger	segment
foggy	magnet	shaggy
foghorn	magpie	signal
fragment	meager	soggy
frigate	misguide	stagger
headgear	muggy	stagnant
hogshead	nagging	sugar
Hugo	nosegay	swagger
ignite	nugget	swaggered
ignore	pagan	tiger
ingot	piggy	toga
jagged	pigment	tollgate
jigger	pignut	trigger
jiggle	pigpen	triggered
jigsaw	pigskin	tugboat
jogging	pigtail	vagus
juggle	quagmire	vigor
lagger	ragman	wagging
lagging	ragtime	wagon
lagoon	Reagan	Yoga
leaguer	regain	yogi
legal	regale	Yogi
leghorn	regard	zygote
Logan	regards	_____
logger	rigor	_____
logging	roguish	_____

G /g/ Medial—three syllables

Abigail	bowlegged	conjugate
Agatha	bugaboo	corrugate
agonize	Carnegie	demigod
agony	castigate	diagnose
arrogance	category	dignify
beginning	chuck wagon	dignity
begonia	clogginess	disgusted
billy goat	cognizance	disregard

dogmatic
doll buggy
eagerly
egotist
elegance
fatiguing
four-legged
gigantic
hexagon
hobgoblin
ignorance
ignorant
illegal
instigate
legacy
legally
legation
ligament
lumbago
magazines
magnify
magnolia
marigold
megaphone
misgiving

misgivings
misgovern
Mother Goose
navigate
negative
New Guinea
Niagara
Oregon
outgoing
outrigger
pagoda
pentagon
pigheaded
pogo stick
Portugal
prodigal
prognosis
recognize
regalia
regardless
regatta
regular
regulate
renegade
rigorous

seagoing
self-regard
signature
signify
spaghetti
Sugar Land
synagogue
Thanksgiving
tiger-eye
tiger moth
toboggan
together
two-legged
unguarded
unguided
untangled
vagabond
vigorous
vinegar
whirligig
woolgather

_____
_____
_____
_____

G /g/ Medial—four syllables

allegation
alligator
altogether
antagonist
antagonize
baby buggy
beginner's luck
coagulate
Copenhagen
delegation
derogative
egotism

enigmatic
esophagus
Gulf of Guinea
illegally
investigate
legality
magnificent
mahogany
merry-go-round
monogamous
navigation
navigator

negotiate
obligation
polygamous
prolongation
propaganda
protagonist
regality
significance
significant
tiger beetle
tiger lily
togetherness

unregarded   vinegary   _____
video game   _____   _____

G /g/ Medial—five syllables

egomania   ingurgitation   _____
egotistical   _____   _____

G /g/ Final—one syllable

bag	Greg	rogue
beg	hag	rug
big	hog	sag
bog	hug	shag
brag	jag	shrug
brig	jig	slug
brogue	jog	smog
bug	jug	smug
clog	keg	snag
cog	lag	snug
crag	league	sprig
Craig	leg	stag
dig	log	swag
dog	lug	swig
Doug	Mag	tag
drag	Meg	thug
dug	mug	trig
egg	nag	tug
fig	peg	twig
flag	Peg	vague
flog	pig	vogue
fog	plague	wag
frog	plug	Whig
fugue	prig	wig
gag	rag	yegg
gig	rig	_____

G /g/ Final—two syllables

agog	bedbug	bowleg
bean-bag	bigwig	brown bag
bear hug	bird dog	bulldog

clothes bag
colleague
dog tag
eggnog
fatigue
game bag
ground fog
groundhog
guide dog
hand bag
hedgehog
hot dog
humbug

ice bag
ice fog
intrigue
jet lag
June bug
lunch bag
nutmeg
prologue
ragtag
renege
sand bag
sand bug
shag rug

shindig
shoe bag
sled dog
spark plug
tea bag
The Hague
time-lag
trash bag
unclog
washrag
wigwag
zigzag
_____

G /g/ Final—three syllables

analog
bunny hug
carpetbag
catalog
chili dog
deviled egg
dialogue
ditty bag
doodlebug
duffel bag
garbage bag
guinea pig
jitterbug
ladybug
laundry bag

lightning bug
litter bag
litterbug
moneybag
monologue
paper bag
Persian rug
plastic bag
polliwog
prairie dog
punching bag
sandwich bag
shopping bag
shoulder bag
sleeping bag

synagogue
travelogue
underdog
vacuum bag
water bag
water bug
water dog
waterlog
whirligig
Winnipeg
_____
_____
_____
_____
_____

G /g/ Final—four syllables

card catalog
carry-on bag
desk catalog

gift catalog
potato bug
prescription drug

seeing-eye dog
traveling bag
_____

GER /gɚ/ Medial—three syllables

rigorous
vigorous

GER /gɚ/ Final—two syllables

beggar	jigger	rigor
bigger	lager	stagger
chigger	leaguer	tiger
cougar	logger	vigor
dagger	lugger	_____
eager	meager	_____

GER /gɚ/ Final—three syllables

cheeseburger	Limburger	vinegar
hamburger	outrigger	_____

NGER /ŋɚ/ Medial—three syllables

fingerling	fingerprint	lingering
fingernail	fingerspell	_____

NGER /ŋɚ/ Final—two syllables

finger	longer	wringer
hanger	ringer	younger
hunger	singer	_____
linger	swinger	_____

GL /gl/ Initial—one syllable

glad	glean	gloss
glade	gleaned	glove
glance	glee	gloves
glanced	glen	glow
gland	Glenn	glue
glare	glib	glued
glared	glide	glum
glass	glimpse	glume
glaze	gloat	_____
glazed	globe	_____
gleam	gloom	_____

GL /gl/ Initial—two syllables

glacier	glad rags	glancing
gladden	Gladys	glaring
gladness	glamor	glary

glasses	Glenda	gloomy
glasshouse	Glendale	glory
glassine	glided	glossy
glassware	glide plane	glottis
glasswork	glider	Glover
glassy	gliding	glowing
glazement	glimmer	glowworm
glazier	glisten	glucose
glazing	glitter	gluing
gleaning	gloaming	gluten
glee club	global	glutton
gleeful	globate	_____

GL /gl/ Initial—three syllables

glamorize	glimmering	glorify
glamorous	glistening	glorious
glandular	glitter ice	glossary
glass blowcr	glittery	glossier
glass blowing	globe-trotter	glycerin
glass cutter	glomerate	glyptodont
glaucoma	gloomier	_____
gleefully	Gloria	_____

GL /gl/ Initial—four syllables

gladiator	Gloriana	glossology
gladiola	glorifier	_____
glamorously	gloriously	_____

GL /gl/ Medial—two syllables

aglow	giggly	scrub gloves
boggling	haggling	spyglass
bugler	hourglass	straggling
Douglas	igloo	sunglow
dress gloves	joggling	unglue
eaglet	juggler	unglued
eagling	juggling	wineglass
eyeglass	lymph gland	work gloves
giggler	neglect	wriggler
giggling	piglet	wriggly

GL /gl/ Medial—three syllables

aglimmer	fiberglass	semi-glaze
aglitter	field glasses	semi-glazed
baseball glove	leather gloves	semi-gloss
boondoggler	looking glass	sunglasses
boxing glove	neglectful	water glass
dark glasses	negligence	window glass
everglade	negligent	_____
Everglades	plastic glass	_____
eyeglasses	rubber gloves	_____

GL /gl/ Final—two syllables

beagle	jiggle	straggle
bugle	joggle	struggle
eagle	juggle	waggle
gargle	legal	wiggle
giggle	regal	wriggle
gurgle	smuggle	_____
haggle	snuggle	_____

GL /gl/ Final—three syllables

bedraggle	illegal	prodigal
boondoggle	Portugal	salt bagel

NGL /ŋl/ Medial—two syllables

angler	English	mingling
angling	jingler	wrangler
Anglo	jingling	wrangling
England	jungly	_____

NGL /ŋl/ Medial—three syllables

Anglican	drinking glass	English horn
anglicize	Englander	Englishman
anglify	Englisher	New England

NGL /ŋl/ Final—two syllables

angle	jangle	mingle
dangle	jingle	shingle
dingle	jungle	single

spangle	tingle	_____
tangle	wrangle	_____

NGL /ŋl/ Final—three syllables

commingle	quadrangle	untangle
entangle	rectangle	_____
Kris Kringle	right angle	_____
left angle	triangle	_____

NGTH /ŋθ/ Medial—two syllables

lengthen	lengthy	_____
lengthways	strengthen	_____
lengthwise	_____	_____

NGTH /ŋθ/ Final—one syllable

length	_____	_____
strength	_____	_____

NGTH /ŋθ/ Final—two syllables

full-length	wave-length	_____
half-length	whole-length	_____

GR /gr/ Initial—one syllable

grab	grass	grill
grace	grate	grilled
Grace	grave	grim
grade	gray	grime
grades	graze	grin
graft	grease	grind
grain	great	grip
gram	Greece	gripe
grand	green	grit
grange	greet	groan
grant	Greg	groom
Grant	grew	groomed
grape	grey	groove
grapes	grid	grooved
graph	grief	grope
grasp	grieve	gross

grouch

ground

grounds

group

grouse

grove

grow

growl

grown

growth

grub

grudge

gruff

grump

grunt

_____

_____

_____

GR /gr/ Initial—two syllables

grabbing

graceful

gracious

grackle

grader

grade school

grading

grafting

Graham

grammar

grandad

grandeur

grandma

grandniece

grandpa

Grand Prix

grand slam

grandson

grandstand

grand tour

granite

grantee

grantor

granule

grapefruit

grapevine

graphic

graphite

grasping

grassland

grass snake

grassy

grateful

grating

gravel

graveyard

gravy

grazing

greasing

greasy

Great Dane

greater

greatest

Great Falls

Great Lakes

greatly

greedy

greenbacks

greenhouse

greeting

greetings

gremlin

Greta

Gretchen

greyhound

griddle

Griffin

Griffith

grillwork

grimace

grimy

grinder

grinding

grindstone

grinning

griping

gripping

gristle

gritty

grizzle

grizzled

grizzly

grocer

groggy

grooming

groomsman

grooving

groovy

groping

grotesque

grotto

grouchy

ground crew

grounder

ground floor

ground fog

groundhog

ground rules

ground wave

groundwire

groundwork

Grover

growing

grown-up	grumble	grunion
grubby	grumpy	_____
gruesome	Grundy	_____

GR /gr/ Initial—three syllables

gracias	grandnephew	grizzly bear
graciously	grandparents	groceries
gradual	granny knot	grocery
graduate	granulate	ground cover
granary	grasshopper	Ground Hog Day
Grandberry	gratify	grounds keeper
Grand Canyon	gratitude	ground squirrel
grandchildren	gravity	ground zero
granddaughter	Great Britain	grueling
grandfather	Great Divide	_____
grandiose	Gregory	_____
grand jury	gridiron	_____
grandmother	Griselda	_____

GR /gr/ Initial—four syllables

gradually	Grand Old Party	gravitation
graduation	grand piano	great-grandparent
graduator	Granite City	gregarious
grammarian	graphology	grotesquerie
grammatical	gratifying	group therapy
grandfather clock	gratuitous	_____

GR /gr/ Medial—two syllables

aggrieve	congress	flagrant
aggrieved	degrade	foreground
agree	degree	fragrance
agreed	digress	fragrant
aground	disgrace	hungry
angry	downgrade	ingrain
background	egress	Ingram
begrudge	egret	ingrate
bluegrass	engrave	Ingrid
blue-green	engross	ingroup
bridegroom	fairground	land grant

migrate	progress	tigress
mongrel	regrade	upgrade
outgrow	regress	vagrant
outgrowth	regret	_____
Pilgrim	regroup	_____
program	school ground	_____

GR /gr/ Medial—three syllables

aggregate	disgruntle	photograph
aggression	emigrant	regression
aggressive	evergreen	Rio Grande
agreement	Evergreen	segregate
allegro	filigree	seismograph
anagram	homograph	study group
au gratin	immigrant	telegram
autograph	immigrate	telegraph
cablegram	ingrowing	underground
centigrade	integrate	undergrown
centigram	kilogram	undergrowth
citrus grove	lettergram	ungraceful
concord grapes	Mardi Gras	ungracious
congregate	migration	ungrateful
congressman	milligram	upgrading
congruent	monogram	vagrancy
congruous	overgrown	wintergreen
diagram	overgrowth	_____
dictograph	paragraph	_____
disagree	pedigree	_____
disgraceful	phonograph	_____

GR /gr/ Medial—four syllables

aggravation	coffee grinder	federal grant
agriculture	conflagration	geography
allegretto	congratulate	incongruent
audiogram	congregation	incongruous
biographer	congressional	ingratiate
biographic	congruity	ingratitude
biography	disagreement	ingredient
calligrapher	disintegrate	integration

integrative
integrity
mimeograph
organ grinder
photographer
photography
regretfully
regrettable
retrogression

segregated
segregation
stenographer
subaggregate
subgranular
technography
telegrammic
telegrapher
telegraphic

telegraphy
tympanogram
typographer
typography
undergrading
ungraciously
ungrantable
ungraspable

_____

GR /gr/ Medial—five syllables

agricultural
bibliography
biographical
diagrammatic
disagreeable
disintegrated

disintegration
geographical
incongruity
ingratiating
ingratiation
oceanographer

oceanographic
oceanography
topographical
undergraduate
ungrammatical

_____

RG /rg/ Medial—two syllables

argue
bargain
Bergen
cargo
ergo
forget
forgive

forgot
gargle
gurgle
jargon
Largo
Morgan
mortgage

organ
sorghum
stargaze
target
tour guide
Virgo

_____

RG /rg/ Medial—three syllables

argument
burgundy
cheeseburger
embargo
forgetful
forgetting

forgiven
forgiveness
forgotten
hamburger
Limburger
Margaret

organdy
organic
organize
pipe organ
undergo

_____

RG /rg/ Medial—four syllables

burgomaster
disorganize
forget-me-not

forgettable
forgivable
kindergarten

organ grinder
organism
organizer

undergarment _____ _____
unforgiven _____ _____

RG /rg/ Medial—five syllables
organization _____ _____
unforgettable _____ _____

RG /rg/ Final—one syllable
berg   erg   _____
burg   morgue   _____

RG /rg/ Final—two syllables
Clarksburg   Lordsburg   Salzburg
Goldberg   Newberg   Strasbourg
Hamburg   Oldsberg   Strindberg
iceberg   Pittsburgh Tilburg
Lemberg   Romberg   Youngberg
Lindberg   Roseburg   _____

RG /rg/ Final—three syllables
Brandenburg Hindenburg Regensburg
Cederberg   Luxembourg Reichenberg
Edinburg   Oldenburg   Rosenburg
Gettysburg   Petersburg Swedenborg
Heidelberg   Phillipsburg Williamsburg

RG /rg/ Final—four syllables
East Harrisburg _____ _____
Johannesburg   _____ _____

GW /gw/ Initial—one syllable
Guam   Guelph Gwin
guan   Guinn   Gwyn
guar   Gwen   _____

GW /gw/ Initial—two syllables
guaco   guanine Gwenda
guana   guano   _____
guanay   guava   _____

GW /gw/ Initial—three syllables

guacharo	Guayama	Guinevere
guanaco	guayule	Gwendolyn
Guarani	Guenevere	_____

GW /gw/ Initial—four syllables

guacamole	Guadalupe	_____
Guadalcanal	Guantanamo	_____
Guadalquivir	Guatemala	_____

GW /gw/ Initial—five syllables

guacamole dip	Guadalupe Palm	_____
Guadalajara	Guantanamo Bay	_____

GW /gw/ Medial—two syllables

agua	languet	sanguine
aguar	languid	ungual
anguine	languish	unguent
anguish	lingua	unguis
anguished	lingual	wigwag
dogwood	linguist	wigwam
hogwash	penguin	_____
jaguar	pinguid	_____
language	ragweed	_____

GW /gw/ Medial—three syllables

alguazil	language arts	tagua nut
alguien	language cards	teguexin
bilingual	languages	unguical
distinguish	languishing	_____
extinguish	languishment	_____
iguana	linguiform	_____
inguinal	linguistics	_____
La Guaira	sign language	_____

GW /gw/ Medial—four syllables

Aguadilla	La Guardia	sanguineous
Agua Fria	language patterns	unguentary
extinguisher	language workbook	_____

GY /gj/ Medial—two syllables

egg yolk	figured	_____
figure	figures	_____

GY /gj/ Medial—three syllables

figure eight	figure out	regular
figure-ground	figure skate	regulate
figurehead	figuring	transfigured

GY /gj/ Medial—four syllables

father figure	regulated	triangular
figure skating	regulating	_____
regularly	regulation	_____

GZ /gz/ Medial—two syllables

exact	exert	exist
exalt	exhaust	exult
exam	exhort	zigzag
exempt	exile	_____

GZ /gz/ Medial—three syllables

eczema	exemption	exhibit
exacting	exertion	existence
exaction	exertive	existent
exactly	exhaustion	exotic
examine	exhaustive	exultant
example	exhaustless	_____

GZ /gz/ Medial—four syllables

exactitude	exemplify	exorbitance
exaggerate	exemptible	exorbitant
examinant	exhaustible	exordium
examinate	exhibitive	exuberance
examinee	exhibitor	exuberant
exasperate	exhilarant	exuberate
executant	exhilarate	exultancy
executive	exhortation	exultation
executrix	existential	_____
exemplary	exonerate	_____

GZ /gz/ Medial—five syllables

exaggeration	executory	exonerator
exaggerative	exercitation	exorbitancy
exaggerator	exhibitory	exotically
examinable	exhilaration	exuberancy
examination	exhilarative	_____
exasperation	exoneration	_____

GZ /gz/ Final—one syllable

bags	jogs	rogues
begs	kegs	rugs
bogs	lags	sags
bugs	legs	tags
cogs	logs	togs
digs	lugs	tugs
dogs	mugs	wags
eggs	nags	wigs
gags	pegs	_____
hogs	pigs	_____
hugs	rags	_____
jigs	rigs	_____

H

Pronounced: /h/
Spelled: h, wh, g, j

H /h/ Initial—one syllable

hack	he	hill
Hack	head	him
had	health	hind
hail	heap	hinge
hair	hear	hint
Hal	hearse	hip
half	heart	his
hall	heat	hiss
halt	heath	hit
ham	heave	hitch
hand	heel	hive
hang	heels	ho
Hank	height	hoard
Hans	heist	hoarse
hard	helm	hoax
hare	help	hob
harp	hem	hock
harsh	hemp	hoe
has	hen	hog
hash	hence	hoist
haste	her	hold
hat	Herb	hole
hatch	herd	home
haul	here	hone
haunt	hers	honk
have	hi	hood
hawk	hid	hoof
hay	hide	hook
Hayes	high	hoop
haze	hike	hoot

hop	huff	hush
hope	hug	husk
horn	hulk	hut
horse	Hulk	hutch
hose	hull	hymn
host	hum	who
hot	hump	whole
hound	hunch	who'll
house	hung	whom
how	hunt	whose
Hoyle	hurl	_____
hub	hurt	_____

H /h/ Initial—two syllables

habit	hanger	hatchet
hacksaw	hanker	Hattie
haddock	Hannah	haughty
hailstone	hapless	hausfrau
hailstorm	happy	havoc
hair-do	harangue	hayrack
Haiti	hardback	hayride
halfback	hard hats	haystack
half-hour	hardhead	hazard
half time	Harding	Hazel
halfway	hardwood	headache
hallway	Harlem	headboard
halter	Harlen	headlight
hammer	Harley	headset
hammock	harmful	health farm
hamper	harness	health food
hamster	Harold	healthy
handbag	harpoon	hearing
handball	harried	heartburn
handknit	Harris	heartsick
handlace	Harry	heat rash
handle	Harvard	heathen
handsaw	Harvey	heather
handset	hassock	Heather
handshake	hatbox	heatstroke

heatwave	hilltop	horrid
Hebrew	hilly	horseback
heckle	Hilton	horseshoe
hedge hog	himself	hot bath
hedgehop	Hindu	hot dog
Hedy	hippo	hotel
heedful	Hiram	hot rod
Heidi	hitchhike	Hot Springs
heifer	hoary	housetop
heighten	hobby	housewife
heinous	hockey	housing
Helen	hodgepodge	Houston
Helga	hoeing	hovel
hello	hogan	hover
Helma	Holland	Howard
helmet	hollow	howling
helping	holly	humble
hemlock	Holly	hummock
henna	holster	Humphrey
Henry	holy	hundred
Herbert	homeland	hungry
Herman	homely	Huntsville
hermit	homemade	hurdle
heron	homer	hurrah
herself	Homer	hurry
Hester	homeroom	hydrant
Hibbing	home run	hygiene
hidden	homespun	hymnal
hiding	homework	hymnbook
hi-fi	honey	hyper
high jump	Hong Kong	hyphen
high rise	hoodwink	hypo
high school	hoofer	Jai Alai
high tide	hookup	Jose
high time	Hopi	whole wheat
highway	hopping	wholesale
hiker	hopscotch	wholesome
Hilda	Horace	who's who
hillside	hornet	

H /h/ Initial—three syllables

Gila Bend	hearing aid	horizon
habitat	heating pad	horned lizard
hair dryer	heavyweight	horseradish
hairdresser	helium	hospital
half-and-half	hemisphere	housemother
half brother	herbicide	Hovercraft
half-dollars	hermitage	however
halibut	heroic	Hudson Bay
Hall of Fame	Hidalgo	hula-hoop
Halloween	high jumper	hula skirt
hamburger	high water	humdinger
handicap	Hilary	hummingbird
handicraft	Hildegard	hurricane
handiwork	hippogriff	hyacinth
handkerchief	history	hydrogen
handlebar	hitch hiker	hydroplane
handwriting	hobby horse	hyena
Hanukkah	hockey skate	hypnosis
haphazard	hockey stick	hypnotic
happiness	holiday	hypnotize
harbinger	holiness	hypocrite
hardscrabble	hollyhock	Julio
Harlingen	Hollywood	whodunit
harmonize	homecoming	whoever
harmony	homemaker	wholehearted
harpsichord	Honduras	_____
Harriet	honeybee	_____
Harrison	honeycomb	_____
Hawaii	honeydew	_____
Hawaiian	Hoover Dam	_____

H /h/ Initial—four syllables

gila monster	hepatitis	horticulture
habberdasher	heredity	hot-air balloon
hallelujah	historian	hydrometer
harmonica	historical	hyperfunction
hearing-impaired	histrionic	hypergolic
helicopter	Honolulu	hypocrisy

hypodermic	hypothermal	_____
hypolithic	hypothesis	_____
hypotenuse	hypothesize	_____

H /h/ Initial—five syllables

hemophilia	hippopotamus	hydrotherapy
hermetically	hooliganism	hypochondriac
herpetology	hydrodynamics	_____

H /h/ Medial—two syllables

aha	fire hat	porthole
ahead	fishhook	pothole
ahem	Fordham	redhead
ahoy	forehand	rehash
Amherst	forehead	rehear
Baja	greenhouse	rehearse
beehive	groundhog	reheat
behave	hedgehop	roundhouse
behind	heigh-ho	sandhog
behold	high heels	Sandhurst
behoove	hitchhike	sea horse
bellhop	inhale	treehouse
birdhouse	keyhole	unhook
blackhead	lighthouse	uphill
blockhouse	manhole	wahoo
boohoo	manhunt	White House
chuckhole	mayhem	yahoo
cohort	mishap	yoo-hoo
cowhide	mohair	_____
doghouse	O'Hare	_____
doll house	one-half	_____
downhill	packhorse	_____
eyehole	playhouse	_____

H /h/ Medial—three syllables

abhorrent	beholden	clothes hanger
Abraham	buttonhole	cohesion
anyhow	Captain Hook	cubbyhole
behavior	city hall	dehydrate

Elihu	Ohio	rocking horse
grasshopper	overhaul	sand hopper
hobby horse	Pearl Harbor	study hall
hula hoop	pigeonhole	tomahawk
inhaler	porterhouse	unhappy
inherent	potholder	unholy
inherit	rehearsal	unwholesome
inhibit	rehearsing	_____
O'Hara	Robin Hood	_____

H /h/ Medial—four syllables

aircraft hangar	inhibition	safety helmet
Beverly Hills	inhibitor	_____
exhalation	Irish wolfhound	_____
inhalation	mahogany	_____
inharmonic	Red Riding Hood	_____

J

Pronounced: /dʒ/
Spelled: ch, d, dg, dge, di, g, gg, j

J /dʒ/ Initial—one syllable

gee	jaw	Joan
gel	jaws	job
gem	jay	Job
gene	Jay	jock
Gene	Jayne	Jock
gent	jazz	Joe
George	Jean	jog
germ	Jeanne	jogged
gibe	jeans	John
gin	jeep	join
gist	jeer	joist
gym	jeers	joke
gyp	Jeff	jolt
jab	jell	Jon
jabbed	jerk	Josh
jack	jerked	jot
Jack	Jess	jounce
jacks	jest	jounced
jade	jet	joust
jag	Jew	Jove
Jake	jib	jowl
jam	jibe	joy
jamb	jibed	Joy
James	jig	Joyce
jammed	jigged	Judd
Jan	Jill	Jude
Jane	jilt	judge
jar	Jim	judged
jarred	jinx	jug
jaunt	Jo	juice

jump	junked	_____
jumped	just	_____
June	jut	_____
junk	jute	_____

J /dʒ/ Initial—two syllables

gender	jackstraw	Jerri
genie	Jacob	Jerry
genius	jagged	Jersey
gentle	jaguar	Jesse
genus	jailbird	Jessie
Georgette	Jamestown	jester
Georgia	Jamie	Jesus
Gerald	Janet	Jethro
gerbil	jangle	jetsam
German	jangled	jet set
Germane	Janice	jetty
gerund	Japan	jewcl
gesture	jargon	jiffy
giant	Jarvis	jigger
giblet	jasmine	jiggle
Gina	Jason	jigsaw
ginger	jasper	jimmied
Ginger	Jasper	jimmy
ginseng	jaundice	Jimmy
giraffe	jaundiced	jitney
gymnast	javelin	jittered
gypsum	jawbone	jitters
gypsy	Jaycees	Joanne
gyrate	jayhawk	jockey
jabber	jaywalk	Joel
jackal	jealous	joggle
jacket	Jeanine	joggled
Jack Frost	Jeffrey	Johnson
Jackie	jellied	Joline
jackknife	jelly	jolly
jackknifed	Jenny	Joseph
jackpot	Jensen	jostle
Jackson	Jerome	jostled

journal	Julia	junket
journey	Julian	junk food
joyful	Julie	Juno
joyous	Julius	jurist
joyride	jumble	juror
Judah	jumbled	jury
judgment	jumbo	justice
Judith	jumper	Justin
Judson	junction	_____
Judy	juncture	_____
juggle	Juneau	_____
juggled	June bug	_____
juggler	jungle	_____
juicy	junior	

J /dʒ/ Initial—three syllables

gelatin	jamboree	jubilee
Gemini	janitor	judicial
general	Japanese	jugular
generate	Jasper Park	jujitsu
generous	jawbreaker	julienne
genetic	jazzercise	Juliet
Geneva	jealousy	juniper
Genevieve	Jefferson	jury room
genial	jellybeans	justified
gentleman	jellyfish	justify
genuine	Jennifer	juvenile
Geraldine	Jeopardy	juxtapose
Germany	Jessica	_____
germicide	jettison	_____
germinate	jitterbug	_____
giant crab	Johanna	_____
gigantic	Johnny Reb	_____
gingerbread	Jonathan	_____
gymnastics	Josephine	_____
jackrabbit	Joshua	_____
Jacksonville	journalist	_____
Jacqueline	jovial	_____
jalopy	jubilance	_____

J /dʒ/ Initial—four syllables

generalize	gymnasium	jurisprudence
generally	jack-in-the-box	jurisprudent
generation	jack-o'-lantern	jury duty
geography	javelin throw	justifying
geologist	Jerusalem	juvenescence
geology	joshua tree	juvenescent
geometry	journalism	juxtaposing
gesticulate	jubilation	_____
giant slalom	junior college	_____
gigantism	junior high school	_____
gingerbread man	jurisdiction	_____

J /dʒ/ Medial—two syllables

adjoin	digit	hodgepodge
adjoined	disjoin	judges
adjourn	disjoined	judging
adjunct	disjoint	judgment
adjust	dodge ball	ledger
ageless	dodger	legend
agent	Dodgers	legion
age-old	dodging	lodger
agile	dredger	lodging
aging	edges	logic
ajar	edgewise	magic
badger	Edgewood	major
badgered	Egypt	midget
blue jay	eject	misjudge
Bridget	Eugene	object
bridgework	fidget	pageant
budget	fledgling	page boy
bulges	fragile	pages
bulging	frigid	pigeon
cages	fudging	pledger
codger	gadget	pledging
cogent	hedgehog	prejudge
cudgel	hedgehop	prejudged
deject	hedges	project
digest	high jump	pudgy

rajah	rigid	subject
regent	Roger	suggest
region	snow job	tragic
reject	sojourn	urgent
rejoice	soldier	vigil
rejoiced	squeegee	wage scale
rejoin	stagecoach	wager
rejudge	staging	wages
ridgepole	stodgy	

J /dʒ/ Medial—three syllables

adages	effigy	majestic
adjutant	ejection	majesty
agency	elegy	majorette
agitate	engagement	management
algebra	eugenic	manager
allegiance	eulogize	meninges
arranges	eulogized	nitrogen
astringent	eulogy	Norwegian
bandaging	fugitive	objected
bluejacket	G.I. Joe	objection
cabbages	high jumper	objective
cogitate	high jumping	origin
collegian	hydrogen	outrageous
collegiate	imagine	oxygen
cottage cheese	imagined	passageway
cotton gin	imaging	pigeonhole
courageous	indigence	pigeon-toed
credulous	indigent	plagiarize
deluges	indulgence	plagiarized
digestion	indulgent	procedure
diligence	jumping-jack	prodigious
divulgence	legible	prodigy
divulges	logical	progeny
Dodge City	longitude	projectile
dowager	magenta	pugilist
drudgery	magical	refugee
drum major	magician	regency
educate	magistrate	Regency

regiment	sledge hammer	vigilant
regional	strategic	villager
register	strategy	voyager
registered	suggestion	Voyager
registrar	teenager	windjammer
rejection	tragedy	_____
religion	vegetate	_____

J /dʒ/ Medial—four syllables

adjacency	eligible	pedagogy
adjudicate	encouragement	photogenic
advantageous	exaggerate	prejudicial
Age of Reason	geology	psychology
agility	homogenize	pugilistic
agitation	hygienic	refrigerate
agitator	illegible	regenerate
algebraic	incogitant	regimental
Algeria	incredulous	registration
apologize	intelligence	rejuvenate
apologized	intelligent	vegetables
astrologer	legislation	vegetation
belligerent	maharaja	vigilante
biology	majority	yellow jacket
cajolery	maladjusted	yellow jasmine
cogitation	Middle Ages	zoology
corrigible	mythology	_____
degenerate	neurology	_____
digestible	original	_____
dirigible	originate	_____
education	otology	_____
educator	pathology	_____

J /dʒ/ Medial—five syllables

anthropology	genealogy	physiology
apologetic	ideology	Sagittarius
criminology	imagination	sociology
etiology	incorrigible	subjectivity
etymology	indigestible	_____
exaggeration	ineligible	_____

J /dʒ/ Final—one syllable

age	gauge	ridge
badge	grudge	sage
bilge	hedge	siege
bridge	huge	sledge
budge	judge	sludge
bulge	ledge	smudge
cage	lodge	stage
dodge	Madge	stooge
Dodge	midge	trudge
dredge	Midge	wage
drudge	nudge	wedge
edge	page	_____
fledge	pledge	_____
fudge	rage	_____

J /dʒ/ Final—two syllables

abridge	damage	language
adage	deluge	leakage
allege	divulge	linkage
avenge	dosage	luggage
backstage	drainage	manage
baggage	drawbridge	marriage
bandage	encage	message
begrudge	engage	mileage
besiege	enrage	misjudge
breakage	float bridge	mortgage
Bronze Age	footage	oblige
cabbage	forage	old age
Cambridge	frontage	outage
carriage	garbage	outrage
Carthage	herbage	package
cartridge	hodgepodge	partridge
cleavage	homage	passage
college	hostage	pillage
Coolidge	Ice Age	plumage
cottage	image	porridge
courage	indulge	portage
cribbage	knowledge	postage

prejudge	spillage	upstage
rampage	spoilage	usage
ravage	steerage	vestige
refuge	Stone Age	village
roughage	stoppage	vintage
rummage	storage	voyage
salvage	stowage	wastage
sausage	suffrage	wattage
savage	teenage	wreckage
scrimmage	toll bridge	yardage
selvage	tonnage	_____
silage	trackage	_____
South Bridge	truckage	_____

J /dʒ/ Final—three syllables

acknowledge	disparage	mismanage
acreage	encourage	overage
advantage	cnvisagc	parsonagc
Anchorage	flowerage	patronage
appendage	foliage	percentage
average	golden age	personage
beverage	hemorrhage	pilgrimage
brokerage	heritage	privilege
Brooklyn Bridge	hermitage	Rainbow Bridge
cartilage	horse carriage	self-image
Copper Age	Iron Age	verbiage
coverage	leverage	_____
discourage	lineage	_____
disengage	London Bridge	_____
disoblige	middle age	_____

JER /dʒɚ/ Medial—three syllables

dangerous	gingerly	majorette
ginger ale	gingersnap	_____
gingerbread	injury	_____

JER /dʒɚ/ Medial—four syllables

belligerent	gingerliness	_____
exaggerate	major-domo	_____

JER /dʒɚ/ Final—two syllables

badger	larger	pledger
danger	ledger	ranger
dodger	lodger	Roger
dredger	lounger	soldier
ginger	major	stranger
Ginger	manger	wager
injure	merger	_____

JER /dʒɚ/ Final—three syllables

avenger	messenger	villager
drum major	passenger	voyager
endanger	procedure	Voyager
Lone Ranger	scavenger	_____
manager	teenager	_____

JER /dʒɚ/ Final—four syllables

astrologer	train passenger	_____
supercharger	_____	_____

NJ /ndʒ/ Medial—two syllables

angel	enjoin	pongee
banjo	enjoy	pungent
congeal	enjoyed	ranger
congealed	ginger	rangy
congest	ingest	sponges
conjure	inject	stranger
conjured	injure	tangent
danger	injured	unjust
dingy	lounger	vengeance
dungeon	manger	vengeful
engine	Ninja	_____

NJ /ndʒ/ Medial—three syllables

Angela	avenger	changeable
angelfish	Blue Angels	congested
angelic	Challenger	congestion
Angelus	challenges	conjecture
angina	challenging	conjugal

conjunction	gingerbread	Lone Ranger
dangerous	gingerly	messenger
endanger	gingersnap	passenger
endangered	ingenious	scavenger
engendered	injected	tangerine
engineer	injection	tangible
engineered	injunction	_____
fire engine	injury	_____
ginger ale	injustice	_____

NJ /ndʒ/ Medial—four syllables

conjectural	evangelist	intangible
conjugation	evangelize	meningitis
evangelic	injurious	_____

NJ /ndʒ/ Medial—five syllables

evangelical	laryngectomy	_____
ingenuity	_____	_____

NJ /ndʒ/ Final—one syllable

change	lunge	sponge
flange	mange	strange
fringe	plunge	tinge
grange	range	twinge
hinge	scrounge	_____
lounge	singe	_____

NJ /ndʒ/ Final—two syllables

arrange	estrange	revenge
astringe	exchange	scavenge
avenge	expunge	unhinge
challenge	impinge	_____
derange	lozenge	_____
downrange	orange	_____

NJ /ndʒ/ Final—three syllables

counter change	prearrange	_____
disarrange	rearrange	_____
interchange	_____	_____

RJ /rdʒ/ Medial—two syllables

bargeman	Georgia	perjured
barges	gorgeous	sergeant
charge card	largely	splurging
charger	larger	sturgeon
Chargers	largest	surgeon
charging	Margie	turgid
clergy	margin	urgent
cordial	Margy	Virgil
forger	merger	_____
forging	merging	_____
Georgetown	perjure	_____

RJ /rdʒ/ Medial—three syllables

allergic	energy	overjoy
allergy	enlargement	overjoyed
chargeable	enlarger	perjury
clergyman	forgery	recharger
convergence	insurgent	recharging
converges	lethargic	surgery
crackerjacks	lethargy	surgical
detergent	lumberjack	urgency
discharges	margarine	Virginia
divergent	Margery	_____
emergent	marginal	_____
energize	Marjorie	_____

RJ /rdʒ/ Medial—four syllables

Argentina	reenlargement	Virgin Islands
emergency	supercharger	Virgin Mary
energetic	superjacent	West Virginia

RJ /rdʒ/ Final—one syllable

barge	gurge	serge
charge	large	splurge
dirge	Marge	surge
forge	merge	urge
George	purge	verge
gorge	scourge	_____

RJ /rdʒ/ Final—two syllables

converge	engorge	surcharge
discharge	enlarge	upsurge
diverge	recharge	_____
emerge	submerge	_____

K

Pronounced: /k/
Spelled: c, cc, cch, ch, ck, cq, cque, cu, k, qu

K /k/ Initial—one syllable

cab	cared	cob
cache	cart	cod
cached	carve	code
cad	carved	cog
cage	case	coil
caged	cased	coin
Cain	cash	coined
cake	cashed	cold
Cal	cask	colt
calf	cast	comb
call	cat	combed
called	catch	come
calm	caught	con
calmed	caulk	cone
calves	cause	coo
cam	caused	cooed
came	cave	cook
camp	caved	cooked
camped	caw	cool
can	cawed	cooled
can't	cay	coop
cane	chord	coot
canned	coach	cop
cans	coached	cope
cap	coal	cord
cape	coarse	cords
capped	coast	core
car	coat	cored
card	coax	cork
care	coaxed	corn

corps	culm	Ken
cost	cult	Kent
cot	cup	kept
cote	cupped	ketch
couch	cur	key
cough	curb	kick
coughed	curbed	kicked
could	curd	kid
count	curl	kids
coup	curled	kiln
course	curt	kilt
coursed	Curt	Kim
court	curve	kin
couth	curved	kind
cove	cusp	king
cow	cut	King
cowl	kale	kiss
Cox	Kay	kissed
coy	keel	kit
Coy	keeled	kite
cub	keen	Kurt
cud	keep	Kyle
cuff	keg	_____
cuffed	kelp	_____
cull	kempt	_____

K /k/ Initial—two syllables

cabbage	cafe	campaign
cabby	caffeine	campaigned
cabin	Caleb	camper
cable	calla	campfire
cabled	calling	campground
caboose	callous	camphor
cackle	Calvin	campsite
cackled	cambric	campus
cactus	Cambridge	canal
caddie	camel	cancel
caddied	camp-out	canceled
cadet	camp stove	cancer

Cancer	cardboard	catcher
Candace	careen	catch-up
candid	careened	cater
Candide	career	catered
candle	carefree	Cathy
candy	careful	cattle
Candy	careless	catwalk
canine	Carey	caucus
caning	carfare	caudle
canker	cargo	cauldron
cankered	caring	caution
canning	Carla	cautioned
cannot	carload	cavern
canny	Carmel	cavort
canoe	Carmen	cayenne
canon	carob	chaos
canteen	Carol	chorus
canter	carpet	Coast Guard
cantle	carriage	cobalt
Canton	Carrie	cobble
cantor	carried	cobbled
canvas	carrot	cobbler
canvassed	carry	cobra
canyon	Carter	cobweb
Cape Cod	carton	cockpit
caper	cartoon	cockroach
capon	cartridge	cocksure
caprice	cascade	cocktail
capsize	Casey	cocky
capsized	cashew	cocoa
capsule	cashier	coddle
capsuled	cashiered	coddled
captain	cashmere	codfish
captive	Casper	Cody
capture	cassette	coed
captured	Cassie	coerce
carat	caster	coerced
carbide	castle	coffee
carbon	castoff	cohort

coinage

coin box

cola

cold cuts

colder

cold front

cold pack

cold snap

cold wave

colic

collage

collar

collared

collate

collect

Colleen

college

Collette

collide

collie

cologne

Cologne

colon

colonel

color

colored

column

coma

combine

combined

combo

combust

comeback

comet

comfort

comic

coming

comma

command

commence

commenced

commend

comment

commerce

commit

common

compact

compare

compared

compass

compel

compelled

compete

compile

compiled

complain

complained

complete

complex

complied

comply

compose

composed

compound

comrade

concave

conceal

concealed

conceit

conceive

conceived

concept

concern

concerned

concert

concise

Concord

concrete

concur

concurred

condemn

condemned

condense

condensed

condole

condone

condor

conduce

conduct

condyle

cone shell

coney

confab

confect

confer

conferred

confess

confessed

confide

confine

confined

confirm

confirmed

conflict

conform

confound

confront

confuse

confused

congeal

congealed

Congo

Congress

Connie

conquer

Conrad

consent

conserve	cookbook	cougar
conserved	cooker	cough drop
consign	cookie	council
consist	cooking	counseled
console	Coolidge	counter
consoled	co-op	countess
conspire	copied	country
conspired	copper	county
Constance	copy	couple
consul	Cora	coupled
consult	coral	courage
consume	cordial	courthouse
consumed	cording	courtly
contact	cordless	courtroom
contacts	Corey	courtyard
contain	Cornell	cousin
contained	corner	cover
contempt	cornered	covered
contend	cornet	coward
content	cornfed	cowbell
contest	cornfield	cowboy
contour	corn grits	cower
contract	cornhusks	cowgirl
contrast	cornmeal	cowhand
control	corn oil	cowhide
controlled	corn shock	cowlick
converge	cornstarch	cowskin
converged	Cornwall	cozy
converse	corny	cuddle
conversed	corral	cuddled
convert	corralled	culprit
convex	correct	culture
convey	corrupt	cultured
conveyed	Cortez	cumquat
convict	cosmos	cunning
convince	costume	cupboard
convinced	costumed	cupful
convoy	cottage	curfew
convoyed	cotton	curling

currant	Kaiser	kickboard
current	Kansas	kicker
curried	Karen	kickoff
curry	Karl	kickstand
cursive	Karla	kiddie
cursor	Kashmir	kidding
curtail	kayak	kidskin
curtailed	keener	killjoy
curtain	keeping	kinder
Curtis	Kelly	kindle
curtsy	Kenneth	kindled
cushion	Kenny	kindling
cushioned	Kermit	kindly
cuspid	ketchup	kindness
custard	kettle	king crab
custom	keyboard	kingdom
customs	key chain	kismet
cutlass	keyhole	kissing
cutlet	keynote	kitchen
cutoff	key punch	kitten
cutoffs	key ring	_____
cutout	Key West	_____
cutting	khaki	_____
cutup	kibosh	_____
cutworm	kickball	_____

K /k/ Initial—three syllables

cabinet	Canada	Capricorn
cablegram	canary	Captain Hook
calendar	candy bar	caramel
caliber	canister	caravan
caliche	canopied	carbonate
calico	canopy	cardiac
caloric	cantaloupe	cardinal
calorie	cantata	caretaker
Camelia	capable	carnation
cameo	capital	Carnegie
camera	capitol	carnival
camporee	capricious	carnivore

Caroline
Carolyn
carousel
carpenter
cartilage
casserole
castaway
casual
catalog
catalogued
cataract
cauterize
cauterized
caviar
cavity
chameleon
chaotic
character
chemistry
coconut
collision
collusion
colony
color blind
colorful
color guard
coloring
color wheel
colossal
columbine
Columbus
comedy
commentate
commission
commissioned
committee
companion
company
complexion

complicate
component
composure
computer
concentrate
condition
confession
confessor
confetti
congressman
consensus
consider
considered
consumer
continent
continue
continued
contradict
contrary
contribute
convenient
convention
conveyor
convulsion
convulsive
Copper Age
copperhead
copyright
coral reef
Coral Sea
corduroy
Cornelia
coronet
correction
correspond
corridor
cosmetic
cotton gin
cottonmouth

cottontail
cottonwood
councillor
counselor
counteract
counterfeit
country club
courier
courteous
courtesy
coverage
covering
coyote
cubbyhole
cul-de-sac
culminate
cultivate
cumbersome
curlicue
currency
currently
curvature
custody
customer
cutaway
kangaroo
katydid
kayaking
Kennedy
kennel club
Kentucky
kerosene
kibitzer
kilowatt
kimono
kindhearted
kingfisher

_____

_____

K /k/ Initial—four syllables

Cambodia	Colorado	congresswoman
Capistrano	Columbia	Connecticut
carcinoma	combination	contemptuous
carnivorous	comedian	continental
Carolina	commendation	conversation
catastrophe	commentator	cooperate
category	commiserate	Copenhagen
caterpillar	commissioner	Costa Rica
cauliflower	community	customary
coagulate	comparison	kindergarten
coalition	confirmation	_____
coincidence	congratulate	_____

K /k/ Initial—five syllables

Caledonia	coincidental	conversational
California	commiserating	cooperation
coeducation	congratulations	_____

K /k/ Medial—two syllables

accord	becalm	blocking
accost	becalmed	bobcat
account	became	bookcase
acne	because	bookmark
acorn	Becky	bookshelf
akin	become	boycott
background	bedclothes	bracket
backhand	bicker	brackish
backslide	bickered	brakeman
backstage	biking	breakage
backstroke	blackbird	breakdown
backup	blackboard	breaker
bacon	blackcap	breakfast
bake-off	blacken	breaking
baker	blackened	breakneck
baking	blackhead	breakup
beachcomb	blockade	briquet
beacon	blocker	broadcast
beaker	blockhouse	brocade

broken	encamped	locate
broker	encase	locket
buckboard	encased	locking
bucket	encore	lockjaw
buckeye	flicker	locust
Buckeye	flickered	looker
buckteeth	flicking	looking
buckwheat	focus	lookout
bumpkin	focused	low-cost
checker	fruitcake	lucky
checkers	glucose	lukewarm
checkup	go-cart	maker
chicken	handcar	makeshift
Chico	handcart	making
chock-full	Hawkeye	mucous
cockpit	hawkeyed	mukluk
cocksure	hiccup	napkin
cocoa	hiccupped	nickname
cooker	hockey	nicknamed
cookie	hookup	Nicky
cooking	hooky	Nicole
cracker	income	occur
cracking	jackal	occurred
deacon	jacket	outcast
decade	jackknife	package
decal	jackknifed	packaged
decay	jockey	packet
decayed	kicker	packhorse
decking	kickoff	packing
decode	knickers	packsack
decoy	knocker	peacock
dicker	knocking	pecan
dickered	knockout	picket
docket	lackey	picking
echo	lacquer	pickup
echoed	lacquered	placket
encage	lichen	pocket
encaged	likeness	pockmark
encamp	liking	pockmarked

poker	sackful	sucking
poking	seacoast	taco
poky	second	taken
procure	seconds	takeoff
procured	seeker	taking
pucker	seeking	tokens
puckered	shaker	trucker
pumpkin	shaking	trucking
Quaker	shaky	tucker
raccoon	shortcake	tuckered
racket	sicken	tycoon
racquet	sicker	unkempt
raincoat	sidecar	unkind
raking	slicker	vacant
recall	sneaker	vacate
recalled	snicker	Viking
record	snickered	vocal
recount	soccer	waken
recourse	socket	wakened
recur	speaker	weaken
recurred	speaking	weakened
rickshaw	stockade	weekend
Ricky	stock car	wicked
rocker	stocker	wicker
rocket	Stockholm	wicket
rocking	stocking	wildcat
rocky	stricken	wrecker
Rocky	stucco	_____
rookie	sucker	_____

K /k/ Medial—three syllables

abacus	acolyte	apricot
abdicate	acoustic	awaken
acacia	acreage	awakened
accident	Africa	backgammon
accomplice	allocate	bakery
accomplish	applicant	barricade
acknowledge	appliqué	beachcomber
acknowledged	appliquéd	bed cover

bicuspid
bicycle
bookbinder
bookkeeper
breakable
broccoli
brokerage
bronchial
bronchitis
buccaneer
Buchanan
buckaroo
calico
caretaker
checkerboard
Cherokee
chickadee
Chickasaw
chicken coop
chicken feed
chocolate
chokecherry
coconut
complicate
cowcatcher
cucumber
Dakota
decanter
decorate
delicate
difficult
dislocate
Dracula
dressmaker
duplicate
educate
encounter
encountered
encourage

encouraged
encumber
encumbered
epicure
fabricate
factory
fiasco
firecracker
folk dancing
folk music
four-cycle
game tokens
hackamore
handicap
handicapped
handkerchief
Hanukkah
hickory
hockey stick
holocaust
homemaker
honeycomb
housekeeper
hurricane
Jackelyn
Kentucky
licorice
likeable
likelihood
linebacker
location
loudspeaker
lubricate
macaroon
mackerel
mannequin
McKenzie
McKinley
mechanic

medicate
moccasins
mockingbird
neckerchief
nutcracker
occasion
oncoming
pacemaker
pawnbroker
pelican
piccolo
pillowcase
pocket watch
precaution
psychosis
Rebecca
recommend
recover
recovered
ricochet
ricocheted
rookery
salt shaker
secondly
seersucker
shoemaker
silica
snickering
soccer ball
staccato
stomachache
succotash
talkative
teakettle
trachea
tricycle
unlikely
unlucky
vacation

vindicate
vocalize
vocalized
vocation

walking stick
walk over
watchmaker
wickerwork

womankind
woodpecker
Zachary

_____

K /k/ Medial—four syllables

a cappella
academy
accommodate
accompany
accordion
accountable
agriculture
America
American
amicable
application
area code
authenticate
baby carriage
basilica
bicarbonate
decalcify
despicable
dictionary

difficulty
domesticate
duplication
economize
economized
economy
education
educator
eradicate
helicopter
hocus-pocus
impeccable
incandescent
incapable
incoherent
incorporate
jack-o'-lantern
locality
locomotive

lubrication
macaroni
mechanism
medicated
medication
melancholy
occasional
parochial
persecution
predicament
psychiatry
recuperate
secondary
semicolon
sukiyaki
terra cotta
ukulele
walking safety

_____

K /k/ Medial—five syllables

accommodation
amplification
biochemistry
coeducation
discoloration

disconformity
edification
incalculable
inconsiderate
justification

mechanization
recuperation

_____

_____

_____

K /k/ Final—one syllable

ache
auk
back
bake
balk

beak
beck
bike
black
Blake

bleak
bloc
block
book
brake

break	flick	neck
brick	floc	nick
broke	flock	Nick
brook	fluke	nook
buck	folk	oak
Buck	freak	pack
cake	frock	peak
caulk	Greek	peck
chalk	hack	peek
check	Hack	pick
cheek	hawk	pike
chick	hike	pique
chock	hock	plaque
choke	hook	pluck
chuck	jack	pock
Chuck	Jack	poke
click	Jake	Polk
cloak	joke	puck
cluck	kick	quack
cock	knack	quake
cook	knock	quick
creak	lack	rack
creek	lake	rake
croak	leak	reek
crock	leek	Rick
deck	lick	rock
Dick	like	rook
dike	lock	sac
dock	look	sack
drake	luck	sake
Drake	Luke	seek
duck	Mack	shake
duke	make	sheik
Duke	meek	shock
eke	Mick	shook
fake	mike	shriek
flack	Mike	shuck
flake	mock	sick
fleck	muck	slack

sleek	stick	tuck
slick	stock	tweak
smack	stoke	Vic
smock	streak	wake
smoke	strike	walk
snack	stroke	weak
snake	stuck	week
sneak	suck	whack
soak	tack	wick
sock	take	woke
speak	talk	wrack
speck	teak	wreak
spike	thick	wreck
spoke	tic	yak
spook	tick	yoke
squawk	tikc	yolk
squeak	took	Zach
stack	track	Zeke
stake	trek	_____
stalk	trick	_____
steak	truck	_____

K /k/ Final—two syllables

alack	bed check	cheese cake
alike	bedeck	chopstick
amuck	bedrock	clambake
antic	beefsteak	clinic
antique	bike rack	club steak
attack	blackjack	cold pack
attic	black snake	comeback
awake	blank check	cookbook
awoke	boardwalk	critic
backache	bookrack	crosswalk
backpack	boric	cubic
backstroke	broomstick	cupcake
backtrack	cakewalk	daybreak
Bangkok	cambric	deadlock
bareback	car rack	derrick
basic	catwalk	Derrick

dislike
drastic
drumstick
earache
earthquake
egg yolk
epoch
Eric
evoke
fabric
fire truck
fish hook
flapjack
flashback
flour sack
forsake
frantic
frolic
fullback
garlic
graphic
haddock
halfback
hammock
handbook
hand brake
handshake
hardtack
hassock
hayrack
haystack
headache
heartache
hectic
hemlock
hitchhike
homelike
homesick
horseback

humpback
hunchback
ice pack
ice pick
intake
invoke
jaywalk
jet black
joke book
kayak
king snake
kinsfolk
knickknack
lame duck
lampblack
lilac
lipstick
livestock
lunch break
lyric
magic
mandrake
mastic
medic
metric
mistake
Mohawk
mukluk
music
mystique
namesake
nitric
Norfolk
notebook
oblique
o'clock
opaque
outbreak
outlook

outtalk
padlock
panic
passbook
peacock
pet rock
physique
Pikes Peak
plastic
potluck
provoke
public
racetrack
rain check
ransack
rebuke
remake
repack
revoke
round steak
rustic
scrapbook
scrub oak
seasick
shamrock
shellac
shipwreck
sidewalk
slowpoke
small talk
smokestack
snowflake
spring chick
static
stomach
sun deck
sunstroke
sweepstake
technique

thumbtack
ticktock
tie rack
tie tack
toothache
toothpick
topic
townsfolk

traffic
tunic
unhook
unique
unlock
unpack
windbreak
wisecrack

wolf pack
woodchuck
yardstick
zwieback

——————————
——————————
——————————
——————————

K /k/ Final—three syllables

almanac
artichoke
artistic
athletic
atomic
baby chick
bionic
birthday cake
bivouac
buttonhook
candlestick
candlewick
Captain Hook
cardiac
Catholic
chaotic
chuck-a-luck
coffee break
comic book
cul-de-sac
domestic
fantastic

flutter kick
funny book
galactic
garter snake
gigantic
gunny sack
historic
hockey stick
hognose snake
hollyhock
ladylike
Little Rock
lumberjack
maverick
motorbike
overtake
overtook
Pacific
paperback
piggyback
pogo stick
politic

Pontiac
poppycock
quarterback
railroad track
rattlesnake
republic
sparrow hawk
specific
stomachache
storybook
T-bone steak
terrific
undertake
volcanic
weather cock
wedding cake
womenfolk

——————————
——————————
——————————
——————————

K /k/ Final—four syllables

arithmetic
certified check
chocolate cake
economic
epidemic

hydrologic
hypertonic
hypotonic
magazine rack
mathematic

optimistic
patriotic
South Pacific
supersonic

——————————

KER /kɚ/ Medial—three syllables

acreage	discourage	rookery
Anchorage	handkerchief	snickering
bakery	licorice	soccer ball
brokerage	mackerel	wickerwork
checkerboard	neckerchief	_____

KER /kɚ/ Final—two syllables

acre	flanker	sneaker
anchor	flicker	snicker
baker	hiker	soccer
banker	kicker	speaker
bicker	knocker	stocker
blocker	locker	sucker
breaker	looker	tanker
broker	poker	tucker
canker	Quaker	wicker
choker	rocker	wrecker
clinker	seeker	_____
conquer	shaker	_____
cracker	slicker	_____

KER /kɚ/ Final—three syllables

backpacker	loudspeaker	shoemaker
dressmaker	nutcracker	watchmaker
hitch-hiker	pact maker	windbreaker
homemaker	pawnbroker	woodpecker
linebacker	saltshaker	_____

KL /kl/ Initial—one syllable

clack	clapped	claw
claim	Clark	clawed
claimed	clash	clay
Claire	clashed	Clay
clam	clasp	clean
clamp	clasped	cleaned
clan	class	cleanse
clang	Claude	clear
clap	clause	cleared

cleats	clock	cloy
clef	clocked	cloyed
cleft	clod	club
clench	clog	cluck
clerk	clogs	clue
click	clone	clued
cliff	clop	clump
Cliff	close	clumped
climb	closed	clung
climbed	clot	clutch
clinch	cloth	clutched
cling	clothe	Clyde
Clint	clothes	Kline
clip	cloud	klutz
clipped	clout	_____
clique	clove	_____
cloak	clown	_____
cloaked	clowned	_____

KL /kl/ Initial—two syllables

chloric	cleanup	clinker
chlorine	clearance	Clinton
clackers	clearing	clipboard
claimant	cleaver	clipper
clambake	clement	clippers
clammy	Cleo	clipping
clamor	clergy	clippings
clamshell	Cleveland	clobber
clapping	clever	clockwise
Clara	cliche´	clockwork
Clarence	client	closet
clarice	Clifford	close-up
classic	Clifton	closing
classmate	climate	closure
classroom	climax	clothespin
classy	climber	clothier
clatter	climbing	clothing
clattered	clincher	cloudburst
cleanly	clinic	cloudy

clover
Clovis
clubhouse

club steak
clumsy
cluster

clutter
cluttered
_____

KL /kl/ Initial—three syllables

chlorinate
chloroform
clairvoyance
clam chowder
clam digging
clandestine
Clarendon
clarify
clarinet
classical
classified

classify
Claudia
clavichord
clavicle
claviform
cleanliness
cleft palate
clemency
clergyman
clerical
clientele

cliff dweller
climactic
clinical
clinician
clodhopper
cloverleaf
club sandwich
Klamath Falls
_____
_____
_____

KL /kl/ Medial—two syllables

acclaim
acclaimed
anklet
Auckland
backlash
backlog
ball club
Barclay
becloud
blacklist
book club
booklet
Boys' Club
bridge club
broadcloth
brooklet
buckling
cackling
cheesecloth
chuckler
chuckling

conclude
cycling
cyclone
declare
decline
disclose
dishcloth
dry clean
dry cleaned
duckling
dustcloth
eclipse
eclipsed
enclose
exclaim
exclude
fan club
first class
foreclose
foreclosed
Franklin

freckly
Girls' Club
glee club
health club
heckler
incline
inclined
include
knuckler
knuckling
land claim
likely
loin cloth
mukluks
necklace
Oakland
occlude
o'clock
outclass
pickling
preclude

press club
prickling
prickly
proclaim
proclaimed
quick lime
quickly
reclaim
recline
reclined

seclude
sparkler
sparkling
speckling
sprinkler
sprinkling
tackler
ticklish
time clock
trickling

twinkling
weakling
weakly
wreckless
yacht club

_____
_____
_____
_____
_____

KL /kl/ Medial—three syllables

acclimate
alarm clock
biweekly
bricklayer
Christmas club
country club
dry cleaning
eclectic
ecliptic
enclosure
exclusion
exclusive
foreclosure
Four-H Club
Franklin stove
garden club
health spa club
inclement

inclined plane
inclusion
inclusive
jockey club
junior class
kennel club
Lion's Club
middle class
nuclear
nuclei
nucleus
obliquely
paper clip
prickly heat
prickly pear
proclaimer
proclaiming
Santa Claus

secluded
seclusion
second class
senior class
service club
tablecloth
thunderclap
unbuckling
underclothes
uniquely
unlikely
Women's Club

_____
_____
_____
_____
_____

KL /kl/ Medial—four syllables

acclamation
athletic club
declaration
digital clock
electric clock
enclosable
exclamation

exclusively
grandfather clock
inclinable
inclination
includible
non-classified
Oklahoma

proclamation
proclivity
reclamation
reclining chair
vacuum cleaner

_____
_____

KL /kl/ Final—two syllables

ankle	heckle	speckle
buckle	jackal	sprinkle
cackle	knuckle	stickle
chuckle	local	tackle
circle	nickel	tickle
crackle	pickle	trickle
cycle	prickle	twinkle
fickle	rankle	uncle
fiscal	rascal	vocal
focal	sickle	wrinkle
freckle	snorkel	_____
grackle	spackle	_____

KL /kl/ Final—three syllables

article	metrical	ramshackle
bicycle	miracle	recycle
chemical	monocle	rhythmical
classical	musical	skeptical
clinical	mystical	spectacle
cortical	mythical	spherical
critical	nautical	technical
cubicle	obstacle	tentacle
cuticle	optical	topical
encircle	oracle	tricycle
icicle	particle	two-cycle
lexical	physical	typical
logical	pinnacle	vehicle
lyrical	pinochle	vesicle
magical	practical	_____
medical	radical	_____

KL /kl/ Final—four syllables

angelical	ironical	patriarchal
botanical	kilocycle	political
historical	mechanical	receptacle
honeysuckle	motorcycle	reciprocal
identical	nonsensical	sabbatical
illogical	numerical	semicircle

statistical   _____   _____

unicycle   _____   _____

KL /kl/ Final—five syllables

academical	biographical	mythological
alphabetical	categorical	pathological
analytical	chronological	unequivocal
anatomical	economical	unmechanical
astrological	geographical	unmethodical
astronomical	mathematical	_____

LK /lk/ Medial—two syllables

Alcan	mail car	silk hat
alcove	milkman	silkworm
bulkhead	milkmen	silky
bulk mail	milkshake	sulking
bulky	milk truck	sulky
Elkhart	milkweed	talcum
Elkhorn	polka	welcome
elk rack	railcar	welcomed
hulking	silken	_____

LK /lk/ Medial—three syllables

alcohol	calculate	silk stockings
alkali	Chilkoot Pass	unwelcome
alkaline	Elk City	volcanic
alkalize	Milky Way	volcano
alkalized	silkiness	vulcanize
balcony	silk-screen print	_____

LK /lk/ Medial—four syllables

Alcan Highway	recalculate	_____
calculator	talcum powder	_____

LK /lk/ Final—one syllable

bilk	Hulk	sulk
bulk	ilk	talc
elk	milk	whelk
hulk	silk	yelk

LK /lk/ Final—two syllables

canned milk	real silk	sweet milk
dry milk	skim milk	_____
goat's milk	sour milk	_____
ice milk	spun silk	_____

LK /lk/ Final—three syllables

buttermilk	_____	_____
lowfat milk	_____	_____
malted milk	_____	_____
powdered milk	_____	_____

KR /kr/ Initial—one syllable

Chris	crepe	cruised
Christ	crept	crumb
chrome	crest	crumbed
crab	Crete	crumbs
craft	crew	crunch
crag	crib	crush
Craig	cribbed	crust
cram	crick	crutch
crammed	cried	cry
cramp	crime	kraut
cramped	crisp	_____
crane	crisped	_____
crank	croak	_____
crash	crock	_____
crate	crop	_____
crave	cross	_____
craw	crossed	_____
crawl	crouch	_____
crawled	croup	_____
creak	crow	_____
cream	crowd	_____
crease	crowed	_____
creased	crown	_____
creed	crowned	_____
creek	crude	_____
creep	cruise	_____

KR /kr/ Initial—two syllables

Christa	crescent	crow's nest
Christian	crevasse	crucial
Christine	crewel	crude oil
Christmas	crewman	cruel
Christy	crewmen	cruise car
chroma	cribbage	cruiser
Chrysler	cricket	cruise ship
Chrystal	crimson	cruising
crabby	cripple	crumble
cracker	crippled	crumbled
cracking	crisis	crumbly
crackling	crispy	crummy
cradle	crisscross	crumple
cradled	crochet	crunchy
craftsman	crock pot	crusade
crafty	crocus	crushing
craggy	crooked	crystal
cramming	crop dust	Kristi
cramping	cropper	_____
crater	cropping	_____
crayfish	croquet	_____
crayon	crossbow	_____
crazy	crossing	_____
cream cheese	crossroad	_____
create	crosswalk	_____
creature	croutons	_____
credit	crowbar	_____
creeper	crowded	_____
creeping	crowdy	_____
creepy	crowning	_____

KR /kr/ Initial—three syllables

Christina	chromosome	Crater Lake
Christmas card	chrysolite	creation
Christmas Day	crackerjack	creative
Christmas Eve	craftsmanship	creator
Christmas tree	cranberry	credible
Christopher	crash helmet	cremation

crepe paper	crocodile	cruelty
cribbage board	Cro-Magnon	crusader
criminal	crop duster	crustacean
critical	cross-country	crystallize
criticize	crossover	_____
crocheting	cross section	_____
crockery	crucify	_____

KR /kr/ Initial—four syllables

chronology	creditable	cross-country skis
chrysanthemum	credit rating	cross reference
cracker barrel	credit union	crossword puzzle
cranberry tree	criterion	_____
creativeness	critical mass	_____

KR /kr/ Medial—two syllables

accrete	decree	sacred
accrue	discrete	sand crab
accrued	ecru	scarecrow
acrid	fulcrum	sea crab
across	handcraft	secret
aircraft	increase	secrete
aircrew	increased	spacecraft
Akron	king crab	stock room
bankrupt	macron	tree crab
book rack	microbe	witchcraft
cockroach	okra	woodcraft
concrete	packrat	_____
corn crib	pie crust	_____
decrease	recruit	_____
decreased	Red Cross	_____

KR /kr/ Medial—three syllables

accredit	autocrat	giant crab
achromic	bike crossing	handcrafted
acrobat	deer crossing	handicraft
acrylic	democrat	hot cross buns
aircraftman	doublecross	Hovercraft
aircrewman	endocrine	hypocrite

increasing
increment
leather craft
microfilm
microphone
microscope
microwave
moose crossing

nutcracker
oyster crab
pancreas
pleasure craft
plutocrat
sacrifice
Santa Cruz
sauerkraut

secrecy
soft-shell crab
sour cream
synchronize
Veracruz
water craft
_____
_____

KR /kr/ Medial—four syllables

acrobatics
aristocrat
democracy
hypocrisy
increasingly

incredible
incredulous
incriminate
microscopic
plutocracy

railroad crossing
recreation
secretary
_____
_____

KR /kr/ Medial—five syllables

aircraft carrier
aristocratic

incriminating
microdetector

_____
_____

RK /rk/ Medial—two syllables

air-cool
arcade
archive
Arctic
barking
bearcat
Berkeley
carcass
charcoal
circle
circuit
circus
clerking
corkscrew
Corky
darken
darker
darkness

Dorcas
forecast
haircut
harken
jerkin
jerking
jerky
Larkin
larkspur
lurking
marker
market
marking
marquee
murky
orchid
parka
Parker

parking
parkway
perky
shirking
smirking
snorkle
spark plug
sparkle
sparkled
sparklers
sparkling
turkey
Turkey
Turkish
turquoise
workbench
workbook
working

workman	workroom	_____
workmen	workshop	_____

RK /rk/ Medial—three syllables

anarchist	mercury	patchwork quilt
anarchy	Mercury	percolate
Antarctic	monarchist	percussion
archaic	monarchy	porcupine
archangel	motorcade	remarking
beef jerky	motorcar	sarcasm
circular	orchestra	sarcastic
circulate	overcame	Turkish bath
darkener	overcast	woodworking
embarking	overcoat	workable
encircle	overcome	workmanship
marketing	parking lights	work station
Market Street	parking lot	worktable
mazurka	parking place	_____

RK /rk/ Medial—four syllables

air-condition	disembarking	remarkable
altercation	felt-tip marker	semicircle
Antarctica	hierarchy	sheltered workshop
Arcadia	money market	social worker
Arctic Circle	orchestration	summer workshop
Arctic Ocean	Park Avenue	supermarket
charcoal lighter	parking meter	turkey buzzard
circuit breaker	percolator	_____

RK /rk/ Final—one syllable

arc	fork	mark
ark	hark	Mark
bark	irk	park
Burke	jerk	perk
Clark	Kirk	Perk
clerk	lark	pork
cork	lurk	quirk
dark	marc	shark
Dirk	Marc	shirk

smirk	stork	work
spark	torque	York
stark	Turk	_____

RK /rk/ Final—two syllables

birch bark	hallmark	postmark
birthmark	handwork	remark
bookmark	hayfork	salesclerk
bridgework	homework	skylark
check mark	housework	stonework
debark	landmark	town clerk
Denmark	loan shark	trademark
earmark	monarch	uncork
embark	network	woodwork
footmark	Newark	_____
footwork	New York	_____
framework	patchwork	_____
frostwork	pitchfork	_____
guesswork	pockmark	_____

RK /rk/ Final—three syllables

baseball park	meadowlark	social work
Central Park	needlework	Sunset Park
city park	Noah's Ark	tuning fork
disembark	overpark	watermark
fancywork	overwork	waterwork
handiwork	patriarch	_____
hierarchy	pencil mark	_____
Jasper Park	question mark	_____

RK /rk/ Final—four syllables

Denali Park	_____	_____
national park	_____	_____
quotation mark	_____	_____

RKT /rkt/ Final—one syllable

arcked	jerked	sparked
barked	marked	worked
irked	parked	_____

RKT /rkt/ Final—two syllables

embarked	uncorked	_____
postmarked	unmarked	_____
remarked	unworked	_____

KS /ks/ Medial—two syllables

accent	expelled	perplexed
accept	expend	pixy
access	expense	proxy
axis	expert	quicksand
axle	expire	Roxanne
bake sale	Expo	sextet
boxcar	export	sexton
boxer	expose	sixpence
boxful	exposed	sixteen
boxing	expound	sixteenth
boxwood	extant	sixth sense
dachshund	extend	sixty
Dexter	extern	succeed
dextrose	extinct	success
Dixie	extol	taxi
Dixon	extort	Texas
exceed	fixate	toxic
excel	fixing	toxin
except	fixture	vaccine
excerpt	foxhole	waxy
excess	foxhound	_____
exchange	Jackson	_____
exchanged	Knoxville	_____
excise	Maxine	_____
excite	mixer	_____
excuse	mixing	_____
excused	mixture	_____
exhale	mix-up	_____
exhaled	Nixon	_____
expand	oxcart	_____
expanse	oxen	_____
expect	Oxford	_____
expel	oxide	_____

KS /ks/ Medial—three syllables

axiom	exhalant	flexible
complexion	exlibris	galaxy
dexterous	exodus	hexagon
dioxide	exogen	Jacksonville
excavate	exorcise	Lexington
exceeding	expanded	luxury
excellence	expansion	maximum
excellent	expansive	Mexican
excepting	expectant	Mexico
exception	expedite	oxidize
exceptive	expensive	oxygen
excerption	exponent	quicksilver
excessive	exporter	saxophone
exchequer	exposure	successful
excision	expulsion	succession
excitant	extended	successive
excited	extension	successor
excitement	extensive	taxable
exciter	extensor	taxation
exciting	external	taxicab
excursion	extinction	taxpayer
excursive	extinctive	vaccinate
execute	extinguish	vexation
exercise	extortion	_____
exercised	exudate	_____

KS /ks/ Medial—four syllables

accelerate	exchangeable	exotoxin
Alexander	excisable	expectancy
approximate	excitable	expectation
complexity	excitation	expectorant
excavation	excusable	expedience
excavator	execution	expedient
exceedingly	executor	expendable
excellency	exerciser	expenditure
excelsior	exfoliate	experience
exceptional	exhalation	experiment
excessively	exhibition	expiration

exportation
exposition
expositor
extendible
exterior
exterminate
externalize
extinguisher

fox terrier
index finger
luxuriant
luxurious
Mexican food
New Mexico
Old Mexico
proximity

relaxation
Route 66
St. Patrick's Day
success story
Texas Rangers
unexpected
vaccination
_____

KS /ks/ Medial—five syllables

exceptionable
exceptionably
excitableness
excitatory
excommunicate
executable
exfoliation

exhibitioner
exhibitionist
ex officio
expediency
experimental
expiratory
extemporary

extenuation
extermination
Mexican Hat Dance
Mexico City
_____
_____
_____

KS /ks/ Final—one syllable

aches
ax
backs
bakes
beaks
bikes
blacks
blocks
books
box
brakes
breaks
bricks
Bronx
brooks
Brooks
bucks
Bucks
cakes
checks

cheeks
chicks
chokes
chucks
clicks
cloaks
clocks
coax
cokes
cooks
Cox
cracks
creaks
creeks
croaks
crocks
crooks
decks
dikes
docks

drakes
ducks
dukes
fakes
fix
flakes
flax
flecks
flex
flicks
flocks
flukes
folks
fox
francs
freaks
frocks
Greeks
hawks
hex

hikes	minx	spikes
hoax	mix	spooks
hocks	necks	squeaks
hooks	ox	stacks
irks	picks	steaks
Jack's	pox	sticks
jacks	racks	tacks
Jake's	ranks	tax
jinx	rex	Tex
jokes	Rex	ticks
kicks	rocks	tracks
knacks	sacks	tricks
knocks	seeks	trucks
lacks	shakes	tucks
lakes	shocks	vex
lax	six	wakes
likes	slacks	wax
locks	smocks	weeks
looks	smokes	whacks
lox	snacks	wrecks
lux	snakes	yaks
lynx	socks	_____
makes	sphinx	_____

KS /ks/ Final—two syllables

affix	borax	epics
Alex	classics	epochs
annex	clinics	ethics
antiques	coin box	fabrics
apex	comics	Felix
attacks	complex	garlics
attics	convex	hat box
Aztecs	cornflakes	icebox
bandbox	critics	index
barracks	daybreaks	influx
basics	deluxe	invokes
beefsteaks	Derrick's	kayaks
beeswax	derricks	larynx
black snakes	duplex	latex

lyrics
mailbox
mistakes
musk ox
notebooks
padlocks
peacocks
perplex
Phoenix
physics
pillbox
prefix

race tracks
relax
sandbox
scrapbooks
shamrocks
silex
smallpox
snowflakes
sound box
suffix
surtax
sweepstakes

syntax
thorax
thumbtacks
toothpicks
triplex
woodchucks
wordbooks
workbooks
yardsticks
_____
_____
_____

KS /ks/ Final—three syllables

aerobics
almanacs
appendix
artichokes
candlesticks
ceramics
chicken pox

comic books
elastics
equinox
garter snakes
income tax
lumberjacks
motorbikes

orthodox
paperbacks
pogo sticks
politics
railroad tracks
storybooks
_____

KS + Adjoining Clusters, Medial—two clusters

exclaim
exclaimed
exclude
excrete
explain
explode

exploit
explore
express
expressed
extra
extract

extreme
extrude
foxglove
foxtrot
_____
_____

KS + Adjoining Clusters, Medial—three clusters

ecstasy
ecstatic
exclusion
exclusive
expletive
explicit
explorer
explosion

explosive
expressage
expression
expressive
expressly
expressman
express train
expressway

exquisite
extra bold
extraction
extractor
extradite
extravert
extremely
extremist

extricate	extrovert	_____
extrinsic	extrusion	_____

KS + Adjoining Clusters, Medial—four clusters

exclamation	expropriate	extravagant
exclusively	extractable	extraversion
excruciate	extradition	extremity
explanation	extraneous	extroversion
exploitation	extrapolate	_____
explorative	extravagance	_____

KS + Adjoining Clusters, Medial—five clusters

exclamation mark	exploratory	extrasensory
exclamatory	expropriation	extravascular
explanatory	extrajudicial	_____

SK /sk/ Initial—one syllable

scab	scoot	skid
scald	scope	skiff
scale	scorch	skill
scaled	scorched	skilled
scamp	score	skim
scan	scored	skimmed
scanned	scorn	skimp
scant	scorned	skimped
scar	Scotch	skin
scarce	Scott	skinned
scare	scour	skip
scared	scoured	skipped
scarf	scout	skirt
scarred	scouts	skit
scat	scowl	skulk
scheme	scowled	skull
schemed	scuff	skunk
school	scum	skunked
scoff	skate	sky
scold	skeet	_____
scoop	sketch	_____
scooped	ski	_____

SK /sk/ Initial—two syllables

scabbard	schoolroom	Skagway
scabby	schooner	skateboard
scaffold	scolding	skated
scallion	scooter	skater
scallop	scorcher	skating
scalloped	scoreboard	skeptic
scallops	scorecard	sketchbook
scalpel	scornful	sketchy
scamper	scot-free	skidding
scandal	Scotland	skier
scanty	Scotsman	skiing
scapegoat	Scottie	ski jump
scarcely	Scottish	ski lift
scarecrow	Scottsdale	skillet
scarlet	Scottsville	skillful
scary	Scotty	skinny
scatter	scoundrel	skunkweed
scattered	scouting	sky blue
schedule	scuba	skyborn
scheduled	scuffle	skydive
scholar	scuffled	Skylab
schoolboy	sculptor	skylark
school bus	sculpture	skyline
schoolgirl	sculptured	skyward
schoolhouse	scurried	skyway
schooling	scurry	skywrite
schoolmarm	scurvy	_____
schoolmate	scuttle	_____

SK /sk/ Initial—three syllables

scandalize	scholastic	skate-a-thon
scapula	scorekeeper	skatemobile
scatterbrain	Scorpio	skeleton
scattering	scorpion	ski-a-thon
scatter rug	Scotland Yard	skin diving
scavenger	Scott City	ski patrol
schematic	scoutmaster	sky cover
scholarship	scuttlebutt	sky diving

| sky rocket | skywriter | _____ |
| skyscraper | skywriting | _____ |

SK /sk/ Medial—two syllables

asking	frisky	night school
basket	gasket	oilskin
basking	Girl Scouts	Oscar
biscuit	grade school	outskirts
Boy Scouts	grass skirt	pesky
brisket	Haskell	pigskin
buckskin	high school	plaid skirt
calfskin	hopscotch	preschool
cascade	husking	Redskins
casket	husky	rescue
cub Scout	Husky	risky
day school	ice skate	sealskin
discard	kidskin	sheepskin
discount	landscape	threescore
discourse	mascot	tuskless
discuss	miscount	whiskbroom
diskette	muskegs	whisker
dusky	musk ox	whiskers
escape	muskrat	_____
escort	musky	_____

SK /sk/ Medial—three syllables

Alaska	discordance	hockey skate
basketball	discourage	horoscope
basketful	discouraged	hula skirt
basket weave	discover	huskiness
basketwork	discovered	ice skating
breadbasket	discussion	mascara
butterscotch	escapade	masculine
confiscate	escapement	masquerade
discolor	escarpment	May basket
discomfort	Eskimo	microscope
disconcert	fire escape	misconstrue
disconnect	gyroscope	mosquito
discontent	hibiscus	muscular

musketeer
muskmelon
musk oxen
Nebraska
onionskin
periscope
public school

roller skates
spectroscope
stethoscope
Stravinsky
summer school
Sunday School
telescope

wastebasket
whiskerless
whiskery
Wisconsin

_____
_____
_____

SK /sk/ Medial—four syllables
baleen basket
birch bark basket
disconsolate
discontented
discontinue
discovery

Easter basket
Episcopal
escalator
figure skater
figure skating
kaleidoscope

microscopic
picnic basket
private schooling
roller skating
San Francisco

_____

SK /sk/ Final—one syllable
ask
bask
bisque
brisk
brusque
cask
desk

disk
dusk
flask
frisk
husk
mask
mosque

musk
risk
rusk
task
tusk
whisk

_____

SK /sk/ Final—two syllables
corn husk
face mask
file disk

gas mask
grotesque
mollusk

school desk
swim mask
unmask

SK /sk/ Final—three syllables
asterisk
data disk
floppy disk

mammoth tusk
office desk
picturesque

reading desk
_____
_____

KT /kt/ Medial—two syllables
active
cactus
Choctaw

doctor
doctrine
factor

Hector
lecturn
necktie

octane	spectant	victor
octave	tractor	Victor
pectin	vector	_____
practice	victim	_____

KT /kt/ Medial—three syllables

activate	director	nocturnal
actively	doctoral	objected
affected	effective	objective
affective	elective	obstructing
attracted	elector	octagon
attractive	electron	October
bisected	erector	octopus
character	exacting	pact-maker
conducting	exactly	perspective
conductor	factitious	practical
connecting	factory	prospective
connector	hectagon	prospector
deducted	impacted	reactor
destructive	inactive	selective
detective	infected	spectator
dictaphone	inflicting	transacting
dictation	instructor	_____
dictator	neglected	_____

KT /kt/ Medial—four syllables

activity	destructible	respectable
bacteria	directory	retractable
benefactor	objectable	Victoria
deductible	predictable	_____

KT /kt/ Final—one syllable

act	cracked	joked
backed	docked	kicked
biked	ducked	knocked
blocked	duct	leaked
booked	fact	liked
checked	faked	locked
cooked	hiked	looked

packed	sneaked	ticked
pact	soaked	tracked
peaked	spooked	tract
picked	squeaked	tricked
poked	stacked	trucked
raked	staked	tucked
reeked	stocked	walked
rocked	strict	wrecked
sacked	tacked	_____
sect	tact	_____
shocked	talked	_____

KT /kt/ Final—two syllables

abduct	detract	obstruct
abstract	direct	perfect
affect	dissect	predict
afflict	distract	prefect
aspect	district	product
attacked	effect	project
attract	eject	prospect
barebacked	elect	protect
bisect	enact	protract
collect	erect	react
compact	evict	reflect
conduct	evoked	reject
conflict	exact	respect
connect	expect	restrict
constrict	extract	retract
construct	impact	select
contact	induct	subject
contract	infect	subtract
convict	inflict	suspect
correct	inject	transact
deduct	insect	_____
defect	inspect	_____
deflect	instruct	_____
deject	intact	_____
depict	neglect	
detect	object	_____

KT /kt/ Final—three syllables

architect	indirect	reelect
cataract	intellect	self-respect
derelict	interject	subcontract
dialect	intersect	viaduct
disconnect	misdirect	_____
disinfect	overact	_____
incorrect	recollect	_____

KW /kw/ Initial—one syllable

choir	quart	quill
quack	quartz	quilt
quacked	quash	quince
quad	quashed	quints
quaff	quay	quip
quaffed	queen	quipped
quag	quell	quirk
quail	quelled	quirt
quaint	quench	quit
quake	quenched	quite
quaked	quest	quiz
qualm	quick	_____
quark	quid	_____

KW /kw/ Initial—two syllables

quadrant	quarry	queried
quadrate	quartan	query
quadrille	quarter	quester
quadroon	quartet	question
quagga	quartile	questioned
quagmire	quarto	quibble
quaintly	quartzite	quickbread
Quaker	quasi	quicken
quaking	quatrain	quickened
qualmish	quaver	quickie
quantize	queasy	quickly
quantum	Quebec	quicksand
quarrel	Queen Anne	quickstep
quarreled	quencher	quiet

quilted	quintet	quonset
quilting	quisling	quorum
Quincy	quitclaim	quota
quinine	quitter	quotient
quinsy	quiver	_____
quintain	quizzer	_____

KW /kw/ Initial—three syllables

quadrangle	quandary	quick-tempered
quadratic	quantity	quick-witted
quadriceps	quarantine	quiescent
quadrifid	quarrelsome	quietly
quadrillion	quarterback	quintessence
quadruped	quarterdeck	quintuple
quadruple	quarterhorse	quintuplet
quadruplet	quartering	quixotic
Quakertown	quarter note	quizzical
qualified	quavering	quotable
qualify	question mark	quotation
qualities	questionnaire	_____
quality	quicksilver	_____

KW /kw/ Initial—four syllables

quadrangular	qualitative	quinine water
quadrennial	quantifier	quinquennial
quadriplegic	quantitative	quotation mark
quadruplicate	quartermaster	_____
qualifier	questionable	_____

KW /kw/ Initial—five syllables

quadrilateral	quantitatively	_____
qualification	_____	_____

KW /kw/ Medial—two syllables

acquaint	awkward	bequeath
acquire	backward	bequeathed
acquired	backwash	bequest
acquit	backwoods	bookworm
aqua	banquet	brick wall

cakewalk
catwalk
chickweed
equal
equalled
equate
equip
equipped
frequence
frequent
inquest

inquire
inquired
knockwurst
likewise
liquid
loquat
lukewarm
milkweed
misquote
request
require

required
sequel
sequence
sequenced
sequin
shock wave
tranquil
unquote
walkway

_____

_____

KW /kw/ Medial—three syllables

acquaintance
acquainted
acquiesce
acquiesced
acquiring
acquittal
acquittance
acquitted
antiquate
aqualung
aquanaut
aquaplane
aquatic
aquatint
aqueduct
aqueous
aquiline
chuck wagon
chuckwalla
consequence
consequent

disquiet
equaling
equalize
equalized
equated
equating
equation
equator
equerry
equinox
equipage
equipment
equipping
equity
frequency
headquarters
hindquarter
inequal
infrequent
inquirer
inquiring

inquiry
liquefy
liquidate
liquified
loquacious
misquoted
misquoting
requirement
requiring
requisite
requital
requiter
sequential
sequoia
subsequent
tranquilize
tranquilly
unequal
unequaled
unquestioned

_____

KW /kw/ Medial—four syllables

acquiescence
acquiescent
acquisition

acquisitive
antiquary
antiquated

antiquation
antiquity
aquamarine

aquarium
Aquarius
consequential
disqualified
disqualify
disquietude
disquisition
equality
equalizer
equalizing
equidistant
equitable
equitation

equivalence
equivalent
equivocal
equivocate
infrequented
inquisition
inquisitive
inquisitor
liquefaction
liquefying
liquidating
liquidation
liquidity

loquacity
post headquarters
requisition
tranquility
tranquilizer
unfrequented
unqualified
unquenchable
ventriloquist
_____
_____
_____
_____

KW /kw/ Medial—five syllables
antiquarian
disqualifying
equanimity
equatorial
equiangular

equilateral
equilibrium
equivalency
equivocation
unequivocal

unquestionable
_____
_____
_____
_____

KY /kj/ Medial—two syllables
backyard
brickyard

dockyard
stockyard

_____
_____

KY /kj/ Medial—three syllables
calculate
calculus
Hercules
molecule
ocular

oculist
porcupine
secular
speculate
succulent

Tokyo
_____
_____
_____

KY /kj/ Medial—four syllables
accusation
articulate
calculated
calculator
curriculum
executor

gesticulate
lenticular
molecular
particular
ridiculous
security

spectacular
speculation
vermicular
vermiculate
_____
_____

SKR /skr/ Initial—one syllable

scram	screen	scrub
scrap	screw	scrunch
scrape	scribe	_____
scratch	scrimp	_____
scrawl	script	_____
scream	scroll	_____
screech	Scrooge	_____

SKR /skr/ Initial—two syllables

scraggly	screening	scrub nurse
scramble	screenplay	scrumptious
scrambled	screentest	scruple
scrapbook	screwball	_____
scraper	scribble	_____
scrapper	scribbled	_____
scratchy	scrimmage	_____
scrawny	scripture	_____

SKR /skr/ Initial—three syllables

screen writer	scrutinize	_____
screwdriver	scrutiny	_____
scrupulous	_____	_____

SKR /skr/ Medial—two syllables

ascribe	inscribe	subscript
ascribed	muskrat	transcribe
corkscrew	postscript	transcribed
describe	prescribe	_____
described	prescribed	_____
discreet	silkscreen	_____
escrow	subscribe	_____
ice cream	subscribed	_____

SKR /skr/ Medial—three syllables

description	inscription	subscription
descriptive	manuscript	_____
ice-cream man	prescription	_____
ice-cream truck	skyscraper	_____

SKS /sks/ Final—one syllable

asks	flasks	tusks
basks	husks	_____
casks	masks	_____
desks	risks	_____
disks	tasks	_____

SKW /skw/ Initial—one syllable

squab	squawk	squint
squad	squeak	squire
squall	squeal	squirm
square	squeeze	squirt
squash	squelch	squish
squat	squib	_____
squaw	squid	_____

SKW /skw/ Initial—two syllables

squabble	squarely	squeaky
squabbling	square knot	squeamish
squad car	square meal	squeegee
squadron	square mile	squeezer
squalid	square off	squeezing
squally	square root	squelcher
squalor	squarest	squiggle
squander	square yard	squirmy
square dance	squashy	squirrel
square deal	squatted	squirt gun
square feet	squatter	squishy
square foot	squatting	_____
square inch	squatty	_____

SKW /skw/ Initial—three syllables

square away	square rigger	squeezable
square inches	square shooter	_____
square meters	squashiest	_____

L

Pronounced: /l/
Spelled: l, ll

L /l/ Initial—one syllable

lace	late	leech
lack	lathe	leer
lad	laud	left
lade	laugh	leg
lag	laughed	lei
lagged	launch	Len
laid	law	lend
lain	lawn	length
lair	lay	lens
Laird	lea	lent
lake	leach	Lent
lamb	lead	Les
lame	leaf	less
lamed	league	let
lamp	leak	Lew
lance	lean	lice
land	leap	lick
lane	leaped	licked
Lane	learn	lid
lank	learned	lie
lap	lease	lied
laps	leased	lien
lapse	leash	lieu
lard	least	life
large	leave	lift
lark	leaves	light
lash	led	lights
lass	ledge	like
last	lee	liked
latch	Lee	limb

[164]

limbs	loft	low
lime	log	lox
limes	loge	lube
limp	logged	luck
limped	loin	lug
line	long	luge
link	look	lugged
links	looked	Luke
lint	loom	lump
lip	loon	lunch
lisp	loop	lung
list	loose	lunge
lit	loot	lurch
live	lop	lure
lived	lopped	lured
lives	lord	lures
Lloyd	lore	lurk
load	Lorne	lush
loaf	lose	lute
loan	loss	Lux
loath	lost	lye
loathe	lot	lymph
loaves	Lou	Lynn
lob	loud	lynx
lobe	lounge	lyre
lock	louse	_____
lodge	love	_____
lodged	loved	_____

L /l/ Initial—two syllables

labor	lady	landmark
labored	lagging	landscape
lacework	lagoon	language
lacing	Lambert	lantern
lacquer	lame duck	lanyard
lactose	lancer	larger
ladder	landed	largest
laden	land grant	larkspur
ladies	landing	Larry

larva	leachy	lessee
laser	leader	lessen
lasher	lead-in	lesson
lashing	leading	letdown
Lassie	lead-off	letter
lasso	leafage	lettered
lasting	leafy	Lettie
last name	Leah	lettuce
later	leakage	letup
latest	leaning	leucite
latex	lean-to	levee
lather	leap year	lever
lathwork	leapfrog	levy
Latin	learning	Lewis
latter	leasing	liar
lattice	leather	Libby
laughing	leaven	Libra
laughter	leaving	license
launcher	lector	lichen
launder	lecture	licking
laundry	ledger	lifeboat
Laura	leery	life buoy
Laurie	lee tide	lifeguard
lava	leeward	life raft
lavish	leeway	lifetime
lawman	left-hand	life vest
Lawrence	legate	lifter
lawsuit	legend	lift-off
lawyer	legion	ligate
layer	legume	lighten
layered	leisure	lighter
layette	Lemberg	lighthouse
laying	lemming	lighting
layman	lemon	lightning
layoff	Lena	lightweight
layout	Leo	light-year
lay up	Leon	likeness
lazy	Leonard	likewise
leacher	lesion	liking

Lima	loading	looking
limber	loafer	lookout
Limberg	loaning	looming
limbo	loathful	loony
limeade	loathing	looper
limestone	loathsome	loopy
limit	lobby	loper
Lina	lobster	Lopez
Lincoln	locate	loppy
Linda	locker	loquats
lineage	locket	Lordsburg
line drive	locking	lordship
line graph	lockjaw	Lorin
lineman	locksmith	Lorraine
linen	locus	Lory
liner	locust	loser
lineup	lodger	losing
linger	lodging	lost cause
lingo	logbook	lotion
lining	logger	Lottie
linkage	logging	lotto
linseed	logic	louder
lion	log jam	loudmouthed
lipstick	logo	Louis
liquid	log on	Louise
listen	Lois	lounger
listing	loiter	lousy
liter	London	louver
litter	lonesome	lovebirds
liven	longhand	lover
liver	longhorn	loving
livestock	longing	lowboy
live wire	longish	low-cost
livid	long johns	lower
living	long jump	lowest
lizard	long-range	low fat
Lizzie	long shot	low tide
llama	longwise	lozenge
loaded	looker	Lubbock

lucid
lucky
Lucy
luggage
lugger
lumber
lumbered
lummox
lumpish

lumpy
lunar
luncheon
lunchroom
lunchtime
luring
luscious
luster
lustrous

lusty
Luther
luxate
lying
Lyndon
Lyndsay
lyric

_____

_____

L /l/ Initial—three syllables

Labor Day
labor force
Labrador
lacerate
ladybug
lambasted
landing gear
landing strip
landowner
Laramie
Las Vegas
latency
latitude
latticework
laughing gas
laughingstock
launching pad
laundromat
lavender
lawbreaker
lawn mower
lawn tennis
layer cake
layering
layover
lazy bones
lazy tongs
leadership

leather work
leftovers
legacy
legalize
legation
legato
legible
lomonade
lemon juice
lempira
lenient
Leningrad
Lenora
leprosy
Lethargic
Leticia
lettergram
letterhead
lettering
leverage
lexicon
Lexington
liaison
liberate
liberty
library
licensee
licorice

lieutenant
life jacket
lifesaver
lifesaving
ligament
ligature
light-footed
lightheaded
light meter
lightning bug
lightning rod
lima beans
limerick
lime water
limited
limiting
limousine
lineage
linebacker
line drawing
liniment
lip reading
liquidate
Lithia
lithograph
lithoprint
litterbug
Little Rock

livable
liverwurst
living room
load factor
location
locator
lodging house
log cabin
logistics
logogram
logograph
London Bridge
Lone Star State
long distance
longitude
longshoreman
longsighted
long-winded

lopsided
loquacious
Lorinda
lottery
loudspeaker
Louisa
lousiest
lowering
lowermost
Lowery
low pressure
low water
lubricant
luckier
luckiest
lucrative
lucubrate
lumbago

lumbering
lumberjack
lumber mill
lumberyard
luminous
luncheonette
Luxembourg
luxury
lyceum
Lydia
_____
_____
_____
_____
_____
_____
_____
_____

L /l/ Initial—four syllables

labialize
laborious
laceration
laminated
laryngeal
laryngitis
laryngoscope
lateral pass
lathing hatchet
lavatory
law abiding
lazy Susan
legality
legislation
legislative
legislator
legislature
legitimate
lenticular

Liberty Bell
librarian
lickety-split
lifeguard station
life preserver
limitation
Lincoln's Birthday
lineament
linoleum
literacy
literature
lithology
Little Dipper
liturgical
locality
locomotion
locomotive
loganberry
logarithmic

Londonderry
longevity
long-suffering
lopsidedness
Los Angeles
loving kindness
lower classman
low spirited
lunitidal
luxuriance
luxurious
_____
_____
_____
_____
_____
_____
_____
_____

L /l/ Initial—five syllables

laboratory	libertarian	Louisiana
lackadaisical	Lithuania	_____
liability	longitudinal	_____

L /l/ Medial—two syllables

Aileen	below	Cologne
ailing	billow	colon
Alan	Billy	color
alarm	boiler	colors
Alex	boiling	column
Alice	bowler	coolant
alike	bowling	cooler
alive	brilliant	Coolidge
alley	broiler	crawler
allied	bully	daily
allot	caller	Dallas
allow	Cally	daylight
alloy	ceiling	dealer
allure	cellar	delete
ally	cello	Delhi
alone	Ceylon	delight
along	chalet	deluxe
aloud	challenge	dialing
Bailey	Chile	dilute
balance	chili	doily
balanced	chilly	dollar
baler	cola	Dolly
ballad	collage	driller
ballet	collapse	drilling
balloon	collar	drooler
ballot	colleague	duller
bay leaf	collect	dweller
Bayley	Colleen	dwelling
Baylor	college	Elaine
believe	Collette	elapse
bellows	collide	elate
belly	collie	elect
belong	cologne	elite

ellipse	highly	oily
elope	hilly	olive
elude	Holland	Olive
eyelash	hollow	palace
eyelet	holly	pallet
eyelid	Holly	Pauline
failing	holy	peeling
fallen	howler	pellet
fallout	Ireland	Phillip
feelers	island	Phyllis
feeling	Jai Alai	pilar
Felix	jailer	pilings
fellow	jealous	pillar
filings	jelly	pillow
fillet	Joline	pilot
filling	jolly	Poland
filly	Julie	polar
follow	July	poler
folly	Kelly	police
foolish	kilo	polish
freelance	kneeling	Polish
freeload	knowledge	polite
free lunch	mailer	pollen
fully	mailing	pollute
gaily	malice	Polly
gala	mallard	polo
gallant	mallet	polyp
galley	mellow	pullet
gallon	melon	pulley
gallop	mileage	pulling
galore	miler	railing
galosh	miller	rally
goalie	millet	really
hallow	molar	relapse
halo	mollusk	relate
healer	Molly	relax
heeler	Nellie	relay
Helen	newly	release
hello	nylon	relic

relief	smeller	trailer
relieve	smelling	trawler
relieved	smiling	troller
relish	solar	tulip
rely	solemn	Tyler
roller	solid	valance
ruler	solo	valid
ruling	speller	valley
sailing	spelling	value
sailor	spilling	velour
salaam	sprawler	villa
salad	squealer	village
Sally	stealer	villain
salon	stealing	volley
salute	stolen	volume
scaler	stroller	Wallace
scholar	strolling	wallet
scalant	stylish	wallop
sealer	stylist	wallow
select	stylus	Wally
seller	swallow	whaler
shallow	swelling	whaling
shellac	swollen	Willie
Shelley	tailing	willing
shilling	tailor	willow
shoelace	talent	Willy
shriller	taller	woolen
shrillest	tallish	woolly
silence	tallow	yelling
silent	tally	yellow
silly	talon	zealous
silo	Taylor	Zulu
ski lift	teller	_____
skillet	telling	_____
Skylab	thriller	_____
skylark	tiling	_____
skyline	tiller	_____
smaller	toilet	_____
smallish	towline	_____

L /l/ Medial—three syllables

a la carte
abolish
absolute
acknowledge
Adaline
Adela
Alamo
Alaska
Aletta
Alison
Alissa
allergic
allergy
alliance
allowance
aloha
ambulance
Amelia
analyze
angelic
angular
antelope
Apollo
avalanche
bachelor
balancing
ballistics
balloonist
ballyhoo
belated
beloved
billy goat
bobolink
bolero
bologna
bowlegged
broccoli
buffalo

bulletin
bungalow
calendar
calico
calorie
calypso
candlelight
cantaloupe
catalog
cavalier
celebrate
celery
cellophane
Challenger
challenges
challenging
chili sauce
chuck-a-luck
chuckwalla
circulate
civilize
colander
collarbone
collection
collector
collision
colony
colorful
color guard
coloring
Columbus
consoler
controller
counselor
dandelion
Delaware
delicate
delicious

deliver
demolish
Denali
desolate
develop
dialect
dialing
dialogue
diligent
discolor
Disneyland
easily
elastic
election
elective
electric
electrode
elegant
element
elephant
elevate
eleven
entailing
envelope
Evelyn
exhaling
fabulous
fairyland
family
fellowship
filament
finale
finalize
foliage
folio
follower
following
follow-through

follow-up	jalopy	polar ice
formula	jealousy	polarize
four-wheeler	jelly beans	polar lights
freeloader	jet pilot	policeman
galaxy	jeweler	policy
Galena	journalist	polio
Galilee	kilogram	polishing
gallery	kilowatt	politics
galoshes	make-believe	polliwog
gasoline	malamute	polygon
gelatin	Malinda	popular
Gila Bend	mandolin	populous
gondola	marmalade	porcelain
gorilla	marshmallow	propeller
guerrilla	marvelous	qualified
gullible	masculine	quality
Gwendolyn	melody	realize
halibut	metallic	really
Halloween	militia	rebelling
happily	molasses	regular
helium	muscular	regulate
holiday	muskmelon	related
Hollywood	New Zealand	relation
hula hoop	obsolete	relative
hula skirt	ocular	relay race
Illinois	oleo	relevant
illusion	Oliver	relieving
illustrate	Olympics	religion
impala	omelet	religious
inhaling	Pamela	reluctant
insulate	paralyze	retailer
intellect	pelican	roller skates
invalid	penalize	rolling pin
isolate	pendulum	salad bar
Israeli	Philippines	salami
italic	Phillipsburg	salary
Italy	photo lab	sand dollar
Jackelyn	piccolo	satellite
Jacqueline	polar bear	scholarship

sea lion
secular
silhouette
similar
simulate
singular
skeleton
socialize
solar heat
solar house
solarize
soloist
solution
spatula
specialist
specialize
specially
speculate
speedily
spelling bee
sterilize
stimulate
stimulus
succulent
Sun Valley
surveillance
swallowing
swallowtail
syllabus

symbolize
talented
talent show
tamale
telegram
telegraph
telephone
telescope
telethon
televise
three-wheeler
tolerance
tolerant
totally
tricolor
tubular
two-wheeler
umbrella
unbalanced
unduly
unruly
unwilling
utilize
Valeda
valentine
Valerie
vanilla
ventilate
verbally

vigilant
villager
viola
violate
violet
Violet
violin
vitalize
vocalist
vocally
volition
volleyball
volunteer
wallaby
xylophone
Yellowstone
zeppelin

_____
_____
_____
_____
_____
_____
_____
_____
_____
_____
_____

L /l/ Medial—four syllables

a capella
abalone
ability
accelerate
accumulate
actually
affiliate
agility

Alabama
alimony
allegation
alleluia
alligator
aluminum
Amarillo
Amaryllis

Annapolis
armadillo
articulate
ballerina
belligerent
binoculars
biologist
California

capillary
caterpillar
celebration
celebrity
chameleon
chocolate chip
Cinderella
coliseum
colonial
Colorado
coloring book
Columbia
consolidate
constellation
curriculum
deliberate
development
ecology
electrician
elevation
elevator
escalator
evaluate
finality
fortuneteller
geology
helicopter
hilarious
Honolulu
hot-air balloon
humiliate
ideally
illuminate
illustration
incredulous
initialize
inoculate
intelligence
intelligent

intolerant
irregular
jack-o'-lantern
Jerusalem
Jolly Roger
jubilation
kaleidoscope
kilometer
lenticular
linoleum
literally
locality
malaria
Marco Polo
melancholy
metropolis
military
monopoly
multicolor
mythology
Napoleon
naturally
nevertheless
nobility
Olivia
palomino
parallel bars
paralysis
particular
penicillin
peninsula
personally
philodendron
philosopher
philosophy
polar axis
polar region
police station
political

politician
population
practically
prematurely
pussy willow
qualitative
realism
reality
regulation
relationship
resolution
revolution
ridiculous
roller coaster
roller skating
salad dressing
semicolon
semitrailer
spectacular
tarantula
technicolor
technology
telepathy
television
theologian
theology
tolerable
tolerably
twin propeller
typically
ukulele
unparalleled
unpopular
unqualified
usually
utility
utilizing
Valentine's Day
valuable

velocity	vitality	_____
Venezuela	voluminous	_____
ventilation	voluntary	_____
violation	water colors	_____
violinist	yellow jackets	_____

L /l/ Medial—five syllables

acceleration	nationalism	specifically
accidentally	nationality	unbelievable
articulation	necessarily	underdeveloped
delicatessen	occasionally	universally
dilapidated	originally	unreliable
electricity	personality	unusually
immediately	polarization	utilization
incidentally	popularity	versatility
inequality	possibility	visibility
intellectual	preliminary	vocabulary
involuntary	principality	voluntarily
metabolism	qualification	_____
Metropolitan	roller skating rink	_____
miscellaneous	similarity	_____

L /l/ Medial—six syllables

individually	totalitarian	_____
revolutionary	utilitarian	_____
theoretically	variability	_____

L /l/ Final—one syllable

ail	bowl	deal
aisle	braille	dell
all	broil	Dell
bail	bull	dill
bale	call	dole
ball	cell	doll
bell	coal	Doyle
Belle	coil	drawl
bill	cool	drill
Bill	crawl	drool
boil	Dale	dull

dwell	Kyle	sale
eel	mail	Saul
fail	male	scale
fall	mall	school
feel	meal	scowl
fell	Mel	scroll
file	mile	seal
fill	mill	sell
foal	mole	shall
foil	mule	shawl
fool	nail	she'll
foul	Neal	shell
fowl	Nell	shoal
frill	null	shrill
full	oil	sill
Gail	owl	skill
gale	pail	skull
gall	pal	small
Gil	pale	smell
gill	Paul	smile
goal	peal	snail
gull	peel	soil
hail	Phil	sole
Hal	pile	soul
hall	pill	spell
haul	pole	spill
heal	poll	spoil
heel	pool	spool
hill	pull	sprawl
howl	quail	squall
Hoyle	quell	squeal
hull	quill	stale
ill	rail	stall
isle	real	steel
jail	reel	still
jell	role	stole
kale	roll	stool
keel	rule	stroll
kneel	sail	style

swell	trail	whole
tail	twill	who'll
tale	Vail	will
tall	veal	Will
teal	veil	wool
tell	voile	Yale
thrill	wail	yawl
tile	wall	yell
till	well	yule
toil	whale	zeal
toll	wheel	_____
tool	while	_____

L /l/ Final—two syllables

Adele	compile	entail
Airedale	conceal	Estelle
airmail	control	exhale
anthill	cordial	exile
appeal	Cornell	expel
April	corral	eyeball
avail	cowbell	faithful
awhile	cruel	female
baseball	Crystal	fire drill
beach ball	cue ball	fire sale
bedroll	cupful	football
Beryl	curtail	footstool
Bethel	Cyril	fragile
bluebell	Daniel	fuel
Brazil	decal	gazelle
canal	detail	handball
cancel	dial	handbill
capsule	diesel	handrail
Carol	distill	hangnail
cartwheel	dowel	Hazel
cattail	downfall	high school
Cheryl	downhill	hotel
chisel	dual	inkwell
Churchill	eggshell	install
compel	enroll	jackal

jewel	pastel	sleigh bell
Joel	payroll	snowball
joyful	pencil	snowfall
jump ball	pen pal	standstill
keyhole	pigtail	steel wool
kickball	pinball	subsoil
manhole	pinwheel	symbol
Maypole	porthole	tadpole
meanwhile	rainfall	tinfoil
meatball	real	toadstool
misspell	recall	toenail
module	recoil	topsoil
molehill	refill	towel
morale	repeal	town hall
mortal	repel	turmoil
motel	reptile	unroll
mothball	retail	until
muscle	reveal	unvcil
Nashville	Rochelle	unwell
newsreel	royal	vial
Nicole	Russell	viol
nightfall	sackful	vowel
nodule	sandpile	Wendell
Noel	sawmill	windfall
North Pole	schedule	windmill
nutshell	scoopful	_____
oatmeal	sea gull	_____
oil well	seashell	_____
ordeal	sea wall	_____
pailful	Sibyl	_____
parole	ski trail	_____

L /l/ Final—three syllables

Abigail	axial	bronchial
aerial	baby doll	Bunker Hill
alcohol	basketball	burial
Annabelle	bass viol	buttonhole
annual	betrayal	carryall
aureole	bookmobile	casserole

casual	musical	Sunday school
cathedral	mutual	sundial
Cherryvale	nightingale	Sunnyvale
Cherryville	oriel	swimming pool
cottontail	overall	tetherball
denial	overhaul	unequal
disloyal	overrule	unreal
factual	parasol	usual
fairy tale	punctual	versatile
Fayetteville	racquet ball	vestibule
Ferris wheel	radial	viceroyal
fingernail	renewal	virtual
gradual	ridicule	visual
honor roll	ritual	wading pool
hospital	rock-n-roll	withdrawal
ideal	rummage sale	_____
infantile	Samuel	_____
initial	serial	_____
Israel	shrimp cocktail	_____
Jacksonville	ski patrol	_____
jovial	snowmobile	_____
juvenile	soccerball	_____
manual	spinning wheel	_____
Montreal	summer school	_____

L /l/ Final—four syllables

arterial	parochial	vice-principal
certified mail	perpetual	_____
Liberty Bell	tutorial	_____
nursery school	unusual	_____

L /l/ Final—five syllables

ceremonial	intellectual	_____
editorial	Roman numeral	_____
individual	testimonial	_____

L /l/ Recurring—one syllable

Lil	loll	_____
Lille	Lyle	_____

L /l/ Recurring—two syllables

fulfill
ill will
label
ladle
lamplight
landlord
lapel
lapful
Lapland
largely
lastly
lately
lawful
lawless
legal
lentil
lethal
level
libel
lifeless
lifelike

lifeline
lifelong
lightly
likely
Lila
lilac
Lilly
lily
limelight
lingual
lintel
listless
little
lively
local
locale
Lola
lonely
long-lived
loophole
loose-leaf

lovelock
lovelorn
lovely
Lowell
lowlands
lowly
loyal
Lucille
lunch pail
Lulu
Lyell
pell-mell
roll call
solely
steel wool
telltale
toll call
wholesale

_____

_____

_____

L /l/ Recurring—three syllables

April fool
colorful
color wheel
illegal
jelly roll
labeller
labial
ladylike
lamplighter
landlady
Laplander
laryngal
lastingly
latently
lateral

legislate
leveler
levelling
lexical
liable
liberal
likelihood
Lillian
lily pad
lily-white
limitless
lineal
linseed oil
literal
Little League

littler
littlest
livelier
liveliest
livelihood
Llewellyn
localize
locally
logical
logrolling
lollipop
Long Island
long leaf pine
long liner
Longfellow

lovable

loyalist

loyalty

Loyola

luckily

luculent

lullaby

lunular

molecule

olive oil

paddlewheel

parallel

salad oil

sea level

skillfully

wholesaler

willfully

_____

LB /lb/ Medial—two syllables

Albert

album

ball bat

ball boy

bellbird

bell book

bell boy

billboard

callboard

call box

coalbin

Delbert

Elbe

Elbert

Elbie

elbow

file box

Galbraith

Gilbert

Holbrook

mailbag

mailbox

Melba

Melbourne

Milbank

millboard

Millburn

nail bag

Olbers

pillbox

roll bar

sailboat

school band

school board

schoolbooks

school bus

skull bone

spellbound

steel box

tool box

wallboard

whalebone

Wilbanks

Wilbur

_____

LB /lb/ Medial—three syllables

Albany

albatross

Alberta

albino

ball bearings

bell-bottoms

bell buoy

doll buggy

Elberta

Elberton

elbow grease

elbowroom

Gilberta

melba toast

mulberry

Mulberry

nail-biting

wheelbarrow

LB /lb/ Final—one syllable

alb

bulb

Kalb

Kolb

_____

_____

LB /lb/ Final—two syllables

DeKalb

flashbulb

light bulb

wet bulb

_____

_____

BL /bl/ Initial—one syllable

blab	bleed	blond
blabbed	blench	blood
black	blend	bloom
blade	bless	bloomed
Blaine	blessed	blot
Blake	blest	blotch
blame	blew	blotched
blamed	blight	blouse
blanch	blimp	blow
Blanche	blind	blown
bland	blink	blue
blank	blinked	blues
blare	blintz	bluff
blared	blip	bluffed
blast	bliss	blunt
blaze	blithe	blur
blazed	blitz	blurb
bleach	bloat	blurred
bleached	blob	blurt
bleak	bloc	blush
blear	block	blushed
bleat	blocked	Blythe
bled	blocks	

BL /bl/ Initial—two syllables

blackball	blacklist	blasé
blackballed	blackmail	blaspheme
black bear	blackmailed	blasphemed
black belt	blackout	blast off
blackbird	Black Sea	blatant
blackboard	black sheep	blazer
blacken	blacksmith	blazon
Blackett	blackthorn	blazoned
black eye	blacktop	bleachers
black flag	black whale	bleary
Blackfoot	blameless	blemish
blackhead	blanket	blemished
blacking	blarney	blessed

blessing
blinder
blinders
blindfold
blinding
blinker
blinkers
blissful
blister
blistered
blithesome
blizzard
blockade
blocker
blockhead
blockhouse
bloodhound
bloodline
bloodstream
blood test

blossom
blossomed
blotchy
blotter
blower
blowgun
blowout
blowpipe
blowtorch
blubber
blubbered
bluebell
blue belt
bluebird
blue cheese
blue fish
bluegill
bluegrass
blue jay
blue jeans

blue moon
blueprint
bluer
Blue Ridge
blue shark
blue sky
bluest
bluets
blue whale
bluffer
bluffing
bluing
bluish
blunder
blundered
bluster
blustered
Blytheville
_____
_____

BL /bl/ Initial—three syllables

black and blue
blackberry
black market
black widow
blamelessly
blameworthy
blandishing
blandishment
blasphemy

bleeding heart
blindman's bluff
blockbuster
bloodmobile
blood pressure
Blue Angels
blueberry
bluebonnet
bluebottle

blue color
bluejacket
blue marlin
Blue Mountains
blue ribbon
blustery
_____
_____
_____

BL /bl/ Medial—two syllables

ablaze
abloom
babbling
bubbling
bubbly
cobbler

dabbling
doublet
doubly
dribbling
emblaze
emblem

gambling
giblet
glibly
gobbler
gobbling
goblet

goblin	public	sublet
grabbler	publish	sublime
hobbling	pueblo	tableau
mumbling	Pueblo	tablet
nibbling	rambler	trembling
nimbly	Red Bluff	troubling
nosebleed	sandblast	tumbler
oblate	sand-blind	tumbling
oblige	semblance	warbler
oblique	sibling	warbling
oblong	squabbling	wobbly
problem	sublease	———————

BL /bl/ Medial—three syllables

ablation	Navy blue	red-blooded
ablution	night blindness	republic
cable car	notably	resemblance
emblazing	obligate	San Pablo
emblazon	obliging	shoulder blade
emblem book	obligor	sublimate
emblements	public school	unpublished
establish	publisher	———————
established	publishing	———————

BL /bl/ Medial—four syllables

ablactating	obligation	publishing house
ablepsia	obligato	reestablish
army blanket	oblique angle	republican
baby-blue eyes	obliterate	subliminal
disestablish	publication	———————
emblazonment	public domain	———————
establishment	publicity	———————

BL /bl/ Final—two syllables

Abel	brabble	crumble
able	bramble	cymbal
amble	bubble	dabble
babble	bumble	double
Bible	cable	drabble

dribble	nimble	Sybil
fable	noble	table
feeble	pebble	thimble
fumble	quibble	treble
gable	ramble	tremble
gamble	rebel	tribal
global	rubble	trouble
gobble	ruble	tumble
grumble	rumble	verbal
hobble	sable	wabble
humble	scramble	waddle
jumble	scribal	warble
label	scribble	wobble
libel	squabble	_____
marble	stable	_____
mumble	stubble	_____
nibble	stumble	_____

BL /bl/ Final—three syllables

affable	gullible	resemble
assemble	horrible	sellable
audible	legible	sensible
cannibal	liable	sociable
capable	livable	soluble
constable	lovable	suitable
decibel	notable	syllable
disable	portable	terrible
durable	possible	timetable
edible	preamble	unable
flammable	probable	useable
flexible	quotable	_____

BL /bl/ Final—four syllables

acceptable	convertible	formidable
advisable	dependable	habitable
agreeable	desirable	handleable
answerable	eligible	honorable
available	enjoyable	Honorable
comfortable	favorable	hospitable

illegible
impossible
incredible
inedible
inflammable
invisible
miserable
perishable
practicable
preferable
presentable
profitable

questionable
reasonable
reassemble
receivable
reliable
remarkable
respectable
responsible
separable
tolerable
unchangeable
unmatchable

unprintable
unquenchable
unspeakable
unsuitable
unthinkable
valuable
variable
vegetable
veritable
vulnerable
_____
_____

BL /bl/ Final—five syllables

dishonorable
indivisible
inevitable
inhospitable
innumerable
inoperable
irresistible

recoverable
unalterable
unapproachable
unavoidable
unbelievable
undesirable
unmistakable

unprofitable
unquestionable
unreasonable
unreliable
unutterable
unwarrantable
_____

LD /ld/ Medial—two syllables

Alden
alder
Baldwin
boulder
Boulder
builder
building
build-up
childhood
childish
children
cold cuts
colder
coldest
cold front
cold pack

cold snap
cold wave
Elden
elder
Elder
eldest
fielded
fielder
field goal
field trip
file disk
folder
folding
gelding
golden
goldfinch

goldfish
gold mine
gold pan
gold rush
gold stream
holder
holding
hold-up
mildew
molding
olden
older
oldest
scalding
scolding
seldom

Sheldon	Welden	wild west
shielded	welder	yielded
shoulder	welding	yielding
smolder	wildcat	_____
Waldon	wildfire	_____
welded	wildlife	_____

LD /ld/ Medial—three syllables

beholden	golden age	shipbuilder
blindfolded	goldenrod	shouldering
bulldozer	gold nugget	unfolding
bulldozing	gold panner	unwieldy
cul-de-sac	grandchildren	unyielding
deviled eggs	left fielder	upholder
elderly	old-fashioned	wilderness
Eldora	right fielder	wildflower
field glasses	shareholder	withholding
field worker	shelled pecans	World Series
folding chair	shelled walnuts	_____

LD /ld/ Final—one syllable

bald	guild	shield
billed	held	skilled
bold	hold	sold
build	mild	spilled
called	mold	told
child	mulled	veiled
cold	old	weld
field	polled	wield
filed	pulled	wild
filled	rolled	world
fold	scald	yield
gild	scold	_____
gold	shelled	_____

LD /ld/ Final—two syllables

afield	airfield	Arnold
age-old	appalled	backfield
ahold	appealed	beheld

behold	infield	twofold
billfold	infold	unfold
blindfold	left field	unsold
coal field	marbled	untold
cornfield	marveled	upheld
corralled	outfield	uphold
Donald	rebuild	windshield
downfield	retold	withheld
enfold	right field	withhold
foothold	Ronald	_____
foretold	Sea World	_____
Gerald	stepchild	_____
grandchild	stronghold	_____
Harold	threefold	_____
household	threshold	_____

LD /ld/ Final—three syllables

battlefield	initialed	marigold
center field	interfold	soccer field
centerfold	landing field	_____
emerald	MacDonald	_____
football field	manifold	_____

DL /dl/ Medial—two syllables

badly	madly	toddler
Bradley	meddling	toddling
deadline	medley	twiddling
deadlock	midland	wedlock
deadly	needless	widely
gladly	needling	windlass
Hadley	oddly	_____
headlight	paddling	_____
headline	padlock	_____
heedless	red light	_____
huddling	sadly	_____
hurdler	seedless	_____
idling	seedling	_____
kindling	soundly	_____
loudly	swindling	_____

DL /dl/ Medial—three syllables

bridal veil	idleness	Middle East
candlestick	meddlesome	Middle West
candlewick	middle age	_____
handlebars	middle ear	_____

DL /dl/ Final—two syllables

bridal	kindle	riddle
bridle	ladle	saddle
bundle	medal	sandal
candle	meddle	scandal
caudal	middle	spindle
cradle	model	swindle
dwindle	muddle	tidal
fiddle	needle	toddle
griddle	noodle	twiddle
handle	paddle	vandal
huddle	pedal	wheedle
hurdle	peddle	yodel
idle	poodle	_____
idol	puddle	_____

LDZ /ldz/ Final—one syllable

builds	holds	scolds
fields	molds	worlds
folds	scalds	yields

LF /lf/ Medial—two syllables

Alfred	self-care	sulfine
baleful	self-ease	sulfite
bullfinch	self-fed	sulfur
bullfrog	self-help	welfare
elfin	selfish	willful
elfish	self-pride	wolf cub
elfkin	self-serve	wolfhound
elflock	self-taught	wolfish
golfer	shellfish	wolf pack
golfing	sulfa	_____
Gulf Stream	sulfate	_____

LF /lf/ Medial—three syllables

alfalfa	self-control	self-righteous
alphabet	self-defense	self-searching
bellflower	self-esteem	self-serving
Bellflower	self-giving	self-support
bisulphate	self-glory	skillfully
bullfiddle	self-image	skillfulness
self-addressed	self-imposed	sulfatic
self-assured	selfishly	sulfitic
self-aware	self-pity	sulfuric
self-composed	self-possessed	unselfish
self-concept	self-regard	_____
self-conscious	self-reproach	_____
self-contained	self-respect	_____

LF /lf/ Medial—four syllables

alphabetic	self-confidence	self-evident
self-appointed	self-determined	self-reliance
self-assurance	self-directed	self-sacrifice
self-awareness	self-discipline	self-sufficient

LF /lf/ Final—one syllable

elf	Ralph	wolf
golf	self	_____
gulf	shelf	_____

LF /lf/ Final—two syllables

Adolf	himself	Rudolph
Adolphe	itself	thyself
bookshelf	myself	werewolf
engulf	oneself	white wolf
gray wolf	ourself	yourself
herself	Randolph	_____

FL /fl/ Initial—one syllable

flab	flair	flakes
flagged	flaired	flame
flagged	flak	flamed
flail	flake	flank

flap	flick	flout
flapped	flies	flow
flare	flight	flown
flared	flinch	Floyd
flash	fling	flu
flashed	flint	flub
flask	flip	flue
flat	flipped	fluff
flaunt	flirt	fluffs
flaw	flit	fluke
flax	Flo	flume
flay	float	flung
flea	flock	flunk
fleck	flood	flush
fled	floor	flute
flee	flop	flux
fleece	flopped	fly
fleet	floss	phlegm
flesh	flounce	phlox
flew	flounced	_____
flex	flour	_____

FL /fl/ Initial—two syllables

flabby	flashback	flavor
flaccid	flashbulb	flaxseed
Flag Day	flash card	flection
flagging	flashcube	fledgling
flagman	flash flood	fleecy
flagpole	flashgun	Flemish
flagrant	flashing	fleshy
Flagstaff	flashlight	Fletcher
flaky	flashy	flexion
flameproof	flatbed	flicker
flaming	flatboat	flier
flanker	flatcar	flight path
flannel	flatfoot	flighty
flapjack	flatter	flimsy
flapper	flattop	flip-flops
flare-up	flautist	flipper

flippers	floppy	flue pipe
flipping	Flora	fluffy
flitter	floral	fluid
float bridge	Florence	flunky
floater	florid	flurry
floating	florist	fluster
float plane	flossy	flutist
flocking	flounder	flutter
floodlight	flourish	flying
floorboard	flow chart	flywheel
floor lamp	flower	_____
floor show	flowing	_____
floozy	fluent	_____

FL /fl/ Initial—three syllables

flabbergast	flexible	fluctuate
flagrantly	flight control	fluency
flamboyant	floating dock	flufficr
flamenco	flood control	fluid ounce
flamethrower	floodwater	fluorine
flamingo	floorwalker	flutter kick
flammable	floppy disk	flyable
flannelette	Florentine	fly-casting
flashier	florescent	flycatcher
flatiron	Florida	flying fish
flattery	flotation	phlegmatic
flavoring	flotilla	_____
flea-bitten	flower girl	_____
flea market	flowerpot	_____

FL /fl/ Initial—four syllables

floriculture	flying safety	_____
fluctuation	flying saucer	_____

FL /fl/ Medial—two syllables

afflict	chiefly	deflect
aflame	conflict	firefly
afloat	cornflakes	flip-flops
blowfly	deflate	horsefly

housefly
ice floe
inflame
inflate
inflict
leaflet

muffler
pamphlet
reflect
roughly
snowflake
souffle'

stiffly
top-flight

_____
_____
_____
_____

FL /fl/ Medial—three syllables

affliction
affluence
affluent
butterfly
camouflage
cornflower
deflation
deflection

deflower
disfluent
dragonfly
genuflect
ice flowers
inflation
inflection
influence

overflow
reflection
reflector
sunflower
wallflower

_____
_____
_____

FL /fl/ Medial—four syllables

cauliflower
conflagration
genuflection
inflammable

inflammation
inflatable
inflexible
influential

influenza
superfluous

_____
_____

FL /fl/ Final—two syllables

armful
artful
awful
baffle
baleful
careful
changeful
cheerful
doleful
doubtful
dreadful
Eiffel
faithful
fateful
fitful

forceful
fretful
frightful
fruitful
gainful
gleeful
graceful
grateful
handful
harmful
healthful
heedful
helpful
hopeful
hurtful

joyful
mournful
mouthful
muffle
needful
pailful
painful
peaceful
playful
raffle
restful
rightful
rueful
ruffle
sackful

scoopful	thoughtful	wishful
scuffle	trifle	woeful
shuffle	tuneful	wrathful
skillful	useful	wrongful
sniffle	waffle	youthful
spiteful	wakeful	_____
spoonful	wasteful	_____
stifle	watchful	_____
thankful	willful	_____

FL /fl/ Final—three syllables

beautiful	eventful	resourceful
bountiful	fanciful	respectful
colorful	forgetful	sorrowful
deceitful	masterful	teaspoonful
disdainful	meaningful	unlawful
disgraceful	merciful	unthankful
distasteful	pitiful	untruthful
distressful	plentiful	wonderful
distrustful	reproachful	_____
dutiful	resentful	_____

FL /fl/ Final—four syllables

tablespoonful	_____	_____
uneventful	_____	_____
unmerciful	_____	_____

GL /gl/ Initial—one syllable

glad	glean	gloss
glade	gleaned	glove
glance	glee	gloves
glanced	glen	glow
gland	Glenn	glue
glare	glib	glued
glared	glide	glum
glass	glimpse	glume
glaze	gloat	_____
glazed	globe	_____
gleam	gloom	_____

GL /gl/ Initial—two syllables

glacier
gladden
gladness
glad rags
Gladys
glamor
glancing
glaring
glary
glasses
glasshouse
glassine
glassware
glasswork
glassy

glazement
glazier
glazing
gleaning
glee club
gleeful
Glenda
Glendale
glided
glide plane
glider
gliding
glimmer
glisten
glitter

gloaming
global
globate
gloomy
glory
glossy
glottis
Glover
glowing
glowworm
glucose
gluing
gluten
glutton

_____

GL /gl/ Initial—three syllables

glamorize
glamorous
glandular
glass blower
glass blowing
glass cutter
glaucoma
gleefully

glimmering
glistening
glitter ice
glittery
globe-trotter
glomerate
gloomier
Gloria

glorify
glorious
glossary
glossier
glycerin
glyptodont

_____

_____

GL /gl/ Initial—four syllables

gladiator
gladiola
glamorously

Gloriana
glorifier
gloriously

glossology

_____

_____

GL /gl/ Medial—two syllables

aglow
boggling
bugler
Douglas
dress gloves
eaglet

eagling
eyeglass
giggler
giggling
giggly
haggling

hourglass
igloo
joggling
juggler
juggling
lymph gland

neglect	straggling	wineglass
piglet	sunglow	work gloves
scrub gloves	unglue	wriggler
spyglass	unglued	wriggly

GL /gl/ Medial—three syllables

aglimmer	eyeglasses	plastic glass
aglitter	fiberglass	rubber gloves
baseball glove	field glasses	semi-glaze
boondoggler	leather gloves	semi-glazed
boxing glove	looking glass	semi-gloss
dark glasses	neglectful	sunglasses
everglade	negligence	water glass
Everglades	negligent	window glass

GL /gl/ Final—two syllables

beagle	jiggle	straggle
bugle	joggle	struggle
eagle	juggle	waggle
gargle	legal	wiggle
giggle	regal	wriggle
gurgle	smuggle	_____
haggle	snuggle	_____

GL /gl/ Final—three syllables

bedraggle	illegal	prodigal
boondoggle	Portugal	salt bagel

NGL /ŋl/ Medial—two syllables

angler	English	mingling
angling	jingler	wrangler
Anglo	jingling	wrangling
England	jungly	_____

NGL /ŋl/ Medial—three syllables

Anglican	Englander	New England
anglicize	Englisher	_____
anglify	English horn	_____
drinking glass	Englishman	_____

NGL /ŋl/ Final—two syllables

angle	mingle	wrangle
dangle	shingle	
dingle	single	
jangle	spangle	
jingle	tangle	
jungle	tingle	

NGL /ŋl/ Final—three syllables

commingle	quadrangle	untangle
entangle	rectangle	
Kris Kringle	right angle	
left angle	triangle	

LK /lk/ Medial—two syllables

Alcan	milkman	silky
alcove	milkmen	sulking
bulkhead	milkshake	sulky
bulk mail	milk truck	talcum
bulky	milkweed	welcome
Elkhart	polka	welcomed
Elkhorn	railcar	
elk rack	silken	
hulking	silk hat	
mail car	silkworm	

LK /lk/ Medial—three syllables

alcohol	Chilkoot Pass	volcanic
alkali	Elk City	volcano
alkaline	Milky Way	vulcanize
alkalize	silkiness	
alkalized	silk-screen print	
balcony	silk stockings	
calculate	unwelcome	

LK /lk/ Medial—four syllables

Alcan Highway	talcum powder
calculator	
recalculate	

LK /lk/ Final—one syllable

bilk	ilk	whelk
bulk	milk	yelk
elk	silk	_____
hulk	sulk	_____
Hulk	talc	_____

LK /lk/ Final—two syllables

canned milk	real silk	sweet milk
dry milk	skim milk	_____
goat's milk	sour milk	_____
ice milk	spun silk	_____

LK /lk/ Final—three syllables

buttermilk	malted milk	_____
lowfat milk	powdered milk	_____

KL /kl/ Initial—one syllable

clack	Clay	clique
claim	clean	cloak
claimed	cleaned	cloaked
Claire	cleanse	clock
clam	clear	clocked
clamp	cleared	clod
clan	cleats	clog
clang	clef	clogs
clap	cleft	clone
clapped	clench	clop
Clark	clerk	close
clash	click	closed
clashed	cliff	clot
clasp	Cliff	cloth
clasped	climb	clothe
class	climbed	clothes
Claude	clinch	cloud
clause	cling	clout
claw	Clint	clove
clawed	clip	clown
clay	clipped	clowned

cloy	clump	Kline
cloyed	clumped	klutz
club	clung	_____
cluck	clutch	_____
clue	clutched	_____
clued	Clyde	_____

KL /kl/ Initial—two syllables

chloric	cleaver	clippings
chlorine	clement	clobber
clackers	Cleo	clockwise
claimant	clergy	clockwork
clambake	Cleveland	closet
clammy	clever	close-up
clamor	cliché	closing
clamshell	client	closure
clapping	Clifford	clothespin
Clara	Clifton	clothier
Clarence	climate	clothing
clarice	climax	cloudburst
classic	climber	cloudy
classmate	climbing	clover
classroom	clincher	Clovis
classy	clinic	clubhouse
clatter	clinker	club steak
clattered	Clinton	clumsy
cleanly	clipboard	cluster
cleanup	clipper	clutter
clearance	clippers	cluttered
clearing	clipping	_____

KL /kl/ Initial—three syllables

chlorinate	clarify	clavicle
chloroform	clarinet	claviform
clairvoyance	classical	cleanliness
clam chowder	classified	cleft palate
clam digging	classify	clemency
clandestine	Claudia	clergyman
Clarendon	clavichord	clerical

clientele	clinician	Klamath Falls
cliff dweller	clodhopper	_____
climactic	cloverleaf	_____
clinical	club sandwich	_____

KL /kl/ Medial—two syllables

acclaim	eclipsed	proclaim
acclaimed	enclose	proclaimed
anklet	exclaim	quick lime
Auckland	exclude	quickly
backlash	fan club	reclaim
backlog	first class	recline
ball club	foreclose	reclined
Barclay	foreclosed	seclude
becloud	Franklin	sparkler
blacklist	freckly	sparkling
book club	Girls' Club	speckling
booklet	glee club	sprinkler
Boys' Club	health club	sprinkling
bridge club	heckler	tackler
broadcloth	incline	ticklish
brooklet	inclined	time clock
buckling	include	trickling
cackling	knuckler	twinkling
cheesecloth	knuckling	weakling
chuckler	land claim	weakly
chuckling	likely	wreckless
conclude	loin cloth	yacht club
cycling	mukluks	_____
cyclone	necklace	_____
declare	Oakland	_____
decline	occlude	_____
disclose	o'clock	_____
dishcloth	outclass	_____
dry clean	pickling	_____
dry cleaned	preclude	_____
duckling	press club	_____
dustcloth	prickling	_____
eclipse	prickly	_____

KL /kl/ Medial—three syllables

acclimate
alarm clock
biweekly
bricklayer
Christmas club
country club
dry cleaning
eclectic
ecliptic
enclosure
exclusion
exclusive
foreclosure
Four-H Club
Franklin stove
garden club
health spa club

inclement
inclined plane
inclusion
inclusive
jockey club
junior class
kennel club
Lion's Club
middle class
nuclear
nuclei
nucleus
obliquely
paper clip
prickly heat
prickly pear
proclaimer

proclaiming
Santa Claus
secluded
seclusion
second class
senior class
service club
tablecloth
thunderclap
unbuckling
underclothes
uniquely
unlikely
Women's Club
_____
_____
_____

KL /kl/ Medial—four syllables

acclamation
athletic club
declaration
digital clock
electric clock
enclosable
exclamation
exclusively

grandfather clock
inclinable
inclination
includible
non-classified
Oklahoma
proclamation
proclivity

reclamation
reclining chair
vacuum cleaner
_____
_____
_____
_____
_____

KL /kl/ Final—two syllables

ankle
buckle
cackle
chuckle
circle
crackle
cycle
fickle
fiscal

focal
freckle
grackle
heckle
jackal
knuckle
local
nickel
pickle

prickle
rankle
rascal
sickle
snorkel
spackle
speckle
sprinkle
stickle

tackle	twinkle	wrinkle
tickle	uncle	_____
trickle	vocal	_____

KL /kl/ Final—three syllables

article	metrical	ramshackle
bicycle	miracle	recycle
chemical	monocle	rhythmical
classical	musical	skeptical
clinical	mystical	spectacle
cortical	mythical	spherical
critical	nautical	technical
cubicle	obstacle	tentacle
cuticle	optical	topical
encircle	oracle	tricycle
icicle	particle	two-cycle
lexical	physical	typical
logical	pinnacle	vehicle
lyrical	pinochle	vesicle
magical	practical	_____
medical	radical	_____

KL /kl/ Final—four syllables

angelical	kilocycle	receptacle
botanical	mechanical	reciprocal
historical	motorcycle	sabbatical
honeysuckle	nonsensical	semicircle
identical	numerical	statistical
illogical	patriarchal	unicycle
ironical	political	_____

KL /kl/ Final—five syllables

academical	categorical	unequivocal
alphabetical	chronological	unmechanical
analytical	economical	unmethodical
anatomical	geographical	_____
astrological	mathematical	_____
astronomical	mythological	_____
biographical	pathological	_____

LER /lɚ/ Medial—three syllables

allergic	gallery	scholarship
allergy	polar bear	tolerance
celery	polarize	tolerant
collarbone	polar lights	_____
colorful	roller skates	_____
coloring	salary	_____

LER /lɚ/ Medial—four syllables

artillery	polar axis	tolerable
capillary	polar region	tolerably
intolerant	roller skating	_____

LER /lɚ/ Medial—five syllables

intolerable	roller skating rink	_____
polarization	similarity	_____
popularity	_____	_____

LER /lɚ/ Final—two syllables

antler	jailer	smaller
baler	mailer	smeller
Baylor	miller	solar
bowler	Miller	speller
broiler	molar	sprawler
caller	parlor	squealer
cellar	peddler	stroller
collar	piler	tailor
color	pillar	taller
cooler	polar	Taylor
crawler	poler	teller
dealer	poplar	thriller
dollar	roller	tiller
driller	ruler	trailer
drooler	sailor	trawler
duller	scaler	troller
dweller	scholar	Tyler
feeler	sealer	whaler
healer	seller	_____
heeler	shriller	_____

LER /lɚ/ Final—three syllables

angular	modular	secular
bachelor	muscular	similar
consoler	ocular	singular
controller	patroller	three-wheeler
counselor	popular	tricolor
discolor	propeller	tubular
four-wheeler	regular	two-wheeler
jeweler	retailer	wholesaler
littler	sand dollar	_____

LER /lɚ/ Final—four syllables

caterpillar	particular	twin propeller
fortuneteller	semitrailer	unpopular
irregular	spectacular	watercolor
lenticular	storm cellar	_____
multicolor	technicolor	_____

LM /lm/ Medial—two syllables

ailment	filmstrip	stalemate
Alma	hallmark	Talmud
almond	helmet	Thelma
Belmont	Palmer	trailman
Delmar	schoolmarm	Wilma
Elma	schoolmate	_____
Elmer	Selma	_____

LM /lm/ Medial—three syllables

almanac	derailment	palmetto
almighty	enrollment	repealment
almond paste	entailment	revealment
concealment	fulfillment	_____
congealment	installment	_____
curtailment	instillment	_____

LM /lm/ Final—one syllable

elm	realm	_____
film	whelm	_____
helm	_____	_____

ML /ml/ Final—two syllables

camel	mammal	_____
dismal	normal	_____
formal	thermal	_____

ML /ml/ Final—three syllables

abnormal	decimal	subnormal
animal	enamel	_____
caramel	informal	_____

NL /nl/ Final—two syllables

channel	hymnal	shrapnel
colonel	journal	signal
final	kennel	spinal
flannel	kernel	tunnel
funnel	panel	_____

NL /nl/ Final—three syllables

arsenal	infernal	paternal
cardinal	internal	personal
criminal	marginal	rational
doctrinal	maternal	seasonal
eternal	national	sectional
external	nocturnal	sentinel
fictional	nominal	terminal
fractional	optional	_____
functional	ordinal	_____

NL /nl/ Final—four syllables

additional	irrational	provisional
congressional	nutritional	sensational
diagonal	occasional	_____
emotional	octagonal	_____
exceptional	original	_____

LP /lp/ Medial—two syllables

alpine	helpful	kelp crab
gulping	helping	kelpfish
helper	helpless	palpate

pulpit	sculpture	_____
scalpel	yelping	_____
sculptor	_____	_____

LP /lp/ Final—one syllable

alp	palp	yelp
gulp	pulp	_____
help	scalp	_____
kelp	whelp	_____

PL /pl/ Initial—one syllable

place	played	plowed
placed	plea	pluck
plaid	plead	plug
plain	please	plugged
plaint	pleased	plum
plait	pleat	plumb
plan	pledge	plume
plane	pledged	plumed
planed	plied	plump
plank	plight	plunge
planned	plink	plunged
plant	plinth	plunk
plants	plod	plus
plaque	plop	plush
plat	plopped	ply
plate	plot	_____
play	plow	_____

PL /pl/ Initial—two syllables

placard	plaintive	plankton
place kick	Plainview	planner
place mat	Plainville	planning
place name	planar	plantar
placer	planer	planter
placid	planet	plant food
placing	plangent	plasma
placket	planing	plaster
plaintiff	planking	plastic

plateau	playtime	plower
plated	playwear	plowshare
plateful	playwright	plugging
plate glass	plaza	plug in
platelet	pleaded	plumage
plate mark	pleading	plumber
plater	pleasant	plumbing
platform	pleasing	plummet
plating	pleasure	plumpness
Plato	pledger	plunder
platoon	plenty	plunger
platter	pleural	plunging
playback	plexus	plural
player	pliant	plushy
playful	pliers	plus sign
playground	plodded	Pluto
playhouse	plodder	plying
playmate	plodding	Plymouth
playoff	plopping	plywood
playpen	plotted	_____
playroom	plotter	_____
playsuit	plotting	_____
playthings	plover	_____

PL /pl/ Initial—three syllables

placebo	plasterboard	pleurisy
place hitter	platinous	plexiglass
place holder	platinum	pliable
place-kicker	platonic	pliancy
placement test	platypus	plowable
placer gold	plausible	plundering
Placerville	play-by-play	pluralize
plagiarize	playacting	plutocrat
plainclothesman	playfully	Plutonic
plainspoken	playing card	Plymouth Rock
plaintively	playing field	_____
planetoid	pleasantry	_____
plantable	plenteous	_____
plantation	plentiful	_____

PL /pl/ Initial—four syllables

plagiarism	platform rocker	pleximeter
planarian	Pleasant Island	plotting paper
planetary	pleasurable	plurality
planimeter	plenipotent	plutonium
plasticity	plentifully	_____

PL /pl/ Initial—five syllables

planetarium	pledge of allegiance	_____
player piano	plutonically	_____

PL /pl/ Medial—two syllables

airplane	displace	poplar
air plant	display	replace
air plot	displease	replant
amply	eggplant	replay
aplite	employ	replete
aplomb	explain	reply
applaud	explode	sapling
applause	exploit	seaplane
applied	explore	simply
apply	fireplace	ski plane
birthplace	float plane	sleepless
complain	gangplank	someplace
complaint	grappling	stapler
complete	home plate	stoplight
complex	hopeless	supplant
comply	houseplant	supply
deplane	ice plant	surplus
deplete	imply	top line
deplore	jet plane	upline
deploy	perplex	upload
deplume	pipeline	_____

PL /pl/ Medial—three syllables

accomplish	applicant	complement
amplify	applique'	completion
anyplace	applying	complexion
appliance	complacent	complicate

compliment	explosion	simplify
contemplate	explosive	supplement
diploma	heating plant	supplicant
diplomat	implement	triplicate
discipline	incomplete	unemployed
double play	multiply	unpleasant
duplicate	octuplet	water plant
employee	quintuplet	_____
employment	replenish	_____
explicit	resplendent	_____

PL /pl/ Medial—four syllables

amplifier	explanation	unemployment
application	exploration	_____
cassette player	multiplier	_____
complexity	simplicity	_____

PL /pl/ Final—two syllables

ample	opal	simple
apple	Opal	staple
chapel	people	steeple
couple	pimple	temple
cripple	purple	topple
crumple	ripple	triple
dimple	rumple	Whipple
gospel	sample	_____
grapple	scalpel	_____
maple	scruple	_____

PL /pl/ Final—three syllables

deep purple	multiple	quadruple
disciple	pineapple	quintuple
example	principal	rose apple
free sample	principle	_____

PL /pl/ Final—four syllables

acne pimple	cornmeal scrapple	lovely dimple
bottle nipple	Episcopal	mini-sample
candied apple	keep it simple	more than ample

municipal
participle

rotten apple
spotted dapple

vice-principal
_____

LR /lr/ Medial—two syllables
all right
ballroom
railroad

schoolroom
seal ring
toll road

walrus
_____
_____

LR /lr/ Medial—three syllables
already
cavalry
civil rights

coral reef
cradle roll
gravel road

jewelry
middle ring
rivalry

RL /rl/ Medial—two syllables
airlift
airline
Arlene
Arlon
barely
barley
Berlin
burlap
burly
careless
Carla
carload
Charlene
Charlie
Charline
Charlotte
clearly
curling
curly
Darlene

darling
Earlene
early
fairly
fearless
furlong
furlough
garland
garlic
Girl Scouts
Harlan
Harlem
Harley
heirloom
hourly
marlin
merely
Merlin
moorland
nearly

oarlock
parlor
pearly
poorly
scarlet
Shirley
squarely
starlight
starling
starlit
sterling
surely
swirly
Verlene
whirlpool
whirlwind
yearling
yearly
_____
_____

RL /rl/ Medial—three syllables
Arlington
barleycorn
Barley Green

blue marlin
brotherly
charlatan

charley horse
Charlottesville
Charlottetown

cheerleaders
curlicue
eagerly
early bird
entirely
fatherly
garlic bread
garlic salt
gingerly
Harlingen
hourly wage
Kimberly
mannerly
masterly
maturely
miserly

motherly
neighborly
northerly
obscurely
orderly
overland
overlap
overlay
overlie
overload
overlook
overly
Parliament
Pearl Harbor
power line
powerless

properly
quarterly
scholarly
securely
severely
sisterly
Sutherland
tenderly
utterly
whirlabout
whirligig
whirlpool bath
whirlybird
wonderland
_____
_____

RL /rl/ Medial—four syllables

curling iron
everlasting
New Orleans

northwesterly
sitting parlor
southeasterly

sterling silver
_____
_____

RL /ɚl/ Final—one syllable

Beryl
burl
Burl
Carl
curl
Earl
furl
girl

gnarl
hurl
Karl
Merle
pearl
Pearl
purl
skirl

snarl
swirl
twirl
whirl
whorl
_____
_____
_____

RL /ɚl/ Final—two syllables

blue pearl
unfurl

untwirl
white pearl

young girl
_____

RL /ɚl/ Final—three syllables

baby girl
baton twirl

Campfire Girl
knit and purl

Minnie Pearl
yellow pearl

RLZ /ɚlz/ Final—one syllable

Charles	hurls	twirls
curls	pearls	whirls
Earl's	purls	whorls
girls	snarls	_____
gnarls	swirls	_____

REL /rl̩/ Final—two syllables

barrel	mural	spiral
choral	oral	squirrel
coral	peril	sterile
floral	quarrel	_____
moral	rural	_____

REL /rl̩/ Final—three syllables

admiral	immoral	natural
apparel	imperil	numeral
corporal	lateral	pastoral
cultural	liberal	sculptural
funeral	mackerel	several
general	mineral	_____

REL /rl̩/ Final—four syllables

bilateral	inaugural	unnatural
collateral	intramural	vice-admiral
conjectural	rear admiral	_____

SL /sl/ Initial—one syllable

slab	slaw	slid
slack	sled	slide
slacks	sleek	slides
slam	sleep	slight
slang	sleet	slim
slant	sleeve	slime
slap	sleigh	sling
slash	sleight	slip
slat	slept	slit
slate	slew	sloop
slave	slick	slope

slot	sluice	slush
sloth	slum	sly
slouch	slump	_____
slow	slung	_____
sludge	slunk	_____
slug	slur	_____
slugs	slurp	_____

SL /sl/ Initial—two syllables

slacken	slicing	sloth bear
slacker	slicker	slothful
slalom	slide rule	slouchy
slapstick	sliding	Slovak
slashing	slighting	slowdown
sledder	slightly	slowpoke
sledding	slimy	slow sign
sled dog	slingshot	slow-up
sleeky	slinking	sludgy
sleeper	slinky	sluggish
sleepers	slipknot	slumber
sleep-in	slipper	slurring
sleepless	slippers	_____
sleepwear	slither	_____
sleepy	sliver	_____
sleety	slobber	_____
sleeveless	slogan	_____
sleigh bells	sloping	_____
slender	sloppy	_____
slicer	sloshy	_____

SL /sl/ Initial—three syllables

slalom course	slide viewer	slow-witted
sledgehammer	sliding scale	sluggishness
sleeping bag	slip cover	slumberland
sleepwalking	slippery	slushiest
sleepyhead	slot machine	_____
slenderize	slovenly	_____
sliceable	slow-motion	_____
slide trombone	slow-moving	_____

SL /sl/ Medial—two syllables

asleep	jostling	tussling
bobsled	juiceless	useless
bracelet	landslide	voiceless
bustling	Lesley	Wesley
crosslight	loosely	whistler
crossline	nicely	whistling
crossly	North slope	wrestler
dislike	onslaught	wrestling
dislodge	priceless	_____
dog sled	rustling	_____
enslave	ski slope	_____
grand slam	snowslide	_____
hustling	translate	_____

SL /sl/ Medial—three syllables

carelessly	super slide	wrestling coach
cross-legged	translation	wrestling match
dislocate	translative	wrestling shoes
disloyal	translator	wrestling team
enslavement	translocate	_____
expressly	translucence	_____
misleading	translucent	_____
purposeless	uselessly	_____
purposely	wrestling camp	_____

SL /sl/ Medial—four syllables

dislocation	_____	_____
legislation	_____	_____
legislative	_____	_____

SL /sl/ Final—two syllables

axle	dorsal	parcel
basal	fossil	pencil
bristle	gristle	trestle
bustle	jostle	vessel
capsule	missile	wrestle
castle	morsel	_____
counsel	mussel	_____

SL /sl/ Final—three syllables

blood vessel	dismissal	utensil
carousel	dispersal	_____
colossal	rehearsal	_____

LS /ls/ Medial—two syllables

also	falsely	wholesome
balsam	hillside	_____
Elsa	pulsate	_____
elsewhere	Tulsa	_____
Elsie	ulcer	_____
falsehood	wholesale	_____

LS /ls/ Medial—three syllables

balsam fir	falsify	wholesaler
Coral Sea	quarrelsome	Wilson
falsetto	Uncle Sam	_____

LS /ls/ Final—one syllable

else	_____	_____
false	_____	_____
pulse	_____	_____

LS /ls/ Final—two syllables

convulse	_____	_____
impulse	_____	_____
repulse	_____	_____

SHL /ʃl/ Final—two syllables

bushel	marshal	spatial
crucial	partial	special
facial	racial	_____
glacial	social	_____

SHL /ʃl/ Final—three syllables

commercial	impartial	potential
essential	initial	provincial
financial	judicial	torrential
fire marshal	official	_____

SHL /ʃl/ Final—four syllables

antisocial	differential	prejudicial
artificial	influential	presidential
beneficial	nonessential	residential
consequential	preferential	_____

SPL /spl/ Initial—one syllable

splash	splice	splits
splat	spliced	splotch
splay	splint	splurge
spleen	split	_____

SPL /spl/ Initial—two syllables

splashdown	splendor	split shift
splash guard	splicer	splitting
splatter	splicing	splutter
splendid	splinter	_____

SPL /spl/ Initial—three syllables

splintery	split entry	split second
split entrance	split level	_____

LT /lt/ Medial—two syllables

alter	guilty	salted
alto	halter	shelter
Colton	hilltop	smelter
cultist	Hilton	voltage
delta	melted	Walter
falter	molten	welter
faultless	poultry	yuletide
filter	quilting	_____

LT /lt/ Medial—three syllables

alternate	faultfinding	novelty
altitude	loyalty	penalty
Central Time	malted milk	resulting
cultism	multiple	revolted
cultivate	multiply	royalty
dial tone	multitude	saltshaker

specialty   welterweight   _____

voltmeter   _____   _____

LT /lt/ Medial—four syllables

altimeter	cultivator	multiplier
altogether	difficulty	seat belt safety

LT /lt/ Final—one syllable

belt	jolt	smelt
bolt	kilt	spilt
built	knelt	stilt
colt	lilt	tilt
dealt	malt	vault
dwelt	melt	volt
fault	molt	Walt
felt	pelt	welt
guilt	quilt	wilt
halt	salt	Wilt
hilt	shalt	_____
jilt	silt	_____

LT /lt/ Final—two syllables

adult	default	result
asphalt	exalt	revolt
bank vault	exult	rock salt
black belt	fan belt	seat belt
blue belt	farm belt	tumult
cobalt	insult	white belt
consult	pole vault	_____
Corn Belt	Renault	_____

LT /lt/ Final—three syllables

difficult	patchwork quilt	thunderbolt
garlic salt	Roosevelt	_____
leather belt	somersault	_____

LTH /lθ/ Medial—two syllables

filthy	healthy	Waltham
healthful	stealthy	wealthy

LTH /lθ/ Medial—three syllables

filthiest	unhealthy	_____
stealthiest	wealthier	_____
unhealthful	wealthiest	_____

LTH /lθ/ Final—one syllable

filth	stealth	wealth
health	tilth	_____

LTS /lts/ Final—one syllable

belts	melts	tilts
bolts	molts	vaults
colts	pelts	welts
faults	quilts	wilts
jolts	salts	_____
kilts	silts	_____
malts	stilts	_____

LTS /lts/ Final—two syllables

adults	insults	revolts
consults	pole vaults	seat belts

TL /tl/ Medial—two syllables

atlas	outlet	potluck
butler	outline	settler
lightly	outlook	_____
outlaw	potlatch	_____

TL /tl/ Medial—three syllables

anciently	outlining	quietly
Atlanta	outlying	sedately
Atlantic	perfectly	_____
irately	politely	_____

TL /tl/ Final—three syllables

belittle	parental	skeletal
capital	pedestal	subtitle
entitle	rose beetle	_____
immortal	segmental	_____

TL /tl/ Final—four syllables

accidental	horizontal	sentimental
congenital	incidental	thermos bottle
continental	monumental	tittle tattle
elemental	noncommittal	_____
fundamental	oriental	_____

LV /lv/ Medial—two syllables

Alva	salvage	solvent
Alvin	salvaged	solving
Calvin	salvo	velvet
Cleveland	shelving	_____
culvert	silver	_____
		_____

LV /lv/ Medial—three syllables

Alvina	quicksilver	solvable
dissolving	resolving	Sylvia
evolvement	revolving	velveteen
galvanic	salvation	velvety
galvanize	silver fox	wolverine
insolvent	silver-plate	_____
involvement	silversmith	_____
involving	silverware	_____
pulverize	silvery	_____

LV /lv/ Final—one syllable

delve	solve	_____
salve	twelve	_____
shelve	valve	_____

LV /lv/ Final—two syllables

absolve	dissolve	resolve
bivalve	evolve	revolve
devolve	involve	_____

LVD /lvd/ Final—one syllable

delved	_____	_____
shelved	_____	_____
solved	_____	_____

LVD /lvd/ Final—two syllables

absolved	involved	unsolved
dissolved	resolved	_____
evolved	revolved	_____

LVZ /lvz/ Final—one syllable

delves	shelves	wolves
elves	solves	_____
selves	valves	_____

LVZ /lvz/ Final—two syllables

dissolves	ourselves	themselves
evolves	resolves	yourselves
involves	revolves	_____

VL /vl/ Final—two syllables

bevel	marvel	shovel
civil	navel	shrivel
devil	novel	swivel
gavel	oval	weevil
gravel	ravel	_____
hovel	revel	_____
level	rival	_____

VL /vl/ Final—three syllables

approval	festival	steam shovel
arrival	interval	unravel
boll weevil	removal	upheaval
carnival	revival	_____

LY /lj/ Medial—two syllables

all year	Dahlia	stallion
billiards	failure	trillion
billion	Julia	valiant
bouillon	Julian	value
bullion	million	valued
coal yard	millionth	William
collier	school yard	zillion
Collier	school year	_____

LY /lj/ Medial—three syllables

alienate	Centralia	regalia
Amelia	Cornelia	valiancy
Australia	cotillion	valiantly
Australian	familial	valuate
azalea	familiar	valueless
battalion	four billion	valuing
billiard ball	magnolia	Vermillion
billionaire	medallion	Williamsburg
bouillon cube	millionaire	_____
Camellia	rebellion	_____

LY /lj/ Medial—four syllables

billiard table	Julius Caesar	valuation
chameleon	salutation	valuator
familiarize	valuable	_____

LZ /lz/ Medial—two syllables

bailsman	salesman	_____
fool's cap	school zone	_____
fool's gold	_____	_____

LZ /lz/ Final—one syllable

aisles	drills	grills
bails	eels	growls
bales	fails	gulls
balls	falls	hails
bells	feels	halls
Bill's	files	heels
bills	fills	hills
boils	foals	holes
bowls	foils	hulls
calls	fools	jails
Charles	fouls	kneels
chills	frills	males
coils	gales	meals
deals	gals	miles
dills	gills	mills
dolls	goals	moles

nails	scowls	stalls
oils	seals	stools
pails	sells	strolls
peals	shrills	styles
piles	sills	tails
pills	skills	tales
poles	skulls	tells
polls	smells	thrills
pools	smiles	tiles
pulls	snails	toils
quails	snarls	tolls
quills	soils	tools
rails	soles	walls
reels	souls	wells
roles	spells	whales
rolls	spills	wheels
rules	spoils	wills
sails	spools	wools
sales	squalls	yells
scales	squeals	———————

LZ /lz/ Final—two syllables

angels	dawdles	ladles
annals	details	middles
ant hills	dwellers	needles
barrels	eggshells	nettles
baseballs	equals	noodles
battles	females	paddles
bluebells	fiddles	petals
bottles	finals	poodles
bundles	footballs	portholes
bushels	formals	pretzels
camels	fossils	prevails
candles	fuels	profiles
capsules	gruels	propels
carols	handles	pupils
cattails	hymnals	quarrels
cradles	jewels	quetzals
cymbals	kindles	rascals

rattles	sandals	tattles
rebels	sawmills	tittles
recalls	scandals	toadstools
refills	seagulls	toddles
rentals	seashells	toenails
reptiles	settles	tonsils
retails	signals	towels
reveals	Sioux Falls	windmills
riddles	skittles	_____
rivals	snowballs	_____
roll calls	softballs	_____
saddles	tadpoles	_____

LZ /lz/ Final—three syllables

aerials	cardinals	generals
animals	Cardinals	principals
annuals	carnivals	projectiles
axials	carousels	rehearsals
basketballs	casseroles	rituals
bass viols	cathedrals	spectacles
Blue Angels	coveralls	syllables
bookmobiles	enamels	utensils
burials	fairy tales	volleyballs
buttonholes	festivals	_____
cannonballs	fingernails	_____

ZL /zl/ Final—two syllables

chisel	frizzle	nuzzle
damsel	fusil	puzzle
dazzle	grizzle	schnozzle
diesel	guzzle	sizzle
drizzle	Hazel	weasel
easel	muzzle	_____
fizzle	nasal	_____
frazzle	nozzle	_____

ZL /zl/ Final—three syllables

appraisal	disposal	refusal
arousal	embezzle	witch hazel

M

Pronounced: /m/
Spelled: m, mm, mn, mb, lm, gm, chm

M /m/ Initial—one syllable

Ma	marsh	mess
Mac	Marv	met
mace	mash	mice
mad	mashed	mid
made	mask	Midge
Madge	masked	might
maid	mass	mike
mail	massed	Mike
mailed	mat	mile
main	Mat	milk
maize	match	milked
make	matched	mill
male	mate	milled
mall	math	mime
malt	Matt	mimed
Mame	may	mind
man	May	mine
mane	maze	mined
mange	mazed	mint
manned	me	mire
map	meal	mired
mar	mean	miss
Marc	meant	Miss
march	meat	missed
March	meet	mist
marchcd	Mel	mite
mare	melt	mitt
mark	men	mix
Mark	mesh	mixed
marred	meshed	moan

moaned	moped	muffed
mod	mopped	mug
mode	more	mull
mold	moss	mulled
mole	most	mum
Mom	moth	mush
monk	mount	muss
month	mouse	must
mood	mouth	mutt
moon	mouthed	my
moor	move	Myles
moored	moved	myrrh
moose	much	myth
mop	mud	_____
mope	muff	_____

M /m/ Initial—two syllables

Mabel	marbles	master
macaw	Marcus	mastered
machine	Marie	mattress
Madame	marine	Maureen
Madrid	market	Maurice
maelstrom	marriage	maybe
Magi	married	May Day
magnet	marrow	mayor
mailman	marry	measure
Main Street	Marshall	measured
maintain	marten	meaty
major	Martha	medal
majored	martial	member
malice	martin	membrane
mammal	Martin	mental
mammoth	Marty	menu
mandate	martyr	merit
Mandel	Marvin	mermaid
mankind	Mary	merry
manner	mascot	metal
manners	masher	meter
many	mason	Mickey

middle
migraine
migrate
Milan
mildew
mildewed
mileage
milkmaid
milkman
milky
miller
Miller
Millie
Milton
minstrel
minute
mirror
mirrored
mister
Mitchell
mitten
mitzvah
model
modeled
modem
Molly
molten

Monday
money
monied
monkey
monkeyed
Monroe
monster
Monty
morbid
morose
Morris
Morse code
mother
motor
motored
mountain
moustache
mouthful
mouth guard
mouthwash
movement
movie
moving
Mr.
Mrs.
mudguard
mudhole

muffin
muffler
muggy
mukluk
mummy
mundane
Murray
muscle
mushing
mushroom
musk ox
muskrat
muslin
mustang
mustard
muster
mutton
muzzle
myna
Myrna
Myron
Myrtle
myself
mystic
mystique

_____

_____

M /m/ Initial—three syllables

MacArthur
machinate
machinist
mackerel
mackinaw
Mackintosh
macrograph
Madeline
Madison
Madonna

madrigal
magazine
magician
magistrate
magnitude
mailwoman
malfunction
management
manager
mandible

mandolin
maneuver
maneuvered
mannequin
manual
Manucl
marching band
March of Dimes
mariner
marital

marshmallow
Maryland
masculine
matronly
maverick
McKenzie
McKinley
meander
meandered
measurement
mechanic
mechanize
mechanized
medial
medieval
medium
melody
menial
Mercedes
mercury
Meredith
messenger
Messiah
meteor

Mexico
Miami
miasma
Micro Age
microfilm
microphone
microscope
microwave
Milky Way
millionaire
minister
ministry
Miranda
misfortune
Missouri
mobile home
moccasin
modulate
mollified
mollify
monitor
Montana
Monterey
Montpelier

monument
mortified
mortify
Mother's Day
motorbike
motorboat
motorcade
motorcar
motor home
motorist
motorize
multiplied
multiply
muscle-bound
musical
musician
musketeer
mussel crab
myopic
mystical
_____
_____
_____
_____

M /m/ Initial—four syllables

macaroni
machination
machinery
macroscopic
magnanimous
magnificent
malaria
mandibular
Manitoba
Massachusetts
mass emergy
medially
mediocre

melodrama
meticulous
metropolis
Mexican food
migratory
military
millinery
Minnesota
misadventure
misconception
miserable
misinterpret
misrepresent

Mississippi
modality
monastery
Mongolia
monotonous
monumental
morality
myopia
mysterious
mythology
_____
_____
_____

M /m/ Initial—five syllables

Macedonia	metropolitan	monoplegia
magnification	miscegenation	monotheism
major general	miscellaneous	monotonously
manipulation	misrepresented	multiplication
manual training	Mississippian	musicology
manufacturer	misunderstanding	mysteriously
mathematical	modification	_____
mechanization	monogenesis	_____
Memorial Day	monomania	_____
memorization	monophobia	_____

M /m/ Medial—two syllables

aiming	combing	hammer
almost	comet	hammock
amcn	comic	hemlock
amend	coming	himself
amends	command	homage
amid	commend	homely
amidst	commerce	homer
amiss	common	Homer
among	damage	human
amount	demand	humid
Amy	dimmer	humor
asthma	dimming	image
beaming	dreamer	Jamey
bloomer	dreaming	Jamie
booming	drummer	jasmine
camel	Edmond	jimmy
cement	Emma	Jimmy
chamois	famine	lament
checkmate	famous	layman
chimney	flaming	lemon
clamming	foaming	limeade
clammy	foamy	limit
clamor	grammar	Mama
climate	grimace	Mamie
climber	grimy	mammal
climbing	gummy	milkman

Mimi	scrimmage	Thomas
moment	seaman	thumbing
Mommy	segment	timer
naming	shammy	Timmy
numbing	shimmer	tombstone
Omar	simmer	tomcat
omen	Simon	Tommi
pieman	skimmer	Tommy
pigmy	someone	trimmer
playmates	stammer	trimming
plumage	steamer	Truman
plumber	steaming	tumor
plummet	streamer	woman
primer	submerge	women
Raymond	summer	yeoman
reamer	summit	Yuma
Remus	swimmer	_____
roomer	swimming	_____
rumor	tamer	_____
Sammy	Tammy	_____

M /m/ Medial—three syllables

adamant	comedy	family
admiral	commission	feminine
admonish	committee	feminist
a la mode	consumer	flamenco
alchemist	customer	flamingo
Amanda	demeanor	gamma ray
Amazon	democrat	Gemini
Amelia	demonstrate	hemisphere
amethyst	diminish	homecoming
amnesia	domestic	homemaker
animal	dominate	homophone
argument	dominos	humorous
boomerang	edema	imitate
camera	Edmonton	imminent
ceramic	emerald	infamous
cinnamon	emery	laminate
circumstance	familiar	laundromat

lawnmower
limerick
limited
memorize
memory
newcomer
numeral
numerous
ominous
optimist
persimmon
preempted
redeemer
salami
Samoa

Samoan
samovar
sediment
self-image
seminar
shoemaker
simulate
sledge hammer
somersault
submarine
submission
submissive
summerhouse
summer school
summer stock

summertime
supplement
symmetry
talisman
tamale
tenement
Timothy
tomato
tournament
ultimate
whimsical
Women's Club
Wyoming
_____
_____

M /m/ Medial—four syllables

accommodate
administer
admonition
Alabama
alimony
Amarillo
amaryllis
America
amphibian
anathema
animation
anomalous
anomaly
anonymous
Bohemian
catamaran

chameleon
climbing safety
commentator
commercially
commissioner
conglomerate
demolition
economist
eminently
gemologist
homophonous
humility
immensity
insomnia
insomniac
intimidate

magnanimous
monumental
noncommittal
panorama
paramedic
parameter
patrolwoman
phenomenon
predicament
proximity
public domain
seminary
timidity
unanimous
_____
_____

M /m/ Medial—five syllables

abominable
accommodation
administration
admonishingly

ameliorate
axiomatic
bimolecular
binomially

condominium
denomination
enumerated
geometrical

hippopotamus	sedimentary	_____
immediately	seminarian	_____
innumerable	simultaneous	_____
Memorial Day	unanimously	_____
momentarily	_____	_____
myringatomy	_____	
ramification	_____	
rudimentary	_____	_____

M /m/ Final—one syllable

aim	dime	hymn
am	dome	I'm
balm	doom	jam
beam	dram	Jim
Bim	dream	Kim
blame	drum	lam
bloom	fame	lamb
boom	flame	lame
brim	foam	limb
broom	frame	lime
brougham	from	loam
bum	fume	loom
calm	game	malm
cam	gem	Mame
came	gleam	Mom
chime	gloom	mum
chrome	gnome	name
chum	gram	Nome
clam	grim	numb
Clem	grime	ohm
climb	groom	palm
comb	Guam	Pam
come	gum	plum
cram	gym	plumb
cream	ham	pram
dam	hem	prim
dame	him	prime
deem	home	psalm
dim	hum	qualm

ram	slum	Tom
ream	some	tomb
rhyme	steam	tram
rim	stem	trim
roam	stream	vim
Rome	strum	whim
room	sum	whom
Sam	swam	yam
same	swim	zoom
scram	tam	_____
scream	tame	_____
seam	team	_____
seem	teem	_____
sham	them	_____
shame	theme	_____
skim	thumb	_____
slam	thyme	_____
slim	Tim	_____
slime	time	_____

M /m/ Final—two syllables

Adam	bottom	denim
album	bridegroom	dictum
alum	broadloom	doldrum
annum	brougham	emblem
anthem	buckram	esteem
atom	carom	extreme
balsam	chartroom	fathom
bathroom	chasm	first name
becalm	checkroom	flotsam
became	coatroom	forum
become	condemn	frenum
bedlam	courtroom	gypsum
bedroom	coxcomb	half time
bedtime	custom	heirloom
Belgium	daydream	high time
blossom	daytime	homeroom
boredom	defame	humdrum

ice cream
income
jetsam
last name
lifetime
madame
maxim
mayhem
modem
moonbeam
mushroom
phantom
phoneme
phylum
problem
random

redeem
salaam
spasm
springtime
sternum
Stockholm
stockroom
storeroom
sunbeam
supreme
symptom
system
tandem
theorem
twosome
wholesome

wigwam
William
wisdom

_____
_____
_____
_____
_____
_____
_____
_____
_____
_____
_____
_____

M /m/ Final—three syllables

Abraham
accustom
addendum
amalgam
anagram
anteroom
antonym
baptism
Bethlehem
Boulder Dam
bubble gum
Buckingham
buddhism
cablegram
calcium
Central Time
cerebrum
chewing gum
Christendom
cofferdam
decorum

diadem
diagram
dining room
elbowroom
facism
frolic
Hall of Fame
helium
homonym
honeycomb
Hoover Dam
jejunum
living room
maximum
minimum
monogram
overtime
pantomime
paradigm
pseudonym
radium

reading room
Rotterdam
sodium
soft-shell clam
sour cream
stadium
sugarplum
summertime
synonym
telegram
truism
wrestling team

_____
_____
_____
_____
_____
_____
_____
_____
_____

M /m/ Final—four syllables

aluminum	gymnasium	paroxysm
aquarium	heroism	petroleum
arboretum	hinduism	proscenium
beryllium	ideogram	realism
cerebellum	Jerusalem	symposium
chauvinism	jingoism	terrarium
chrysanthemum	journalism	video game
coliseum	Judaism	_____
compendium	linoleum	_____
consortium	mongolism	_____
family room	neoplasm	_____
feudalism	pacifism	_____

M /m/ Final—five syllables

Anglicanism	crematorium	scholasticism
auditorium	hesperidium	subjectivism
behaviorism	Protestantism	_____
Catholicism	recidivism	_____
condominium	romanticism	_____

MB /mb/ Medial—two syllables

amber	emboss	nameboard
Amber	gambit	number
Bambi	game bag	numbered
bamboo	game bird	Romberg
Bombay	gumbo	rumba
chamber	imbibe	samba
chambers	imbibed	slumber
combine	Lambert	slumbered
combined	Lemberg	somber
combo	limber	tambour
combust	Limberg	timber
comeback	limbo	trombone
Dumbo	Lombard	umber
embank	lumbar	_____
embark	lumber	_____
embed	mambo	_____
ember	member	_____

MB /mb/ Medial—three syllables

ambition	hamburger	reimburse
bambino	Kimberly	remember
bamboo shoots	Limburger	remembered
bamboozle	lumbering	September
Columbus	lumberjack	sombrero
combustion	lumbermill	somebody
cucumber	lumberyard	tambourine
cumbersome	membership	unnumbered
December	November	Zambezi
embankment	numbering	Zambia
embargo	numberline	_____
embarrass	ombudsman	_____
embassy	outnumber	_____
gamboling	rambunctious	_____

MB /mb/ Medial—four syllables

ambassador	Columbia	mumbo jumbo
ambiguous	combination	_____
Cambodia	combustible	_____

MBER /mbɚ/ Final—two syllables

amber	lumber	timber
Amber	member	umber
chamber	number	_____
ember	slumber	_____
limber	somber	_____

MBER /mbɚ/ Final—three syllables

cucumber	outnumber	_____
December	remember	_____
November	September	_____

MER /mer/ /mɚ/ Medial—three syllables

admiral	formerly	numerous
armory	humorous	somersault
boomerang	limerick	_____
emerald	memory	_____
emery	numerate	_____

MER /mer/ /mɚ/ Medial—four syllables

America	emergency	_____
American	_____	_____

MER /mɚ/ Final—two syllables

armor	Homer	skimmer
clamor	humor	stammer
climber	murmur	steamer
drummer	plumber	streamer
Elmer	primer	summer
farmer	reamer	swimmer
former	roomer	tamer
grammar	rumor	tumor
hammer	shimmer	_____
homer	simmer	_____

MER /mɚ/ Final—three syllables

beachcomber	newcomer	sledgehammer
consumer	performer	_____
customer	redeemer	_____

ML /ml/ Final—two syllables

camel	mammal	_____
dismal	normal	_____
formal	thermal	_____

ML /ml/ Final—three syllables

abnormal	decimal	subnormal
animal	enamel	_____
caramel	informal	_____

LM /lm/ Medial—two syllables

ailment	filmstrip	stalemate
Alma	hallmark	Talmud
almond	helmet	Thelma
Belmont	Palmer	trailman
Delmar	schoolmarm	Wilma
Elma	schoolmate	_____
Elmer	Selma	_____

LM /lm/ Medial—three syllables

almanac	derailment	palmetto
almighty	enrollment	repealment
almond paste	entailment	revealment
concealment	fulfillment	_____
congealment	installment	_____
curtailment	instillment	_____

LM /lm/ Final—one syllable

elm	helm	whelm
film	realm	_____

MP /mp/ Medial—two syllables

bumper	dampen	jumping
bumpy	dampened	jump rope
campaign	dumping	jump seat
camper	dumpling	jump suit
campground	dumpster	jumpy
camping	dump truck	limpet
camp-out	dumpy	limpid
campus	empire	limping
clamping	grumpy	lumpy
clumpy	hamper	pamper
compact	impact	pampered
compare	impair	pampers
compared	impaired	Pompey
compass	impale	pompous
compel	impaled	primping
compete	impart	pumping
complain	impasse	pumpkin
complaint	impeach	rampart
complete	impeached	rumpling
complex	impede	sampan
compound	impel	sampler
compute	impelled	scamper
cramping	impend	scrimping
crimpy	impose	shrimping
crumple	jump ball	skimpy
crumply	jumper	slumping

stamping
stumping
tamper
tampered
temper
tempered
tempest

template
temple
tempted
thumping
tramping
trumpet
trumping

vampire
whimper

_____

_____

_____

_____

_____

MP /mp/ Medial—three syllables

accomplice
accomplish
amplify
assumption
attempted
bumper guard
bumper jack
camporee
compactor
companion
company
compassion
competent
component
composite
composure
computer

consumption
contemplate
decompose
decomposed
distemper
empower
encompass
example
exempted
exemption
high jumper
impacted
imported
imposter
jumping bean
jumping jack
No Dumping

Olympics
pompadour
preempted
presumption
pumpkin pie
redemption
resumption
tamper-proof
temperance
temperate
temptation

_____

_____

_____

_____

_____

_____

MP /mp/ Medial—four syllables

companionship
compensation
composition
contemplation
Humpty Dumpty
impalpable

imperious
intemperate
pomposity
pumpernickel
reimposing
temperament

temperature
temporary
unimportant

_____

_____

_____

MP /mp/ Medial—five syllables

contemporary
impenetrable
imperishable

temperamental
temporization

_____

_____

_____

MP /mp/ Final—one syllable

amp	hemp	scamp
blimp	hump	shrimp
bump	imp	skimp
camp	jump	slump
champ	lamp	stamp
chump	limp	stomp
clamp	lump	stump
clump	plump	thump
cramp	primp	tramp
crimp	pump	trump
damp	ramp	_____
dump	romp	_____
grump	rump	_____

MP /mp/ Final—two syllables

boot camp	girls' camp	revamp
boys' camp	high jump	ski jump
broad jump	leg cramp	sun lamp
encamp	long jump	tire pump
floor lamp	off ramp	_____
gas pump	on ramp	_____

MP /mp/ Final—three syllables

Boy Scout camp	rubber stamp	table lamp
city dump	safety lamp	wrestling camp
garbage dump	stomach cramp	_____
Girl Scout camp	sugar lump	_____
postage stamp	summer camp	_____

MPS /mps/ Final—one syllable

amps	crimps	mumps
blimps	dumps	primps
bumps	glimpse	pumps
champs	imps	ramps
chumps	jumps	romps
clamps	lamps	shrimps
clumps	limps	skimps
cramps	lumps	slumps

stamps	tramps	_____
stumps	trumps	_____
thumps	_____	_____

RM /rm/ Medial—two syllables

airmail	fireman	permit
airman	firemen	spearmint
armful	foreman	sperm whale
armhole	foremost	surmise
armor	formal	surmount
armored	format	termite
army	former	thermal
Burma	garment	thermos
Burmese	German	torment
Carmel	gourmet	turmoil
Carmen	harmful	unarmed
charming	harmless	vermin
dormant	hermit	Vermont
Erma	hormone	warmly
ermine	Irma	warm-up
farm belt	mermaid	wormwood
farmer	Norma	_____
farming	normal	_____
farmland	Norman	_____

RM /rm/ Medial—three syllables

alderman	Germany	retirement
armament	germinate	snake charmer
armistice	harmonize	storm cellar
armorer	harmony	storm center
armory	informal	storm warning
Bermuda	marmalade	storm window
cormorant	performance	terminal
enormous	performer	terminate
farming land	permanent	thermostat
fire marshall	permission	uniformed
firmament	pharmacist	vermillion
formation	pharmacy	_____
formula	Prince Charming	_____

RM /rm/ Medial—four syllables

affirmative	fermentation	permeable
armadillo	germination	supermarket
Armistice Day	harmonica	termination
army blanket	infirmary	thermometer
conformation	infirmity	uniformly
dormitory	permanently	_____

RM /rm/ Medial—five syllables

formalization	thermal barrier	_____
terminology	uniformity	_____
		_____

RM /rm/ Final—one syllable

arm	form	swarm
charm	germ	warm
dorm	harm	worm
farm	squirm	_____
firm	storm	_____

RM /rm/ Final—two syllables

affirm	earthworm	reform
alarm	hailstorm	sandstorm
bookworm	inchworm	silkworm
confirm	infirm	snowstorm
conform	inform	tapeworm
cutworm	perform	windstorm
deform	platform	_____
dust storm	rainstorm	_____

RM /rm/ Final—three syllables

angleworm	thunderstorm	_____
fire alarm	uniform	_____
pachyderm	_____	_____

SM /sm/ Initial—one syllable

smack	smear	smiled
small	smell	smirch
smart	smelt	smirk
smash	smile	smit

smite	smoke	smudge
smith	smoked	smug
Smith	smooch	_____
smock	smooth	_____
smog	smote	_____

SM /sm/ Initial—two syllables

smacker	smeary	smoke screen
smacking	smeller	smokestack
smaller	smelling	Smoky
smallest	smelly	smolder
small fry	smelter	smoldered
small game	smidgen	smoother
smallpox	smiling	smoothly
small talk	smirky	smother
small-town	Smithville	smothered
smarter	smithy	smudgy
smartly	smiting	smugger
smartness	smitten	smuggest
smart set	smocking	smugly
smash-up	smoggy	smugness
smatter	smokehouse	_____

SM /sm/ Initial—three syllables

smart aleck	smoke chaser	smothering
smattering	smoke jumper	smudgily
smearier	smokier	smudginess
smelling salts	smokiest	_____
smilingly	smoldering	_____
smithereens	smorgasbord	_____

SM /sm/ Medial—two syllables

baseman	dismiss	placemat
basement	dismount	pressman
blacksmith	goldsmith	tinsmith
Christmas	huntsman	transmit
classman	iceman	_____
classmate	locksmith	_____
dismay	outsmart	_____

SM /sm/ Medial—three syllables

businessman	first baseman	second baseman
Christmas card	locksmith shop	silversmith
Christmas Eve	Mr. Smith	third baseman
Christmas seals	pacemaker	_____
Christmas tree	policeman	_____
coppersmith	policemen	_____

SM /sm/ Medial—four syllables

embarrassment	senior classman	_____
junior classman	upper classman	_____
lower classman	_____	_____

MY /mj/ Medial—two syllables

farmyard	_____	_____
_____	_____	_____

MY /mj/ Medial—three syllables

amulet	simulate	stimulus
communist	stimulant	_____
emulate	stimulate	_____

MY /mj/ Medial—four syllables

Bohemian	_____	_____
stimulation	_____	_____

MZ /mz/ Medial—two syllables

doomsday	Jamestown	time zone
groomsman	thumbs down	_____
helmsman	thumbs up	_____

MZ /mz/ Final—one syllable

beams	comes	dims
bums	crams	domes
calms	creams	dooms
charms	crimes	drams
chimes	crumbs	dreams
clams	deems	drums
climbs	dimes	flames

foams	limbs	seems
fumes	limes	shames
games	looms	stems
gems	palms	sums
gums	Pam's	tames
gyms	psalms	teams
hams	rams	Thames
hems	reams	themes
homes	Reims	thumbs
hums	rhymes	times
James	rims	trams
jams	roams	trims
Jim's	rooms	_____
lambs	Sam's	_____

MZ /mz/ Final—two syllables

Adams	daydreams	windchimes
assumes	exams	_____
bedrooms	schoolrooms	_____

N

Pronounced: /n/
Spelled: n, nn, gn, kn, pn, ne

N /n/ Initial—one syllable

gnar	name	nine
gnarl	Nan	ninth
gnarled	nap	nip
gnash	Nash	nix
gnat	Neal	no
gnaw	neap	nod
gnome	near	noise
gnu	neat	Nome
knap	neck	none
knave	Ned	nook
knead	need	noon
knee	Neil	nor
kneel	Nell	North
knell	nerve	nose
knew	nest	not
knife	net	note
knight	new	noun
knit	news	now
knob	next	numb
knock	nibs	nun
knoll	nice	nurse
knot	Nick	nut
know	niece	————
known	night	————
nail	Nile	————

N /n/ Initial—two syllables

gnarling	gnathic	Gnostics
gnarring	gnawing	knapsack
gnashing	gnomish	knavish

[247]

kneecap	nation	night guard
knee-deep	native	nightmare
knee-high	naughty	Nina
knee-hole	navy	nineteen
knee-jerk	nearly	ninety
kneeler	nebbish	Ninja
kneepad	necklace	Nita
knickers	necktie	Nixon
knickknack	nectar	Noah
knife-edge	needle	noble
knighthood	neglect	nobly
knightly	Negus	noel
knitting	neighbor	Noel
knockdown	Neika	noisy
knocker	neither	nonsense
knocking	Nellie	noodle
knock-kneed	Nelson	Norbert
knockout	Nemo	Norma
knockwurst	neon	normal
knothole	nephew	Norman
knotted	nervy	northern
know-how	network	North Pole
knowing	neuter	North Sea
knowledge	neutral	North Shore
knuckle	neutron	North Star
nail brush	never	Norway
nail file	Newark	Norwich
naive	Newman	nosebleed
naked	New Year's	nostril
nameboard	New York	nothing
Nancy	Newark	notice
Nanette	Newman	notion
napkin	nibble	nouveau
Naples	nickel	novel
narrow	nickname	novice
nasal	Nicky	nowhere
Nashville	Nicole	nugget
natal	nightfall	number
Nathan	nightgown	nutmeg

nutty

nylon

pneuma

N /n/ Initial—three syllables

nail polish	negative	night watchman
Nairobi	negligee	nitrogen
nanogram	negligent	nobody
Nantucket	neighborhood	nocturnal
Naomi	nemesis	nomadic
narcissus	Netherlands	nominee
nasturtium	nether world	nostalgia
Natalie	networking	notary
national	neurosis	noteworthy
nationwide	Nevada	novelty
natively	New Delhi	November
natural	New England	nucleus
naturelike	newfangled	nursery
nausea	Newfoundland	nutcracker
nautical	New Hampshire	nutrition
Nautilus	New Jersey	pneumatic
Navajo	newspaper	pneumograph
Nebraska	New Year's Day	pneumonia
nectarine	New Year's Eve	
needlepoint	New Zealand	
needlework	nicety	

N /n/ Initial—four syllables

Nagasaki	nefarious	Nicaragua
Napoleon	negotiate	nobility
naturalist	neighborhood watch	nomenclature
naturalize	neolithic	noncommittal
navigation	neology	nonobjective
navigator	neurologist	nonresistant
Neanderthal	neurology	nonrestrictive
necessary	neurosurgeon	nonviolence
necessitate	neutrality	northwesterner
necessity	New Mexico	noticeable
necropolis	newspaperman	notorious

numerical	pneumothorax	_____
pneumococcus	_____	_____
pneumogastric	_____	_____

N /n/ Medial—two syllables

Anna	dinner	lunar
any	donor	manna
banner	doughnut	manner
beanie	downfall	mannered
Benny	drainage	manor
boner	Enid	many
bonnet	Fannie	meaner
Bonnie	final	minor
bonus	finer	minute
bunny	finish	money
canal	Finnish	Nanette
canning	Francis	Nannie
cannon	frowning	owner
cannot	funny	panel
canoe	gainer	panic
channel	Gina	panning
Cheney	honey	peanut
chimney	honor	penny
china	innate	Phoenix
China	inner	plainer
cleaner	Janet	planet
cleaners	Jeanette	pony
cleanup	Jeanie	pruning
Connie	jennet	rainbow
cunning	Jenny	rainy
Dana	Juneau	Reno
Danish	keener	renowned
Danny	kennel	runner
Deming	Kenneth	running
Dena	Kenny	schooner
denim	Lana	sign-off
Dennis	Lena	sign-up
deny	lightning	Sinai
diner	liner	Sonny

sooner	tenor	winning
Sooner	tinny	_____
spinner	tiny	_____
spinning	tonic	_____
sunny	Venus	_____
tanner	wiener	_____
tanning	winner	_____
tennis	Winnie	_____

N /n/ Medial—three syllables

Adonis	honeycomb	pinnacle
airliner	honeydew	plenary
animal	honor roll	prisoner
Anita	initial	questioner
Annabelle	initialed	roadrunner
another	inner ear	Robin Hood
banana	inner tube	runner-up
beginner	innocent	scenery
benefit	Iron Age	serenade
Benita	Johnny Reb	sinister
Canada	juniper	strenuous
canary	Kennedy	sunglasses
chicken pox	kennel club	Sunnyvale
China Sea	lanolin	synagogue
Chinatown	lawnmower	teenager
cinnamon	lemonade	tyranny
Denali	lineage	universe
dinosaur	lioness	venison
dishonor	luncheonette	Vietnam
dry cleaner	magnitude	volcano
foreigner	maneuver	wagoner
funeral	Manila	Winnipeg
Galena	manual	_____
Gemini	Manuel	_____
general	mariner	_____
generous	mineral	_____
gold panner	monitor	_____
Hanukkah	opener	_____
honeybee	pineapple	_____

N /n/ Medial—four syllables

anatomy	initialize	practitioner
Annapolis	machinery	refinery
Arizona	manifesting	spontaneous
banana split	manipulate	table tennis
commissioner	manually	unhappiness
continental	Mona Lisa	unmannerly
generation	monastery	vulnerable
generator	monopoly	Winnebago
Honolulu	monumental	_____
honorable	municipal	_____
inaugurate	peanut butter	_____
incandescent	poison ivy	_____

N /n/ Medial—five syllables

animatedly	inadequately	miniaturize
developmental	inarticulate	Unitarian
elementary	inordinatcly	veterinary
inability	manufacturing	_____
inaccessible	mineralogist	_____

N /n/ Final—one syllable

an	chain	done
Ann	chin	down
ban	clan	drain
bean	clean	drown
been	clown	dune
Ben	coin	fan
bin	cone	fawn
Blaine	crane	fin
blown	crown	fine
bone	Dan	Fran
brain	dawn	fun
bran	Dawn	gain
brawn	dean	Gene
brown	Dean	glean
bun	den	Glenn
can	dine	gone
cane	Don	gown

grain	noon	shine
green	noun	shone
grin	nun	shown
groan	on	shrine
grown	one	shun
hen	own	sign
hone	pain	sin
in	pan	skein
inn	pane	skin
Jan	pawn	son
Jane	pen	soon
Jean	phone	Spain
Jeanne	pin	span
Joan	pine	spawn
John	plain	spin
June	plan	spine
keen	plane	spoon
Ken	prone	sprain
kin	prune	spun
lane	pun	stain
Lane	rain	Stan
lawn	ran	stone
lean	reign	sun
lien	rein	swan
line	Rhine	swine
loan	Rhone	tan
lone	roan	ten
loon	Ron	than
Lynn	run	then
main	sane	thin
Maine	scan	throne
man	scene	thrown
mane	screen	tin
mean	seen	tine
men	seine	ton
mine	Seine	tone
moon	Shane	town
Nan	Shawn	train
nine	shin	tune

twin	vein	won
twine	vine	yawn
vain	wane	Zane
van	when	zone
Van	whine	_____
vane	win	_____

N /n/ Final—two syllables

Aaron	butane	deadline
adjoin	button	deepen
again	cabin	define
Aileen	caffeine	deplane
airman	cake pan	design
airplane	Calvin	divan
Akron	campaign	divine
Aldcn	canteen	Doreen
alone	cartoon	downtown
atone	Ceylon	dragoon
attain	Charline	Earlene
baboon	chicken	eighteen
backbone	children	Elaine
bacon	chlorine	Elden
bailsman	chow mein	engine
balloon	Clifton	Erin
bargain	Clinton	Eugene
bassoon	clothespin	explain
bastion	coastline	fireman
baton	Colleen	flatten
beacon	cologne	foreseen
bearskin	Cologne	fortune
began	combine	garden
begin	common	gold mine
Berlin	complain	goose down
Bethune	constrain	Gordon
betwecn	contain	hailstone
bonbon	convene	harpoon
Brian	Dagan	headstone
bunyon	Darlene	Helen
Burton	Dawson	Herman

Hilton	notion	satin
home run	ocean	sealskin
homespun	open	seven
human	outshine	Sharon
humane	Owen	Sheldon
Irene	pecan	shoeshine
Jackson	pie pan	sideline
Japan	pigeon	soapstone
Jason	pigpen	soybean
Jensen	pipeline	squirt gun
Johnson	platoon	Steven
Joline	pontoon	sunshine
Karen	postpone	suntan
key chain	praline	Susan
limestone	prison	Susanne
Lincoln	puffin	sustain
lion	raccoon	Sylvan
listen	rattan	terrain
log on	raven	thirteen
Lorin	ravine	topline
Lorraine	recline	trombone
lotion	refine	Truman
Lyndon	refrain	tycoon
machine	regain	unknown
mailman	remain	urbane
marine	rerun	Verlene
Marine	resign	wagon
martin	restrain	Waldon
Martin	ribbon	Warren
membrane	Robbin	Welden
milestone	robin	whalebone
Milton	Roman	within
moisten	rotten	woman
motion	ruin	women
mountain	run-in	yachtsman
napkin	Ryan	yeoman
nation	Saigon	Zion
Nixon	salmon	_____
Norman	sandman	_____

N /n/ Final—three syllables

Adaline	emotion	margarine
African	enlighten	Mexican
afternoon	entertain	mezzanine
Alison	evergreen	Michigan
allophone	fire engine	microphone
Amazon	fire station	moccasin
aspirin	firewoman	monotone
attention	fisherman	overgrown
Audubon	formation	overran
autobahn	frying pan	overthrown
baritone	gabardine	patrolman
battalion	galleon	pelican
Bernadine	Galveston	Philippine
bobby pin	gasoline	Phoenician
Buchanan	gas station	physician
bus station	gelatin	policeman
carnation	gentleman	porcupine
Caroline	Geraldine	position
Chinatown	go-between	power line
chuck wagon	Halloween	putting green
Cimarron	Harrison	read-a-thon
cinnamon	hurricane	rejection
clergyman	hydroplane	relation
collarbone	ice-cream cone	religion
collation	Indian	remission
collection	Jackelyn	reunion
collegian	javelin	reversion
collision	Jefferson	roasting pan
confession	jellybean	safety pin
confusion	Josephine	saxophone
decision	kerosene	scatterbrain
derision	location	sea lion
determine	log cabin	Sheraton
dictaphone	Madison	signalman
discipline	magazine	skeleton
division	Magdalene	snowmachine
Edison	mailwoman	space station
emblazon	marathon	spick and span

submarine
sugarcane
super fine
superman
Superman
suspension
tambourine
telephone
telethon
train station

triathlon
turpentine
unforeseen
unison
Van Buren
Vatican
venison
violin
vitamin
Washington

water crane
weather vane
windowpane
wolverine
xylophone
zeppelin

_____
_____
_____
_____

N /n/ Final—four syllables

adding machine
amputation
animation
benediction
chameleon
complication
Copenhagen
deviation
domination
elevation
fermentation
generation

germination
hibernation
hot-air balloon
indecision
lamination
lifeguard station
nomination
patrolwoman
patrolwomen
phenomenon
police station
policewoman

policewomen
politician
public domain
sanitation
satisfaction
supervision
syncopation
television
Victorian

_____
_____
_____

ND /nd/ Medial—two syllables

Andy
bandage
bandstand
branding
Brandon
Brenda
bundle
Candace
candle
candy
Candy
cinder
Cindy

condemn
condor
dandy
fender
flounder
foundry
gander
Gandhi
Glenda
Glendale
grinder
grounded
grounder

handbag
handball
handbook
handcuff
handful
handle
handsaw
handshake
handsome
handspring
handy
hinder
Hindi

Hindu
hundred
indeed
indent
indulge
jaundiced
kindly
kindness
landing
landlord
landscape
landslide
Landy
launder
laundry
Linda
London
mandate
Mandy
Monday

plunder
ponder
Randolph
random
Randy
reindeer
render
rounded
rounding
round trip
roundup
sand crab
sandbox
sandbug
sandbur
sander
Sandy
sender
send-off
slander

slender
splendor
Sunday
sunder
tandem
tender
thunder
tundra
undamped
under
undone
undress
vendor
Wendy
window
windup
windy
wonder

_____

_____

ND /nd/ Medial—three syllables

Amanda
amendment
appendage
appendix
bandaging
candy bar
condition
conducive
conduction
conductor
endurance
handicap
handicraft
handiwork
handwriting
handwritten
Honduras

India
Indian
inundate
landlady
Laplander
laundromat
left-handed
London Bridge
mandarin
meander
plundering
sandalwood
sandbagging
sand dollar
sandpaper
sandpiper
storm window

Sunday School
sundial
tendency
tenderfoot
thunderbolt
thunderclap
thunderhead
thunderous
thunderstorm
thunderstruck
tinderbox
underbrush
underclothes
underdog
underfoot
underground
underline

undermine	understood	unfounded
underneath	undertake	wanderer
underpass	undertook	wanderlust
undersea	undertow	wonderful
undershirt	underwear	_____
underside	underweight	_____
understand	underwent	_____
understate	underworld	_____

ND /nd/ Medial—four syllables

candelabra	indelible	Indonesia
Cinderella	indentation	kindergarten
condemnation	independent	mendaciously
conditional	Indiana	mendacity
incandescent	indicative	undulating
indecently	indiscretion	_____

ND /nd/ Medial—five syllables

appendicitis	indeterminate	underestimate
condominium	indiscriminate	underexposure
hypochondriac	industrialist	underprivileged
incandescently	Indy 500	understandingly
incendiary	serendipity	_____
indefensible	underachiever	_____
independency	underdeveloped	_____

ND /nd/ Final—one syllable

and	end	hound
band	find	kind
bend	fined	land
bind	fond	lend
bland	found	mend
blend	fund	mind
blind	gland	mound
blond	grand	pond
bond	grind	pound
bound	ground	rend
brand	hand	rind
canned	hind	round

sand	stand	weaned
send	strand	wind
skinned	tend	wound
sound	trend	yawned
spanned	vend	_____
spend	wand	_____

ND /nd/ Final—two syllables

abound	expand	quicksand
aground	extend	Raymond
airbound	fairground	rebound
almond	farmland	refund
amend	Finland	remand
ascend	firebrand	remind
astound	foreground	respond
attend	grassland	right-hand
backbend	greyhound	Roland
background	headband	rotund
backhand	highland	second
bandstand	Holland	shorthand
behind	homeland	side band
beyond	husband	snowblind
bloodhound	inland	snowbound
Cleveland	intend	spellbound
combined	Ireland	stagehand
command	island	thousand
commend	jocund	unbind
compound	kickstand	unwind
confound	left-hand	up-end
contend	legend	upland
dachshund	longhand	waistband
dead end	mainland	woodland
defend	mankind	wristband
demand	Midland	_____
depend	misspend	_____
descend	offend	_____
diamond	Portland	_____
England	pretend	_____
errand	profound	_____

ND /nd/ Final—three syllables

apprehend	marching band	Sugar Land
beforehand	Maryland	Sutherland
comprehend	New England	Switzerland
condescend	Newfoundland	Tamarind
contraband	New Zealand	underground
correspond	overland	underhand
countermand	recommend	understand
dividend	Rhode Island	upper hand
fairyland	rhythm band	vagabond
Gila Bend	rubber band	wonderland
integrand	savings bond	wraparound
intertwined	secondhand	_____

ND /nd/ Final—four syllables

merry-go-round	_____	_____
misunderstand	_____	_____
superintend	_____	_____

NER /nɚ/ Medial—three syllables

energy	honor roll	runnerup
funeral	inner ear	scenery
general	mineral	spinneret
generous	partnership	_____

NER /nɚ/ Medial—four syllables

energetic	honorable	unmannerly
generation	machinery	vulnerable
generator	refinery	_____

NER /nɚ/ Final—two syllables

banner	gunner	owner
burner	honor	partner
cleaner	inner	plainer
corner	liner	runner
diner	lunar	schooner
dinner	manner	sooner
donor	manor	Sooner
gainer	minor	spinner

tanner	Turner	——————
tenor	vintner	——————
turner	winner	——————

NER /nɚ/ Final—three syllables

airliner	foreigner	questioner
beginner	gold panner	roadrunner
container	governor	wagoner
dishonor	long liner	Westerner
dry cleaner	opener	——————
Easterner	prisoner	——————

NER /nɚ/ Final—four syllables

commissioner	——————	——————
mid-westerner	——————	——————
practitioner	——————	——————

NJ /ndʒ/ Medial—two syllables

angel	enjoin	pongee
banjo	enjoy	pungent
congeal	enjoyed	ranger
congealed	ginger	rangy
congest	ingest	sponges
conjure	inject	stranger
conjured	injure	tangent
danger	injured	unjust
dingy	lounger	vengeance
dungeon	manger	vengeful
engine	Ninja	——————

NJ /ndʒ/ Medial—three syllables

Angela	challenges	dangerous
angelfish	challenging	endanger
angelic	changeable	endangered
Angelus	congested	engendered
angina	congestion	engineer
avenger	conjecture	engineered
Blue Angels	conjugal	fire engine
Challenger	conjunction	ginger ale

gingerbread	injury	tangible
gingerly	injustice	_____
gingersnap	Lone Ranger	_____
ingenious	messenger	_____
injected	passenger	_____
injection	scavenger	_____
injunction	tangerine	_____

NJ /ndʒ/ Medial—four syllables

conjectural	evangelist	intangible
conjugation	evangelize	meningitis
evangelic	injurious	_____

NJ /ndʒ/ Medial—five syllables

evangelical	_____	_____
ingenuity	_____	_____
laryngectomy	_____	_____

NJ /ndʒ/ Final—one syllable

change	mange	tinge
flange	plunge	twinge
fringe	range	_____
grange	scrounge	_____
hinge	singe	_____
lounge	sponge	_____
lunge	strange	_____

NJ /ndʒ/ Final—two syllables

arrange	estrange	revenge
astringe	exchange	scavenge
avenge	expunge	unhinge
challenge	impinge	_____
derange	lozenge	_____
downrange	orange	_____

NJ /ndʒ/ Final—three syllables

counter change	prearrange	_____
disarrange	rearrange	_____
interchange	_____	_____

NL /nl̩/ Final—two syllables

channel	hymnal	spinal
colonel	journal	tunnel
final	kennel	_____
flannel	panel	_____
funnel	signal	_____

NL /nl̩/ Final—three syllables

arsenal	infernal	paternal
cardinal	internal	personal
criminal	marginal	rational
doctrinal	maternal	seasonal
eternal	national	sectional
external	nocturnal	sentinel
fictional	nominal	terminal
fractional	optional	_____
functional	ordinal	_____

NL /nl̩/ Final—four syllables

additional	irrational	provisional
congressional	nutritional	sensational
diagonal	occasional	_____
emotional	octagonal	_____
exceptional	original	_____

RN /rn/ Medial—two syllables

Arnold	cornet	garnish
barnyard	cornfield	harness
Bernard	cornflakes	horned toad
Bernice	corn oil	hornet
burned-out	cornstarch	journal
burner	darning	journey
burning	doorknob	kernel
colonel	earnest	learning
cornbread	earnings	Lorna
corncob	Ernest	morning
Cornell	furnace	mourning
corner	furnish	Myrna
cornered	garnet	ornate

surname	turnkey	Vernon
tarnish	turn on	warning
thorny	turnout	worn-out
turncoat	turnpike	_____
turner	turnstile	_____
turnip	varnish	_____

RN /rn/ Medial—three syllables

alternate	internal	stubbornness
Bernadine	internee	tornado
carnation	internist	tournament
Carnegie	internment	tourniquet
carnival	journalist	turnover
cornerstone	journeyman	turntable
corn popper	maternal	unfurnished
Easterner	nocturnal	Westerner
eternal	ornament	westernmost
external	paternal	_____
fraternal	returning	_____
furnishings	Southern Cross	_____
furniture	Southerner	_____
government	southernmost	_____
infernal	storm warning	_____

RN /rn/ Medial—four syllables

alternately	carnivorous	returnable
alternative	internalize	vernacular
alternator	morning glory	_____

RN /rn/ Final—one syllable

barn	learn	urn
born	Lorne	Verne
burn	mourn	warn
churn	scorn	worn
corn	stern	yarn
darn	sworn	yearn
earn	thorn	_____
fern	torn	_____
horn	turn	_____

RN /rn/ Final—two syllables

acorn	Hawthorn	return
adjourn	inborn	Saturn
adorn	intern	shopworn
airborne	iron	shorthorn
auburn	lantern	sojourn
Auburn	LaVerne	southern
cavern	long horn	stubborn
cistern	modern	sunburn
concern	newborn	upturn
eastern	pattern	western
fire thorn	popcorn	windburn
fog horn	pronghorn	_____
French horn	Rayburn	_____
govern	reborn	_____

RN /rn/ Final—three syllables

Capricorn	unconcern	_____
southeastern	unicorn	_____
southwestern	_____	_____

NS /ns/ Medial—two syllables

answer	fencer	rancid
cancer	fencing	ransom
Cancer	glancer	Sensei
censor	insert	senses
chancer	inside	Spencer
concede	insist	sponsor
concept	insult	stencil
concern	Jensen	tensor
concert	Johnson	tinsel
consent	lancer	tonsils
console	lonesome	unsafe
consult	mincemeat	unseal
consume	monsoon	unseen
council	pencil	_____
dancer	prancer	_____
denser	princess	_____
fancy	Quincy	_____

NS /ns/ Medial—three syllables

advancement	density	one-sided
advancer	dispenser	potency
agency	enhancer	principal
announcer	entrancer	principle
chancellor	fiancée	reconcile
commencement	frequency	Regency
concession	incentive	romancer
condenser	incident	sensible
consider	insincere	sensitive
consonant	insulate	transgressor
consumer	insulted	uncertain
consumption	linseed oil	unselfish
counselor	nonsupport	unsightly
currency	offensive	vacancy

NS /ns/ Medial—four syllables

coincidence	Pensacola	sensational
consecutive	precedency	social science
deficiency	preconceiving	unsatisfied
emergency	preconception	unsuitable
insignia	principalship	unsuspected
intensity	radiancy	_____
peninsula	reconsider	_____

NS /ns/ Final—one syllable

bounce	lance	rinse
chance	Lance	sense
dance	mince	since
dense	once	tense
fence	ounce	thence
France	pounce	whence
glance	prance	wince
hence	prince	_____

NS /ns/ Final—two syllables

absence	balance	conscience
advance	commence	Constance
announce	condense	convince

defense	license	science
denounce	nonsense	sentence
dispense	nuisance	sequence
distance	offense	silence
enhance	past tense	tuppence
entrance	patience	twopence
finance	presence	vengeance
Florence	pretense	_____
fragrance	pronounce	_____
immense	province	_____
incense	prudence	_____
instance	response	_____
intense	romance	_____

NS /ns/ Final—three syllables

abundance	dependence	prevalence
acceptance	difference	radiance
admittance	disturbance	recurrence
allegiance	endurance	redundance
alliance	evidence	reference
allowance	ignorance	residence
ambulance	impatience	resistance
annoyance	importance	reverence
appearance	influence	subsistence
appliance	innocence	surveillance
audience	insurance	tolerance
circumstance	maintenance	turbulence
common sense	mispronounce	utterance
conference	occurrence	variance
confidence	performance	vigilance
consequence	precedence	_____
convenience	preference	_____

NS /ns/ Final—four syllables

circumference	obedience	self-reliance
independence	predominance	significance
indifference	preponderance	_____
inheritance	self-assurance	_____
intelligence	self-confidence	_____

SN /sn/ Initial—one syllable

snack	sneaked	snook
snacked	sneer	snoop
snag	sneeze	snoot
snagged	sneezed	snooze
snail	snell	snore
snake	snelled	snout
snap	snide	snow
snapped	snip	snowed
snare	snipe	snub
snared	snipes	snubbed
snarl	snipped	snug
snatch	snitch	_____
sneak	snob	_____

SN /sn/ Initial—two syllables

snack bar	snazzy	snowbound
snaffle	sneakers	snow-capped
snagging	sneaking	snowdrift
snaggy	sneezy	snowfall
snakebite	snicker	snowflake
snake dance	sniffle	snow-go
snakeskin	snippy	snow job
snaky	snobbish	snowman
snapback	snobby	snowplow
snap bean	snooper	snowshoe
snapper	Snoopy	snowstorm
snapping	snooty	snowsuit
snappish	snorkel	snow tires
snappy	snowball	Snow White
snapshots	snowbank	snubby
snare drum	snowbird	snuggle
snatchy	snow boots	_____

SN /sn/ Initial—three syllables

snaggletooth	snapdragon	sneakiest
snaggletoothed	snappier	snickering
snake charmer	snappiness	snout beetle
snakier	snazzier	snowball fight

snow blindness	snowmobile	_____
snowblower	snowy owl	_____
snow bunting	_____	_____

SN /sn/ Initial—four syllables

snapping beetle	_____	_____
snapping turtle	_____	_____
snowy egret	_____	_____

NSER /nsɚ/ Final—two syllables

answer	denser	Spencer
cancer	fencer	sponsor
Cancer	glancer	tensor
censor	lancer	_____
chancer	prancer	_____
dancer	spencer	_____

NSER /nsɚ/ Final—three syllables

advancer	dispenser	extensor
announcer	enhancer	romancer
condenser	entrancer	_____

NT /nt/ Medial—two syllables

ante	county	hunter
antler	dainty	hunting
banter	dental	huntress
cantor	dented	into
center	dentist	junta
centered	Denton	mantle
central	enter	mental
chanting	entrance	mentor
contempt	entry	minted
contend	fainted	Monty
content	frantic	nineteen
contest	frontal	nincty
context	gentle	onto
contort	granted	painted
contour	grantor	painter
country	hinted	painting

pantry	rental	Trenton
plaintiff	rented	vantage
plaintive	saintly	vented
planter	Santa	vintage
planting	scented	wanted
pointer	shanty	wanton
pointing	slanted	winter
pontiff	splinter	_____
printed	squinted	_____
printer	squinter	_____
printing	syntax	_____
punted	tantrum	_____
quaintly	tinted	_____

NT /nt/ Medial—three syllables

advantage	gigantic	repented
Antarctic	imprinted	repenting
Atlantic	incentive	resented
attentive	indented	resentful
carpenter	interact	resentment
centerpiece	intercede	romantic
Centerville	intercept	Santa Claus
Central Park	intercom	Santa Cruz
Central Time	interest	Santa Fe
consented	interface	self-centered
container	interfere	seventeen
contented	interfold	seventy
contention	intersect	storm center
contentment	interval	tentative
contestant	interview	tormentor
continent	invented	transplanting
continue	inventor	wintergreen
counterfeit	Kentucky	wintertime
enchanted	Kon Tiki	_____
encounter	misprinted	_____
enterprise	parental	_____
entertain	presenting	_____
eventful	re-enter	_____
fantasy	repentant	_____

NT /nt/ Medial—four syllables

accidental	disadvantage	radiantly
adventurer	egocentric	regimental
antagonist	governmental	representant
antagonize	horizontal	rudimental
antecedent	instrumental	sacramental
cantilever	integrity	sentimental
commentary	interesting	supplemental
contaminate	intermission	trans-Atlantic
contemplating	intersection	transcendental
continental	intimidate	uneventful
contingency	monumental	unprevented
continual	oriental	unrepentant
continuous	ornamental	Valentine's Day
continuum	pedimental	ventriloquist
conventional	pigmentation	yellow bunting
departmental	presentation	_____
differential	radiant heat	_____

NT /nt/ Medial—five syllables

antibiotic	experiential	representation
contaminated	intermediate	supplementary
contemporary	international	temperamental
differentiate	involuntary	testamentary
disinterested	orientation	_____
documentary	parliamentary	_____
elementary	Protestantism	_____

NT /nt/ Final—one syllable

ant	dent	grunt
aunt	don't	haunt
bent	faint	hint
blunt	feint	hunt
brunt	flint	jaunt
bunt	front	lent
can't	gaunt	lint
cent	gent	meant
chant	grant	mint
count	Grant	mount

paint	rent	stunt
pant	runt	taunt
pent	saint	tent
pint	scant	tint
plant	scent	vent
point	sent	want
print	shunt	went
punt	slant	won't
quaint	spent	_____
quint	sprint	_____
rant	squint	_____

NT /nt/ Final—two syllables

absent	distant	pageant
accent	eggplant	parchment
account	enchant	parent
affront	entente	patent
agent	event	patient
ailment	extent	pavement
amount	ferment	payment
anoint	foment	peasant
appoint	For Rent	pennant
ascent	frequent	percent
aslant	gallant	pheasant
basement	garment	pigment
Belmont	hydrant	pinpoint
blueprint	imprint	placement
brilliant	indent	pleasant
buoyant	infant	poignant
cement	instant	potent
client	intent	preprint
cogent	invent	present
cold front	judgment	prevent
comment	merchant	prudent
consent	moment	quadrant
constant	movement	quotient
content	newsprint	rampant
descent	oil paint	recent
discount	ointment	recount

remnant
resent
rodent
sea front
segment
sergeant
serpent
servant
shipment
silent

spearmint
stagnant
standpoint
statement
strident
stringent
student
talent
tenant
torrent

transient
transplant
treatment
urgent
vacant
valiant
Vermont
vibrant

_____

_____

_____

NT /nt/ Final—three syllables

abundant
accident
accountant
adjacent
adornment
advanccmcnt
affluent
allotment
amazement
amendment
amusement
announcement
apartment
apparent
appointment
arrangement
atonement
commencement
compartment
competent
compliment
component
consonant
contentment
continent
convenient
decedent

dependent
descendant
detergent
different
diligent
dissonant
document
dominant
efficient
elephant
elopement
emigrant
encroachment
enjoyment
enrollment
filament
ignorant
immigrant
implement
improvement
impudent
incident
indignant
inherent
innocent
insolvent
installment

instrument
investment
lenient
lieutenant
ligament
malignant
management
measurement
monument
nourishment
nutrient
occupant
operant
opponent
orient
ornament
palpitant
parliament
peppermint
permanent
persistent
petulant
precedent
president
prominent
Protestant
punishment

radiant
recurrent
refreshment
regiment
relevant
reluctant
represent
requirement
resentment
resident
resistant

respondent
restaurant
retirement
reverent
ruminant
sediment
sentiment
subjacent
subsequent
succulent
sufficient

supplement
sycophant
tenement
testament
tolerant
tournament
variant
vigilant
violent
wonderment
_____

NT /nt/ Final—four syllables

accomplishment
adolescent
advertisement
apportionment
astonishment
determinant
entertainment
environment
equivalent
establishment
expedient
experiment

extravagant
independent
indifferent
ingredient
intelligent
intolerant
iridescent
magnificent
noncombatant
obedient
participant
precipitant

predicament
predominant
preponderant
presentiment
reinforcement
significant
single parent
subservient
superjacent
temperament
understatement
vice-president

NT /nt/ Final—five syllables

insignificant
interdependent

superintendent
_____

_____
_____

NTH /nθ/ Medial—two syllables

anthem
anther
enthuse

enthused
menthol
monthly

panther
unthink
_____

NTH /nθ/ Medial—three syllables

Anthony
Cynthia
Samantha

synthesis
synthesize
synthetic

unthankful
unthinking
unthoughtful

NTH /nθ/ Medial—four syllables

anthology	enthusiast	pyracantha
Corinthian	mentholated	_____
Corinthians	parenthesis	_____

NTH /nθ/ Final—one syllable

month	plinth	_____
ninth	tenth	_____

NTH /nθ/ Final—two syllables

billionth	fifteenth	seventh
Corinth	fourteenth	sixteenth
dozenth	millionth	thirteenth
eighteenth	nineteenth	_____

NTH /nθ/ Final—three syllables

amaranth	hyacinth	seventeenth
eleventh	labyrinth	_____

NGTH /ŋθ/ Medial—two syllables

lengthen	lengthy	_____
lengthways	strengthen	_____
lengthwise	_____	_____

NGTH /ŋθ/ Final—one syllable

length	_____	_____
strength	_____	_____

NGTH /ŋθ/ Final—two syllables

full-length	wave-length	_____
half-length	whole-length	_____

NY /nj/ Medial—two syllables

banyan	genial	lanyard
barnyard	genius	minion
bunion	junior	Muñoz
Bunyan	Junior	onion
canyon	Kenya	Runnion
Daniel	Kenyon	senior

senõr	Tanya	
Spaniard	unused	
spaniel	vineyard	

NY /nj/ Medial—three syllables

ammonia	golden years	sinuate
annual	Grand Canyon	Virginia
banyan tree	ingenious	zinnia
begonia	lunula	
Black Canyon	lunular	
congenial	manuscript	
convenience	minuet	
convenient	monument	
dominion	Paul Bunyan	
geniuses	señora	

NY /nj/ Medial—four syllables

annual wage	filet mignon	unusual
annually	gardenia	Virginia Beach
biannual	genuinely	West Virginia
Boulder Canyon	January	
centennial	manufacture	
cocker spaniel	monumental	
continual	señorita	
Dominion Day	triannual	

NZ /nz/ Medial—two syllables

benzene	Kansas	
Bronze Age	Wednesday	
clansman		
frenzy		

NZ /nz/ Final—one syllable

bans	canes	coins
Benz	cans	cones
bins	chains	crowns
bones	chins	Dan's
bronze	cleans	deans
buns	clowns	dines

drains	pens	tans
fans	phones	teens
fines	pines	tens
fins	pins	thins
gains	plains	tins
grains	planes	tones
groans	plans	tons
jeans	prunes	trains
lanes	puns	tunes
lawns	queens	twins
leans	rains	vans
lines	shines	vines
loans	shins	wanes
manes	signs	wins
mines	skins	zones
moans	sons	_____
moons	spans	_____
Nan's	spins	_____
nines	spoons	_____
nouns	stains	_____
pains	stones	_____
pans	swans	_____

NZ /nz/ Final—two syllables

balloons	Marines	retains
batons	mountains	ribbons
blue jeans	napkins	robins
buttons	nations	sevens
cake pans	notions	sidelines
cartoons	oceans	soybeans
chickens	opens	swim fins
complains	outshines	trombones
detains	pecans	wagons
Great Plains	pie pans	_____
hailstones	pigeons	_____
heavens	platoons	_____
kitchens	puffins	_____
lions	ravens	_____
machines	remains	_____

NDZ /ndz/ Final—one syllable

bends	lends	spends
binds	mends	stands
ends	minds	tends
finds	ponds	winds
glands	rends	_____
grinds	rinds	_____
hands	sands	_____
kinds	sends	_____
lands	sounds	_____

NG

Pronounced: /ŋ/
Spelled: n, ng, ngue

NG /ŋ/ Medial—two syllables

anger
angle
angler
angling
anguish
Angus
banging
bangle
Bangor
Bengal
bongo
England
English
finger
fungus
gangplank
hanger
hunger
jangle

jingle
jungle
kingdom
kingly
linger
longer
mangle
mingle
mongoose
Ping Pong
ringer
singer
songster
springy
stringer
stronger
strongly
swinger
Tango

tingle
wrangler
wringer
younger
youngest
youngster
Youngstown

_____
_____
_____
_____
_____
_____
_____
_____
_____
_____
_____

NG /ŋ/ Medial—three syllables

Anglican
Angola
angora
belonging
Buckingham
bungalow
chewing gum
dungaree
elongate

fingerling
fingernail
fingerpaint
fingerprint
fingertip
flamingo
hearing aid
heating pad
kangaroo

lingering
marching band
Singapore
untangled
Washington

_____
_____
_____

NG /ŋ/ Final—one syllable

bang	pang	strong
Bing	ping	stung
bring	pong	sung
clang	prong	swing
cling	rang	tang
ding	ring	thing
dong	rung	thong
fang	sang	throng
fling	sing	tong
gang	slang	tongue
gong	sling	wing
hang	song	wring
hung	sprang	wrong
king	spring	_____
long	sprung	_____
lung	sting	_____
Ming	string	_____

NG /ŋ/ Final—two syllables

asking	buzzing	diving
baking	caring	docking
batting	carving	doing
beaming	catching	driving
bedding	charging	duckling
being	charming	eating
belong	chuckling	evening
bending	clamming	failing
biking	climbing	falling
blessing	clowning	feeding
blinding	coming	feeling
boating	cording	fencing
booting	crackling	finding
bowling	cramping	fishing
boxing	curling	fitting
bucking	cycling	flying
buckling	dancing	fouling
bullring	ding-dong	frying
buying	dining	giving

gliding
going
golfing
grabbing
greeting
guarding
guessing
guiding
Harding
having
hearing
helping
hiding
holding
Hong Kong
hopping
housing
jiving
jogging
judging
jumping
key ring
laughing
leading
leading
lifting
linking
living
loading
locking
lodging
looking
loving
making
morning
moving
paddling
painting
passing

Ping Pong
placing
playing
pounding
pressing
pulling
pushing
racing
raining
riding
ringing
roping
rounding
routing
rowing
ruling
running
sailing
saying
seeing
serving
setting
shaking
sharing
shining
shoestring
sitting
skating
skiing
sledding
sleeping
sleeting
sliding
snowing
sparring
speeding
standing
steering
stepping

stopping
stretching
surfing
swimming
tackling
talking
tanning
throwing
tingling
topping
touching
trailing
training
trotting
trying
tumbling
tying
wading
waiting
walking
watching
wearing
winning
wishing
working
wrestling
yachting
——————————
——————————
——————————
——————————
——————————
——————————
——————————
——————————
——————————
——————————
——————————

NG /ŋ/ Final—three syllables

arriving
awarding
backpacking
balancing
bandaging
bellowing
bobsledding
broadjumping
cancelling
canoeing
carousing
car racing
challenging
childbearing
coercing
collapsing
colluding
coloring
corroding
departing
dialing
dog mushing
dog sledding
drag racing
endearing
exciting

galloping
gardening
handwriting
hayriding
high diving
high jumping
hollering
homecoming
horse racing
hot rodding
ice skating
jump roping
kayaking
lassoing
listening
lumbering
marauding
measuring
performing
picnicking
place kicking
pole-vaulting
polishing
promoting
remaking
rewarding

rock climbing
skateboarding
skindiving
sky diving
snorkeling
spear fishing
square dancing
storm warning
sunbathing
surfboarding
tap dancing
Thanksgiving
tightroping
traveling
unfolding
unmaking
unmasking
visiting
wedding ring
weight lifting
windsurfing
Wyoming
_____
_____
_____
_____

NG /ŋ/ Final—four syllables

awakening
clarifying
classifying
coinciding
convalescing
deep sea fishing
exercising
figure skating
harmonizing
hockey skating

horseback riding
mountain climbing
pacifying
photographing
rectifying
river rafting
roller skating
salad dressing
salmon fishing
satisfying

scuba diving
stock car racing
televising
underlying
undertaking
verifying
water skiing
_____
_____
_____

NGL /ŋl/ Medial—two syllables

angler	jingler	wrangling
angling	jingling	_____
Anglo	jungly	_____
England	mingling	_____
English	wrangler	_____

NGL /ŋl/ Medial—three syllables

Anglican	Englander	New England
anglicize	Englisher	_____
anglify	English horn	_____
drinking glass	Englishman	_____

NGL /ŋl/ Final—two syllables

angle	mingle	wrangle
dangle	shingle	_____
dingle	single	_____
jangle	spangle	_____
jingle	tangle	_____
jungle	tingle	_____

NGL /ŋl/ Final—three syllables

commingle	quadrangle	untangle
entangle	rectangle	_____
Kris Kringle	right angle	_____
left angle	triangle	_____

NGTH /ŋθ/ Medial—two syllables

lengthen	lengthy	_____
lengthways	strengthen	_____
lengthwise	_____	_____

NGTH /ŋθ/ Final—one syllable

length	_____	_____
strength	_____	_____

NGTH /ŋθ/ Final—two syllables

full-length	wave-length	_____
half-length	whole-length	_____

NGZ /ŋz/ Final—one syllable

bangs	pangs	things
brings	pings	tongs
fangs	rings	wings
gangs	sings	wrongs
gongs	songs	_____
hangs	stings	_____
kings	swings	_____

NGZ /ŋz/ Final—two syllables

cravings	pavings	_____
drawings	savings	_____
paintings	_____	_____

NK

Pronounced: /ŋk/ and /nk/
Spelled: nk, nch, nc

NK /nk/, /ŋk/ Medial—two syllables

anchor	flanker	thinker
anchored	frankly	tinker
ankle	Hong Kong	tinkle
Bangkok	honking	tinkled
bank draft	inkling	trinket
banker	junket	twinkle
banking	junky	twinkled
bank loan	kinky	twinkling
bankrupt	lanky	winking
blanket	Lincoln	wrinkle
blinker	linkage	wrinkled
blinking	linking	Yankee
bronco	linkup	yanking
Bronco	monkey	————————
bunkbed	pancake	————————
canker	ranking	————————
cankered	rankle	————————
chunky	rankled	————————
clanking	shrinking	————————
clinker	sinker	————————
concave	sinking	————————
Concord	slinky	————————
concur	sprinkle	————————
conquer	sprinkled	————————
cranking	sprinkling	————————
dinky	spunky	————————
donkey	stinker	————————
drinker	stinking	————————
drinking	tanker	————————
encode	thank you	————————

NK /ŋk/ Final—one syllable

bank	honk	sink
blank	hunk	skink
blink	ink	skunk
brink	junk	slank
bunk	kink	slink
chink	lank	slunk
chunk	link	spank
clank	mink	spunk
clink	monk	stank
crank	pink	stink
dank	plank	sunk
drank	plunk	tank
drink	prank	thank
dunk	punk	think
flank	rank	trunk
flunk	rink	twink
franc	sank	wink
frank	shank	yank
Frank	shrank	Yank
hank	shrink	zinc
Hank	shrunk	_____

NK /ŋk/ Final—two syllables

Burbank	gas tank	prethink
chain link	lime drink	soft drink
chipmunk	oil tank	unlink
embank	outflank	World Bank
enrank	outrank	_____
fruit drink	out think	_____
fuel tank	point-blank	_____

NK /ŋk/ Final—three syllables

apple drink	interlink	river bank
bobolink	kitchen sink	savings bank
City Bank	lemon drink	water tank
countersink	orange drink	_____
grapefruit drink	pressure tank	_____

P

Pronounced: /p/
Spelled: p, pe, pp

P /p/ Initial—one syllable

pace	parch	peak
paced	parched	peaked
pack	pare	peal
packed	pared	pealed
pact	park	pear
pad	parked	pearl
page	part	Pearl
Page	pass	pearls
paged	passed	pears
paid	past	peat
pail	paste	peck
pain	pat	pecked
pained	Pat	peek
paint	patch	peeked
pair	patched	peel
paired	pate	peeled
pal	path	peep
pale	Paul	peeped
paled	pause	peer
pall	paused	peered
palled	pave	peers
palm	paved	peg
palmed	paw	Peg
Pam	pawed	pegged
pan	pawn	pelt
Pan	pawned	pen
pang	pay	penned
panned	pea	pep
pant	peace	per
par	peach	perch

perched	pit	pounds
perk	pitch	pour
Perk	pitched	poured
pert	Poe	pout
pet	point	pox
Pete	poise	poxed
pick	poised	pub
picked	poke	puck
pie	pole	puff
piece	poled	pug
pieced	Polk	pull
pier	poll	pulled
Pierce	polled	pulp
pig	pond	pulse
pike	pone	pulsed
pile	pool	pun
piled	pooled	punch
pill	poor	punk
pills	pop	punt
pin	Pop	pup
pinch	popped	purge
pinched	porch	purged
pine	pore	purl
pined	pork	purled
ping	port	purse
pink	pose	push
pinned	posed	pushed
pint	post	put
pip	pouch	putt
pipe	pouched	pyre
piped	pounce	_____
pique	pounced	_____
piqued	pound	_____

P /p/ Initial—two syllables

paca	packer	paddy
pacer	packet	padlock
package	padded	padre
packaged	paddle	pagan

pageant	pardon	pasture
painful	pardoned	pastured
painless	parent	pasty
paintbrush	parfait	patchwork
painted	paring	patent
painter	Paris	pathos
palace	parish	pathway
palate	parka	patience
paleface	parking	patient
pallet	parkway	Patrick
pallor	parley	patrol
palsied	parlor	patrolled
palsy	parole	patron
paltry	parquet	Patsy
Pammy	parried	patter
pampas	parrot	pattered
pamper	parry	pattern
pampered	parsley	patterned
pamphlet	parsnip	patty
pancake	parson	Patty
panda	partake	pauper
panel	partial	pavement
paneled	partly	paving
panic	partner	pawnshop
panicked	partook	payee
pansy	part-time	payment
panther	passage	payroll
pantry	passe′	peaceful
pantsuit	passing	peacock
papa	passion	peanut
papal	passive	Peanuts
paper	passkey	peasant
papered	passport	pebble
papoose	password	pebbled
pappy	pasteboard	pecan
parade	pastel	pedal
parboil	pastime	pedaled
parboiled	pastor	peddle
parcel	pastry	peddled

peeling	perished	pilfer
peephole	perjure	pilgrim
peevish	perjured	pillage
peewee	perky	pillar
Peking	permit	pillared
pellet	perplex	pillow
pelvis	perplexed	pilot
penal	Perry	pimple
penance	Persia	pimpled
penchant	persist	pincers
pencil	person	pinch-hit
penciled	persuade	pinchers
pendant	Peru	Ping Pong
pending	pesky	pinhead
penguin	pester	pinhole
penknife	pestered	pinkeye
pennant	petal	pinkie
penny	Peter	pinpoint
pension	petite	pinto
pensioned	petty	pin-up
pensive	pewter	pinwheel
penthouse	picket	pious
peon	pickle	pipeline
people	pickled	piquant
peopled	pickup	pirate
pepper	picnic	Pisa
peppered	picnicked	Pisces
perceive	picot	piston
perceived	picture	pitcher
percent	pictured	pitchfork
perfect	Pierre	pitfall
perform	pigeon	pithy
performed	piggish	Pittsburgh
perfume	pigment	pity
perfumed	pigpen	pivot
perhaps	pigskin	pixy
peril	pigsty	pizza
periled	pigtail	pocket
perish	pigtailed	pockmark

pockmarked	poplar	pot roast
poem	poplin	potter
poet	poppy	poultice
poignant	pop-up	poulticed
pointed	porous	poultry
pointer	porpoise	pouter
pointing	porridge	powder
pointless	portage	powdered
poison	portal	Powell
poisoned	porter	power
poker	porthole	powered
pokey	portion	powwow
poky	Portland	public
Poland	portly	publish
polar	portrait	published
polecat	portray	pucker
police	portrayed	puckered
policed	posse	pudding
polish	possess	puddle
polished	possessed	puddled
polite	possum	pudgy
polka	postage	pueblo
pollen	postal	Pueblo
pollute	postcard	puffball
Polly	posted	puffin
polo	poster	puffy
polyp	postman	pugnose
pomade	postmark	pugnosed
pompon	postpaid	pullet
pompous	postpone	pulley
poncho	postponed	pulpit
ponder	posture	pulsate
pondered	posy	puma
pontiff	potash	pumice
pontoon	potent	pumiced
pony	pothook	pumpkin
poodle	potion	punch card
popcorn	potlatch	puncture
Popeye	potluck	punctured

pungent
punish
punished
puppet
puppy
purchase
purchased
purloin

purple
purpose
pursue
pursued
pursuit
push-up
putter
puttered

putty
puzzle
pygmy
pylon
python

_____
_____
_____

P /p/ Initial—three syllables

pachyderm
Pacific
pacifist
pacify
paddle wheel
pageantry
pagoda
pajamas
Pakistan
palatial
Palestine
palisade
pallbearer
palmetto
palmistry
palpable
palpitate
Pamela
Panama
pancreas
Pandora
paneling
panicky
pantaloon
pantomime
pantomimed
papaya
paperback
paperboy

paperweight
paprika
papyrus
parable
parachute
paradise
paradox
paraffin
paragon
paragraph
parakeet
parallel
paralleled
paralyze
paralyzed
paranoid
parapet
parasite
parasol
parental
parity
parsonage
Parthenon
particle
partition
partnership
passable
passably
passageway

Passaic
passenger
passerby
passionate
Passover
pasteurize
pasteurized
pastoral
paternal
Paterson
pathetic
patriarch
Patricia
patriot
patrolman
patronage
patronize
patronized
pawnbroker
Pearl Harbor
peccary
pectoral
peculiar
pedestal
pedigree
pemmican
penalize
penalized
penalty

penciling

pendulous

pendulum

penetrate

penitent

penmanship

penniless

pensioner

pentagon

peppermint

percentage

perception

percolate

percussion

perfection

perforate

performance

performing

perilous

period

periscope

perjury

permission

peroxide

persecute

persevere

persevered

persimmon

persistent

personal

personnel

persuasion

pertinent

peskiness

pessimist

pestilence

petition

petitioned

petrified

petrify

petticoat

pettiness

piano

picturesque

piggyback

piggy bank

pilgrimage

pillowcase

pimento

pinafore

pincushion

pineapple

pinfeather

pinnacle

pinochle

pinsetter

pioneer

piracy

pirouette

pitiful

pocketbook

pocketknife

pocket watch

podium

poetry

pogo stick

poisonous

polar bear

policeman

policy

polio

polishing

politics

polka dot

pollinate

polliwog

polygon

pompadour

pony ride

popover

popular

populate

porcelain

porcupine

portable

portico

portrayal

Portugal

position

positioned

positive

possession

possessive

possiblc

possibly

postage stamp

postglacial

posthumous

postmaster

postmortem

post office

potato

potential

potpourri

pottery

Poughkeepsie

poverty

powder puff

powdery

powerful

powerhouse

powerless

power line

power saw

publicize

publicized

publicly

public school
publisher
pugnacious
pulverize
pulverized
pumpkin pie

punching bag
punctual
punctuate
punishment
purveyor
pushover

pussyfoot
putting green
pyramid

_____

_____

_____

P /p/ Initial—four syllables

pacifier
palomino
palpitation
panacea
panorama
panoramic
paralysis
parasitic
pardonable
paregoric
parenthesis
parishioner
parochial
participant
participate
participle
particular
Pasadena
paternity
pathology
patriotic
patrolwoman
peanut butter
pedestrian
pediatrics
pedodontist
Penelope
penetrable
penetration
penicillin
peninsula

perceptible
percolator
peremptory
perennial
perfectible
perfectionist
perfidious
performing arts
perfunctory
perimeter
periodic
periphery
perishable
periwinkle
permeable
permissible
perpetual
perpetuate
perplexity
perseverance
personable
personalize
personalized
personify
perspiration
pessimism
petroleum
piccalilli
pictorial
Pinnochio
pistachio

pitter-patter
pizzicato
podiatrist
poinsettia
poison ivy
police station
policewoman
policewomen
politician
Polynesia
polytechnic
pontifical
popularize
portulaca
potassium
potato chips
potentially
publication
public domain
publicity
Puerto Rico
pulmonary
pumpernickel
punctuation
punishable
purgatory
pussy willow
pyemia
pyorrhea
pyracantha
pyramidal

pyrogenic	_____	_____
pyrography	_____	_____
pyrolysis	_____	_____
pyrotechnic	_____	_____

P /p/ Initial—five syllables

Panama Canal	paternalism	pianissimo
Pan American	pathological	pituitary
pandemonium	patriotism	polysyllabic
parallelism	pecuniary	polysyllable
parallelogram	pediatrician	Pomeranian
parliamentary	penitentiary	possibility
participial	Pennsylvania	punctuality
particularly	perfectionism	pyromania
pasteurization	perpendicular	_____
Patagonia	personality	_____

P /p/ Medial—two syllables

apace	coupled	flapper
apart	coupon	flipper
apiece	crackpot	gaping
appear	creeper	gripper
appeared	crockpot	groping
append	dapper	guidepost
biped	deeper	happy
blooper	depart	hippo
Cape Cod	depend	hippy
caper	depict	Hopi
capon	depose	hopper
chipper	deposed	hopping
Chopin	depot	Jaipur
chopper	dipper	Japan
chopping	dipping	jodhpurs
choppy	dripping	keeper
clipper	dropout	keep out
clipping	dropping	key punch
copied	dustpan	kopeck
coping	epic	leaping
copy	epoch	leopard

Lopez	quipster	soppy
mapping	rapid	stepchild
moping	rapport	stepson
moppet	repaid	stop-off
mopping	repair	stopper
napkin	repaired	stopping
napping	repay	super
nipping	repeal	supper
nippy	repealed	suppose
opah	repeat	supposed
opal	repel	taper
Opal	repelled	teapot
opaque	repent	tepee
open	report	toothpaste
opened	riper	topping
opine	riposte	toupee
opined	ripper	trapeze
oppose	roper	trapper
opposed	roping	trapping
Papa	scapegoat	Trappist
paper	scrapbook	two-piece
papered	scraper	upbeat
papoose	scraping	upbraid
pepper	scrapping	upbuild
peppered	scrappy	update
peppy	seepage	updraft
pepsin	seeping	upend
peptic	shipper	upgrade
Ping Pong	shipping	upheave
piper	sipping	upheld
popcorn	skipper	uphill
poppy	slapping	uphold
pop-up	sleeper	uplift
prepaid	sleeping	upmost
proper	slipper	upon
pupa	slipping	upper
puppet	soapbox	vapor
puppy	soapy	whopper
quipping	sopping	wiper

wrapper	zipper	_____
wrapping	_____	_____
wrap-up	_____	_____
zip code	_____	_____

P /p/ Medial—three syllables

apartment	emperor	pineapple
apathy	epicure	popover
apostle	epiderm	properly
apparel	epigram	property
apparent	episode	recapping
appealing	floppy disk	recipe
appearing	frying pan	repaying
appendix	grasshopper	repeated
appetite	guinea pig	repellent
apple pic	haphazard	repentance
appointment	hypocrite	repentant
boarding pass	inn keeper	repertoire
canape	Japanese	reporter
canopy	juniper	republic
capital	lollipop	repulsing
capitol	newspaper	repulsion
cherry pie	octopus	repulsive
Chippewa	open door	safety pin
choppier	opening	sandpaper
choppiest	opera	sandpiper
chopping block	operate	separate
chopping wood	opinion	Singapore
cooperage	opponent	skyscraper
Copper Age	opposite	slippery
copperhead	papaya	soda pop
copybook	paperback	state trooper
copyright	paper bag	stepping stone
corn popper	paperboy	stopover
crepe paper	paper clip	stupendous
deported	paper dolls	superman
diaper	papering	Superman
dissipate	peppermint	supersede
drapery	Peter Pan	superstar

supervise	typewriter	Winnipeg
timekeeper	uppermost	woodpecker
Topeka	vaporize	zeppelin
topical	wallpaper	zoo keeper
tropical	whippoorwill	_____

P /p/ Medial—four syllables

Annapolis	epidermis	superego
apologize	epiglottis	superficial
apology	flipping a coin	superior
apparatus	handicapping	superlative
apparition	incipient	supermarket
appetizer	Lilliputian	tissue paper
candy striper	litmus paper	topography
capacity	manipulate	vaporific
capitulate	metropolis	vaporizer
Copenhagen	monopoly	whippersnapper
depopulate	municipal	Winnie-the-Pooh
disappearance	operator	wrapping paper
disposable	paper cutter	_____
epicanthus	paper towels	_____
epicenter	paratrooper	_____
epidemic	stapedial	_____

P /p/ Medial—five syllables

appendectomy	happy-go-lucky	stapedectomy
appendicitis	hippopotamus	unpopulated
cosmopolitan	lapis lazuli	_____
epicardium	metropolitan	_____
epicurean	opinionated	_____
episcopalian	opportunity	_____

P /p/ Final—one syllable

ape	chap	coop
beep	cheap	cop
Bip	chip	cope
bop	chop	coupe
cap	clap	creep
cape	clip	crepe

crop	nape	soap
croup	neap	sop
cup	nip	soup
deep	peep	steep
dip	pep	step
drape	pipe	stoop
drip	plop	stop
droop	pop	strap
drop	Pope	strip
flap	prop	stripe
flip	pup	sup
flop	rap	swap
gap	reap	sweep
gape	rip	swipe
grape	ripe	swoop
grip	rope	tap
gripe	sap	tape
grope	scoop	tip
group	scope	top
hap	scrap	trap
heap	scrape	trip
hip	scrip	troop
hoop	seep	type
hop	shape	up
hope	sheep	weep
Hope	ship	whip
jeep	shop	whoop
jump	sip	wipe
keep	skip	wrap
Kip	Skip	yap
lap	slap	yipe
leap	sleep	zap
lip	slip	zip
loop	sloop	_____
lope	slop	_____
map	slope	_____
mop	snap	_____
mope	snip	_____
nap	snipe	_____

P /p/ Final—two syllables

Aesop	gossip	seascape
airdrop	grown-up	shipshape
asleep	gumdrop	shoeshop
backdrop	half-slip	shortstop
backstop	hard up	sign-up
backup	hedgehop	sit-up
bagpipe	hilltop	ski slope
bean soup	hookup	sport shop
bear trap	housetop	stopgap
bebop	jump rope	stovepipe
bishop	ketchup	subgroup
blow up	keyed up	swap shop
book drop	landscape	syrup
breakup	makeup	teacup
build-up	markup	tightrope
bus stop	mishap	tip-top
carhop	mousetrap	toss-up
catch-up	nightcap	township
checkup	pawn shop	toy shop
clean up	peace pipe	tulip
close-up	pet shop	turnip
cold snap	Phillip	unwrap
co-op	pickup	upkeep
cough drop	polyp	warmed-up
cowslip	pop-up	warm-up
doorstep	pork chop	warship
doorstop	post-op	whitecap
dust mop	pre-op	windpipe
eavesdrop	push-up	windup
elope	rag mop	workshop
equip	rattrap	worship
escape	recoup	wrap-up
firetrap	regroup	write-up
flagship	reship	_____
flip-flop	round trip	_____
flue pipe	roundup	_____
footstep	sand trap	_____
gallop	scallop	_____

P /p/ Final—three syllables

antelope
astroscope
baseball cap
bathing cap
battleship
beauty sleep
belly flop
buckle-up
buttercup
candy shop
cantaloupe
cassette tape
censorship
chicken coop
chimney sweep
city map
cityscape
coffee cup
develop
envelope
exhaust pipe
fellowship
fingertip
fire escape
floral shop
follow-up
Gaza Strip
gingersnap
gyroscope

handicap
horoscope
hula hoop
landing strip
laundry soap
leadership
linotype
lollipop
malaprop
marksmanship
masking tape
membership
microscope
misanthrope
mountaintop
onion dip
organ pipe
otoscope
overlap
overripe
oversleep
overstep
ownership
paper clip
partnership
penmanship
periscope
photo shop
pleasure trip

pogonip
prototype
rattletrap
runner-up
scholarship
seamanship
semi-ripe
sewer pipe
shoulder strap
soda pop
spectroscope
sponsorship
sportsmanship
stethoscope
stewardship
Sunset Strip
telescope
teletype
thunderclap
turboprop
U.S. map
water drop
weather strip
workmanship

_____
_____
_____
_____
_____

P /p/ Final—four syllables

adhesive tape
audiotape
chocolate chip
cinemascope
citizenship
companionship
Cumberland Gap

curio shop
electroscope
electrotype
flippity-flop
guardianship
heliotrope
jet landing strip

kaleidoscope
laryngoscope
Little Bo Peep
measuring cup
measuring tape
novelty shop
potato chip

potato crop	tomato soup	_____
stereotype	videotape	_____

PER /pɚ/ Medial—three syllables

aspirin	paperclip	Superman
Copper Age	papering	supersede
copperhead	peppermint	supervise
drapery	properly	temperate
emperor	property	uppermost
opera	slippery	vaporize
paperback	superman	_____

PER /pɚ/ Medial—four syllables

copper-plated	operator	temperative
experiment	superego	vaporizer
intemperate	superficial	_____

PER /pɚ/ Final—two syllables

blooper	keeper	taper
chipper	paper	trooper
chopper	pepper	upper
clipper	proper	vapor
copper	riper	viper
creeper	roper	whisper
dipper	scraper	whopper
flapper	shipper	wiper
flipper	skipper	wrapper
gripper	slipper	zipper
helper	stopper	_____
hopper	stupor	_____
jasper	super	_____
Jasper	supper	_____

PER /pɚ/ Final—three syllables

crepe paper	juniper	state trooper
diaper	newspaper	timekeeper
grasshopper	sandpaper	wallpaper
improper	sandpiper	_____
innkeeper	skyscraper	_____

PER /pɚ/ Final—four syllables

candy striper	tissue paper	_____
litmus paper	wrapping paper	_____
paratrooper	writing paper	_____

PL /pl/ Initial—one syllable

place	played	plowed
placed	plea	pluck
plaid	plead	plug
plain	please	plugged
plaint	pleased	plum
plait	pleat	plumb
plan	pledge	plume
plane	pledged	plumed
planed	plied	plump
plank	plight	plunge
planned	plink	plunged
plant	plinth	plunk
plants	plod	plus
plaque	plop	plush
plat	plopped	ply
plate	plot	_____
play	plow	_____

PL /pl/ Initial—two syllables

placard	planet	plated
place kick	plangent	plateful
place mat	planing	plate glass
place name	planking	platelet
placer	plankton	plate mark
placid	planner	plater
placing	planning	platform
placket	plantar	plating
plaintiff	planter	Plato
plaintive	plant food	platoon
Plainview	plasma	platter
Plainville	plaster	playback
planar	plastic	player
planer	plateau	playful

playground
playhouse
playmate
playoff
playpen
playroom
playsuit
playthings
playtime
playwear
playwright
plaza
pleaded
pleading
pleasant
pleasing
pleasure

pledger
plenty
pleural
plexus
pliant
pliers
plodded
plodder
plodding
plopping
plotted
plotter
plotting
plover
plower
plowshare
plugging

plug in
plumage
plumber
plumbing
plummet
plumpness
plunder
plunger
plunging
plural
plushy
plus sign
Pluto
plying
Plymouth
plywood

_____

PL /pl/ Initial—three syllables

placebo
place hitter
place holder
place-kicker
placement test
placer gold
Placerville
plagiarize
plainclothesman
plainspoken
plaintively
planetoid
plantable

plantation
plasterboard
platinous
platinum
platonic
platypus
plausible
playacting
play-by-play
playfully
playing card
playing field
pleasantry

plenteous
plentiful
pleurisy
plexiglass
pliable
pliancy
plowable
plundering
pluralize
plutocrat
Plutonic
Plymouth Rock

_____

PL /pl/ Initial—four syllables

plagiarism
planarian
planetary
planimeter
plasticity

platform rocker
Pleasant Island
pleasurable
plenipotent
plentifully

pleximeter
plotting paper
plurality
plutonium

_____

PL /pl/ Initial—five syllables

planetarium	pledge of allegiance	_____
player piano	plutonically	_____

PL /pl/ Medial—two syllables

airplane	display	replant
air plant	displease	replay
air plot	eggplant	replete
amply	employ	reply
aplite	explain	sapling
aplomb	explode	seaplane
applaud	exploit	simply
applause	explore	ski plane
applied	fireplace	sleepless
apply	float plane	someplace
birthplace	gangplank	stapler
complain	grappling	stoplight
complaint	home plate	supplant
complete	hopeless	supply
complex	houseplant	surplus
comply	ice plant	top line
deplane	imply	upline
deplete	jet plane	upload
deplore	perplex	_____
deploy	pipeline	_____
deplume	poplar	_____
displace	replace	_____

PL /pl/ Medial—three syllables

accomplish	complexion	employment
amplify	complicate	explicit
anyplace	compliment	explosion
appliance	contemplate	explosive
applicant	diploma	heating plant
applique´	diplomat	implement
applying	discipline	incomplete
complacent	double play	multiply
complement	duplicate	octuplet
completion	employee	quintuplet

replenish
resplendent
simplify

supplement
supplicant
triplicate

unemployed
unpleasant
water plant

PL /pl/ Medial—four syllables

amplifier
application
cassette player

complexity
explanation
exploration

multiplier
simplicity
unemployment

PL /pl/ Final—two syllables

ample
apple
chapel
couple
cripple
crumple
dimple
gospel
grapple

maple
opal
Opal
people
pimple
purple
ripple
rumple
sample

scalpel
scruple
simple
staple
steeple
temple
topple
triple
Whipple

PL /pl/ Final—three syllables

deep purple
disciple
example
free sample

multiple
pineapple
principal
principle

quadruple
quintuple
rose apple

_____

PL /pl/ Final—four syllables

acne pimple
bottle nipple
candied apple
cornmeal scrapple
Episcopal

keep it simple
lovely dimple
mini-sample
more than ample
municipal

participle
rotten apple
spotted dapple
vice-principal

_____

LP /lp/ Medial—two syllables

alpine
gulping
helper
helpful
helping

helpless
kelp crab
kelpfish
palpate
pulpit

scalpel
sculptor
sculpture
yelping

_____

LP /lp/ Final—one syllable

alp	palp	yelp
gulp	pulp	_____
help	scalp	_____
kelp	whelp	_____

MP /mp/ Medial—two syllables

bumper	dumpy	Pompey
bumpy	empire	pompous
campaign	grumpy	primping
camper	hamper	pumping
campground	impact	pumpkin
camping	impair	rampart
camp-out	impaired	rumpling
campus	impale	sampan
clamping	impaled	sampler
clumpy	impart	scamper
compact	impasse	scrimping
compare	impeach	shrimping
compared	impeached	skimpy
compass	impede	slumping
compel	impel	stamping
compete	impelled	stumping
complain	impend	tamper
complaint	impose	tampered
complete	jump ball	temper
complex	jumper	tempered
compound	jumping	tempest
compute	jump rope	template
cramping	jump seat	temple
crimpy	jump suit	tempted
crumple	jumpy	thumping
crumply	limpet	tramping
dampen	limpid	trumpet
dampcncd	limping	trumping
dumping	lumpy	vampire
dumpling	pamper	whimper
dumpster	pampered	_____
dump truck	pampers	_____

MP /mp/ Medial—three syllables

accomplice	computer	jumping jack
accomplish	consumption	No Dumping
amplify	contemplate	Olympics
assumption	decompose	pompadour
attempted	decomposed	preempted
bumper guard	distemper	presumption
bumper jack	empower	pumpkin pie
camporee	encompass	redemption
compactor	example	resumption
companion	exempted	tamper-proof
company	exemption	temperance
compassion	high jumper	temperate
competent	impacted	temptation
component	imported	_____
composite	imposter	_____
composure	jumping bean	_____

MP /mp/ Medial—four syllables

companionship	imperious	temperature
compensation	intemperate	temporary
composition	pomposity	unimportant
contemplation	pumpernickel	_____
Humpty Dumpty	reimposing	_____
impalpable	temperament	_____

MP /mp/ Medial—five syllables

contemporary	temperamental	_____
impenetrable	temporization	_____
imperishable	_____	_____

MP /mp/ Final—one syllable

amp	clump	hump
blimp	cramp	imp
bump	crimp	jump
camp	damp	lamp
champ	dump	limp
chump	grump	lump
clamp	hemp	plump

primp	shrimp	thump
pump	skimp	tramp
ramp	slump	trump
romp	stamp	_____
rump	stomp	_____
scamp	stump	_____

MP /mp/ Final—two syllables

boot camp	girls' camp	revamp
boys' camp	high jump	ski jump
broad jump	leg cramp	sun lamp
encamp	long jump	tire pump
floor lamp	off ramp	_____
gas pump	on ramp	_____

MP /mp/ Final—three syllables

Boy Scout camp	rubber stamp	table lamp
city dump	safety lamp	wrestling camp
garbage dump	stomach cramp	_____
Girl Scout camp	sugar lump	_____
postage stamp	summer camp	_____

MPS /mps/ Final—one syllable

amps	glimpse	romps
blimps	imps	shrimps
bumps	jumps	skimps
champs	lamps	slumps
chumps	limps	stamps
clamps	lumps	stumps
clumps	mumps	thumps
cramps	primps	tramps
crimps	pumps	trumps
dumps	ramps	_____

PR /pr/ Initial—one syllable

Prague	pranced	prawn
praise	prank	prawns
praised	prate	pray
prance	Pratt	prayed

preach	prince	prop
preached	print	propped
preen	prize	props
press	prized	prose
pressed	pro	proud
prey	probe	prove
price	probed	prow
priced	prod	prowl
pride	prof	prude
pried	prom	prune
pries	prompt	pruned
priest	prone	pry
prime	prong	_____
primed	proof	_____
primp	proofed	_____

PR /pr/ Initial—two syllables

practice	premise	presume
prairie	prepaid	pretend
praline	prepare	pretense
pratique	prepared	pretest
prattle	prepay	pretext
prattler	preschool	pretty
preacher	prescribe	pretzel
precede	presence	prevail
precept	present	prevent
precinct	presents	preview
precious	preserve	priceless
precise	preshrunk	prickle
preclude	preside	prickly
predict	press club	priesthood
preempt	presser	primal
preface	pressing	primate
prefect	pressman	primer
prefer	pressroom	priming
prefix	pressure	primrose
prejudge	presswork	princess
prelude	prestige	printed
premier	presto	printer

printing	profuse	prosper
printout	program	protect
prior	progress	protein
prism	project	protest
prison	prolong	proton
pristine	promise	protract
private	promote	protrude
probate	prompted	proverb
problem	prompter	provide
proceed	promptly	province
proceeds	pronghorn	provoke
process	pronoun	prowess
proclaim	pronounce	proxy
proctor	pronounced	prudence
Proctor	proofread	Prudence
procure	propel	prudent
produce	proper	prudish
product	prophct	pruning
profess	propose	_____
profile	propound	_____
profit	proscribe	_____
profound	prospect	_____

PR /pr/ Initial—three syllables

practical	predestine	prescription
prairie dog	predicate	presently
preamble	prediction	preserver
prearrange	predispose	president
precaution	preemption	pressurize
precedence	preexist	prestigious
precedent	preference	presumption
preceding	preferment	pretentious
precipice	prefigure	prevalence
precision	prejudice	prevention
precocious	prematurc	previous
preconceive	premiership	prickly pear
preconcert	premium	primary
precursor	prenatal	primitive
predator	preordain	principal

principle
printing press
prisoner
privacy
privately
privation
privilege
probable
probably
probation
proboscis
procedure
procession
processor
prodigal
prodigious
prodigy
producer
production
productive
profession
professor
proficient
profitee
profusion
progeny

prognosis
prognostic
progressive
prohibit
projected
projectile
projector
prolific
promenade
prominent
promising
promptitude
promulgate
pronouncement
propagate
propeller
proper name
property
prophecy
prophesy
prophetess
prophetic
propolis
proponent
proportion
proposal

propulsion
prosaic
prosecute
prosody
prospective
prosperous
protection
protective
protege
Protestant
protocol
protoplast
prototype
protractor
protrusion
provender
provided
providence
providing
provincial
provision
provoking
prudential
_____
_____
_____

PR /pr/ Initial—four syllables

practicable
practical joke
practically
practical nurse
practitioner
prairie chicken
praying mantis
precarious
precedency
precipitant
precipitate

precipitous
preconception
predatory
predecessor
predetermine
predicament
predominance
predominant
preeminent
preexistence
preexistent

prefabricate
preferable
preferential
prefiguring
preformation
prefulfillment
pregalvanize
prehardener
preharmony
prehistoric
preholiday

preignition
preimposing
preinclining
preindicate
preinstruction
prejudicial
prematurely
premedical
premeditate
premonition
preoccupied
preparation
preponderance
preponderate
preposition
preposterous
prerequisite
prerogative
presentable
presentation
preservation

preservative
presidency
presidential
presumable
presumptuous
prevaricate
prima donna
primarily
prime minister
principally
priority
processional
proclamation
procrastinate
procreation
productively
professional
profitable
prohibition
prohibitive
proletary

proliferate
prolongation
promissory
promontory
propaganda
propensity
proportional
proposition
proprietor
proscenium
prosecution
prosperity
protuberance
protuberant
proverbial
provisional
provocation
provocative
proximity

_____

_____

PR /pr/ Initial—five syllables

precipitation
predestination
prehistorical
preliminary
premeditation

preparatory
prepositional
Presbyterian
principality
probability

productivity
prognostication
promissory note
pronunciation

_____

PR /pr/ Medial—two syllables

appraise
appraised
apprize
approach
approved
April
apron
blueprint
bombproof

Capri
compress
culprit
cypress
Cypress
depress
depressed
deprive
deprived

dustproof
express
fireproof
footprint
impress
imprint
improve
oppress
rainproof

repress	shipwreck	surprise
reprieve	shipwrecked	surprised
reprint	soundproof	upright
reprise	sun proof	_____
reproach	suppress	_____
reprove	supreme	_____

PR /pr/ Medial—three syllables

appraisal	expression	paprika
apprehend	expressive	represent
approval	expressway	repression
apricot	fingerprint	reprimand
April Fool	high pressure	reprinted
bulletproof	impression	reprisal
by-product	impressive	reprobate
capricious	imprison	reproduce
Capricorn	impromptu	soprano
comprehend	improper	tamper-proof
deprecate	improvement	unprepared
depressant	improvise	waterproof
depression	interpret	weatherproof
depressive	jet propelled	_____
disapprove	low pressure	_____
enterprise	mispronounce	_____

PR /pr/ Medial—four syllables

appreciate	depreciate	reciprocate
apprehension	disapproval	reproduction
apprenticeship	impregnable	supremacy
approbation	impressionist	vice-president
appropriate	life preserver	word processor
approximate	proprietor	_____
April Fools' Day	reciprocal	_____

PR /pr/ Medial—five syllables

appreciation	impracticable	inappropriate
apprehensible	impressionable	interpretation
appropriation	impropriety	irrepressible
depreciation	improvisation	irreproachable

reprehensible	uncompromising	_____
representative	unprecedented	_____

RP /rp/ Medial—two syllables

airplane	perplex	tarpon
airport	porpoise	terpene
burping	purple	torpid
carpet	purpose	torpor
chirping	serpent	turpeth
fireplace	sharpen	war paint
hairpin	sharper	warpath
harping	surpass	warping
harpist	surplus	_____
harpoon	tarpan	_____

RP /rp/ Medial—three syllables

absorption	Scorpio	surplus store
carpenter	scorpion	tarpaulin
centerpiece	sharpener	torpedo
corporal	sharpening	turpentine
harpsichord	sharpshooter	unsharpened
power pack	sharpsighted	unsurpassed
purposely	sharpwitted	_____

RP /rp/ Medial—four syllables

caterpillar	perpetual	torpedo boat
incorporate	surpassable	_____

RP /rp/ Final—one syllable

burp	sharp	Thorpe
carp	slurp	twirp
chirp	tarp	warp
harp	thorp	_____

PS /ps/ Medial—two syllables

capsize	dip stick	hopscotch
capsule	dropsy	keepsake
chopsticks	gypsum	knapsack
deep South	gypsy	lapsing

lipstick	stop sign	typeset
Mopsy	tipsy	upset
pipsqueak	topsail	upstairs
slapstick	topside	upstart
soapsuds	topsoil	upswing
step stool	Topsy	

PS /ps/ Medial—three syllables

asepsis	relapsing	upsetting
autopsy	synopsis	upstanding
biopsy	tipsiness	upsurging
chop suey	tipsy cake	upsweeping
collapsing	top secret	upswelling
elapsing	top sergeant	upswinging
ellipsis	typesetter	
Phillipsburg	typesetting	

PS /ps/ Medial—four syllables

epilepsy	upside-down cake	
topsy-turvy	upsy-daisy	
upsettable		

PS /ps/ Final—one syllable

alps	grapes	mops
Alps	gripes	naps
caps	grips	nips
chaps	gropes	peeps
chips	groups	pipes
chops	hopes	pups
copes	hops	raps
crops	jeeps	reaps
cups	jumps	rips
dips	keeps	ropes
drapes	laps	saps
drips	lapse	scalps
drops	leaps	scoops
flaps	lips	scopes
flips	loops	scrapes
flops	maps	scraps

seeps	snaps	traps
ships	snipes	trips
shops	snips	troops
sips	steps	weeps
skips	straps	whips
slaps	stripes	wipes
sleeps	swaps	wraps
slips	tapes	zips
sloops	taps	_____
slopes	tips	_____
slumps	tops	_____

PS /ps/ Final—two syllables

biceps	gossips	sit-ups
collapse	grown-ups	triceps
eclipse	push-ups	tulips
elapse	raindrops	turnips
cllipsc	rclapsc	unwraps
escapes	round trips	wallops
forceps	roundups	_____
gallops	scallops	_____

PS /ps/ Final—three syllables

antelopes	_____	_____
cantaloupes	_____	_____
fire escapes	_____	_____

SP /sp/ Initial—one syllable

spa	spat	spiced
space	spawn	spike
spade	speak	spill
spake	spear	spilled
span	speck	spilt
spanned	speech	spin
spar	spcll	spinc
spare	spelled	spire
spared	spend	spit
sparred	spent	spite
sparse	spice	spitz

spoil	spoon	spunk
spoiled	spoor	spur
spoke	sport	spurge
spokes	sports	spurred
sponge	spot	spurs
sponged	spouse	spurt
spoof	spout	spy
spook	spud	_____
spool	spun	_____

SP /sp/ Initial—two syllables

space bar	Spartan	spendthrift
spacecraft	spasm	sperm whale
space flight	spastic	spicy
spaceman	spatial	spider
spaceport	spatter	spiky
spaceship	spawning	spillage
space suit	speaker	spilling
spacial	speakers	spillway
spacing	speaking	spinach
spacious	spearfish	spinal
spadeful	spearhead	spindle
spadework	spearmint	spindling
spancel	special	spineless
spangle	specie	spinet
Spaniard	specious	spinner
spaniel	speckle	spinning
Spanish	spectre	spin out
spanner	spectrum	spinster
spareribs	speechless	spiral
sparing	speedboat	spirit
spark coil	speedster	spitball
sparker	speedtrap	spiteful
sparkle	speedway	spitfire
sparkler	speedy	spittoon
sparkling	speed zone	spoilage
spark plug	spellbound	spoiling
sparring	speller	spoken
sparrow	spelling	spokesman

sponger	sport shirt	spunky
spongy	sportsman	Sputnik
sponsor	sportswear	sputter
spooky	sporty	spy glass
spoon bread	spot check	spying
spoonful	spotlight	_____
sportful	spotted	_____
sporting	spotter	_____
sports car	spotty	_____
sportscast	spun glass	_____

SP /sp/ Initial—three syllables

space heater	specify	spiritless
space station	specimen	sponsoring
space writer	spectacle	sponsorship
spaghetti	spectator	spookier
Spanish food	spectrogram	sporadic
Spanish rice	spectrograph	sporting goods
sparable	spectroscope	sportscaster
sparrow hawk	speculate	sportsmanship
spasmodic	speedily	sportswriter
spatula	speed limit	spunkier
speakable	spelling bee	_____
spear fishing	spider web	_____
specialist	spinal cord	_____
specialize	spinal nerve	_____
specialty	spinning wheel	_____
specific	spirited	_____

SP /sp/ Initial—four syllables

spectacular	speedometer	spiritual
spectrometer	spider monkey	spirometer
speech therapist	spinal column	spontaneous
speech therapy	spiral notebook	_____

SP /sp/ Initial—five syllables

Special Olympics	specification	_____
specialization	_____	_____
specifically	_____	_____

SP /sp/ Medial—two syllables

aspen	dispute	respect
Aspen	gospel	respire
Casper	grasping	respite
crispy	high-speed	respond
despair	inspect	response
despise	inspire	Shakespeare
despised	Jasper	teaspoon
despite	larkspur	turnspit
despoil	misplace	waspish
despoiled	misspell	waspy
dispatch	passport	whisper
dispatched	peace pipe	_____
dispel	prospect	_____
dispose	prosper	_____

SP /sp/ Medial—three syllables

aerospace	loudspeaker	retrospect
aspirin	mispronounce	suspenders
baby spoon	outer space	suspension
desperate	outspoken	suspicion
disparate	prospective	suspicious
disposal	prospector	tablespoon
hospital	prosperous	transparent
inspection	respectful	whispering
Jasper Park	respective	_____

SP /sp/ Medial—four syllables

asparagus	disproportion	perspiration
conspiracy	disputable	prosperity
correspondence	especially	respectable
despairingly	espionage	respectively
desperado	high-spirited	respiration
desperation	hospitable	respirator
despicable	hospitalize	responsible
dispensary	inspiration	tablespoonful
dispensation	litmus paper	unspeakable
disposable	low-spirited	_____
disposition	perspicacious	_____

SP /sp/ Medial—five syllables
hospitality   respiratory
indisputable
irresponsibly

SP /sp/ Medial—six syllables
inspirationally
respectability
responsibility

SP /sp/ Final—one syllable
clasp   grasp   wasp
crisp   lisp   wisp
gasp   rasp

SPL /spl/ Initial—one syllable
splash   splice   splits
splat   spliced   splotch
splay   splint   splurge
spleen   split

SPL /spl/ Initial—two syllables
splashdown   splendor   split shift
splash guard   splicer   splitting
splatter   splicing   splutter
splendid   splinter

SPL /spl/ Initial—three syllables
splintery   split level
split entrance   split second
split entry

SPR /spr/ Initial—one syllable
sprain   sprig   sprung
sprang   spring   spry
sprawl   sprint
spray   sprite
spread   sprout
spree   spruce

SPR /spr/ Initial—two syllables

spraddle	springboard	sprinkler
sprayer	Springfield	sprinkling
spray gun	springing	sprocket
spreader	springtime	_____
spreadsheet	sprinkle	_____

SPR /spr/ Medial—two syllables

bedspread	hot springs	Rock Springs
hair spray	Hot Springs	_____
handspring	offspring	_____

SPR /spr/ Medial—three syllables

Brussels sprouts	shopping spree	Union Springs
ocean spray	Silver Spring	_____

PT /pt/ Final—one syllable

chapped	napped	slipped
chipped	nipped	snapped
chopped	peeped	snipped
clapped	piped	stepped
clipped	plopped	stopped
crept	popped	strapped
dipped	propped	swapped
dripped	rapped	swooped
dropped	reaped	taped
flapped	ripped	tapped
flipped	roped	tipped
flopped	scooped	topped
griped	scoped	trapped
gripped	scraped	tripped
heaped	scrapped	typed
hoped	script	wept
hopped	seeped	wiped
kept	shipped	wrapped
lapped	shopped	yipped
leaped	sipped	zapped
mapped	skipped	zipped
mopped	slept	_____

PT /pt/ Final—two syllables

abrupt	corrupt	gossiped
accept	disrupt	postscript
adapt	Egypt	precept
adept	erupt	subscript
adopt	escaped	unwrapped
bankrupt	except	_____
concept	galloped	_____

PT /pt/ Final—three syllables

intercept	_____	_____
non-adept	_____	_____

PY /pj/ Medial—two syllables

leap year	_____	_____
shipyard	_____	_____

PY /pj/ Medial—three syllables

deputize	populace	stipulate
deputy	popular	_____
impudence	populate	_____
impudent	populous	_____

PY /pj/ Medial—four syllables

manipulate	popular vote	_____
popularize	population	_____
popularly	stipulation	_____
popular song	unpopular	_____

R

Pronounced: /r/
Spelled: r, rr, rh

R /r/ Initial—one syllable

race	rave	ride
rack	raw	ridge
Rae	ray	ridged
raft	Ray	rig
rag	reach	rigged
rage	read	right
raid	real	rights
rail	realm	rim
rain	ream	rimmed
raise	reap	rims
rake	red	rind
ram	reed	ring
rammed	Reed	rings
ramp	reeds	rink
Rams	reef	rinse
ran	reel	rip
ranch	reels	ripe
rang	reign	ripped
range	rein	rise
ranged	rent	risk
rank	rest	rite
rant	Rhine	road
rap	rhyme	roam
rapped	rib	roast
rash	ribbed	robe
rasp	rice	robed
rat	rich	rock
rate	Rich	Rock
rates	Rick	rocked
rats	rid	rocks

rod	rough	Ruth
Rod	round	rye
rode	rouse	wrack
roe	rout	wraith
rogue	route	wrap
role	rove	wrapped
Rolf	row	wrath
roll	rowed	wreath
rolls	Roy	wreck
Rome	rub	wren
Ron	rubbed	wrench
roof	rude	wrest
roofed	Rude	wretch
rook	rue	wring
room	ruff	wrist
rooms	rug	writ
roost	rule	write
root	ruled	writhe
roots	rules	wrong
Roots	rump	wrote
rope	run	wrought
roped	rung	wrung
rose	runt	wry
Rose	rush	_____
Ross	rushed	_____
rot	rust	_____
rote	rut	_____

R /r/ Initial—two syllables

rabbi	raffle	rainfall
rabbit	rafting	rainy
rabid	ragged	raisin
rabies	ragtime	Raleigh
raccoon	ragweed	rally
Rachel	railing	ramble
racial	railway	rambling
racing	raiment	rampage
racket	rainbow	rampant
radish	raincoat	rancid

Randolph	recant	relayed
random	recede	release
Randy	receipt	released
ranging	receive	relic
ransack	recent	relief
ransom	recess	relieve
rapid	recite	relieved
rapture	reckless	relish
rascal	reckon	rely
ratchet	reclaim	remains
rating	recline	remind
ratio	recoil	remnant
ration	recount	remote
rattan	redeem	remove
rattle	red hot	renew
ravage	Redlands	repaid
ravel	Red Sea	repay
raven	Redskins	repeal
ravine	reduce	repeat
raving	redwing	repel
rawhide	redwood	replace
Rawlings	refill	reply
Raymond	refine	reptile
rayon	refined	request
react	reflect	rescue
reading	refuge	rescued
ready	refund	resent
Reagan	refuse	reset
reason	regain	resign
Reba	regime	resist
rebate	region	resolve
rebel	reject	resort
rebirth	rejoice	resound
reborn	rejoiced	respect
rebound	relapse	restless
rebuild	relate	result
rebuke	relax	retail
rebut	relaxed	retain
recall	relay	retained

Reuben	Robbin	Roslyn
reveal	robin	rosy
revenge	robot	rotate
review	robust	rotten
revise	Rochelle	rotund
revive	rocket	roughage
revived	rockfish	roughen
revoke	Rockies	rounded
revolt	rocking	roundhouse
Rhea	rock salt	rounding
rhinestone	Rockville	roundup
Rhoda	Rockwell	routine
Rhonda	rocky	rowboat
rhythmic	Rocky	rowdy
ribbon	rodent	Roxanne
riches	Rodney	royal
Richie	Roland	rubbish
ricksha	roll call	rubble
Ricky	rollick	ruby
ridden	rolling	Ruby
riddle	roll-out	ruddy
rigging	Roman	Rudolph
righteous	romance	Rudy
right-hand	rompers	ruffle
rigid	Ronald	ruffled
ringlet	roofing	Rugby
ripen	rookie	rugged
Ripley	roommate	ruin
ripping	roomy	ruling
ripple	rootbeer	rumba
ripsaw	rootstock	rummage
riptide	roping	rummy
risking	Rosa	run-down
Rita	rosebud	running
rival	rosebush	runoff
rivet	Roseland	runway
roadside	Rosette	rupee
roadway	rosewood	Russell
roasting	rosin	Russia

Russian	wrapping	wrist watch
rustic	wrap-up	write-off
rusty	wrathful	writeup
Rusty	wreckage	writing
Ruth Ann	wrestle	written
ruthful	wrestling	wrongful
Ruthie	wretched	_____
ruthless	wriggle	_____
wrangle	wrinkle	_____
wrangling	wrinkly	_____

R /r/ Initial—three syllables

racquetball	reassume	redundance
radial	Rebecca	reelect
radiance	rebellion	reflection
radiant	rebellious	refugee
radiate	receiving	Regency
radical	reception	regiment
radio	receptive	regulate
radium	recession	related
radius	recital	relation
ramify	reckoning	relative
ramshackle	recognize	relatives
ratify	recollect	relaying
rational	recombine	releasing
rattlesnake	recommend	relevant
raveling	recommit	relief map
ravenous	recompense	religion
reaction	reconcile	religious
readjust	rectangle	reluctant
ready-made	rectify	remaining
reagent	rectitude	remedy
realign	recumbent	removal
realist	recurrence	rendezvous
realize	recurrent	republic
really	recycle	resemblance
rearrange	redeeming	resemble
reascend	redemption	resentment
reasoning	reduction	residence

resident
resistance
resonate
respectful
respective
retina
reunion
reunite
reveille
revenue
rheumatic
Rhode Island
ricochet
ridicule
right angle

right handed
ritual
road atlas
Robin Hood
rodeo
rolling pin
romantic
Roosevelt
rotation
Rowena
Roxana
royalty
rummage sale
runabout
runaway

runaways
running mate
wrestling camp
wrestling coach
wrestling match
wrestling shoes
wrestling team
wretchedness
wrongdoing
wrongfully
_____
_____
_____
_____
_____

R /r/ Initial—four syllables

radiancy
rapidity
reactivate
reality
reasonable
reassemble
receivable
receptacle
recessional
recipient
recitation
reclamation
recognition
recognizance

recollection
reconnaissance
reconstitute
regulation
relationship
repetition
republican
reputation
residential
resolution
respectable
respectively
revolution
rhesus monkey

Rhodesia
ridiculous
riding safety
Rocky Mountains
Rosh Hoshanah
ruination
Rumanian
rutabaga
_____
_____
_____
_____
_____
_____

R /r/ Initial—five syllables

radioactive
rationality
reactionary
reawakening
recapitulate
reciprocity

recommendation
reconstituted
respiratory
roasting marshmallows
Roman Catholic
Roman numeral

rudimentary
_____
_____
_____
_____

R /r/ Initial—six syllables
reconciliation _____ _____
reconsideration _____ _____
Republican Party _____ _____

R /r/ Medial—two syllables

Aaron	carob	during
airy	Carol	earring
arid	carols	eerie
Aries	carriage	era
arise	Carrie	erase
arose	carried	Eric
around	carrot	Erie
arouse	carry	Erin
arrange	Cary	erode
arranged	charades	errand
arrest	cheery	Europe
arrive	Cheri	every
arrived	cherish	fairy
arrow	cherry	Far East
baron	cherub	Farrah
barracks	Cheryl	fearing
barrage	chorus	ferry
barrel	clearing	firing
barren	Cora	flooring
beret	coral	Flora
berry	Corey	Florence
Berry	corral	florist
Beryl	correct	flurry
boric	corrode	foreign
boring	corrupt	forest
borough	courage	For Rent
borrow	currant	forum
buried	current	Four-H
burro	Cyril	furring
burrow	dairy	furrow
bury	daring	furry
Cairo	direct	fury
caring	Doreen	garage

Gary	maroon	sari -
Gerald	marriage	scurry
Geri -	married	serene -
giraffe	marrow	series
glory	marry	sharing
Harold	Mary	Sharon -
Harris	merit	Sherese -
harrow -	merry	sheriff
Harry	mirage	Sherrill
hayrack	moral	Sherry
hayride	morale	siren
hearing	Morris	sorrow
herald -	morrow -	sorry
hero	mural	spareribs
heron -	narrate	sparrow
herring	narrow	spearing
high rise	narrows -	spiral
hiring	ncaring	spirit
hurrah	nourish	squirrel
hurried	oral	starry
hurry	orange	steering
Ireland -	parade	stirrup
iris	parent	storage
Iris -	Paris	storeroom
Irish	parish	stories
Jerry	parole	story
joy ride	parrot	surrey -
jury	payroll	surround
Karen	peril	syringe
key ring	perish	syrup
Larry	~~Perry~~	tarring -
Laura	Peru	Taurus
laurel -	Pharaoh	tearing
Lawrence -	pirate	tea room
Lorin -	plural	terrace
Lorraine	porridge	Terri
Lory -	quarrel	Terry -
lyric	quarry	thorax
marine	Sarah	thorough

tiring
Torah
touring
tourist
tureen
turret
varied
vary

Vera
very
warrant
Warren
wary
weary
wiring
wiry

worried
worry
zero
Zorro

_____
_____
_____
_____

R /r/ Medial—three syllables

accurate
aerial
aerobics
aerospace
Anchorage
apparel
apparent
area
arena
aroma
arresting
arrival
arrowhead
arroyo
authorize
ball bearing
baritone
barricade
battery
bayberry
blackberry
blueberry
boundary
burial
calorie
camera
camporee
canary
caramel

caravan
caribou
Caroline
carry-all
casserole
celery
century
ceramics
cereal
chariot
Cherokee
cherry pie
Cherryvale
Cherryville
chokeberry
clarinet
clarity
coloring
copyright
Coral Sea
coral snake
correction
correspond
courageous
currency
daredevil
dewberry
diary
direction

director
dogberry
Dorothy
durable
duration
embarrass
emerald
encourage
everyday
everyone
everything
Fahrenheit
fairyland
fairytale
ferocious
Ferris wheel
fire engine
fire escape
fishing rod
Florida
furious
garrison
Gloria
glorify
glorious
glossary
godparent
gooseberry
gorilla

guarantee
gyroscope
hackberry
Harriet
Harrison
hearing aid
heritage
heroic
heroine
hickory
Honduras
horizon
horrible
horrify
hurricane
immoral
incorrect
indirect
inherent
inherit
inquiry
insurance
interrupt
Iron Age
irrigate
irritate
Israel
Israeli
Johnny Reb
juneberry
kangaroo
kerosene
Korea
lariat
luxury
lyrical
marigold
Marilyn
marimba

marina
Marine Corps
mariner
Marion
maritime
Maryland
masquerade
memorize
Missouri
mulberry
Nairobi
narration
narrative
nourishment
occurrence
occurring
operate
orangeade
Oregon
orient
origin
oriole
papyrus
parachute
parading
paradise
paraffin
parakeet
parallel
paralyze
parasite
parasol
parroting
period
periscope
pokeberry
pony ride
purify
Puritan

purity
pyramid
quandary
salary
saturate
señora
separate
serenade
serial
serious
Sheraton
skyrocket
snow flurry
sorrowful
spherical
storybook
summarize
summary
Syria
tambourine
teaberry
terrible
terrific
terrify
theorem
theorist
theorize
theory
therapist
Theresa
thoracic
thoroughfare
tomorrow
torrential
touring car
tyranic
tyrannize
tyranny
untiring

unwary	veranda	wearisome
unwearied	verify	wheelbarrow
Uranus	verily	worrisome
Uriah	very good	Zachary
Van Buren	victory	_____
variance	waiting room	_____
variant	wearily	_____
various	weariness	_____

R /r/ Medial—four syllables

aerophoto	evaporate	notorious
Amarillo	everybody	numerical
amaryllis	geranium	operating
America	heredity	operation
American	horizontal	orangutan
Aquarius	huckleberry	oriental
area code	inaugurate	original
arithmetic	infuriate	originate
Arizona	inheritance	panorama
artificial	interruption	parachuting
aspiration	inventory	paralysis
atmospheric	irrigation	parenthesis
authority	January	parochial
baby carriage	legendary	perimeter
ballerina	loganberry	perishable
barracuda	luxurious	sanctuary
category	macaroni	secondary
ceremony	malaria	security
Colorado	maple syrup	seminary
comparison	marionette	seniority
compulsory	material	señorita
Costa Rica	memorial	separation
curriculum	meridian	single parent
declaration	meteorite	solitary
decoration	military	South Korea
desirable	minority	stationary
dictionary	missionary	stationery
encouragement	momentary	tarantula
engineering	necessary	theoretic

therapeutic
tyrannical
variable
variation

variety
veritable
vicarious
Victoria

victorious
voluntary
waffle iron

_____

R /r/ Medial—five syllables

auditorium
cafeteria
deteriorate
elementary
hieroglyphic
imaginary
inauguration
interrogative

irresistible
Memorial Day
necessarily
penitentiary
respiratory
rudimentary
Sagittarius
theoretical

unwarrantable
variegated
vegetarian
verification
vocabulary
voluntarily

_____

_____

R /r/ Medial—six syllables

Mediterranean
peculiarity

totalitarian
utilitarian

_____

_____

R /r/ Final—one syllable

air
are
bar
bare
bear
blare
blur
boar
bore
bur
Burr
car
care
cheer
choir
chore
clear
core
czar

dare
dear
deer
door
ear
fair
far
fare
fear
fir
fire
flair
floor
fore
four
fur
gear
glare
hair

hare
hear
heir
her
here
hire
hour
jar
lair
leer
lore
lure
mar
mare
mere
more
near
nor
oar

or	smear	swore
ore	snare	tear
our	sneer	their
pair	soar	there
par	sore	tire
pare	sour	tore
pear	spar	tour
peer	spare	veer
pier	spear	war
poor	sphere	ware
pore	spire	wear
pour	spore	where
pure	spur	whir
purr	square	wire
scar	squire	wore
scare	stair	year
score	star	your
share	stare	you're
shear	steer	_____
sheer	stir	_____
shore	sure	_____
sir	swear	_____

R /r/ Final—two syllables

acquire	bazaar	demure
adhere	before	deplore
admire	beware	desire
adore	bizarre	despair
afar	bonfire	detour
affair	bookstore	devour
afire	boxcar	downpour
ajar	briar	drugstore
appear	campfire	eclair
ashore	cashier	elsewhere
aspire	cashmere	empire
assure	compare	encore
attire	conspire	endure
aware	contour	ensure
backfire	declare	entire

esquire
expire
explore
Fillmore
flatcar
folklore
frontier
galore
guitar
half-hour
health fair
ignore
impair
implore
impure
indoor
inquire
inspire
insure
jaguar
killdeer
Lamar
larkspur
leap year

live wire
mature
memoir
mohair
monsieur
mule deer
New Year
nightmare
North Star
nowhere
obscure
occur
offshore
outdoor
outpour
outroar
outsoar
quasar
sapphire
satyr
seashore
secure
señor
Shakespeare

sincere
snack bar
software
somewhere
sonar
space bar
spitfire
squad car
stock car
stoneware
tambour
threescore
umpire
unfair
vampire
velour
veneer
welfare
_____
_____
_____
_____
_____
_____

R /r/ Final—three syllables

amateur
anywhere
atmosphere
Baltimore
billionaire
cable car
candy bar
cassimere
cavalier
caviar
chicken wire
commodore
Delaware

dinosaur
disappear
domineer
engineer
evening star
falling star
gondolier
handlebar
hemisphere
humidor
insecure
insincere
Leanor

manicure
matador
medicare
middle ear
millionaire
mountaineer
pinafore
pioneer
questionnaire
salad bar
seminar
shooting star
Singapore

solitaire
sophomore
souvenir

sycamore
Theodore
unaware

volunteer
_____
_____

R /r/ Final—four syllables

conquistador
El Salvador
U.S.S.R.

_____ _____
_____ _____
_____ _____

R /r/ Recurring—two syllables

career
carfare
clearer
dearer
error
fiercer
furor
horror
juror
mirror
nearer
racer
radar
rafter
railroad
rambler
rammer
ramrod
rancher
ranger
rapport
rater
rather
rattler
razor
reader
reamer
reaper
rector

recur
recurred
refer
reindeer
render
renter
repair
require
rerun
respire
restore
restroom
retire
rewrite
rider
rigger
ringer
riper
riser
river
roaster
robber
rocker
roller
roomer
rooster
root beer
Rory
roster

rotor
rover
Rover
rower
rubber
rudder
ruler
rumor
runner
rupture
rural
sheerer
tartar
terror
uproar
warfare
warrior
wrangler
wrapper
wrecker
wrestler
wringer
wrinkler
writer

_____
_____
_____
_____
_____

R /r/ Recurring—three syllables

admirer
adorer
armorer
barrier
carrier
caterer
conjurer
conqueror
emperor
explorer
foreigner
furrier
hereafter
laborer
loiterer
lumberer
mariner
moreover
raspberry
reactor
realtor
reappear
reassure
recapture
receiver
recorder
recover
rectory
recurring
redeemer

reducer
referee
reference
register
regular
relay race
remainder
remember
remover
repairer
repeater
replier
requirement
requirer
rescuer
resider
resister
respecter
responder
responsor
restaurant
restorer
retailer
retainer
retirement
retiring
reverence
reverent
reverie
Rhone River

ring finger
ringleader
river boat
riverside
Riverside
roadrunner
rock 'n roll
rocking chair
roller skates
rookery
rosary
Rose Marie
Rose Mary
rotary
rubber band
rubber stamp
runner-up
rural route
terrier
thereafter
typewriter
underwear
wanderer
warrior
wherever
wonderer
wraparound
wrought iron
zero hour

R /r/ Recurring—four syllables

adventurer
barometer
candy wrapper
direct current
directory
exterior

inferior
interior
irregular
merry-go-round
radiator
rear admiral

receivership
reconsider
recovery
rectangular
recuperate
refinery

respiration	Rotarian	territory
rhinoceros	secretary	toreador
roller coaster	sound barrier	ulterior
Roman Empire	superior	wrapping paper

RB /rb/ Medial—two syllables

air base	derby	orbit
airborne	disturbed	sherbet
air bus	doorbell	turban
arbor	Fairbanks	turbid
barbed wire	forbear	turbine
barbells	forbid	turbot
barber	forborne	urban
bareback	garbage	verbal
Burbank	gerbil	verbose
carbon	harbor	warble
choirboy	Herbert	warbler
Corbet	marble	yearbook
Corbin	morbid	_____
Corby	nearby	_____

RB /rb/ Medial—three syllables

Ann Arbor	harboring	urbanite
Barbara	orbital	urbanize
barbaric	overbear	verbalize
barbecue	tetherball	verbally
barber chair	turbulence	verbatim
barber shop	turbulent	_____
fur bearer	undisturbed	_____

RB /rb/ Medial—four syllables

barbecue sauce	orbicular	urbanity
carbon paper	overbearing	verbosity
carburetor	roller derby	_____

RB /rb/ Final—one syllable

barb	curb	Herb
Barb	garb	verb
blurb	herb	_____

RB /rb/ Final—two syllables

absorb	potherb	superb
adverb	proverb	_____
disturb	rhubarb	_____
exurb	suburb	_____

BR /br/ Initial—one syllable

brace	breathe	broke
braced	bred	Bronx
brad	breech	bronze
Brad	breed	bronzed
brag	breeze	brooch
bragged	Brent	brood
braid	Bret	brook
braille	brew	Brooks
brain	brewed	broom
braise	bribe	broth
braised	bribed	brought
brake	Brice	brow
brakes	brick	brown
bran	bricked	browse
branch	bride	browsed
brand	bridge	Bruce
Brant	brief	bruise
brash	briefed	bruised
brass	brig	brunch
brat	bright	brunt
brave	brim	brush
brawl	brimmed	brushed
brawn	brine	brusque
bray	bring	brute
brayed	brink	Bryce
braze	brisk	_____
breach	broach	_____
breached	broached	_____
bread	broad	_____
breadth	brogue	_____
break	broil	_____
breath	broiled	_____

BR /br/ Initial—two syllables

bracelet	breastbone	brigade
bracer	breastplate	Brigham
braces	breaststroke	brighten
bracing	breathing	brightened
bracken	breathless	brilliance
bracket	breeches	brilliant
brackish	breeder	brimful
Bradford	breeding	brimstone
Bradley	breezy	brindle
braggart	Brenda	briny
Brahma	brethren	brisket
brainless	brewer	bristle
brainstorm	Brian	bristled
brainwash	briar	Britain
brain wave	brickbat	British
brainy	brickwork	brittle
brakeage	brickyard	broadcast
brake drum	bridal	broadcloth
brake dye	bridegroom	broaden
brakeman	bridesmaid	broadened
brake shoe	bridge house	broad jump
bramble	bridge lamp	broadloom
brandish	Bridgeport	broadside
brandished	bridge sign	Broadway
brand-new	Bridget	brocade
brass band	Bridgeton	brochure
brassy	Bridge View	brogan
bravo	Bridgeville	broiler
brazen	bridgework	broken
brazier	bridging	broker
Brazil	bridle	bromide
breadfruit	bridled	bromine
breakage	bridling	bronchi
breakdown	briefcase	bronco
breaker	briefing	Bronze Age
breakfast	briefly	brooded
breakneck	briefness	brooder
breakup	brier	brooding

brooklet	brownish	Brussels
Brooklyn	brown rice	Brutus
broomstick	bruin	Bryan
brother	Bruins	Bryant
browbeat	brunette	_____
brownie	brush fire	_____
Brownie	brush work	_____

BR /br/ Initial—three syllables

bravado	brigadier	brokerage
bravery	brilliancy	bronchial
Brazil nut	bringing-up	bronchitis
breakable	British Isles	Brooklyn Bridge
breakwater	Britisher	brotherhood
breathtaking	broadcaster	brotherly
brevity	broadcasting	brouhaha
bribery	broad jumper	Brussels sprouts
bric-a-brac	broad-minded	_____
bricklayer	broccoli	_____
bridle path	broken down	_____

BR /br/ Medial—two syllables

abrade	embrace	sagebrush
Abram	eyebrow	sea breeze
abreast	fabric	shoebrush
abridge	fibrous	sweetbread
abridged	float bridge	toll bridge
abroad	Gambrel	toothbrush
abrupt	hairbrush	vibrant
cambric	Hebrew	vibrate
Cambridge	hybrid	whisk broom
clothes brush	inbred	white bread
cobra	Libra	windbreak
cornbread	membrane	zebra
daybreak	nail brush	_____
Debra	outbreak	_____
debrief	paint brush	_____
debris	purebred	_____
drawbridge	rye bread	_____

BR /br/ Medial—three syllables

Abraham	Labrador	umbrella
abrasive	library	unabridged
abridgment	London Bridge	unbroken
algebra	lubricate	underbrush
Brooklyn Bridge	Nebraska	upbringing
celebrate	paint brushes	vertebra
embracement	pawnbroker	vertebral
embracer	Rainbow Bridge	vertebrate
embrasure	rebroadcast	vibration
embroider	scatterbrain	whole wheat bread
Gabriel	sombrero	_____
gingerbread	thoroughbred	_____

BR /br/ Medial—four syllables

abbreviate	celebration	Golden Gate Bridge
abranchial	celebrity	invertebrate
abreaction	embraceable	librarian
candelabra	embracery	lubrication
celebrated	embroidery	Natural Bridge

RCH /rtʃ/ Medial—two syllables

archduke	lurching	porches
archer	marches	purchase
Archie	marching	purchased
arching	merchant	researched
archway	nurture	scorching
birch bark	nurtured	searchlight
churches	orchard	starchy
Churchill	parchment	surcharge
fortune	perchance	torchlight
kerchief	perches	virtue
lurcher	perching	_____

RCH /rtʃ/ Medial—three syllables

archbishop	archerfish	cheddar cheese
archdeacon	archery	departure
archduchess	Archibald	fortunate
archduchy	arch support	handkerchief

interchange
marching band
March of Dimes
merchandise
misfortune
neckerchief

nurturing
orange orchard
overcharge
pear orchard
purchaser
purchasing

sea urchin
starchiest
virtual
_____
_____
_____

RCH /rtʃ/ Medial—four syllables

apple orchard
archery set
birch bark basket
fortunately
fortune cookie
fortune hunter

fortuneteller
fortunetelling
grapefruit orchard
merchant marine
mortuary
purchasable

purchase order
torchlight parade
unfortunate
_____
_____
_____

RCH /rtʃ/ Final—one syllable

arch
birch
church
lurch
march

March
parch
perch
porch
scorch

search
smirch
starch
torch
_____

RCH /rtʃ/ Final—two syllables

blowtorch
cornstarch

out march
research

white birch
_____

RCHT /rtʃt/ Final—one syllable

arched
marched
parched

perched
scorched
searched

starched
_____
_____

RD /rd/ Medial—two syllables

Airedale
birdhouse
birdie
birdseed
border
burden
card tricks

cardboard
cording
cordless
cordwood
garden
guarded
guardhouse

guardrail
hair-do
hard-boiled
harden
hardhead
Harding
hardly

hardship	order	warder
hardware	ordered	wardrobe
hardwood	pardon	yardage
hardy	sturdy	yard light
herdsman	tardy	yardstick
hors d'oeuvre	third base	Zardax
hurdle	third class	_____
hurdler	Third World	_____
ordain	Verde	_____
ordeal	warden	_____

RD /rd/ Medial—three syllables

bird watcher	guardian	regarding
borderline	Hoover Dam	regardless
cardinal	Labor Day	reorder
card table	ordering	rewording
concordance	orderly	rose garden
concordant	ordinal	Saturday
corduroy	ordinance	standardize
disorder	ordinate	standard time
disordered	overdo	stewardess
gabardine	overdone	stewardship
gardener	overdue	unguarded
Garden Grove	preordain	wardenship
gardening	recorder	_____
Garden State	recording	_____

RD /rd/ Medial—four syllables

accordion	guard of honor	standardizing
coordinate	guardianship	Verde River
disorderly	inboard motor	_____
Garden City	ordinary	_____
gardenia	ordination	_____
garden party	outboard motor	_____

RD /rd/ Medial—five syllables

coordination	ordinarily	_____
guardian angel	overburdensome	_____
ordinal number	_____	_____

RD /rd/ Final—one syllable

bard	guard	spared
beard	hard	sparred
bird	heard	stared
board	herd	steered
bored	hoard	stirred
Byrd	horde	stored
card	lard	third
chard	lord	toward
chord	moored	ward
cleared	poured	weird
cord	roared	word
ford	scared	yard
Ford	scarred	_____
gird	scored	_____
gourd	shared	_____

RD /rd/ Final—two syllables

aboard	cardboard	graveyard
accord	charge card	Harvard
afford	chessboard	hazard
appeared	Clifford	Howard
award	clipboard	inboard
awkward	Coast Guard	inward
backboard	colored	keyboard
backward	Concord	kickboard
backyard	cornered	landlord
barnyard	courtyard	leeward
Bedford	coward	Leonard
Bernard	cupboard	leopard
Big Bird	custard	lifeguard
billboard	dashboard	lizard
blackbird	discard	Lombard
blackboard	eastward	mallard
blizzard	Edward	Maynard
bluebird	flashcard	measured
bombard	front yard	mouth guard
Buford	game bird	mud guard
buzzard	gizzard	mustard

nameboard	safeguard	thundered
night guard	scoreboard	timecard
numbered	scorecard	tutored
onward	seaboard	unheard
orchard	shepherd	upward
outboard	shipyard	vineyard
outward	skateboard	wallboard
Oxford	skyward	washboard
pampered	songbird	watchword
password	southward	watered
postcard	Spaniard	wayward
prepared	splattered	westward
punch card	springboard	Willard
Radford	standard	wizard
rear guard	Stanford	_____
record	starboard	_____
regard	steward	_____
reward	stockyard	_____
Rexford	surfboard	_____
Richard	switchboard	_____
rip cord	tagboard	_____
Ruford	tattered	_____

RD /rd/ Final—three syllables

aboveboard	hummingbird	smorgasboard
afterward	leotard	spinal cord
birthday card	lumberyard	substandard
bodyguard	mockingbird	thank-you card
boulevard	outnumbered	union card
checkerboard	overboard	unnumbered
Christmas card	remembered	unwatered
color guard	report card	Weatherford
cribbage board	Rocky Ford	_____
disregard	room and board	_____
diving board	rose-colored	_____
drawing board	rust-colored	_____
early bird	Rutherford	_____
harpsichord	Scotland Yard	_____
horned lizard	shuffleboard	_____

RDZ /rdz/ Final—one syllable

bards	cords	wards
beards	gourds	words
birds	guards	yards
boards	hoards	_____
cards	lords	_____
chords	towards	_____

RDZ /rdz/ Final—two syllables

backyards	leopards	skateboards
blackbirds	lifeguards	songbirds
bluebirds	lizards	Spaniards
buzzards	orchards	surfboards
clipboards	postcards	timecards
cupboards	punch cards	vineyards
discards	rear guards	wizards
flashcards	rewards	_____
kick boards	score cards	_____
leewards	shepherds	_____

DR /dr/ Initial—one syllable

drab	dredge	drop
draft	dredged	dropped
drag	drench	drought
drain	dress	drove
drake	dressed	drown
Drake	drew	drowse
dram	dried	drudge
drank	drift	drug
drape	drill	drum
draped	drilled	drummed
draw	drink	drunk
drawl	drip	drupe
drawn	dripped	dry
dread	drive	_____
dream	droll	_____
dreamed	drone	_____
dreams	drool	_____
dreamt	droop	_____

DR /dr/ Initial—two syllables

draftsman	dredger	dropping
drafty	dredging	drowsy
dragging	dresser	druggist
dragnet	dressing	drugstore
dragon	dribble	druid
dragoon	drier	drummer
drag race	driest	drumstick
drag strip	drifter	dry cell
drainage	drifting	dry clean
drainpipe	driftwood	drydock
drama	drilling	dryer
drastic	drip-dry	dry goods
drawback	drive-in	dry ice
drawbridge	driven	dry milk
drawer	driver	dryness
drawing	drive-through	_____
drawstring	driveway	_____
dreadful	drizzle	_____
dreamer	droopy	_____
dreaming	dropkick	_____
dreamland	droplet	_____
dreary	droplight	_____

DR /dr/ Initial—three syllables

Dracula	dressmaker	drudgery
draft dodger	dressing gown	drum major
dragonfly	dressing room	drummer boy
Drakensburg	dressing up	dry cleaner
dramatic	drillmaster	dry cleaning
dramatist	drinkable	dry goods store
dramatize	drive-in bank	dry measure
drapery	driver's seat	_____
drawing board	driving range	_____
drawing card	drollery	_____
drawing frame	drop kicker	_____
drawing room	dropsical	_____
dreadfully	drop table	_____
dreamily	drowsiness	_____

DR /dr/ Initial—four syllables

draconian	Dravidian	dry battery
dramatical	drawing table	_____
dramaturgy	dromedary	_____
drastically	drosophila	_____

DR /dr/ Medial—two syllables

address	fruit drink	scoundrel
adrift	gumdrop	snare drum
Andrew	headdress	snowdrift
Audrey	hindrance	soft drink
bass drum	hum-drum	sundress
bed rest	hundred	sun-dried
bedroll	hundredth	sundries
bedroom	hydrant	sundrops
Cedric	hydrate	sundry
children	hydro	tawdry
coughdrop	laundry	tendril
dandruff	lime drink	tundra
daydream	line drive	undress
dewdrop	Madrid	withdraw
drip-dry	Mildred	withdrawn
eardrop	nose drops	withdraws
eardrops	Pedro	withdrew
eardrum	quadrant	wondrous
eye drops	quadrille	Woodrow
fire drill	raindrops	_____
foundry	Sandra	_____

DR /dr/ Medial—three syllables

Adrian	hair dresser	orange drink
Andrea	hair dryer	overdrawn
apple drink	hydraulics	overdrive
bongo drums	hydrogen	quadrangle
cathedral	hydrophone	quadruped
dehydrate	hydroplane	quadruple
eye dropper	kettle drum	quadruplet
Fredericksburg	lemon drink	race driver
grapefruit drink	line drawing	San Pedro

screwdriver	withdrawal	_____
snapdragon	withdrawing	_____
truck driver	_____	_____

DR /dr/ Medial—four syllables

adrenalin	overdrawing	quadruplicate
dehydrated	Padre Island	rhododendron
driving safety	philodendron	salad dressing
hydroponics	photodrama	taxi driver
lemon-lime drink	pineapple drink	_____
melodrama	quadrennial	_____

DR /dr/ Medial—five syllables

ambulance driver	hydrophobia	quadrilateral
hydrodynamics	hypochondriac	_____

RF /rf/ Medial—two syllables

airfield	fearful	starfish
barefaced	forfeit	surface
barefoot	Garfield	surfboard
careful	orphan	surfer
cheerful	parfait	surfing
curfew	perfect	_____
earful	perform	_____
earphone	perfume	_____

RF /rf/ Medial—three syllables

butterfat	interfere	performer
carefully	interfold	performing
carefulness	labor force	tenderfoot
colorful	orphanage	underfoot
counterfeit	perfection	waterfall
fire fighter	perfectly	_____
forfeiture	perforate	_____
interface	performance	_____

RF /rf/ Medial—four syllables

butterfinger	morphology	_____
imperfection	performing arts	_____

FR /fr/ Initial—one syllable

frail	French	frond
frame	fresh	front
Fran	fret	frost
franc	fried	froth
France	friend	frown
Frank	fright	froze
fraud	frill	fruit
fray	fringe	fry
freak	frisk	phrase
Fred	Fritz	_____
free	frock	_____
freeze	frog	_____
freight	from	_____

FR /fr/ Initial—two syllables

fraction	Freeport	Frieda
fracture	freestyle	friendly
fragile	free throw	friendship
fragment	free time	frigate
fragrance	freeway	frighten
fragrant	free will	frigid
framework	freezer	frisky
framing	freighter	fritter
Frances	Fremont	frizzy
franchise	French fries	frogman
Francis	French horn	frolic
Frankfurt	French toast	frontage
Franklin	Frenchman	frontal
frantic	frenum	fronted
Frazer	frenzied	frontier
freakish	frenzy	front page
freckle	frequent	front room
Freda	freshen	frostbite
freedom	freshman	frosted
freefall	fretful	frosting
freehand	friar	frosty
free-lance	friction	frozen
free lunch	Friday	frugal

fruitcake
fruit cup

frustrate
fryer

frying

_____

FR /fr/ Initial—three syllables

fractional
fragmental
frankfurter
fraternal
Frederica
Frederick
Fredricksburg
freewheeling
frequency
fresh water

fricative
frictional
friction tape
friendliness
frivolous
frizzier
frolicking
frolicsome
frontal lobe
front runner

frost warning
frostbitten
fruitfulness
fruit salad
frustrating
frustration
frying pan
phrenetic
phrenitis

_____

FR /fr/ Initial—four syllables

fractionary
fragility
fragmentary

fraternity
fraternizing
frighteningly

phraseogram
phrenology

_____

FR /fr/ Medial—two syllables

affray
affront
afraid
A-frame
Alfred
befriend
belfry
boyfriend
breadfruit
bullfrog
carefree
cold front

confront
deep freeze
deepfry
defraud
defray
defrost
fish fry
girl friend
grapefruit
Hausfrau
Humphrey
infract

infringe
Jack Frost
Jeffrey
leapfrog
refrain
refresh
scot-free
sea front
Wilfred
Winfred

_____

_____

FR /fr/ Medial—three syllables

affricate
Africa
antifreeze
deep freezer

defrosted
defroster
defrosting
Good Friday

infraction
infrared
infrequent
infringement

refreshing	unfriendly	Winifred
refreshments	unfrozen	_____
sassafras	unfruitful	_____
unafraid	waterfront	_____

FR /fr/ Medial—four syllables

confrontation	refrigerate	unfrequented
infractible	San Francisco	unfriendliest
infrequently	South Africa	unfruitfulness
refreshingly	tutti frutti	

FR /fr/ Medial—five syllables

infrangibleness	refrigeration	_____
refractivity	refrigerative	_____
refractometer	refrigerator	_____

RG /rg/ Medial—two syllables

argue	garglc	stargaze
bargain	gurgle	target
Bergen	jargon	tour guide
cargo	Largo	Virgo
ergo	Morgan	_____
forget	mortgage	_____
forgive	organ	_____
forgot	sorghum	_____

RG /rg/ Medial—three syllables

argument	forgiven	organdy
burgundy	forgiveness	organic
cheeseburger	forgotten	organize
embargo	hamburger	pipe organ
forgetful	Limburger	undergo
forgetting	Margaret	_____

RG /rg/ Medial—four syllables

burgomaster	forgivable	organizer
disorganize	kindergarten	undergarment
forget-me-not	organ grinder	unforgiven
forgettable	organism	_____

RG /rg/ Medial—five syllables
organization
unforgettable

RG /rg/ Final—one syllable
| berg | erg |
| burg | morgue |

RG /rg/ Final—two syllables
Clarksburg	Lordsburg	Salzburg
Goldberg	Newberg	Strasbourg
Hamburg	Oldsberg	Strindberg
iceberg	Pittsburgh	Tilburg
Lemberg	Romberg	Youngberg
Lindberg	Roseburg	

RG /rg/ Final—three syllables
Brandenburg	Luxembourg	Rosenburg
Cederberg	Oldenburg	Swedenborg
Edinburg	Petersburg	Williamsburg
Gettysburg	Phillipsburg	
Heidelberg	Regensburg	
Hindenburg	Reichenberg	

RG /rg/ Final—four syllables
East Harrisburg
Johannesburg

GR /gr/ Initial—one syllable
grab	grant	graze
grace	Grant	grease
Grace	grape	great
grade	grapes	Greece
grades	graph	green
graft	grasp	greet
grain	grass	Greg
gram	grate	grew
grand	grave	grey
grange	gray	grid

grief
grieve
grill
grilled
grim
grime
grin
grind
grip
gripe
grit
groan
groom
groomed
groove
grooved
grope
gross
grouch
ground
grounds
group
grouse
grove
grow
growl
grown
growth
grub
grudge
gruff
grump
grunt

_____
_____
_____

GR /gr/ Initial—two syllables

grabbing
graceful
gracious
grackle
grader
grade school
grading
grafting
Graham
grammar
grandad
grandma
grandniece
grandpa
Grand Prix
grand slam
grandson
grandstand
grand tour
granite
grantee
grantor
granule
grapefruit
grapevine
graphic
graphite
grasping
grassland
grass snake
grassy
grateful
grating
gravel
graveyard
gravy
grazing
greasing
greasy
Great Dane
greater
greatest
Great Falls
Great Lakes
greatly
greedy
greenbacks
greenhouse
greeting
greetings
gremlin
Greta
Gretchen
greyhound
griddle
Griffin
Griffith
grillwork
grimace
grimy
grinder
grinding
grindstone
grinning
griping
gripping
gristle
gritty
grizzle
grizzled
grizzly
grocer
groggy
grooming

groomsman
grooving
groovy
groping
grotesque
grotto
grouchy
ground crew
grounder

ground floor
ground fog
groundhog
ground rules
ground wave
groundwire
groundwork
Grover
growing

grown-up
grubby
gruesome
grumble
grumpy
Grundy
grunion

_____

_____

GR /gr/ Initial—three syllables

gracias
graciously
gradual
graduate
granary
Grandberry
Grand Canyon
grandchildren
granddaughter
grandfather
grandiose
grand jury

grandmother
grandnephew
grandparents
granny knot
granulate
grasshopper
gratify
gratitude
gravity
Great Britain
Great Divide
Gregory

gridiron
Griselda
grizzly bear
groceries
grocery
ground cover
Ground Hog Day
grounds keeper
ground squirrel
ground zero
grueling

_____

GR /gr/ Initial—four syllables

gradually
graduation
graduator
grammarian
grammatical
grandfather clock

Grand Old Party
grand piano
Granite City
graphology
gratifying
gratuitous

gravitation
great-grandparent
gregarious
grotesquerie
group therapy

_____

GR /gr/ Medial—two syllables

aggrieve
aggrieved
agree
agreed
aground
angry

background
begrudge
bluegrass
blue-green
bridegroom
congress

degrade
degree
digress
disgrace
downgrade
egress

egret
engrave
engross
fairground
flagrant
foreground
fragrance
fragrant
hungry
ingrain
Ingram

ingrate
Ingrid
ingroup
land grant
migrate
mongrel
outgrow
outgrowth
Pilgrim
program
progress

regrade
regress
regret
regroup
school ground
tigress
upgrade
vagrant

_____

_____

_____

GR /gr/ Medial—three syllables

aggregate
aggression
aggressive
agreement
allegro
anagram
au gratin
autograph
cablegram
centigrade
centigram
citrus grove
concord grapes
congregate
congressman
congruent
congruous
diagram
dictograph
disagree

disgraceful
disgruntle
emigrant
evergreen
Evergreen
filigree
homograph
immigrant
immigrate
ingrowing
integrate
kilogram
lettergram
Mardi Gras
migration
milligram
monogram
overgrown
overgrowth
paragraph

pedigree
phonograph
photograph
regression
Rio Grande
segregate
seismograph
study group
telegram
telegraph
underground
undergrown
undergrowth
ungraceful
ungracious
ungrateful
upgrading
vagrancy
wintergreen

_____

GR /gr/ Medial—four syllables

aggravation
agriculture
allegretto
audiogram

biographer
biographic
biography
calligrapher

coffee grinder
conflagration
congratulate
congregation

congressional
congruity
disagreement
disintegrate
federal grant
geography
incongruent
incongruous
ingratiate
ingratitude
ingredient
integration
integrative

integrity
mimeograph
organ grinder
photographer
photography
regretfully
regrettable
retrogression
segregated
segregation
stenographer
subaggregate
subgranular

technography
telegrammic
telegrapher
telegraphic
telegraphy
tympanogram
typographer
typography
undergrading
ungraciously
ungrantable
ungraspable

_____

GR /gr/ Medial—five syllables

agricultural
bibliography
biographical
diagrammatic
disagreeable
disintegrated

disintegration
geographical
incongruity
ingratiating
ingratiation
oceanographer

oceanographic
oceanography
topographical
undergraduate
ungrammatical

_____

RJ /rdʒ/ Medial—two syllables

bargeman
barges
charge card
charger
Chargers
charging
clergy
cordial
forger
forging
Georgetown

Georgia
gorgeous
largely
larger
largest
Margie
margin
Margy
merger
merging
perjure

perjured
sergeant
splurging
sturgeon
surgeon
turgid
urgent
Virgil

_____

_____

_____

RJ /rdʒ/ Medial—three syllables

allergic
allergy
chargeable

clergyman
convergence
converges

crackerjacks
detergent
discharges

divergent	lethargy	recharger
emergent	lumberjack	recharging
energize	margarine	surgery
energy	Margery	surgical
enlargement	marginal	urgency
enlarger	Marjorie	Virginia
forgery	overjoy	_____
insurgent	overjoyed	_____
lethargic	perjury	_____

RJ /rdʒ/ Medial—four syllables

Argentina	supercharger	West Virginia
emergency	superjacent	_____
energetic	Virgin Islands	_____
reenlargement	Virgin Mary	_____

RJ /rdʒ/ Final—one syllable

barge	gurge	serge
charge	large	splurge
dirge	Marge	surge
forge	merge	urge
George	purge	verge
gorge	scourge	_____

RJ /rdʒ/ Final—two syllables

converge	engorge	surcharge
discharge	enlarge	upsurge
diverge	recharge	_____
emerge	submerge	_____

RK /rk/ Medial—two syllables

air-cool	charcoal	darker
arcade	circle	darkness
archive	circuit	Dorcas
Arctic	circus	forecast
barking	clerking	haircut
bearcat	corkscrew	harken
Berkeley	Corky	jerkin
carcass	darken	jerking

jerky
Larkin
larkspur
lurking
marker
market
marking
marquee
murky
orchid
parka
Parker

parking
parkway
perky
shirking
smirking
snorkle
spark plug
sparkle
sparkled
sparklers
sparkling
turkey

Turkey
Turkish
turquoise
workbench
workbook
working
workman
workmen
workroom
workshop
_____
_____

RK /rk/ Medial—three syllables

anarchist
anarchy
Antarctic
archaic
archangel
beef jerky
circular
circulate
darkener
embarking
encircle
marketing
Market Street
mazurka
mercury

Mercury
monarchist
monarchy
motorcade
motorcar
orchestra
overcame
overcast
overcoat
overcome
parking lights
parking lot
parking place
patchwork quilt
percolate

percussion
porcupine
remarking
sarcasm
sarcastic
Turkish bath
woodworking
workable
workmanship
work station
worktable
_____
_____
_____
_____

RK /rk/ Medial—four syllables

air-condition
altercation
Antarctica
Arcadia
Arctic Circle
Arctic Ocean
charcoal lighter
circuit breaker

disembarking
felt-tip marker
hierarchy
money market
orchestration
Park Avenue
parking meter
percolator

remarkable
semicircle
sheltered workshop
social worker
summer workshop
supermarket
turkey buzzard
_____

RK /rk/ Final—one syllable

arc	Kirk	shirk
ark	lark	smirk
bark	lurk	spark
Burke	marc	stark
Clark	Marc	stork
clerk	mark	torque
cork	Mark	Turk
dark	park	work
Dirk	perk	York
fork	Perk	_____
hark	pork	_____
irk	quirk	_____
jerk	shark	_____

RK /rk/ Final—two syllables

birch bark	guesswork	pitchfork
birthmark	hallmark	pockmark
bookmark	handwork	postmark
bridgework	hayfork	remark
check mark	homework	salesclerk
debark	housework	skylark
Denmark	landmark	stonework
earmark	loan shark	town clerk
embark	monarch	trademark
footmark	network	uncork
footwork	Newark	woodwork
framework	New York	_____
frostwork	patchwork	_____

RK /rk/ Final—three syllables

baseball park	meadowlark	social work
Central Park	needlework	Sunset Park
city park	Noah's Ark	tuning fork
disembark	overpark	watermark
fancywork	overwork	waterwork
handiwork	patriarch	_____
hierarchy	pencil mark	_____
Jasper Park	question mark	_____

RK /rk/ Final—four syllables

Denali Park   _____   _____

national park   _____   _____

quotation mark   _____   _____

RKT /rkt/ Final—one syllable

arcked	jerked	sparked
barked	marked	worked
irked	parked	_____

RKT /rkt/ Final—two syllables

embarked	uncorked	_____
postmarked	unmarked	_____
remarked	unworked	_____

KR /kr/ Initial—one syllable

Chris	creed	crowd
Christ	creek	crowed
chrome	creep	crown
crab	crepe	crowned
craft	crept	crude
crag	crest	cruise
Craig	Crete	cruised
cram	crew	crumb
crammed	crib	crumbed
cramp	cribbed	crumbs
cramped	crick	crunch
crane	cried	crush
crank	crime	crust
crash	crisp	crutch
crate	crisped	cry
crave	croak	kraut
craw	crock	_____
crawl	crop	_____
crawled	cross	_____
creak	crossed	_____
cream	crouch	_____
crease	croup	_____
creased	crow	_____

KR /kr/ Initial—two syllables

Christa	creeper	crosswalk
Christian	creeping	croutons
Christine	creepy	crowbar
Christmas	crescent	crowded
Christy	crevasse	crowdy
chroma	crewel	crowning
Chrysler	crewman	crow's nest
Chrystal	crewmen	crucial
crabby	cribbage	crude oil
cracker	cricket	cruel
cracking	crimson	cruise car
crackling	cripple	cruiser
cradle	crippled	cruise ship
cradled	crisis	cruising
craftsman	crispy	crumble
crafty	crisscross	crumbled
craggy	crochet	crumbly
cramming	crock pot	crummy
cramping	crocus	crumple
crater	crooked	crunchy
crayfish	crop dust	crusade
crayon	cropper	crushing
crazy	cropping	crystal
cream cheese	croquet	Kristi
create	crossbow	_____
creature	crossing	_____
credit	crossroad	_____

KR /kr/ Initial—three syllables

Christina	craftsmanship	crepe paper
Christmas card	cranberry	cribbage board
Christmas Day	crash helmet	criminal
Christmas Eve	Crater Lake	critical
Christmas tree	creation	criticize
Christopher	creative	crocheting
chromosome	creator	crockery
chrysolite	credible	crocodile
crackerjack	cremation	Cro-Magnon

crop duster	crucify	crystallize
cross-country	cruelty	_____
crossover	crusader	_____
cross section	crustacean	_____

KR /kr/ Initial—four syllables

chronology	creditable	cross-country skis
chrysanthemum	credit rating	cross reference
cracker barrel	credit union	cross-country skis
cranberry tree	criterion	crossword puzzle
creativeness	critical mass	_____

KR /kr/ Medial—two syllables

accrete	decreased	recruit
accrue	decree	Red Cross
accrued	discrete	sacred
acrid	ecru	sand crab
across	fulcrum	scarecrow
aircraft	handcraft	sea crab
aircrew	increase	secret
Akron	increased	secrete
bankrupt	king crab	spacecraft
book rack	macron	stock room
cockroach	microbe	tree crab
concrete	okra	witchcraft
corn crib	packrat	woodcraft
decrease	pie crust	_____

KR /kr/ Medial—three syllables

accredit	doublecross	leather craft
achromic	endocrine	microfilm
acrobat	giant crab	microphone
acrylic	handcrafted	microscope
aircraftman	handicraft	microwave
aircrewman	hot cross buns	moose crossing
autocrat	Hovercraft	nutcracker
bike crossing	hypocrite	oyster crab
deer crossing	increasing	pancreas
democrat	increment	pleasure craft

plutocrat	soft-shell crab	_____
sacrifice	sour cream	_____
Santa Cruz	synchronize	_____
sauerkraut	Veracruz	_____
secrecy	water craft	_____

KR /kr/ Medial—four syllables

acrobatics	incredible	railroad crossing
aristocrat	incredulous	recreation
democracy	incriminate	secretary
hypocrisy	microscopic	_____
increasingly	plutocracy	_____

KR /kr/ Medial—five syllables

aircraft carrier	incriminating	_____
aristocratic	microdetector	_____

RL /rl/ Medial—two syllables

airlift	Earlene	pearly
airline	early	poorly
Arlene	fairly	scarlet
Arlon	fearless	Shirley
barely	furlong	squarely
barley	furlough	starlight
Berlin	garland	starling
burlap	garlic	starlit
burly	Girl Scouts	sterling
careless	Harlan	surely
Carla	Harlem	swirly
carload	Harley	Verlene
Charlene	heirloom	whirlpool
Charlie	hourly	whirlwind
Charline	marlin	yearling
Charlotte	merely	yearly
clearly	Merlin	_____
curling	moorland	_____
curly	nearly	_____
Darlene	oarlock	_____
darling	parlor	_____

RL /rl/ Medial—three syllables

Arlington	hourly wage	Pearl Harbor
Barley Green	Kimberly	power line
barleycorn	mannerly	powerless
blue marlin	masterly	properly
brotherly	maturely	quarterly
charlatan	miserly	scholarly
charley horse	motherly	securely
Charlottesville	neighborly	severely
Charlottetown	northerly	sisterly
cheerleaders	obscurely	Sutherland
curlicue	orderly	tenderly
eagerly	overland	utterly
early bird	overlap	whirlabout
entirely	overlay	whirligig
fatherly	overlie	whirlpool bath
garlic bread	overload	whirlybird
garlic salt	overlook	wonderland
gingerly	overly	_____
Harlingen	Parliament	_____

RL /rl/ Medial—four syllables

curling iron	northwesterly	sterling silver
everlasting	sitting parlor	_____
New Orleans	southeasterly	_____

RL /rəl/ /ɝl/ Final—one syllable

Beryl	gnarl	snarl
burl	hurl	swirl
Burl	Karl	twirl
Carl	Merle	whirl
curl	pearl	whorl
Earl	Pearl	_____
furl	purl	_____
girl	skirl	_____

RL /rəl/ /ɝl/ Final—two syllables

blue pearl	untwirl	young girl
unfurl	white pearl	_____

RL /ɝl/ Final—three syllables

baby girl	knit and purl	_____
baton twirl	Minnie Pearl	_____
Campfire Girl	yellow pearl	_____

REL /rəl/ Final—two syllables

barrel	mural	spiral
choral	oral	squirrel
coral	peril	sterile
floral	quarrel	_____
moral	rural	_____

REL /rəl/ Final—three syllables

admiral	imperil	pastoral
apparel	lateral	sculptural
corporal	liberal	several
cultural	mackerel	_____
funeral	mineral	_____
general	natural	_____
immoral	numeral	_____

REL /rəl/ Final—four syllables

bilateral	inaugural	unnatural
collateral	intramural	vice-admiral
conjectural	rear admiral	_____

RLZ /rlz/ Final—one syllable

Charles	pearls	whorls
curls	purls	_____
Earl's	snarls	_____
girls	swirls	_____
gnarls	twirls	_____
hurls	whirls	_____

LR /lr/ Medial—two syllables

all right	seal ring	_____
ballroom	toll road	_____
railroad	walrus	_____
schoolroom	_____	_____

LR /lr/ Medial—three syllables

already
cavalry
civil rights
coral reef

cradle roll
gravel road
jewelry
middle ring

rivalry
_____
_____
_____

RM /rm/ Medial—two syllables

airmail
airman
armful
armhole
armor
armored
army
Burma
Burmese
Carmel
Carmen
charming
dormant
Erma
ermine
farm belt
farmer
farming
farmland

fireman
firemen
foreman
foremost
formal
format
former
garment
German
gourmet
harmful
harmless
hermit
hormone
Irma
mermaid
Norma
normal
Norman

permit
spearmint
sperm whale
surmise
surmount
termite
thermal
thermos
torment
turmoil
unarmed
vermin
Vermont
warmly
warm-up
wormwood
_____
_____
_____

RM /rm/ Medial—three syllables

alderman
armament
armistice
armorer
armory
Bermuda
cormorant
enormous
farming land
fire marshal
firmament

formation
formula
Germany
germinate
harmonize
harmony
informal
marmalade
performance
performer
permanent

permission
pharmacist
pharmacy
Prince Charming
retirement
snake charmer
storm cellar
storm center
storm warning
storm window
terminal

terminate _____ _____
thermostat _____ _____
uniformed _____ _____
vermillion _____ _____

RM /rm/ Medial—four syllables

affirmative	germination	termination
armadillo	harmonica	thermometer
Armistice Day	infirmary	uniformly
army blanket	infirmity	_____
conformation	permanently	_____
dormitory	permeable	_____
fermentation	supermarket	_____

RM /rm/ Medial—five syllables

formalization	thermal barrier	_____
terminology	uniformity	_____

RM /rm/ Final—one syllable

arm	form	swarm
charm	germ	warm
dorm	harm	worm
farm	squirm	_____
firm	storm	_____

RM /rm/ Final—two syllables

affirm	earthworm	reform
alarm	hailstorm	sandstorm
bookworm	inchworm	silkworm
confirm	infirm	snowstorm
conform	inform	tapeworm
cutworm	perform	windstorm
deform	platform	_____
dust storm	rainstorm	_____

RM /rm/ Final—three syllables

angleworm	thunderstorm	_____
fire alarm	uniform	_____
pachyderm	_____	_____

RN /rn/ Medial—two syllables

Arnold	darning	mourning
barnyard	doorknob	Myrna
Bernard	earnest	ornate
Bernice	earnings	surname
burned-out	Ernest	tarnish
burner	furnace	thorny
burning	furnish	turncoat
colonel	garnet	turner
cornbread	garnish	turnip
corncob	harness	turnkey
Cornell	horned toad	turn on
corner	hornet	turnout
cornered	journal	turnpike
cornet	journey	turnstile
cornfield	kernel	varnish
cornflakes	learning	Vernon
corn oil	Lorna	warning
cornstarch	morning	worn-out

RN /rn/ Medial—three syllables

alternate	government	Southern Cross
Bernadine	infernal	Southerner
carnation	internal	southernmost
Carnegie	internee	storm warning
carnival	internist	stubbornness
cornerstone	internment	tornado
corn popper	journalist	tournament
Easterner	journeyman	tourniquet
eternal	maternal	turnover
external	nocturnal	turntable
fraternal	ornament	unfurnished
furnishings	paternal	Westerner
furniture	returning	westernmost

RN /rn/ Medial—four syllables

alternately	carnivorous	returnable
alternative	internalize	vernacular
alternator	morning glory	_____

RN /rn/ Final—one syllable

barn	learn	urn
born	Lorne	Verne
burn	mourn	warn
churn	scorn	worn
corn	stern	yarn
darn	sworn	yearn
earn	thorn	_____
fern	torn	_____
horn	turn	_____

RN /rn/ Final—two syllables

acorn	Hawthorn	return
adjourn	inborn	Saturn
adorn	intern	shopworn
airborne	iron	shorthorn
auburn	lantern	sojourn
Auburn	LaVerne	southern
cavern	long horn	stubborn
cistern	modern	sunburn
concern	newborn	upturn
eastern	pattern	western
fire thorn	popcorn	windburn
fog horn	pronghorn	_____
French horn	Rayburn	_____
govern	reborn	_____

RN /rn/ Final—three syllables

Capricorn	southwestern	unicorn
southeastern	unconcern	_____

RP /rp/ Medial—two syllables

airplane	harping	serpent
airport	harpist	sharpen
burping	harpoon	sharper
carpet	perplex	surpass
chirping	porpoise	surplus
fireplace	purple	tarpan
hairpin	purpose	tarpon

terpene
torpid
torpor
turpeth

war paint
warpath
warping
_____

_____
_____
_____
_____

RP /rp/ Medial—three syllables

absorption
carpenter
centerpiece
corporal
harpsichord
power pack
purposely

Scorpio
scorpion
sharpener
sharpening
sharpshooter
sharpsighted
sharpwitted

surplus store
tarpaulin
torpedo
turpentine
unsharpened
unsurpassed

RP /rp/ Medial—four syllables

caterpillar
incorporate
perpetual

surpassable
torpedo boat
_____

_____
_____
_____

RP /rp/ Final—one syllable

burp
carp
chirp
harp

sharp
slurp
tarp
thorp

Thorpe
twirp
warp
_____

PR /pr/ Initial—one syllable

Prague
praise
praised
prance
pranced
prank
prate
Pratt
prawn
prawns
pray
prayed
preach

preached
preen
press
pressed
prey
price
priced
pride
pried
pries
priest
prime
primed

primp
prince
print
prize
prized
pro
probe
probed
prod
prof
prom
prompt
prone

prong	prose	prune
proof	proud	pruned
proofed	prove	pry
prop	prow	_____
propped	prowl	_____
props	prude	_____

PR /pr/ Initial—two syllables

practice	presents	primrose
prairie	preserve	princess
praline	preshrunk	printed
pratique	preside	printer
prattle	press club	printing
prattler	presser	printout
preacher	pressing	prior
precede	pressman	prism
precept	pressroom	prison
precinct	pressure	pristine
precious	presswork	private
precise	prestige	probate
preclude	presto	problem
predict	presume	proceed
preempt	pretend	proceeds
preface	pretense	process
prefect	pretest	proclaim
prefer	pretext	proctor
prefix	pretty	Proctor
prejudge	pretzel	procure
prelude	prevail	produce
premier	prevent	product
premise	preview	profess
prepaid	priceless	profile
prepare	prickle	profit
prepared	prickly	profound
prepay	priesthood	profuse
preschool	primal	program
prescribe	primate	progress
presence	primer	project
present	priming	prolong

promise
promote
prompted
prompter
promptly
pronghorn
pronoun
pronounce
pronounced
proofread
propel
proper
prophet

propose
propound
proscribe
prospect
prosper
protect
protein
protest
proton
protract
protrude
proverb
provide

province
provoke
prowess
proxy
prudence
Prudence
prudent
prudish
pruning

_____
_____
_____
_____

PR /pr/ Initial—three syllables

practical
prairie dog
preamble
prearrange
precaution
precedence
precedent
preceding
precipice
precision
precocious
preconceive
preconcert
precursor
predator
predestine
predicate
prediction
predispose
preemption
preexist
preference
preferment
prefigure

prejudice
premature
premiership
premium
prenatal
preordain
prescription
presently
preserver
president
pressurize
prestigious
presumption
pretentious
prevalence
prevention
previous
prickly pear
primary
primitive
principal
principle
printing press
prisoner

privacy
privately
privation
privilege
probable
probably
probation
proboscis
procedure
procession
processor
prodigal
prodigious
prodigy
producer
production
productive
profession
professor
proficient
profitee
profusion
progeny
prognosis

prognostic
progressive
prohibit
projected
projectile
projector
prolific
promenade
prominent
promising
promptitude
promulgate
pronouncement
propagate
propeller
proper name
property

prophecy
prophesy
prophetess
prophetic
propolis
proponent
proportion
proposal
propulsion
prosaic
prosecute
prosody
prospective
prosperous
protection
protective
protege

Protestant
protocol
protoplast
prototype
protractor
protrusion
provender
provided
providence
providing
provincial
provision
provoking
prudential

_____
_____
_____

PR /pr/ Initial—four syllables

practicable
practical joke
practically
practical nurse
practitioner
prairie chicken
praying mantis
precarious
precedency
precipitant
precipitate
precipitous
preconception
predatory
predecessor
predetermine
predicament
predominance
predominant
preeminent

preexistence
preexistent
prefabricate
preferable
preferential
prefiguring
preformation
prefulfillment
pregalvanize
prehardener
preharmony
prehistoric
preholiday
preignition
preimposing
preinclining
preindicate
preinstruction
prejudicial
prematurely

premedical
premeditate
premonition
preoccupied
preparation
preponderance
preponderate
preposition
preposterous
prerequisite
prerogative
presentable
presentation
preservation
preservative
presidency
presidential
presumable
presumptuous
prevaricate

prima donna
primarily
prime minister
principally
priority
processional
proclamation
procrastinate
procreation
productively
professional
profitable
prohibition

prohibitive
proletary
proliferate
prolongation
promissory
promontory
propaganda
propensity
proportional
proposition
proprietor
proscenium
prosecution

prosperity
protuberance
protuberant
proverbial
provisional
provocation
provocative
proximity

_____
_____
_____
_____
_____

PR /pr/ Initial—five syllables

precipitation
predestination
prehistorical
preliminary
premeditation

preparatory
prepositional
Presbyterian
principality
probability

productivity
prognostication
promissory note
pronunciation

_____

PR /pr/ Medial—two syllables

appraise
appraised
apprize
approach
approved
April
apron
blueprint
bombproof
Capri
compress
culprit
cypress
Cypress
depress
depressed
deprive

deprived
dustproof
express
fireproof
footprint
impress
imprint
improve
oppress
rainproof
repress
reprieve
reprint
reprise
reproach
reprove
shipwreck

shipwrecked
soundproof
sun proof
suppress
supreme
surprise
surprised
upright

_____
_____
_____
_____
_____
_____
_____
_____

PR /pr/ Medial—three syllables

appraisal	expression	paprika
apprehend	expressive	represent
approval	expressway	repression
apricot	fingerprint	reprimand
April Fool	high pressure	reprinted
bulletproof	impression	reprisal
by-product	impressive	reprobate
capricious	imprison	reproduce
Capricorn	impromptu	soprano
comprehend	improper	tamper-proof
deprecate	improvement	unprepared
depressant	improvise	waterproof
depression	interpret	weatherproof
depressive	jet propelled	_____
disapprove	low pressure	_____
enterprise	mispronounce	_____

PR /pr/ Medial—four syllables

appreciate	depreciate	reciprocate
apprehension	disapproval	reproduction
apprenticeship	impregnable	supremacy
approbation	impressionist	vice-president
appropriate	life preserver	word processor
approximate	proprietor	_____
April Fools' Day	reciprocal	_____

PR /pr/ Medial—five syllables

appreciation	impropriety	reprehensible
apprehensible	improvisation	representative
appropriation	inappropriate	uncompromising
depreciation	interpretation	unprecedented
impracticable	irrepressible	_____
impressionable	irreproachable	_____

RS /rs/ Medial—two syllables

arson	cursor	fireside
corsage	dorsal	forceps
cursive	firesale	foresaw

foresee
foreseen
foresight
forsake
for sale
forsook
herself
horseback
horsefly
horseman
horseshoe
horse show
mercy

morsel
Morse Code
ourselves
parcel
parsley
parsnip
parson
perceive
percent
person
perspire
pursue
pursuit

scarcely
tiresome
torso
verso
versus
Warsaw
yourself

_____
_____
_____
_____
_____

RS /rs/ Medial—three syllables

arsenal
arsenic
cumbersome
diversely
fire safety
forsaken
horsepower
intercede
Jefferson
lumbersome
Mercedes
narcissus
near-sighted
nursery
overseas
oversight

overstate
parcel post
parsonage
percentage
persecute
persimmon
persistent
personal
personnel
porcelain
power saw
precursor
rehearsal
rehearsing
reverses
reversing

riverside
Riverside
salesperson
somersault
supersede
supervise
underset
unforeseen
varsity
versatile
versify

_____
_____
_____
_____
_____

RS /rs/ Medial—four syllables

adversary
controversy
diversity
impersonate
marsupial
nursery rhymes

nursery school
persecution
personally
supersonic
superstition
universal

unmerciful
versifier
vice versa
water safety

_____
_____

RS /rs/ Medial—five syllables

anniversary	universally	versification
diversifying	university	_____
personality	versatility	_____

RS /rs/ Final—one syllable

coarse	horse	sparse
course	nurse	verse
curse	pierce	worse
fierce	Pierce	_____
force	purse	_____
hearse	scarce	_____
hoarse	source	_____

RS /rs/ Final—two syllables

adverse	enforce	saw horse
Air Force	golf course	school nurse
averse	imburse	sea horse
coerce	immerse	submerse
concourse	inverse	transverse
converse	race course	traverse
disburse	recourse	_____
disperse	rehearse	_____
diverse	remorse	_____
divorce	resource	_____
endorse	reverse	_____

RS /rs/ Final—three syllables

charley horse	labor force	rocking horse
fire safety	office nurse	slalom course
first aid course	police force	student nurse
hobby horse	quarter horse	universe
intersperse	reinforce	_____

RSII /rʃ/ Medial—two syllables

airship	martial	worship
earshot	partial	_____
Marsha	portion	_____
marshal	warship	_____

RSH /rʃ/ Medial—three syllables

censorship	martial law	proportion
commercial	membership	scholarship
contortion	overshade	sponsorship
distortion	overshine	undershirt
fire marshal	overshoes	undershot
foreshadow	overshoot	undershrub
leadership	overshot	watershed
Marshal Sea	ownership	_____
marshmallow	partnership	_____
martial arts	pastorship	_____

RSH /rʃ/ Medial—four syllables

antique airship	overshadow	treasurership
chancellorship	thundershower	undersheriff
Marshall Islands	torsionally	_____

RSH /rʃ/ Final—one syllable

harsh	_____	_____
kirsch	_____	_____
marsh	_____	_____

SHR /ʃr/ Initial—one syllable

shrank	shrill	shrub
shred	shrimp	shrug
shrew	shrine	shrugged
shrewd	shrines	shrugs
shrews	shrink	shrunk
shriek	shrive	_____
shrift	shroud	_____
shrike	shrove	_____

SHR /ʃr/ Initial—two syllables

shredded	shrimp boat	shriveled
Shreveport	shrimper	shriven
shrewdly	Shriners	shrubby
shrewdness	shrinkage	shrugging
shrewish	shrinking	shrunken
shrillest	shrivel	_____

SHR /ʃr/ Initial—three syllables
shriveling
shrubbery

SHR /ʃr/ Medial—two syllables

enshrine	preshrink	washrag
mushroom	preshrunk	washroom
preshred	unshred	

SKR /skr/ Initial—one syllable

scram	screech	scroll
scrap	screen	Scrooge
scrape	screw	scrub
scratch	scribe	scrunch
scrawl	scrimp	
scream	script	

SKR /skr/ Initial—two syllables

scraggly	scrawny	scrimmage
scramble	screening	scripture
scrambled	screenplay	scrub nurse
scrapbook	screentest	scrumptious
scraper	screwball	scruple
scrapper	scribble	
scratchy	scribbled	

SKR /skr/ Initial—three syllables

screen writer	scrutinize	
screwdriver	scrutiny	
scrupulous		

SKR /skr/ Medial—two syllables

ascribe	ice cream	subscribe
ascribed	inscribe	subscribed
corkscrew	muskrat	subscript
describe	postscript	transcribe
described	prescribe	transcribed
discreet	prescribed	
escrow	silkscreen	

SKR /skr/ Medial—three syllables

description	inscription	subscription
descriptive	manuscript	_____
ice-cream man	prescription	_____
ice-cream truck	skyscraper	_____

SPR /spr/ Initial—one syllable

sprain	spree	sprout
sprang	sprig	spruce
sprawl	spring	sprung
spray	sprint	spry
spread	sprite	_____

SPR /spr/ Initial—two syllables

spraddle	springboard	sprinkler
sprayer	Springfield	sprinkling
spray gun	springing	sprocket
spreader	springtime	_____
spreadsheet	sprinkle	_____

SPR /spr/ Medial—two syllables

bedspread	hot springs	Rock Springs
hair spray	Hot Springs	_____
handspring	offspring	_____

SPR /spr/ Medial—three syllables

Brussels sprouts	Silver Spring	_____
ocean spray	Union Springs	_____
shopping spree	_____	_____

STR /str/ Initial—one syllable

straight	straw	stressed
strain	stray	stretch
strained	strayed	stretched
strait	streak	strict
strand	stream	stride
strange	street	strike
strap	strength	string
strapped	stress	strip

stripe	strokes	struck
stripped	stroll	strum
strive	strolled	strung
strobe	strong	strut
stroke	strove	

STR /str/ Initial—two syllables

straggle	stretchy	stroller
stranger	stricken	strolling
strapping	strident	strongbox
streaking	strike out	stronghold
streamer	strike zone	strongly
streamline	string beans	structure
streetcar	stringent	strudel
strengthen	stringing	struggle
stressing	stringy	strumming
stretcher	stripping	strutting
stretching	striving	strychnine
stretch-out	strobe lamp	

STR /str/ Initial—three syllables

straightforward	strawberry	structural
strait jacket	strenuous	
strategy	string quartet	
stratosphere	stroboscope	

STR /str/ Initial—four syllables

streptococcus		
streptomycin		
stringed instruments		

STR /str/ Medial—two syllables

abstract	breaststroke	frustrate
airstrip	constrict	gold stream
astray	construct	high-strung
astride	destroy	instruct
backstroke	distract	minstrel
bloodstream	distress	mistreat
bowstring	downstream	mistress

monstrous	restrain	side street
nostril	restrict	sidestroke
obstruct	rostrum	upstream
ostrich	seamstress	vestry
pastry	shoestring	_____

STR /str/ Medial—three syllables

Astrodome	destructive	orchestra
astronaut	distraction	reconstruct
Australia	distribute	restraining
Austria	doll stroller	restricting
chemistry	Gaza Strip	restriction
comic strip	illustrate	Sunset Strip
construction	industry	tapestry
demonstrate	instruction	_____
destroyer	instructor	_____
destruction	instrument	_____

STR /str/ Medial—four syllables

apostrophe	catastrophe	instrumental
astrology	catastrophic	orchestra pit
astronomer	demonstration	pedestrian
astronomy	distribution	reconstruction
baby stroller	illustration	string orchestra
band instruments	industrial	_____
candy striper	industrious	_____

STR /str/ Medial—five syllables

| administration | boa constrictor | _____ |
| astronomical | instrumentalist | _____ |

RT /rt/ Medial—two syllables

artful	cartoon	courtyard
artist	cartridge	curtain
barter	cartwheel	Curtis
Bertram	certain	dirty
Burton	charter	fertile
Carter	Cortez	forty
carton	courthouse	fourteen

garter	porter	smarter
Gertrude	Porter	smartly
hearty	porthole	sorting
martin	Portland	sport car
Martin	portrait	sporting
Marty	portray	sportive
martyr	quarter	sportsman
mortal	quartet	sporty
mortar	quart jar	squirting
Myrtle	quarto	started
partake	shortage	starter
parted	shortcake	startle
parting	short-changed	thirteen
partly	short-cut	thirteenth
partner	shorten	thirty
partridge	shorthand	tortoise
part-time	shorthorn	turtle
party	shortly	vertex
pertain	shortstop	warthog
portage	shortwave	wiretap
Portage	Shorty	

RT /rt/ Medial—three syllables

advertise	courtesy	light-hearted
Alberta	departed	particle
aorta	department	partition
apartment	deportment	partnership
artichoke	fertilize	portable
article	fortieth	property
artifact	fortify	quarterback
artisan	garter snake	report card
assortment	Gilberta	reporter
bartering	headquarters	reporting
cartilage	heartbroken	Roberta
certainty	heartily	Roquefort cheese
certified	immortal	short circuit
certify	importance	shortening
chartering	important	short-handed
compartment	liberty	short-sighted

short story
soft-hearted
sportsmanlike
sportsmanship
sportswoman
sportswriter

summertime
support group
support staff
thirtieth
tortilla
turtledove

vertebra
vertebral
vertical
vertigo

_____

_____

RT /rt/ Medial—four syllables

advertisement
articulate
artificial
certificate
certified check
certified mail
comfortable
convertible
departable
fertility
invertebrate

Liberty Bell
participate
participle
particular
porterhouse steak
portfolio
property tax
Puerto Rico
refertilize
reportedly
self-imparting

short division
short-handedness
short-sightedness
smart-alecky
unfortified
unimportant
unsportsmanlike
well-fortified
well-supported

_____

_____

RT /rt/ Medial—five syllables

false advertising
opportunity
past participle

pertinacity
quarterly report
uncomfortable

_____

_____

_____

RT /rt/ Final—one syllable

art
Bart
Bert
blurt
cart
carte
chart
court
Curt
dart
dirt
flirt
fort

girt
heart
hurt
Kurt
mart
part
pert
port
quart
quirt
shirt
short
skirt

smart
snort
sort
sport
spurt
squirt
start
tart
thwart
wart

_____

_____

_____

RT /rt/ Final—two syllables

advert	escort	pushcart
airport	evert	report
Albert	exert	resort
alert	expert	revert
apart	export	Robert
assert	extort	seaport
athwart	filbert	Shreveport
avert	Gilbert	sportshirt
comfort	go-cart	stalwart
concert	Head Start	subvert
convert	Herbert	support
Delbert	Hubert	sweatshirt
depart	impart	sweetheart
deport	import	transport
desert	inert	transvert
dessert	insert	T-shirt
distort	invert	unhurt
divert	Lambert	yogurt
dress shirt	outsmart	_____
effort	oxcart	_____
Elbert	passport	_____

RT /rt/ Final—three syllables

a la carte	introvert	shopping cart
counterpart	liverwort	tennis court
davenport	martial art	trailer court
disconcert	miniskirt	undershirt
extrovert	preconcert	_____
hula skirt	retrovert	_____

TR /tr/ Initial—one syllable

trace	trail	tramp
traced	trailed	tramped
track	trails	trance
tracked	train	trap
tract	trained	trapped
trade	trait	trash
trades	tram	trawl

tray	trimmed	truce
tread	trip	truck
treat	tripe	trucked
treats	tripped	trudge
tree	Trish	true
trek	trite	trump
trench	trod	trumped
trend	troll	trunk
Trent	troop	trunks
tress	troops	truss
tribe	trot	trust
trice	troth	truth
trick	trough	truths
tried	trounce	try
tries	trout	_____
trill	trow	_____
trim	Troy	_____

TR /tr/ Initial—two syllables

tracing	trainman	transgress
tracker	traitor	transient
tracking	tramcar	transit
trackless	tramline	translate
track meet	trammel	transmit
traction	tramper	transmute
tractor	trample	transom
Tracy	trampler	transpire
trademark	trampling	transplant
trade name	tramway	transport
tradesman	tranquil	transpose
trade wind	transact	transverse
trading	transcend	trapdoor
traduce	transcribe	trapeze
traffic	transcript	trapper
tragic	transept	trapping
trailer	transfer	trappings
trainee	transfix	trash can
trainer	transform	travel
training	transfuse	traveled

traverse	tricky	troubled
trawler	trident	troubling
treadle	trifle	troublous
treadmill	trifler	trouncing
treason	trifling	trousers
treasure	trigger	trousseau
treating	trillion	trowel
treatment	trimmer	truant
treaty	trimming	trucking
treble	trimmings	truckle
tree house	trinket	truckled
trekking	trio	truck route
trellis	triple	truck stop
tremble	triplet	Trudy
trembling	triplex	truffle
tremor	tripod	truly
trenchant	tripping	Truman
trencher	triumph	trumpet
Trenton	trivet	trundle
trespass	trodden	trustee
trestle	Trojan	trustees
triad	trolley	trustful
trial	trombone	trusting
tribal	trooper	trusty
tribesman	troopship	truthful
tribesmen	trophy	trying
tribune	tropic	tryout
tribute	trotter	_____
trickle	trotting	_____
trickster	trouble	_____

TR /tr/ Initial—three syllables

traceable	traducement	trailer park
trachea	traducer	train station
trackable	tragedy	trainable
tractable	tragical	training aid
trade union	trailblazer	training school
trading post	trailer camp	traitorous
tradition	trailer court	trammeling

trampoline
tranquilest
tranquilize
transaction
transcendent
transcribing
transcription
transference
transferring
transfigured
transformer
transfusion
transgression
transgressor
transition
transitive
translation
translator
translucent
transmission
transmitter

transonic
transparent
transpolar
trapezoid
traveler
treacherous
treasure chest
treasure house
treasure hunt
treasure map
treasurer
treasury
tremendous
tremulous
trespassing
triangle
triathlon
tribunal
trickery
tricolor
tricycle

trilogy
Trinidad
trinity
triplicate
triumphal
triumphant
trivial
tropical
troubadour
troublesome
truculence
truculent
truism
trumpery
trumpeter
trundle bed
trustworthy
truthfulness
_____
_____
_____

TR /tr/ Initial—four syllables

tracking station
traditional
tragedian
tragedienne
tragically
trajectory
tranquility
tranquilizer
trans-Andean
transatlantic
transcendental

transferable
transferential
transforamtion
transitional
transitory
transmigration
transmutation
transparency
transplantation
transportation
treasonable

trepidation
triangular
tribulation
tributary
triennial
triplicating
triumphal arch
_____
_____
_____
_____

TR /tr/ Initial—five syllables

tracheotomy
traditionally
transcendentalist

transcontinental
transfiguration
triangulation

trigonometry
triviality
_____

TR /tr/ Medial—two syllables

actress	fire truck	protract
attract	horse trail	protrude
betray	intrigue	race track
central	matrix	retract
citrus	matron	retreat
contract	mattress	retrieve
control	metric	round trip
country	neutral	sentry
detract	neutron	ski trail
detrain	nitrate	spectrum
Detroit	pantry	subtract
doctrine	partridge	sultry
dog track	Patrick	tantrum
entrance	patrol	tightrope
entry	patrolled	untried
extra	patron	untrue
extract	pine tree	untruth
extreme	portrait	waitress
field trip	portray	_____
firetrap	poultry	_____

TR /tr/ Medial—three syllables

attraction	infantry	patriot
attractive	inside track	Patriots
Australia	intricate	patrolman
Beatrice	introduce	penetrate
Central Park	maple tree	petrify
concentrate	matriarch	poetry
contraction	metrical	postmistress
contradict	metronome	protractor
contrary	nitrogen	railroad track
country club	nutrient	rainbow trout
countryside	nutrition	reentry
detraction	nutritious	retraction
detriment	orchestra	retrenchment
electric	outrageous	retrieval
electron	patriarch	retriever
extremely	Patricia	retrieving

retrograde	state trooper	victrola
retrogress	subcontract	_____
retrospect	subtraction	_____
ski patrol	subtropics	_____
spectroscope	untruthful	_____

TR /tr/ Medial—four syllables

catastrophe	introduction	remote control
concentration	matriarchy	retribution
contribution	matriculate	retroactive
control tower	matrimony	retroflexion
controversy	metric system	retrogression
electrical	metropolis	retroversion
electrician	no trespassing	St. Patrick's Day
electronics	paratrooper	subtropical
entrepreneur	patriotic	ultrasonic
extravagance	patrolwoman	unobtrusive
extravagant	pedestrian	ventriloquist
geometry	petrified wood	_____
illustrated	petroleum	_____

TR /tr/ Medial—five syllables

electricity	pediatrician	_____
metropolitan	_____	_____

RTS /rts/ Final—one syllable

arts	forts	skirts
blurts	hearts	sorts
carts	parts	sports
charts	ports	spurts
courts	quarts	squirts
darts	shirts	warts
flirts	shorts	_____

RTS /rts/ Final—two syllables

airports	deserts	exports
alerts	desserts	imports
concerts	distorts	inserts
departs	experts	inverts

passports	seaports	_____
reports	supports	_____
resorts	transports	_____
reverts	_____	_____

RST /rst/ Final—one syllables

burst	hurst	thirst
cursed	Hurst	worst
first	nursed	_____
forced	pierced	_____

RST /rst/ Final—two syllables

airburst	enforced	sunburst
cloudburst	imbursed	unversed
coerced	immersed	_____
dispersed	outburst	_____
divorced	rehearsed	_____
endorsed	reversed	_____

RTH /rð/ Medial—two syllables

farther	norther	_____
farthest	northern	_____
farthing	swarthy	_____
further	worthy	_____

RTH /rð/ Medial—three syllables

airworthy	northernmost	worthiest
blameworthy	noteworthy	worthily
farthermost	seaworthy	worthiness
furthermore	swarthier	Worthington
northerly	thankworthy	_____
Northern Cross	trustworthy	_____
northern lights	unworthy	_____
Northerner	worthier	_____

RTH /rð/ Medial—four syllables

nevertheless	_____	_____
unseaworthy	_____	_____
unworthiness	_____	_____

RTH /rθ/ Medial—two syllables

Arthur
Bertha
birthday
birthmark
birthplace
birthrate
birthright
Carthage
Eartha
earthborn
earthbound
earthen
earthling
earthly
earthnut

earthquake
earthward
earthworm
earthy
forethought
forthright
forthwith
fourth grade
hearthstone
Martha
Northcutt
northeast
northland
North Pole
Northport

North Shore
North Slope
North Star
northward
northwest
Swarthmore
Swarthout
unearthed
worthless
worthwhile
_____
_____
_____
_____
_____

RTH /rθ/ Medial—three syllables

afterthought
arthritic
arthritis
birthday card
earthenware
earth science
earthshaking
forthcoming

MacArthur
northeastern
northeastward
Northampton
northwestern
Northwestern
orthodox
orthoscope

overthrow
Parthenon
Port Arthur
unearthing
unearthly
_____
_____
_____

RTH /rθ/ Medial—four syllables

birthday party
earth satellite
Happy Birthday
Martha's Vineyard
merthiolate
North Africa

North Dakota
orthodontics
orthodontist
orthogenic
orthographic
orthography

orthopedic
orthopedics
unearthliness
_____
_____
_____

RTH /rθ/ Medial—five syllables

North America
North American
North Carolina

orthochromatic
orthodontia
orthogenesis

orthogenetic
orthographical
_____

RTH /rθ/ Final—one syllable

berth	forth	north
birth	fourth	swarth
dearth	girth	worth
earth	hearth	_____
firth	mirth	_____

RTH /rθ/ Final—two syllables

childbirth	Kenworth	Wentworth
Ellsworth	rebirth	Woolworth
Emsworth	thenceforth	_____
Fort Worth	unearth	_____
henceforth	Wadsworth	_____

THR /θr/ Initial—one syllable

thrall	thrill	throng
thrash	thrilled	through
thread	thrills	throve
threads	thrive	throw
threat	thrived	thrown
three	throat	thrum
thresh	throb	thrummed
threw	throbbed	thrush
thrice	throne	thrust
thrift	throned	_____

THR /θr/ Initial—two syllables

thralldom	threepence	thrilling
thrasher	three-ply	thriver
thrashing	threescore	thriving
threadbare	threesome	throaty
threaded	threesquare	throbbing
threader	thresher	thrombus
threading	threshold	throttle
threadlike	thriftless	throttling
thread mark	thrift shop	throughout
thready	thrift store	through street
threaten	thrifty	throwback
threefold	thriller	thrower

throw in	thrumming	_____
throwing	thrusting	_____
throw rug	thruway	_____

THR /θr/ Initial—three syllables

threatening	three-wheeler	throatier
three-bagger	thresher shark	throatiest
three-base hit	thriftier	thrombosis
three-decker	thriftiest	throwaway
three-quarters	thriftily	_____

THR /θr/ Initial—four syllables

threateningly	three-ring circus	throat microphone
three-legged race	threshing machine	_____

THR /θr/ Medial—two syllables

anthrax	free throw	spendthrift
bathrobe	Guthrie	unthread
bathroom	heartthrob	unthrone
cutthroat	Jethro	walk-through
drive-through	look-through	Winthrop
enthrall	outthrew	wood thrush
enthrone	outthrow	_____

THR /θr/ Medial—three syllables

anthracite	brown thrasher	overthrow
anthropoid	flamethrower	Plymouth Rock
arthritic	follow-through	unthreaded
arthritis	hermit thrush	_____

THR /θr/ Medial—four syllables

erythrocyte	misanthropic	_____
javelin throw	philanthropist	_____

RV /rv/ Medial—two syllables

carver	dervish	harvest
carving	fervid	Harvey
carvings	fervor	Irving
corvette	Harvard	Kerrville

larva	servant	swerving
marvel	server	
Marvin	service	
Mervin	serving	
nervous	starving	
perverse	survey	
scurvey	survive	

RV /rv/ Medial—three syllables

Centerville	observing	survey crew
conserver	preserver	surveying
conserving	preserving	surveyor
deserver	reserving	survival
deserving	reservoir	surviving
enervate	self-service	survivor
fervently	serviceman	survivors
marveling	servicemen	unnerving
marvelous	services	Waterville
Minerva	servicing	wood carving
observance	servitude	
observant	starvation	
observer	supervise	

RV /rv/ Medial—four syllables

conservation	observation	soapstone carvings
conservative	perseverence	subservient
conservator	preservation	survey party
effervescent	reservation	survival kit
enervated	reservations	survivorship
enervation	serviceable	topsy-turvy
intervention	service station	
life preserver	servicewoman	
nervous system	servicewomen	

RV /rv/ Final—one syllable

carve	starve	
curve	swerve	
nerve	verve	
serve		

RV /rv/ Final—two syllables

conserve	observe	self-serve
deserve	preserve	_____
hors d'oeuvre	reserve	_____

RVD /rvd/ Final—one syllable

carved	starved	_____
curved	swerved	_____
served	_____	_____

RVD /rvd/ Final—two syllables

deserved	preserved	unnerved
observed	reserved	_____

RVZ /rvs/ Final—one syllable

carves	scarves	turves
dwarves	serves	wharves
nerves	starves	_____

RVZ /rvs/ Final—two syllables

conserves	observes	_____
deserves	preserves	_____

RW /rw/ Medial—two syllables

airways	fairway	Norway
careworn	farewell	Sherwood
carwash	fireweed	shoreward
carwax	firewood	therewith
Corwin	fireworks	_____
doorway	forward	_____
Erwin	Irwin	_____

RW /rw/ Medial—three syllables

afterword	thenceforward	underworld
afterworld	underwaist	waterways
netherward	underwear	water wings
silverware	underweight	waterworks
spiderweb	underwent	wonder-world
straightforward	underwood	_____

RW /rw/ Medial—four syllables
underwater _____ _____

RY /rj/ Medial—three syllables
lumberyard   solar year   _____

lunar year   yesteryear   _____

RY /rj/ Medial—four syllables
labor union _____ _____

RZ /rz/ Final—one syllable

airs	gears	scores
bars	glares	scours
bears	hares	shares
blares	hears	shears
blurs	heirs	shirrs
bores	hers	shores
burrs	hires	sirs
cares	hours	slurs
cars	jars	smears
chairs	jeers	snares
cheers	lures	snores
choirs	mares	soars
chores	mars	sores
clears	Mars	sours
cores	nears	spares
dares	oars	spars
doors	ours	spears
ears	pairs	spurs
errs	pears	squares
fairs	peers	stairs
fares	piers	stares
fears	pores	stars
fires	pours	steers
firs	purrs	stirs
flares	rears	tears
floors	roars	theirs
fours	scares	tires
furs	scars	tours

wares	wires	_____
wars	years	_____
wears	yours	_____

RZ /rz/ Final—two syllables

admires	campers	filters
affairs	campfires	fingers
allures	captors	fixtures
altars	captures	Flanders
anchors	carvers	flatcars
angers	cashiers	flickers
answers	casters	fliers
antlers	catchers	flippers
appears	cedars	flounders
arbors	checkers	flowers
aspires	colors	founders
Azores	compares	fractures
backfires	crackers	glaciers
badgers	declares	guitars
barbers	devours	ignores
batters	diners	indoors
bazaars	dinners	lathers
beavers	dippers	matures
beggars	divers	members
bidders	doctors	minors
binders	dollars	molars
bleachers	downstairs	movers
blisters	drawers	odors
boilers	dressers	outdoors
bookstores	drivers	pillars
borders	drummers	pliers
boulders	empires	poplars
boxers	errors	posters
breakers	explores	powders
brokers	farmers	powers
builders	fenders	quarters
burners	fielders	rangers
buzzers	figures	razors
callers	fillers	readers

refers	seashores	tankers
rivers	showers	tweezers
rockers	sisters	umpires
rollers	slippers	upstairs
rompers	slivers	vampires
roosters	sneakers	velours
rulers	sparklers	vespers
rumors	speakers	wafers
scissors	squad cars	_____

RZ /rz/ Final—three syllables

adventures	disappears	receivers
amateurs	discovers	recorders
ancestors	engineers	recovers
announcers	erasers	registers
anteaters	fasteners	remainders
beginners	firecrackers	reporters
bystanders	foreigners	sandpipers
calendars	horse lovers	screwdrivers
campaigners	leftovers	state troopers
candy bars	loudspeakers	studded tires
carpenters	managers	teenagers
carriers	polar bears	unawares
diapers	professors	volunteers
dinosaurs	propellers	_____

ER /ɚ/ Medial—three syllables

lowering	powerful	_____
lowermost	showering	_____
powerboat	towering	_____

ER /ɚ/ Final—two syllables

brier	lower	shower
buyer	mayor	slower
drier	player	thrower
flier	plower	tower
flower	power	viewer
grower	rower	_____
layer	sewer	_____

ER /ɚ/ Final—three syllables

ballplayer	Mayflower	wallflower
flamethrower	rain shower	watchtower
horsepower	sandflower	widower
lawnmower	slide viewer	willpower
light tower	sunflower	_____
manpower	tax payer	_____

ER /ɚ/ Final—four syllables

cassette player	overpower	_____
control tower	thundershower	_____
Eisenhower	wholesale buyer	_____

IER /iɚ/ Final—three syllables

barrier	lovelier	terrier
carrier	luckier	thriftier
courier	merrier	tidier
flightier	meteor	wealthier
furrier	smearier	_____
linear	snazzier	_____

IER /iɚ/ Final—four syllables

air carrier	inferior	ulterior
anterior	interior	unhappier
exterior	superior	_____

IER /iɚ/ Final—five syllables

aircraft carrier	thermal barrier	_____
letter carrier	_____	_____

BER /bɚ/ Medial—three syllables

cheeseburger	liberate	numbering
fiberglass	liberty	number line
gabardine	limburger	rubber band
hamburger	lumbering	rubber stamp
harboring	lumberjack	shrubbery
hibernate	lumberyard	slumberer
Kimberly	membership	tubercle
liberal	neighborhood	tuberous

BER /bɚ/ Medial—four syllables

deliberate	tubercular	_____
remembering	_____	_____

BER /bɚ/ Final—two syllables

barber	labor	slobber
blubber	neighbor	sober
clobber	rubber	tuber
fiber	saber	_____

BER /bɚ/ Final—three syllables

belabor	October	_____
foam rubber	_____	_____

MBER /mbɚ/ Final—two syllables

amber	lumber	timber
Amber	member	umber
chamber	number	_____
ember	slumber	_____
limber	somber	_____

MBER /mbɚ/ Final—three syllables

cucumber	November	remember
December	outnumber	September

CHER /tʃɚ/ Medial—three syllables

archery	futurism	_____
cultural	futurist	_____
futureless	rupturing	_____

CHER /tʃɚ/ Medial—four syllables

naturalist	_____	_____
naturally	_____	_____

CHER /tʃɚ/ Final—two syllables

archer	catcher	facture
bleacher	clincher	feature
butcher	creature	fixture
capture	culture	flincher

fracture	pasture	teacher
future	picture	Thatcher
gesture	pitcher	venture
launcher	posture	voucher
leacher	preacher	watcher
lecture	puncture	_____
luncher	rancher	_____
lurcher	richer	_____
mixture	rupture	_____
moisture	rupture	_____
nature	stature	_____

CHER /tʃɚ/ Final—three syllables

adventure	dogcatcher	ligature
back scratcher	flycatcher	overture
bird watcher	furniture	signature
departure	indenture	_____

CHER /tʃɚ/ Final—four syllables

agriculture	manufacture	_____
legislature	miniature	_____
literature	temperature	_____

DER /dɚ/ Medial—three syllables

elderish	tinderbox	undertake
elderly	underbrush	undertook
eldermost	underclothes	underwear
orderly	underdog	underweight
powderhorn	underfoot	underwent
powdering	underground	wanderer
powdery	underling	wandering
spider web	undermine	wanderlust
tenderfoot	underneath	wanderoo
thunderbolt	underpass	wilderness
thunderclap	undersea	wonderful
thunderhead	undershirt	_____
thunderous	underside	_____
thunderstorm	understand	_____
thunderstruck	understood	_____

DER /dɚ/ Medial—four syllables

elderberry	powdering tub	understanding
elder statesman	powder monkey	undertaker
kindergarten	thundershower	undertaking
misunderstand	undercover	underwater
misunderstood	undergarment	_____
orderliness	underlying	_____

DER /dɚ/ Final—two syllables

alder	folder	rudder
bidder	gander	sander
binder	glider	sender
bladder	grinder	shudder
bleeder	grounder	slander
blender	herder	slender
blinder	hinder	speeder
blunder	ladder	spider
border	launder	splendor
boulder	leader	spreader
chowder	louder	tender
cider	odor	threader
cinder	order	thunder
colder	plodder	tinder
condor	plunder	udder
elder	powder	under
Elder	raider	weeder
fender	reader	_____
fielder	render	_____
flounder	rider	_____

DER /dɚ/ Final—three syllables

asunder	disorder	outsider
bewilder	embroider	remainder
calendar	faultfinder	reminder
cheerleader	free-loader	ringleader
commander	insider	shareholder
consider	islander	stepladder
crusader	lavender	_____
cylinder	left-hander	_____

DER /dɚ/ Final—four syllables
Alexander	ice cream vendor	_____
ambassador	winter splendor	_____

FER /fɚ/ Medial—three syllables
afferent	inference	reference
conference	offering	referent
difference	phosphorus	suffering
different	preference	_____

FER /fɚ/ Medial—four syllables
indifference	long-suffering	referable
indifferent	preferable	referential
inferential	preferential	reoffering

FER /fɚ/ Final—two syllables
buffer	gopher	safer
camphor	infer	scoffer
chauffeur	loader	suffer
confer	loafer	sulphur
deafer	offer	transfer
defer	prefer	wafer
differ	refer	zephyr
gaffer	roofer	_____
golfer	rougher	_____

FER /fɚ/ Final—three syllables
bus transfer	_____	_____
decipher	_____	_____

GER /gɚ/ Medial—three syllables
rigorous	_____	_____
vigorous	_____	_____

GER /gɚ/ Final—two syllables
beggar	dagger	leaguer
bigger	eager	logger
chigger	jigger	lugger
cougar	lager	meager

rigor	tiger	_____
stagger	vigor	_____

GER /gɚ/ Final—three syllables

cheeseburger	Limburger	vinegar
hamburger	outrigger	_____

NGER /ŋgɚ/ Medial—three syllables

fingerling	fingerprint	lingering
fingernail	fingerspell	_____

NGER /ŋgɚ/ Final—two syllables

finger	longer	wringer
hanger	ringer	younger
hunger	singer	_____
linger	swinger	_____

JER /dʒɚ/ Medial—three syllables

dangerous	gingerly	majorette
ginger ale	gingersnap	_____
gingerbread	injury	_____

JER /dʒɚ/ Medial—four syllables

belligerent	gingerliness	_____
exaggerate	major-domo	_____

JER /dʒɚ/ Final—two syllables

badger	larger	pledger
danger	ledger	ranger
dodger	lodger	Roger
dredger	lounger	soldier
ginger	major	stranger
Ginger	manger	wager
injure	merger	_____

JER /dʒɚ/ Final—three syllables

avenger	Lone Ranger	passenger
drum major	manager	procedure
endanger	messenger	scavenger

teenager

villager

voyager

Voyager

JER /dʒɚ/ Final—four syllables
astrologer

supercharger

train passenger

KER /kɚ/ Medial—three syllables

acreage	discourage	rookery
Anchorage	handkerchief	snickering
bakery	licorice	soccer ball
brokerage	mackerel	wickerwork
checkerboard	neckerchief	

KER /kɚ/ Final—two syllables

acre	flicker	soccer
anchor	hiker	speaker
baker	kicker	stocker
banker	knocker	sucker
bicker	locker	tanker
blocker	looker	tucker
breaker	poker	wicker
broker	Quaker	wrecker
canker	rocker	
choker	seeker	
clinker	shaker	
conquer	slicker	
cracker	sneaker	
flanker	snicker	

KER /kɚ/ Final—three syllables

backpacker	loudspeaker	shoemaker
dressmaker	nutcracker	watchmaker
hitch-hiker	pact maker	windbreaker
homemaker	pawnbroker	woodpecker
linebacker	saltshaker	

LER /lɚ/ Medial—three syllables

allergic	gallery	scholarship
allergy	polar bear	tolerance
celery	polarize	tolerant
collarbone	polar lights	_____
colorful	roller skates	_____
coloring	salary	_____

LER /lɚ/ Medial—four syllables

artillery	polar axis	tolerable
capillary	polar region	tolerably
intolerant	roller skating	_____

LER /lɚ/ Medial—five syllables

intolerable	roller skating rink	_____
polarization	similarity	_____
popularity	_____	_____

LER /lɚ/ Final—two syllables

antler	jailer	smaller
baler	mailer	smeller
Baylor	miller	solar
bowler	Miller	speller
broiler	molar	sprawler
caller	parlor	squealer
cellar	peddler	stroller
collar	piler	tailor
color	pillar	taller
cooler	polar	Taylor
crawler	poler	teller
dealer	poplar	thriller
dollar	roller	tiller
driller	ruler	trailer
drooler	sailor	trawler
duller	scaler	troller
dweller	scholar	Tyler
feeler	sealer	whaler
healer	seller	_____
heeler	shriller	_____

LER /lɚ/ Final—three syllables

angular
bachelor
consoler
controller
counselor
discolor
four-wheeler
jeweler
littler

modular
muscular
ocular
patroller
popular
propeller
regular
retailer
sand dollar

secular
similar
singular
three-wheeler
tricolor
tubular
two-wheeler
wholesaler
_____

LER /lɚ/ Final—four syllables

caterpillar
fortuneteller
irregular
lenticular
multicolor

particular
semitrailer
spectacular
storm cellar
technicolor

twin propeller
unpopular
watercolor
_____
_____

MER /mɚ/ Medial—three syllables

admiral
armory
boomerang
emerald

emery
formerly
humorous
limerick

memory
numerate
numerous
somersault

MER /mɚ/ Medial—four syllables

America
American

emergency
_____

_____
_____

MER /mɚ/ Final—two syllables

armor
clamor
climber
drummer
Elmer
farmer
former
grammar
hammer
homer

Homer
humor
murmur
plumber
primer
reamer
roomer
rumor
shimmer
simmer

skimmer
stammer
steamer
streamer
summer
swimmer
tamer
tumor
_____

_____

MER /mɚ/ Final—three syllables

beachcomber	newcomer	sledgehammer
consumer	performer	_____
customer	redeemer	_____

NER /nɚ/ Medial—three syllables

energy	honor roll	runnerup
funeral	inner ear	scenery
general	mineral	spinneret
generous	partnership	_____

NER /nɚ/ Medial—four syllables

energetic	honorable	unmannerly
generation	machinery	vulnerable
generator	refinery	_____

NER /nɚ/ Final—two syllables

banner	inner	schooner
burner	liner	sooner
cleaner	lunar	Sooner
corner	manner	spinner
diner	manor	tanner
dinner	minor	tenor
donor	owner	turner
gainer	partner	Turner
gunner	plainer	vintner
honor	runner	winner

NER /nɚ/ Final—three syllables

airliner	foreigner	questioner
beginner	gold panner	roadrunner
container	governor	wagoner
dishonor	long liner	Westerner
dry cleaner	opener	_____
Easterner	prisoner	_____

NER /nɚ/ Final—four syllables

commissioner	practitioner	_____
mid-westerner	_____	_____

PER /pɚ/ Medial—three syllables

aspirin	paperclip	Superman
Copper Age	papering	supersede
copperhead	peppermint	supervise
drapery	properly	temperate
emperor	property	uppermost
opera	slippery	vaporize
paperback	superman	_____

PER /pɚ/ Medial—four syllables

copper-plated	operator	temperative
experiment	superego	vaporizer
intemperate	superficial	_____

PER /pɚ/ Final—two syllables

blooper	Jasper	super
chipper	keeper	supper
chopper	paper	taper
clipper	pepper	trooper
copper	proper	upper
creeper	riper	vapor
dipper	roper	viper
flapper	scraper	whisper
flipper	shipper	whopper
gripper	skipper	wiper
helper	slipper	wrapper
hopper	stopper	zipper
jasper	stupor	_____

PER /pɚ/ Final—three syllables

crepe paper	juniper	state trooper
diaper	newspaper	timekeeper
grasshopper	sandpaper	wallpaper
improper	sandpiper	_____
innkeeper	skyscraper	_____

PER /pɚ/ Final—four syllables

candy striper	paratrooper	wrapping paper
litmus paper	tissue paper	writing paper

RER /rɚ/ Final—two syllables

barer	juror	wearer
carer	mirror	_____
error	sheerer	_____
horror	terror	_____

RER /rɚ/ Final—three syllables

admirer	conqueror	lumberer
adorer	emperor	usurper
armorer	explorer	wanderer
caterer	laborer	_____
conjurer	loiterer	_____

SER /sɚ/ Medial—three syllables

glossary	nursery	Switzerland
grocery	sponsorship	ulcerate

SER /sɚ/ Medial—four syllables

accessory	nursery school	_____
nursery man	rhinoceros	_____

SER /sɚ/ Final—two syllables

bracer	kisser	racer
chaser	lacer	saucer
closer	leaser	slicer
creaser	lesser	splicer
crosser	nicer	tracer
dicer	pacer	ulcer
dresser	piercer	_____
grocer	placer	_____
guesser	presser	_____

SER /sɚ/ Final—three syllables

aggressor	eraser	professor
assessor	horse racer	progressor
compressor	officer	reducer
conducer	oppressor	successor
embosser	possessor	transgressor
enticer	producer	_____

SER /sɚ/ Final—four syllables

dog sled racer	predecessor	_____
interlacer	reproducer	_____

NSER /nsɚ/ Final—two syllables

answer	denser	Spencer
cancer	fencer	sponsor
Cancer	glancer	tensor
censor	lancer	_____
chancer	prancer	_____
dancer	spencer	_____

NSER /nsɚ/ Final—three syllables

advancer	dispenser	extensor
announcer	enhancer	romancer
condenser	entrancer	_____

SHER /ʃɚ/ Medial—three syllables

fisherman	fishery	_____
fishermen	pressuring	_____

SHER /ʃɚ/ Final—two syllables

crusher	plusher	usher
glacier	pressure	washer
gusher	rusher	_____
kosher	squasher	_____
lasher	thrasher	_____
masher	thresher	_____

SHER /ʃɚ/ Final—three syllables

blood pressure	kingfisher	publisher
Britisher	low-pressure	trash masher
high-pressure	New Hampshire	_____

STER /stɚ/ Medial—three syllables

asterisk	masterpiece	yesterday
castor oil	mastery	_____
history	oyster crab	_____
mastering	westerly	_____

STER /stɚ/ Medial—four syllables

master-at-arms	preposterous	upholstery
masterfully	sister-in-law	_____
prehistory	southeasterly	_____

STER /stɚ/ Final—two syllables

aster	Foster	roadster
blister	hamster	roaster
booster	holster	rooster
Buster	lobster	roster
caster	luster	sister
Chester	master	spinster
cluster	mister	tester
coaster	monster	thruster
Custer	muster	toaster
duster	oyster	twister
Easter	pastor	Webster
faster	pester	youngster
fluster	plaster	_____
foster	poster	_____

STER /stɚ/ Final—three syllables

adjuster	half-sister	sinister
ancestor	minister	Sylvester
bandmaster	postmaster	taskmaster
canister	register	toastmaster
disaster	resister	upholster
forecaster	scoutmaster	Worcester
gangbuster	semester	_____
Grand Master	shipmaster	_____

STER /stɚ/ Final—four syllables

administer	Gila monster	quartermaster
flabbergaster	prime minister	roller coaster

TER /tɚ/ Medial—three syllables

aftermath	artery	butterfly
afterward	attorney	butterscotch
alternate	buttercup	counterfeit

determine
enterprise
entertain
eternal
external
factory
interact
interblend
intercede
intercept
intercom
interest
interfere
interpret
intersect
interval
interview
lateral
lettergram

letterhead
lettering
loitering
lottery
motorboat
motorhome
nectarine
outer space
pottery
quarterback
quarterly
shutterbug
smattering
splintery
utterance
utterly
uttermost
veteran
water bed

waterbird
water bug
watercress
water hole
waterfall
waterfowl
waterfront
waterline
waterlogged
watermark
water plant
waterproof
water rat
watertight
waterway
waterwheel
waterworks
yesterday

_____

TER /tɚ/ Medial—four syllables

alternative
directory
eternity
externalize
illiterate
interesting
intermission

intersection
literature
motorcycle
predetermine
quartermaster
quartersection
watercolor

watering place
water lily
watermelon
water polo
water skiing

_____

_____

TER /tɚ/ Medial—five syllables

disinterested
distributorship
intermediate

international
literarily
uninterrupted

unutterable
veterinary
water buffalo

TER /tɚ/ Final—two syllables

batter
beater
better
bitter

bloater
blotter
brighter
butter

canter
chatter
cheater
clatter

clutter	liter	slaughter
crater	litter	smatter
critter	loiter	spatter
cutter	matter	splatter
daughter	meter	spotter
eater	motor	sputter
fatter	mutter	squatter
fighter	neater	stutter
flatter	otter	sweater
floater	patter	tighter
flutter	pewter	traitor
freighter	platter	tutor
fritter	plotter	twitter
glitter	potter	utter
grater	putter	voter
grcatcr	quitter	waiter
gutter	quoter	water
heater	rotor	whitcr
hitter	scatter	writer
hotter	setter	_____
later	shatter	_____
latter	shutter	_____
letter	sitter	_____
lighter	skater	_____

TER /tɚ/ Final—three syllables

anteater	janitor	storm center
auditor	Jupiter	theater
beanshooter	locater	tidewater
chain letter	monitor	transistor
computer	narrator	translator
creator	newsletter	typesetter
dictator	predator	typewriter
editor	promoter	visitor
cquator	saltwater	wood cutter
fire fighter	Senator	_____
gas meter	shot-putter	_____
globe trotter	spectator	_____
high water	stonecutter	_____

TER /t□/ Final—four syllables

agitator
alligator
alma mater
altimeter
aviator
calculator
centimeter
commentator
competitor
cultivator
decorator
demonstrator
diameter

duplicator
educator
elevator
escalator
excavator
generator
incubator
kilometer
legislator
liberator
moderator
navigator
nominator

numerator
operator
parking meter
peanut butter
percolator
perimeter
radiator
thermometer
_____
_____
_____
_____
_____

TER /t□/ Final—five syllables

accelerator
amphitheater

anemometer
denominator

_____
_____

THER /θ□/ Final—two syllables

Arthur
author
ether

Luther
panther
Reuther

_____
_____
_____

THER /ð□/ Medial—three syllables

bothering
bothersome
brotherhood
brotherly
furtherance
furthermore
furthermost
gathering
heathery

lathering
leatherneck
leatherwork
Netherlands
otherwise
Rutherford
smithereens
smothering
southerly

tetherball
weathercock
Weatherford
weatherglass
weather vane
_____
_____
_____
_____

THER /ð□/ Medial—four syllables

father-in-law
leather jacket
mother-in-law

weatherbeaten
wool gathering
_____

_____
_____
_____

THER /ðɚ/ Final—two syllables

bother	heather	smother
breather	Heather	tether
brother	lather	thither
dither	leather	weather
either	mother	whether
farther	neither	whither
father	other	wither
feather	rather	zither
further	slither	_____
gather	smoother	_____

THER /ðɚ/ Final—three syllables

another	grandmother	stepfather
godfather	half brother	stepmother
godmother	housemother	together
grandfather	stepbrother	_____

THER /ðɚ/ Final—four syllables

altogether	shaving lather	_____
patent leather	stormy weather	_____

VER /vɚ/ Medial—three syllables

advertise	overalls	overlook
average	overboard	overnight
beverage	overcast	overpass
Beverly	overcoat	overrun
bravery	overcome	overseas
conversion	overdo	overshoe
coverage	overdraft	oversight
covering	overdue	overtake
diversion	overflow	overtime
evergreen	overgrow	overture
favorite	overhand	overweight
flavoring	overhaul	overwhelm
Hoover Dam	overhead	overwork
ivory	overhear	overwrite
leverage	overjoy	poverty
liverwurst	overlap	reverence

reverent
several
Silver Age
silverware

silvery
slavery
subversive
thievery

wolverine
_____
_____
_____

VER /vɚ/ Medial—four syllables

Beverly Hills
controversy
conversation
covered wagon
delivery

discovery
diversity
favorable
invertebrate
nevertheless

overpower
receivership
recovery
universal
_____

VER /vɚ/ Final—two syllables

beaver
cleaver
clever
clover
cover
Denver
diver
driver
ever
favor
fever
flavor
giver
Grover

Hoover
hover
lever
liver
louver
lover
mover
never
over
plover
quaver
quiver
river
rover

Rover
savor
sever
shiver
sliver
unfavorable
waiver
waver
weaver
_____
_____
_____
_____
_____

VER /vɚ/ Final—three syllables

deliver
discover
endeavor
forever
hay fever
however
leftover
maneuver
moreover
Passover

preserver
quicksilver
receiver
recover
retriever
Rhone River
screwdriver
skin diver
stopover
turn over

uncover
Vancouver
whatever
whenever
wherever
whichever
whoever
whomever
whyever
_____

VER /vɚ/ Final—four syllables

life preserver	whatsoever	_____
redeliver	whensoever	_____
scuba diver	whosoever	_____

YER /jɚ/ Medial—three syllables

figure eight	figurine	_____
figurehead	_____	_____

YER /jɚ/ Final—two syllables

failure	lawyer	_____
figure	savior	_____
junior	senior	_____

YER /jɚ/ Final—three syllables

behavior	peculiar	_____
employer	refigure	_____
familiar	Tom Sawyer	_____

YER /jɚ/ Final—four syllables

misbehavior	trial lawyer	_____
power failure	unfamiliar	_____

ZER /zɚ/ Medial—three syllables

misery	reservoir	_____
observing	_____	_____

ZER /zɚ/ Medial—four syllables

miserable	observation	reservation
miserably	preservation	_____

ZER /zɚ/ Final—two syllables

blazer	geyser	riser
bruiser	hawser	squeezer
buzzer	laser	uscr
Caesar	loser	visor
cleanser	miser	Windsor
cruiser	quizzer	_____
freezer	razor	_____

ZER /zɚ/ Final—three syllables

accuser	composer	incisor
adviser	deep freezer	trailblazer
bulldozer	divisor	_____

ZER /zɚ/ Final—four syllables

appetizer	polarizer	_____
atomizer	stabilizer	_____
fertilizer	vaporizer	_____

ZHER /ʒɚ/ Medial—three syllables

azurite	measurement	treasury
glaziery	measuring	_____
leisurely	treasurer	_____

ZHER /ʒər/, /ʒɚ/ Medial—four syllables

measuring cup	pleasurable	_____
measuring tape	Treasure Island	_____

ZHER /ʒɚ/ Final—two syllables

closure	pleasure	_____
leisure	treasure	_____
measure	_____	_____

ZHER /ʒɚ/ Final—three syllables

composure	exposure	_____
displeasure	foreclosure	_____
enclosure	remeasure	_____

S

Pronounced: /s/
Spelled: s, ss, sc, sch, c, ce, sw, sp, ps, z, x

S /s/ Initial—one syllable

cell	sash	sell
cells	sat	send
cent	Saul	sent
cinch	save	serf
cite	saved	serve
psalms	saw	served
psyched	say	set
sack	scene	Seth
sacked	scent	sew
sad	sea	sewn
safe	seal	sick
sag	sealed	Sid
sage	seals	side
said	seam	sides
sail	sear	siege
sailed	search	sieve
saint	searched	sift
sake	seat	sigh
sale	see	sight
sales	seed	sign
salt	seeds	signed
salve	seek	signs
Sam	seem	silk
same	seemed	sill
sand	seen	silt
sane	seep	sin
sang	seine	sing
sank	seize	singe
sap	seized	sink
sapped	self	sinned

Sioux	solve	subbed
sip	some	such
sips	son	suck
sir	song	suds
sit	soon	sue
site	soot	Sue
sites	soothe	sued
size	sop	suit
so	sore	suite
soak	sort	sulk
soaked	sought	sum
soap	soul	summed
soar	sound	sun
sob	sounds	sung
sobbed	soup	sunk
sock	sour	sunned
sod	south	surf
soft	sow	surge
soil	sown	_____
sold	soy	_____
sole	sub	_____

S /s/ Initial—two syllables

cedar	civet	saddle
ceiling	civic	sadly
cellar	civil	safer
cement	cycle	safety
center	cycling	saga
central	cyclone	sagebrush
certain	cymbals	sailboat
Ceylon	Cyril	sailfish
cider	pseudo	sailing
cinder	psyched-up	sailor
Cindy	Sabbath	saintly
circle	saber	salaam
circled	sable	salad
circuit	sachet	salesclerk
cited	sacred	salesman
city	sadder	Sally

salmon	scenic	senile
salon	scented	senior
salty	scepter	señor
salute	scissors	sentry
salvage	Seabee	serene
Sammy	sea breeze	sergeant
sampan	seafood	series
sample	sea front	sermon
sampler	sea gull	serpent
sandal	sealer	serum
sandbag	seaplane	servant
sandbar	seaport	serving
sandbug	searchlight	session
sandbur	seashell	setter
sand crab	seashore	setting
sandman	season	settle
sandpail	seat belt	set-up
sandpile	sea trout	seven
sandwich	seaward	seventh
sandy	seaway	sever
Sandy	seaweed	severe
sapling	Sea World	sewage
sapphire	seclude	sewer
sappy	second	sewing
sardine	secret	Sibyl
sari	section	sickle
satchel	sector	side band
satin	secure	sided
Saturn	sedan	sideline
sauna	sedate	sideshow
saunter	seedling	sidewalk
saute	seeing	sideways
savage	seeming	siding
saving	segment	signal
savings	seldom	signing
savor	select	sign-off
sawing	selfish	sign-up
sawmill	semi	silent
saying	senate	silkworm

silky	somewhere	succumb
silly	sonar	sucker
silo	songbird	suckling
silver	Sonja	suction
simmer	sonnet	Sudan
simple	Sonny	sudden
Sinai	sooner	suet
singer	Sooner	Suez
singing	sopping	suffer
single	soppy	suffice
Sioux Falls	sorrow	suited
siphon	sorry	suitor
siren	souffle′	sulfur
sitting	sounding	sulky
sit-up	soundly	sullen
sizzle	soundproof	sultry
soapy	soundwaves	summer
soccer	soupy	summit
social	sourdough	summon
socked-in	South Bridge	summons
socket	southern	sun bath
soda	southpaw	sun bathe
sofa	South Pole	sunbeam
softball	southward	sunburn
soften	soybean	sundae
software	St. Paul	Sunday
soggy	subbing	sun deck
solar	subdue	sunder
soldier	subgroup	sundown
solemn	subject	sundries
solid	sublet	sunfish
solo	sublime	sunken
somber	submerge	sun lamp
someday	submerse	sunlight
somehow	submit	sunlit
someone	subtle	sunny
something	subtract	sun proof
sometime	suburb	sunrise
sometimes	subway	sunshine

sun tan	surfer	suture
super	surfing	Suzanne
superb	surgeon	swordfish
supine	surmise	Sydney
supper	surmount	symbol
supplied	surname	symptom
supplies	surprise	syphon
supply	surrey	syringe
support	surround	syrup
suppose	survey	_____
supreme	survive	_____
surcharge	Susan	_____
surfboard	Susie	_____

S /s/ Initial—three syllables

celebrate	sabotage	Santa Fe
celery	saboteur	satellite
cellophane	saccharin	Saturday
Centerville	sacrament	sauerkraut
centigrade	safety belt	Savannah
centipede	safety pin	savings bond
Central Park	safflower	savory
Central Time	salad bar	scenery
century	salad oil	seafaring
cereal	salami	sea level
certainly	salary	sea lion
certified	saleswoman	seamanship
certify	saliva	sea otter
cinema	salvation	seasoning
cinnamon	Samoa	sea urchin
circular	Samoan	seaworthy
circulate	sand dollar	second hand
citizen	sand piper	sectional
city hall	sandalwood	secular
civilian	sandpaper	sedative
civilize	sanity	sediment
Civil War	San Pedro	segregate
cylinder	Santa Claus	seismograph
Cynthia	Santa Cruz	selection

self-assured
self-composed
self-contained
self-control
self-giving
self-glory
self-image
self-imposed
self-pity
self-regard
self-reproach
semaphore
senator
señora
sentiment
separate
September
sequoia
serape
serenade
serial
settlement
seventeen
seventeenth
seventy
several
signature
sign language
silhouette
Silver Age
silverware
similar
simplify
Singapore
singular
situate
soccerball
soccerfield
sociable

socialize
social work
soda pop
sodium
soft-hearted
soft-shell crab
solar heat
solitaire
solitude
soluble
solution
sombrero
somebody
sonata
sonic boom
son-in-law
sophomore
soprano
sorrowful
soundproofing
sour cream
sousaphone
southerly
Southerner
souvenir
Soviet
subcontract
subdivide
subjection
subjective
subjunctive
submarine
subnormal
subpoena
subtitle
suburban
succotash
succulent
suffering

sufficient
sufficing
suffocate
suggestion
suitable
sulfuric
summarize
summary
summation
summer camp
summertime
sun bathing
sun dial
sunflower
Sunnyvale
Sun Valley
superman
Superman
supplement
supportive
Supreme Court
surrender
surroundings
surveying
Sutherland
sycamore
sycophant
syllable
Sylvia
symbolic
symbolize
symmetry
sympathize
sympathized
sympathy
symphonic
symphony
synagogue
synchronize

syncopate	Syria	_____
synonym	syrupy	_____
synthetic	_____	_____

S /s/ Initial—four syllables

celebration	self-directed	sukiyaki
celebrity	self-evident	supercharger
cemetery	semicolon	superego
centimeter	seminary	superficial
ceremony	señorita	super highway
certificate	sentimental	superimpose
certified check	separation	superior
certified mail	seventieth	supermarket
Cinderella	sewing machine	supervision
circulation	single parent	supremacy
citizenship	social-minded	symbolical
psychology	social welfare	symmetrical
safcty glasses	social worker	sympathetic
safety helmet	soda fountain	sympathizer
salamander	South Korea	sympathizing
satellite dish	South Vietnam	symposium
seasonable	subcommittee	symptomatic
secondary	subcontinent	syncopation
secretary	subdivision	synonymous
sectarian	subjectively	systematize
seeing-eye dog	subliminal	_____
self-appointed	subordinate	_____
self-determined	Suez Canal	_____

S /s/ Initial—five syllables

civilization	subcutaneous	sulfanilamide
psychological	submicroscopic	superintendent
Sagittarius	subminiature	supervisory
sedimentary	subsidiary	_____
self-analysis	subterranean	_____

S /s/ Initial—six syllables

subequatorial	supernumerary	_____
subminiaturize	systematically	_____

S /s/ Medial—two syllables

acid	decent	lacing
ascend	decide	lacy
ascent	descend	Lassie
aside	descent	lasso
assert	dicer	leaser
assign	dissect	leasing
assume	dresser	lessen
basic	dressing	lesser
basin	dress up	lesson
bassoon	essay	Lisa
beside	eyesight	listen
besiege	facet	loosen
Bessie	facing	Lucille
bison	faucet	Lucy
blessing	Flossie	mason
blossom	flossing	massage
bosses	fossil	massive
bossy	fussing	message
bracelet	fussy	messy
bracer	gases	missing
braces	glasses	mossy
Brussels	glisten	muscle
bussing	glossy	muscled
Casey	gossip	mussel
cassette	grassy	myself
castle	grocer	Osage
chasing	guesser	pacer
classic	guessing	pacing
classy	hassock	passage
closer	hayseed	passing
creaser	high sea	peso
crescent	hissing	piecer
crosser	icing	pieces
crossing	icy	Pisces
crusade	Jason	placer
Dawson	Jaycees	placid
deceit	kissing	placing
deceive	lacer	posse

possum	receipt	trestle
precede	receive	Tucson
precept	recent	tussle
precinct	recite	two-some
presser	reset	usage
pressing	Russell	vessel
pricing	tassel	voices
proceed	tossing	voicing
proceeds	toss-up	wayside
racer	tracer	whistle
racing	tracing	_____
recede	Tracy	_____

S /s/ Medial—three syllables

aerosol	cul-de-sac	episode
aggressor	Dawson Creek	eraser
Alison	December	essential
Alissa	deceptive	fantasy
Arkansas	decibel	Ferris wheel
assembly	decided	field glasses
assortment	decimal	garrison
assumption	decipher	gasoline
asylum	decision	glossary
babysit	descendant	gooseberry
bathing suit	desecrate	grasshopper
Bay City	desolate	grocery
bicycle	dinosaur	hairdresser
bus safety	disable	Harrison
casino	disagree	heavyset
casserole	disappear	high-sounding
Chicasaw	disciple	icicle
China Sea	discipline	innocent
classical	disinfect	isolate
classify	disobey	jealousy
compressor	disorder	kerosene
conducer	Edison	legacy
courtesy	embassy	lesson plan
crossover	embosser	lyceum
crusader	enticer	Madison

medicine	precedent	rejoicing
messenger	preceding	tendency
moccasin	preceptor	Tennessee
molasses	precipice	tennis court
mussel crab	principal	tennis shoes
oasis	principle	Teresa
ocelot	procedure	tricycle
officer	producer	two-cycle
opossum	professor	two-sided
oppressor	progressor	U.S.A.
pacemaker	promising	U.S.N.
Pacific	prophecy	Uncle Sam
parasite	prophesy	unfasten
parasol	racing car	unison
passageway	receiver	unloosen
passenger	reception	vacillate
Passover	receptive	windowsill
pharmacy	recipe	worrisome
policeman	recital	_____
policy	recycle	_____
possessor	reducer	_____

S /s/ Medial—four syllables

accuracy	increasingly	presidency
ambassador	interlacer	pussy willow
antecedent	jealousy	receivable
antiseptic	kilocycle	receivership
associate	Minnesota	receptacle
capacity	municipal	reciprocal
cassette player	nervous system	reproducer
classified ad	participate	rhesus monkey
coliseum	participle	U.S.A.F.
commissary	penicillin	U.S.M.C.
desegregate	philosopher	U.S.S.R.
disadvantage	philosophy	ultrasonic
facilitate	policewoman	undecided
Fantasy Land	potassium	unicycle
hacienda	precipitant	vacillation
impossible	precipitate	velocity

vice-president	vitamin C	_____
vicinity	Yosemite	_____
virtuoso	_____	_____

S /s/ Medial—five syllables

animosity	disobedient	promissory note
association	electricity	unnecessary
classification	miscellaneous	unprecedented
confederacy	necessarily	vice presidency
curiosity	potato salad	water moccasin
data processing	precipitation	_____

S /s/ Final—one syllable

ace	fuss	louse
base	gas	mace
bass	geese	mass
Bess	glass	mess
bless	gloss	mice
bliss	goose	miss
blouse	grace	Miss
boss	Grace	moose
brace	grass	moss
brass	grease	mouse
Bruce	Greece	nice
Bryce	grouse	niece
bus	guess	noose
case	Gus	pace
chase	hiss	pass
chess	house	peace
Chris	ice	piece
class	Joyce	place
crease	juice	plus
cross	kiss	press
dice	lace	price
dose	lass	race
dress	lease	rice
face	less	Ross
fleece	lice	Russ
floss	loose	this

thus	us	voice
toss	vase	yes
trace	vice	_____
twice	vise	_____

S /s/ Final—two syllables

access	caress	erase
across	Carlos	Eunice
actress	cautious	express
address	Cayuse	famous
advice	chorus	firehouse
Agnes	Clovis	fireplace
aimless	compass	fitness
air base	compress	focus
air bus	concise	fungus
alas	confess	furnace
Alice	congress	genius
amiss	cordless	goodness
anxious	countless	gorgeous
apiece	courthouse	gracious
Bernice	Curtis	greenhouse
bias	Dallas	harness
birdhouse	decrease	Harris
birthplace	deface	headdress
blue grass	Denise	heiress
boat house	Dennis	helpless
bonus	depress	Highness
bookcase	device	hopeless
breathless	displace	hot house
briefcase	doghouse	hour glass
business	dollhouse	ice house
bypass	Doris	illness
caboose	doubtless	impress
cactus	Douglas	increase
campus	dry ice	invoice
Candice	duchess	iris
canvas	emboss	Iris
carcass	embrace	Janice
careless	endless	jealous

joyous
Kansas
kindness
lattice
lettuce
Lewis
lifeless
lighthouse
likeness
Linus
Lois
lotus
Lucas
malice
mattress
menace
minus
mongoose
Morris
mouthpiece
mucus
necklace
needless
nervous
notice
novice
obese
office
oppress
palace
pampas
papoose
Paris
penthouse

Phyllis
playhouse
police
porpoise
possess
practice
precious
precise
preface
premise
process
produce
profess
profuse
progress
promise
pump house
purchase
purpose
rebus
Red Cross
reduce
release
replace
righteous
roundhouse
Rufus
ruthless
schoolhouse
shameless
shapeless
shoelace
sickness
Taurus

tennis
terrace
thermos
thickness
Thomas
thoughtless
tigress
timepiece
toolhouse
toothless
tortoise
townhouse
treehouse
trellis
two-piece
undress
unlace
unless
useless
Venice
vicious
waitress
Wallace
walrus
warehouse
weakness
White House
witless
witness
wondrous
wordless
workplace
worthless

_____

S /s/ Final—three syllables

about face
accomplice
adios

alias
ambitious
anyplace

apple juice
arthritis
Beatrice

boarding pass
Chilkoot Pass
cleanliness
coffeehouse
Columbus
contagious
courageous
courteous
curious
dangerous
data base
delicious
dental floss
doublecross
embarrass
encompass
enormous
eye witness
fabulous
fiberglass
furious
generous
glorious
happiness
hideous
hiding place
Honduras
horrendous
humorous
igneous

impetus
infectious
ingenious
interface
introduce
lemon juice
lioness
luminous
marvelous
momentous
Mother Goose
mountainous
nautilus
nucleus
numerous
nutritious
obvious
octopus
ominous
open house
orange juice
outrageous
overpass
pancreas
papyrus
paradise
pillowcase
platypus
poisonous
populous

powerhouse
powerless
precipice
precocious
prejudice
previous
printing press
radius
ravenous
rebellious
relay race
religious
reproduce
tedious
tetanus
thoroughness
tidiness
underpass
unkindness
Uranus
various
venturous
vigorous
villainous
virtuous
vivacious
wilderness
wordiness

_____

_____

S /s/ Final—four syllables

adventurous
amaryllis
ambiguous
amphibious
Annapolis
anonymous
apparatus

Aquarius
camera case
continuous
diabetes
diagnosis
hilarious
incredulous

loving kindness
metropolis
miraculous
nevertheless
notorious
opera house
paddle tennis

praying mantis	tumultuous	_____
precarious	unanimous	_____
ridiculous	vicarious	_____
table tennis	victorious	_____
tomato juice	voluminous	_____

S /s/ Final—five syllables

appendicitis	metamorphosis	_____
hippopotamus	simultaneous	_____
magnifying glass	tuberculosis	_____

S /s/ Recurring—one syllable

cease	since	_____
sauce	sis	_____
sense	_____	_____

S /s/ Recurring—two syllables

assess	sack race	solace
basis	sassy	South Seas
biceps	saucepan	subset
cease fire	saucer	subside
ceaseless	saucy	subsoil
Cecil	sausage	succeed
censor	sawhorse	sucrose
census	scentless	suitcase
Christmas	seaside	sunset
circus	secede	suppress
citrus	seesaw	surface
crisis	sentence	surpass
criss cross	sequence	surplus
cypress	service	suspect
Cypress	sickness	suspense
decease	silence	system
Francis	sincere	thesis
glass house	sinus	voiceless
incense	sissy	_____
license	sister	_____
priceless	so-so	_____
recess	soapsuds	_____

S /s/ Recurring—three syllables

assessor	self-addressed	subsidy
Cecilia	self-conscious	subsistence
cellulose	self-defense	subsonic
Celsius	self-esteem	successor
censorship	self-righteous	summer house
centerpiece	self-searching	sumptuous
chili sauce	self-support	sunglasses
Christmas card	sensation	suppressor
Christmas Day	sensible	surfacing
Christmas Eve	sensitive	synopsis
Christmas tree	serious	synthesis
emphasis	serviceman	systemize
five senses	solar house	taco sauce
gaseous	solicit	trespassing
narcissus	S.O.S.	unconscious
processor	Southern Cross	usefulness
sacrifice	St. Louis	_____
sassafras	subconscious	_____
satisfy	subjacent	_____
sea sickness	subsequent	_____
secession	subsidize	_____

S /s/ Recurring—four syllables

accessory	paralysis	semicircle
analysis	parenthesis	sensational
assessable	precipitous	South China Sea
Civil Service	predecessor	South Pacific
dissatisfied	rhinoceros	susceptible
flying saucer	salad dressing	suspension bridge
insecticide	seat belt safety	synonymous
Massachusetts	self-discipline	word processor
necessary	self-sacrifice	_____
necessity	self-sufficient	_____
no trespassing	self-supporting	_____

SF /sf/ Initial—one syllable

sphere	_____	_____
sphinx	_____	_____

SF /sf/ Initial—two syllables
spheric
spheroid

SF /sf/ Initial—three syllables
spherical

SF /sf/ Initial—four syllables
spherically

SF /sf/ Medial—two syllables

asphalt	henceforth	transfix
blaspheme	houseful	transform
cat's fur	peaceful	transfuse
forceful	thenceforth	useful
graceful	transfer	

SF /sf/ Medial—three syllables

atmosphere	gas furnace	transference
blasphemer	hemisphere	transfigure
blasphemous	lithosphere	transformer
blasphemy	misfortune	transfusion
disfavor	phosphorus	usefulness
disfigure	satisfy	
gas fixture	stratosphere	

SF /sf/ Medial—four syllables

asphyxiate	satisfaction	transformation
dysphasia	transferable	transfusible

FS /fs/ Medial—three syllables

cough syrup	lifesaving
life cycles	

FS /fs/ Final—one syllable

beefs	chefs	cuffs
bluffs	chiefs	fluffs
briefs	cliffs	goofs
buffs	coughs	huffs

Jeff's	roofs	staffs
muffs	ruffs	stuffs
proofs	scoffs	whiffs
puffs	scuffs	_____
reefs	spoofs	_____

FS /fs/ Final—two syllables

beliefs	handcuffs	show-offs
cast offs	kerchiefs	takeoffs
cutoffs	layoffs	tariffs
giraffes	play-offs	_____

FS /fs/ Final—three syllables

| photographs | telegraphs | _____ |
| powder puffs | _____ | _____ |

SK /sk/ Initial—one syllable

scab	scoot	skid
scald	scope	skiff
scale	scorch	skill
scaled	scorched	skilled
scamp	score	skim
scan	scored	skimmed
scanned	scorn	skimp
scant	scorned	skimped
scar	Scotch	skin
scarce	Scott	skinned
scare	scour	skip
scared	scoured	skipped
scarf	scout	skirt
scarred	scouts	skit
scat	scowl	skulk
scheme	scowled	skull
schemed	scuff	skunk
school	scum	skunked
scoff	skate	sky
scold	skeet	_____
scoop	sketch	_____
scooped	ski	_____

SK /sk/ Initial—two syllables

scabbard	schoolroom	Skagway
scabby	schooner	skateboard
scaffold	scolding	skated
scallion	scooter	skater
scallop	scorcher	skating
scalloped	scoreboard	skeptic
scallops	scorecard	sketchbook
scalpel	scornful	sketchy
scamper	scot-free	skidding
scandal	Scotland	skier
scanty	Scotsman	skiing
scapegoat	Scottie	ski jump
scarcely	Scottish	ski lift
scarecrow	Scottsdale	skillet
scarlet	Scottsville	skillful
scary	Scotty	skinny
scatter	scoundrel	skunkweed
scattered	scouting	sky blue
schedule	scuba	skyborn
scheduled	scuffle	skydive
scholar	scuffled	Skylab
schoolboy	sculptor	skylark
school bus	sculpture	skyline
schoolgirl	sculptured	skyward
schoolhouse	scurried	skyway
schooling	scurry	skywrite
schoolmarm	scurvy	_____
schoolmate	scuttle	_____

SK /sk/ Initial—three syllables

scandalize	scholastic	skate-a-thon
scapula	scorekeeper	skatemobile
scatterbrain	Scorpio	skeleton
scattering	scorpion	ski-a-thon
scatter rug	Scotland Yard	skin diving
scavenger	Scott City	ski patrol
schematic	scoutmaster	sky cover
scholarship	scuttlebutt	sky diving

sky rocket   skywriter   _____
skyscraper   skywriting   _____

SK /sk/ Medial—two syllables

asking	frisky	night school
basket	gasket	oilskin
basking	Girl Scouts	Oscar
biscuit	grade school	outskirts
Boy Scouts	grass skirt	pesky
brisket	Haskell	pigskin
buckskin	high school	plaid skirt
calfskin	hopscotch	preschool
cascade	husking	Redskins
casket	husky	rescue
cub Scout	Husky	risky
day school	ice skate	sealskin
discard	kidskin	sheepskin
discount	landscape	threescore
discourse	mascot	tuskless
discuss	miscount	whiskbroom
diskette	muskegs	whisker
dusky	musk ox	whiskers
escape	muskrat	_____
escort	musky	_____

SK /sk/ Medial—three syllables

Alaska	discordance	hockey skate
basketball	discourage	horoscope
basketful	discouraged	hula skirt
basket weave	discover	huskiness
basketwork	discovered	ice skating
breadbasket	discussion	mascara
butterscotch	escapade	masculine
confiscate	escapement	masquerade
discolor	escarpment	May basket
discomfort	Eskimo	microscope
disconcert	fire escape	misconstrue
disconnect	gyroscope	mosquito
discontent	hibiscus	muscular

musketeer	spectroscope	whiskery
muskmelon	stethoscope	Wisconsin
musk oxen	Stravinsky	_____
Nebraska	summer school	_____
onionskin	Sunday School	_____
periscope	telescope	_____
public school	wastebasket	_____
roller skates	whiskerless	_____

SK /sk/ Medial—four syllables.

baleen basket	Episcopal	private schooling
birch bark basket	escalator	roller skating
disconsolate	figure skater	San Francisco
discontented	figure skating	_____
discontinue	kaleidoscope	_____
discovery	microscopic	_____
Easter basket	picnic basket	_____

SK /sk/ Final—one syllable

ask	dusk	rusk
bask	flask	task
bisque	frisk	tusk
brisk	husk	whisk
brusque	mask	_____
cask	mosque	_____
desk	musk	_____
disk	risk	_____

SK /sk/ Final—two syllables

corn husk	grotesque	unmask
face mask	mollusk	_____
file disk	school desk	_____
gas mask	swim mask	_____

SK /sk/ Final—three syllables

asterisk	office desk	_____
data disk	picturesque	_____
floppy disk	reading desk	_____
mammoth tusk	_____	_____

KS /ks/ Medial—two syllables

accent	expanse	mix-up
accept	expect	Nixon
access	expel	oxcart
axis	expelled	oxen
axle	expend	Oxford
bake sale	expense	oxide
boxcar	expert	perplexed
boxer	expire	pixy
boxful	Expo	proxy
boxing	export	quicksand
boxwood	expose	Roxanne
dachshund	exposed	sextet
Dexter	expound	sexton
dextrose	extant	sixpence
Dixie	extend	sixteen
Dixon	extern	sixteenth
exceed	extinct	sixth sense
excel	extol	sixty
except	extort	succeed
excerpt	fixate	success
excess	fixing	taxi
exchange	fixture	Texas
exchanged	foxhole	toxic
excise	foxhound	toxin
excite	Jackson	vaccine
excuse	Knoxville	waxy
excused	Maxine	_____
exhale	mixer	_____
exhaled	mixing	_____
expand	mixture	_____

KS /ks/ Medial—three syllables

axiom	excellence	excessive
complexion	excellent	exchequer
dexterous	excepting	excision
dioxide	exception	excitant
excavate	exceptive	excited
exceeding	excerption	excitement

exciter
exciting
excursion
excursive
execute
exercise
exercised
exhalant
exlibris
exodus
exogen
exorcise
expanded
expansion
expansive
expectant
expedite
expensive
exponent
exporter

exposure
expulsion
extended
extension
extensive
extensor
external
extinction
extinctive
extinguish
extortion
exudate
flexible
galaxy
hexagon
Jacksonville
Lexington
luxury
maximum
Mexican

Mexico
oxidize
oxygen
quicksilver
saxophone
successful
succession
successive
successor
taxable
taxation
taxicab
taxpayer
vaccinate
vexation
_____
_____
_____
_____
_____

KS /ks/ Medial—four syllables

accelerate
Alexander
approximate
complexity
excavation
excavator
exceedingly
excellency
excelsior
exceptional
excessively
exchangeable
excisable
excitable
excitation
excusable
execution

executor
exerciser
exfoliate
exhalation
exhibition
exotoxin
expectancy
expectation
expectorant
expedience
expedient
expendable
expenditure
experience
experiment
expiration
exportation

exposition
expositor
extendible
exterior
exterminate
externalize
extinguisher
fox terrier
index finger
luxuriant
luxurious
Mexican food
New Mexico
Old Mexico
proximity
relaxation
Route 66

St. Patrick's Day	unexpected	_____
success story	vaccination	_____
Texas Rangers	_____	_____

KS /ks/ Medial—five syllables

exceptionable	exhibitioner	extenuation
exceptionably	exhibitionist	extermination
excitableness	ex officio	Mexican Hat Dance
excitatory	expediency	Mexico City
excommunicate	experimental	_____
executable	expiratory	_____
exfoliation	extemporary	_____

KS /ks/ Final—one syllable

aches	cloaks	flocks
ax	clocks	flukes
backs	coax	folks
bakes	cokes	fox
beaks	cooks	francs
bikes	Cox	freaks
blacks	cracks	frocks
blocks	creaks	Greeks
books	creeks	hawks
box	croaks	hex
brakes	crocks	hikes
breaks	crooks	hoax
bricks	decks	hocks
Bronx	dikes	hooks
brooks	docks	irks
Brooks	drakes	Jack's
bucks	ducks	jacks
Bucks	dukes	Jake's
cakes	fakes	jinx
checks	fix	jokes
cheeks	flakes	kicks
chicks	flax	knacks
chokes	flecks	knocks
chucks	flex	lacks
clicks	flicks	lakes

lax	rocks	sticks
likes	sacks	tacks
locks	seeks	tax
looks	shakes	Tex
lox	shocks	ticks
lux	six	tracks
lynx	slacks	tricks
makes	smocks	trucks
minx	smokes	tucks
mix	snacks	vex
necks	snakes	wakes
ox	socks	wax
picks	sphinx	weeks
pox	spikes	whacks
racks	spooks	wrecks
ranks	squeaks	yaks
rex	stacks	_____
Rex	steaks	_____

KS /ks/ Final—two syllables

affix	complex	invokes
Alex	convex	kayaks
annex	cornflakes	larynx
antiques	critics	latex
apex	daybreaks	lyrics
attacks	deluxe	mailbox
attics	Derrick's	mistakes
Aztecs	derricks	musk ox
bandbox	duplex	notebooks
barracks	epics	padlocks
basics	epochs	peacocks
beefsteaks	ethics	perplex
beeswax	fabrics	Phoenix
black snakes	Felix	physics
borax	garlics	pillbox
classics	hat box	prefix
clinics	icebox	race tracks
coin box	index	relax
comics	influx	sandbox

scrapbooks
shamrocks
silex
smallpox
snowflakes
sound box
suffix

surtax
sweepstakes
syntax
thorax
thumbtacks
toothpicks
triplex

woodchucks
wordbooks
workbooks
yardsticks
_____
_____
_____

KS /ks/ Final—three syllables

aerobics
almanacs
appendix
artichokes
candlesticks
ceramics
chicken pox
comic books

elastics
equinox
garter snakes
income tax
lumberjacks
motorbikes
orthodox
paperbacks

pogo sticks
politics
railroad tracks
storybooks
_____
_____
_____
_____

KS + Adjoining Clusters, Medial—two syllables

exclaim
exclaimed
exclude
excrete
explain
explode

exploit
explore
express
expressed
extra
extract

extreme
extrude
foxglove
foxtrot
_____
_____

KS + Adjoining Clusters, Medial—three syllables

ecstasy
ecstatic
exclusion
exclusive
expletive
explicit
explorer
explosion
explosive
expressage
expression
expressive

expressly
expressman
express train
expressway
exquisite
extra bold
extraction
extractor
extradite
extravert
extremely
extremist

extricate
extrinsic
extrovert
extrusion
_____
_____
_____
_____
_____
_____
_____
_____

KS + Adjoining Clusters, Medial—four syllables

exclamation	expropriate	extravagant
exclusively	extractable	extraversion
excruciate	extradition	extremity
explanation	extraneous	extroversion
exploitation	extrapolate	_____
explorative	extravagance	_____

KS + Adjoining Clusters, Medial—five syllables

exclamation mark	exploratory	extrasensory
exclamatory	expropriation	extravascular
explanatory	extrajudicial	_____

SL /sl/ Initial—one syllable

slab	sleigh	sloth
slack	sleight	slouch
slacks	slept	slow
slam	slew	sludge
slang	slick	slug
slant	slid	slugs
slap	slide	sluice
slash	slides	slum
slat	slight	slump
slate	slim	slung
slave	slime	slunk
slaw	sling	slur
sled	slip	slurp
sleek	slit	slush
sleep	sloop	sly
sleet	slope	_____
sleeve	slot	_____

SL /sl/ Initial—two syllables

slacken	sledding	sleepless
slacker	sled dog	sleepwear
slalom	sleeky	sleepy
slapstick	sleeper	sleety
slashing	sleepers	sleeveless
sledder	sleep-in	sleigh bells

slender	slippers	slow sign
slicer	slither	slow-up
slicing	sliver	sludgy
slicker	slobber	sluggish
slide rule	slogan	slumber
sliding	sloping	slurring
slighting	sloppy	_____
slightly	sloshy	_____
slimy	sloth bear	_____
slingshot	slothful	_____
slinking	slouchy	_____
slinky	Slovak	_____
slipknot	slowdown	_____
slipper	slowpoke	_____

SL /sl/ Initial—three syllables

slalom course	slide trombone	slow-motion
sledgehammer	slide viewer	slow-moving
sleeping bag	sliding scale	slow-witted
sleepwalking	slip cover	sluggishness
sleepyhead	slippery	slumberland
slenderize	slot machine	slushiest
sliceable	slovenly	_____

SL /sl/ Medial—two syllables

asleep	juiceless	voiceless
bobsled	landslide	Wesley
bracelet	Lesley	whistler
bustling	loosely	whistling
crosslight	nicely	wrestler
crossline	North slope	wrestling
crossly	onslaught	_____
dislike	priceless	_____
dislodge	rustling	_____
dog sled	ski slope	_____
enslave	snowslide	_____
grand slam	translate	_____
hustling	tussling	_____
jostling	useless	_____

SL /sl/ Medial—three syllables

carelessly	purposely	uselessly
cross-legged	super slide	wrestling camp
dislocate	translation	wrestling coach
disloyal	translative	wrestling match
enslavement	translator	wrestling shoes
expressly	translocate	wrestling team
misleading	translucence	_____
purposeless	translucent	_____

SL /sl/ Medial—four syllables

dislocation	legislative	_____
legislation	_____	_____

SL /sl/ Final—two syllables

axle	dorsal	parcel
basal	fossil	pencil
bristle	gristle	trestle
bustle	jostle	vessel
capsule	missile	wrestle
castle	morsel	_____
counsel	mussel ·	_____

SL /sl/ Final—three syllables

blood vessel	dismissal	utensil
carousel	dispersal	_____
colossal	rehearsal	_____

LS /ls/ Medial—two syllables

also	falsehood	ulcer
balsam	falsely	wholesale
Elsa	hillside	wholesome
elsewhere	pulsate	_____
Elsie	Tulsa	_____

LS /ls/ Medial—three syllables

balsam fir	falsify	wholesaler
Coral Sea	quarrelsome	Wilson
falsetto	Uncle Sam	_____

LS /ls/ Final—one syllable

else   _____   _____
false   _____   _____
pulse   _____   _____

LS /ls/ Final—two syllables

convulse   _____   _____
impulse   _____   _____
repulse   _____   _____

SM /sm/ Initial—one syllable

smack	smirk	smooth
small	smit	smote
smart	smite	smudge
smash	smith	smug
smear	Smith	_____
smell	smock	_____
smelt	smog	_____
smile	smoke	_____
smiled	smoked	_____
smirch	smooch	_____

SM /sm/ Initial—two syllables

smacker	smeller	Smoky
smacking	smelling	smolder
smaller	smelly	smoldered
smallest	smelter	smoother
small fry	smidgen	smoothly
small game	smiling	smother
smallpox	smirky	smothered
small talk	Smithville	smudgy
small-town	smithy	smugger
smarter	smiting	smuggest
smartly	smitten	smugly
smartness	smocking	smugness
smart set	smoggy	_____
smash-up	smokehouse	_____
smatter	smoke screen	_____
smeary	smokestack	_____

SM /sm/ Initial—three syllables

smart aleck	smoke chaser	smothering
smattering	smoke jumper	smudgily
smearier	smokier	smudginess
smelling salts	smokiest	_____
smilingly	smoldering	_____
smithereens	smorgasbord	_____

SM /sm/ Medial—two syllables

baseman	dismiss	placemat
basement	dismount	pressman
blacksmith	goldsmith	tinsmith
Christmas	huntsman	transmit
classman	iceman	_____
classmate	locksmith	_____
dismay	outsmart	_____

SM /sm/ Medial—three syllables

businessman	first baseman	second baseman
Christmas card	locksmith shop	silversmith
Christmas Eve	Mr. Smith	third baseman
Christmas seals	pacemaker	_____
Christmas tree	policeman	_____
coppersmith	policemen	_____

SM /sm/ Medial—four syllables

embarrassment	lower classman	upper classman
junior classman	senior classman	_____

SN /sn/ Initial—one syllable

snack	snared	snelled
snacked	snarl	snide
snag	snatch	snip
snagged	sneak	snipe
snail	sneaked	snipcs
snake	sneer	snipped
snap	sneeze	snitch
snapped	sneezed	snob
snare	snell	snook

snoop	snow	_____
snoot	snowed	_____
snooze	snub	_____
snore	snubbed	_____
snout	snug	_____

SN /sn/ Initial—two syllables

snack bar	sneakers	snowdrift
snaffle	sneaking	snowfall
snagging	sneezy	snowflake
snaggy	snicker	snow-go
snakebite	sniffle	snow job
snake dance	snippy	snowman
snakeskin	snobbish	snowplow
snaky	snobby	snowshoe
snapback	snooper	snowstorm
snap bean	Snoopy	snowsuit
snapper	snooty	snow tires
snapping	snorkel	Snow White
snappish	snowball	snubby
snappy	snowbank	snuggle
snapshots	snowbird	_____
snare drum	snow boots	_____
snatchy	snowbound	_____
snazzy	snow-capped	_____

SN /sn/ Initial—three syllables

snaggletooth	snazzier	snow bunting
snaggletoothed	sneakiest	snowmobile
snake charmer	snickering	snowy owl
snakier	snout beetle	_____
snapdragon	snowball fight	_____
snappier	snow blindness	_____
snappiness	snowblower	_____

SN /sn/ Initial—four syllables

snapping beetle	_____	_____
snapping turtle	_____	_____
snowy egret	_____	_____

NS /ns/ Medial—two syllables

answer	fancy	princess
cancer	fencer	Quincy
Cancer	fencing	rancid
censor	glancer	ransom
chancer	insert	Sensei
concede	inside	senses
concept	insist	Spencer
concern	insult	sponsor
concert	Jensen	stencil
consent	Johnson	tensor
console	lancer	tinsel
consult	lonesome	tonsils
consume	mincemeat	unsafe
council	monsoon	unseal
dancer	pencil	unseen
denser	prancer	

NS /ns/ Medial—three syllables

advancement	density	one-sided
advancer	dispenser	potency
agency	enhancer	principal
announcer	entrancer	principle
chancellor	fiancee′	reconcile
commencement	frequency	Regency
concession	incentive	romancer
condenser	incident	sensible
consider	insincere	sensitive
consonant	insulate	transgressor
consumer	insulted	uncertain
consumption	linseed oil	unselfish
counselor	nonsupport	unsightly
currency	offensive	vacancy

NS /ns/ Medial—four syllables

coincidence	insignia	precedency
consecutive	intensity	preconceiving
deficiency	peninsula	preconception
emergency	Pensacola	principalship

radiancy	social science	unsuspected
reconsider	unsatisfied	_____
sensational	unsuitable	_____

NS /ns/ Final—one syllable

bounce	lance	rinse
chance	Lance	sense
dance	mince	since
dense	once	tense
fence	ounce	thence
France	pounce	whence
glance	prance	wince
hence	prince	_____

NS /ns/ Final—two syllables

absence	finance	pronounce
advance	Florence	province
announce	fragrance	prudence
balance	immense	response
commence	incense	romance
condense	instance	science
conscience	intense	sentence
Constance	license	sequence
convince	nonsense	silence
defense	nuisance	tuppence
denounce	offense	twopence
dispense	past tense	vengeance
distance	patience	_____
enhance	presence	_____
entrance	pretense	_____

NS /ns/ Final—three syllables

abundance	annoyance	confidence
acceptance	appearance	consequence
admittance	appliance	convenience
allegiance	audience	dependence
alliance	circumstance	difference
allowance	common sense	disturbance
ambulance	conference	endurance

evidence	performance	reverence
ignorance	precedence	subsistence
impatience	preference	surveillance
importance	prevalence	tolerance
influence	radiance	turbulence
innocence	recurrence	utterance
insurance	redundance	variance
maintenance	reference	vigilance
mispronounce	residence	_____
occurrence	resistance	_____

NS /ns/ Final—four syllables

circumference	obedience	self-reliance
independence	predominance	significance
indifference	preponderance	_____
inheritance	self-assurance	_____
intelligence	self-confidence	_____

SP /sp/ Initial—one syllable

spa	spent	spook
space	spice	spool
spade	spiced	spoon
spake	spike	spoor
span	spill	sport
spanned	spilled	sports
spar	spilt	spot
spare	spin	spouse
spared	spine	spout
sparred	spire	spud
sparse	spit	spun
spat	spite	spunk
spawn	spitz	spur
speak	spoil	spurge
spear	spoiled	spurred
speck	spoke	spurs
speech	spokes	spurt
spell	sponge	spy
spelled	sponged	_____
spend	spoof	_____

SP /sp/ Initial—two syllables

space bar	spearhead	spitball
spacecraft	spearmint	spiteful
space flight	special	spitfire
spaceman	specie	spittoon
spaceport	specious	spoilage
spaceship	speckle	spoiling
space suit	spectre	spoken
spacial	spectrum	spokesman
spacing	speechless	sponger
spacious	speedboat	spongy
spadeful	speedster	sponsor
spadework	speedtrap	spooky
spancel	speedway	spoon bread
spangle	speedy	spoonful
Spaniard	speed zone	sportful
spaniel	spellbound	sporting
Spanish	speller	sports car
spanner	spelling	sportscast
spareribs	spendthrift	sport shirt
sparing	sperm whale	sportsman
spark coil	spicy	sportswear
sparker	spider	sporty
sparkle	spiky	spot check
sparkler	spillage	spotlight
sparkling	spilling	spotted
spark plug	spillway	spotter
sparring	spinach	spotty
sparrow	spinal	spun glass
Spartan	spindle	spunky
spasm	spindling	Sputnik
spastic	spineless	sputter
spatial	spinet	spy glass
spatter	spinner	spying
spawning	spinning	_____
speaker	spin out	_____
speakers	spinster	_____
speaking	spiral	_____
spearfish	spirit	_____

SP /sp/ Initial—three syllables

space heater	specific	spinning wheel
space station	specify	spirited
space writer	specimen	spiritless
spaghetti	spectacle	sponsoring
Spanish food	spectator	sponsorship
Spanish rice	spectrogram	spookier
sparable	spectrograph	sporadic
sparrow hawk	spectroscope	sporting goods
spasmodic	speculate	sportscaster
spatula	speedily	sportsmanship
speakable	speed limit	sportswriter
spear fishing	spelling bee	spunkier
specialist	spider web	_____
specialize	spinal cord	_____
specialty	spinal nerve	_____

SP /sp/ Initial—four syllables

spectacular	speedometer	spiritual
spectrometer	spider monkey	spirometer
speech therapist	spinal column	spontaneous
speech therapy	spiral notebook	_____

SP /sp/ Initial—five syllables

Special Olympics	specifically	_____
specialization	specification	_____

SP /sp/ Medial—two syllables

aspen	dispatched	misplace
Aspen	dispel	misspell
Casper	dispose	passport
crispy	dispute	peace pipe
despair	gospel	prospect
despise	grasping	prosper
despised	high-speed	respect
despite	inspect	respire
despoil	inspire	respite
despoiled	Jasper	respond
dispatch	larkspur	response

Shakespeare	waspish	_____
teaspoon	waspy	_____
turnspit	whisper	_____

SP /sp/ Medial—three syllables

aerospace	mispronounce	suspension
aspirin	outer space	suspicion
baby spoon	outspoken	suspicious
desperate	prospective	tablespoon
disparate	prospector	transparent
disposal	prosperous	whispering
hospital	respectful	_____
inspection	respective	_____
Jasper Park	retrospect	_____
loudspeaker	suspenders	_____

SP /sp/ Medial—four syllables

asparagus	disputable	respectable
conspiracy	especially	respectively
correspondence	espionage	respiration
despairingly	high-spirited	respirator
desperado	hospitable	responsible
desperation	hospitalize	tablespoonful
despicable	inspiration	unspeakable
dispensary	litmus paper	_____
dispensation	low-spirited	_____
disposable	perspicacious	_____
disposition	perspiration	_____
disproportion	prosperity	_____

SP /sp/ Medial—five syllables

hospitality	respiratory	_____
indisputable	_____	_____
irresponsibly	_____	_____

SP /sp/ Medial—six syllables

inspirationally	_____	_____
respectability	_____	_____
responsibility	_____	_____

SP /sp/ Final—one syllable

clasp	grasp	wasp
crisp	lisp	wisp
gasp	rasp	_____

PS /ps/ Medial—two syllables

capsize	knapsack	topsail
capsule	lapsing	topside
chopsticks	lipstick	topsoil
deep South	Mopsy	Topsy
dip stick	pipsqueak	typeset
dropsy	slapstick	upset
gypsum	soapsuds	upstairs
gypsy	step stool	upstart
hopscotch	stop sign	upswing
keepsake	tipsy	_____

PS /ps/ Medial—three syllables

asepsis	relapsing	upsetting
autopsy	synopsis	upstanding
biopsy	tipsiness	upsurging
chop suey	tipsy cake	upsweeping
collapsing	top secret	upswelling
elapsing	top sergeant	upswinging
ellipsis	typesetter	_____
Phillipsburg	typesetting	_____

PS /ps/ Medial—four syllables

epilepsy	upsettable	upsy-daisy
topsy-turvy	upside-down cake	_____

PS /ps/ Final—one syllable

alps	crops	flips
Alps	cups	flops
caps	dips	grapes
chaps	drapes	gripes
chips	drips	grips
chops	drops	gropes
copes	flaps	groups

hopes	ropes	snips
hops	saps	steps
jeeps	scalps	straps
jumps	scoops	stripes
keeps	scopes	swaps
laps	scrapes	tapes
lapse	scraps	taps
leaps	seeps	tips
lips	ships	tops
loops	shops	traps
maps	sips	trips
mops	skips	troops
naps	slaps	weeps
nips	sleeps	whips
peeps	slips	wipes
pipes	sloops	wraps
pups	slopes	zips
raps	slumps	_____
reaps	snaps	_____
rips	snipes	_____

PS /ps/ Final—two syllables

biceps	gossips	sit-ups
collapse	grown-ups	triceps
eclipse	push-ups	tulips
elapse	raindrops	turnips
ellipse	relapse	unwraps
escapes	round trips	wallops
forceps	roundups	_____
gallops	scallops	_____

PS /ps/ Final—three syllables

antelopes	fire escapes	_____
cantaloupes	_____	_____

RS /rs/ Medial—two syllables

arson	cursor	fireside
corsage	dorsal	forceps
cursive	firesale	foresaw

foresee	morsel	scarcely
foreseen	Morse Code	tiresome
foresight	ourselves	torso
forsake	parcel	verso
for sale	parsley	versus
forsook	parsnip	Warsaw
herself	parson	yourself
horseback	perceive	_____
horsefly	percent	_____
horseman	person	_____
horseshoe	perspire	_____
horse show	pursue	_____
mercy	pursuit	_____

RS /rs/ Medial—three syllables

arsenal	overstate	riverside
arsenic	parcel post	Riverside
cumbersome	parsonage	salesperson
diversely	percentage	somersault
fire safety	persecute	supersede
forsaken	persimmon	supervise
horsepower	persistent	underset
intercede	personal	unforeseen
Jefferson	personnel	varsity
lumbersome	porcelain	versatile
Mercedes	power saw	versify
narcissus	precursor	_____
near-sighted	rehearsal	_____
nursery	rehearsing	_____
overseas	reverses	_____
oversight	reversing	_____

RS /rs/ Medial—four syllables

adversary	nursery school	unmerciful
controversy	persecution	versifier
diversity	personally	vice versa
impersonate	supersonic	water safety
marsupial	superstition	_____
nursery rhymes	universal	_____

RS /rs/ Medial—five syllables

anniversary	universally	versification
diversifying	university	_____
personality	versatility	_____

RS /rs/ Final—one syllable

coarse	hoarse	scarce
course	horse	source
curse	nurse	sparse
fierce	pierce	verse
force	Pierce	worse
hearse	purse	_____

RS /rs/ Final—two syllables

adverse	endorse	resource
Air Force	enforce	reverse
averse	golf course	saw horse
coerce	imburse	school nurse
concourse	immerse	sea horse
converse	inverse	submerse
disburse	race course	transverse
disperse	recourse	traverse
diverse	rehearse	_____
divorce	remorse	_____

RS /rs/ Final—three syllables

charley horse	labor force	rocking horse
fire safety	office nurse	slalom course
first aid course	police force	student nurse
hobby horse	quarter horse	universe
intersperse	reinforce	_____

ST /st/ Initial—one syllable

stack	stain	stalk
stacked	stair	stall
staff	stairs	stalled
stag	stake	stamp
stage	staked	stamped
staged	stale	stand

star	stick	stored
starch	stiff	stork
stare	still	storm
stared	stilt	stout
start	sting	stove
state	stink	stow
states	stir	stub
stave	stirred	stubbed
stay	stitch	stud
steak	stock	stuff
steam	stocks	stump
steed	stoke	stun
steel	stole	stung
steep	stomp	stunk
steer	stone	stunned
stem	stood	stunt
stemmed	stool	sty
step	stoop	style
stepped	stop	_____
stern	stopped	_____
stew	store	_____

ST /st/ Initial—two syllables

stable	statement	Stewart
stagecoach	statesman	sticky
stagger	static	stifle
staircase	station	stinger
stallage	statue	stingray
stallion	steadfast	stirrup
stammer	steady	stock car
stampede	steamboat	stocker
standard	steamer	Stockholm
Stanford	steamship	stocking
Stanley	steeple	stockroom
stanza	steerage	stocky
staple	steel wool	stockyard
starboard	sterling	stolen
starfish	Steven	stomach
starling	steward	Stone Age

stoneware
stonework
stoplight
stop-off
stoppage
stopper
stopping
stopwatch
storage
storehouse
storeroom
stories

stormy
story
stovepipe
stowage
stubble
stubborn
stubby
stuck-up
student
studied
study
stuffing

stuffy
stumble
stunning
sturdy
sturgeon
stutter
stylish
stylist
stylize
stylus
stymied

_____

ST /st/ Initial—three syllables

stadium
stalactite
stalagmite
stateswoman
statistics
steam engine
steam shovel
stepbrother
stepfather
stepladder
stepmother
stepping stone

stereo
sterilize
stethoscope
stimulate
stimulus
stock exchange
stock market
stomach ache
stonecutter
stopover
storm cellar
storm center

storm warning
storm window
storybook
stowaway
studio
studious
study group
study hall
stumbling block
stupendous
stuttering

_____

ST /st/ Initial—four syllables

stationary
stationery

station master
station wagon

_____
_____

ST /st/ Medial—two syllables

abstain
bandstand
beefsteak
breastbone
bus stop
cast iron
castoff

Chester
chestnut
chopsticks
coastal
Coast Guard
coastline
constant

costume
crystal
Crystal
custom
destine
distal
distance

distant
distaste
distend
distill
distinct
distort
disturb
drugstore
drumstick
dustcloth
Easter
eastern
eastward
Einstein
estate
Estelle
Ester
footstep
footstool
frostbite
frosting
ghastly
ghost town
grandstand
grindstone
hailstone
hailstorm
hasty
haystack
head start
headstone
homestead
hostage
hostel
hostess
hostile
housetop
Houston
iced tea

install
instance
instant
instead
instep
instinct
justice
keystone
lasting
limestone
lipstick
livestock
milestone
mistake
mister
mistook
misty
mostly
mustang
nasty
North Star
pastel
pastels
pastime
pastor
pester
piston
postage
postal
postcard
posted
posting
postman
postmark
postpaid
postpone
postscript
question
restless

rhinestone
rustic
rusty
Rusty
sandstorm
shoe store
shortstop
smokestack
substance
sustain
sweepstakes
tasty
test tube
toadstool
tombstone
tungsten
turnstile
two-step
vista
waistband
western
West Point
westward
withstand
withstood
wristband
yardstick

_____
_____
_____
_____
_____
_____
_____
_____
_____
_____
_____

ST /st/ Medial—three syllables

accustom	fiesta	postmistress
adjustment	gas station	predestine
armistice	gymnastics	Protestant
artistic	high-stepping	questioner
asbestos	historic	question mark
assistance	hockey stick	questionnaire
assistant	honesty	resistance
astonish	injustice	sarcastic
bus station	installment	shooting star
bystander	instantly	siesta
candlestick	institute	southeastern
castanets	intestine	space station
castaway	investment	substandard
consistent	justify	substantial
constitute	Lone Star State	substation
contestant	long distance	substitute
crop duster	majestic	summer stock
custody	majesty	superstar
customer	mastodon	sustenance
destiny	mistaken	testament
destitute	northwestern	testify
devastate	Northwestern	thermostat
distasteful	obstacle	tossed salad
distemper	outstanding	tostada
distiller	pasteurize	train station
distinction	pedestal	understand
distinguish	persistent	understood
establish	photostat	vestibule
estimate	pogo stick	youth hostel
existence	postage stamp	_____
fantastic	postmaster	_____
festival	post office	_____

ST /st/ Medial—four syllables

consistency	custodian	historian
constituent	customary	hysterical
constitution	establishment	institution
Costa Rica	grocery store	interesting

investigate	questionable	T.V. station
misunderstand	readjustment	testimony
misunderstood	realistic	unaccustomed
optimistic	relay station	understanding
pessimistic	solar system	United States
posterior	superstition	_____

ST /st/ Medial—five syllables

constituency	postmeridian	unquestionable
investigative	predestination	_____

ST /st/ Final—one syllable

baste	gust	pressed
beast	haste	priest
best	hoist	quest
blast	host	raced
blest	iced	rest
boast	jest	roast
boost	just	roost
bussed	last	rust
bust	least	taste
cast	lest	test
chest	list	thrust
coast	lost	toast
cost	mast	twist
crest	messed	vast
crossed	midst	versed
crust	missed	vest
dressed	mist	voiced
dust	moist	waist
east	most	waste
faced	must	west
fast	nest	wist
feast	passed	wrest
fist	past	wrist
frost	paste	yeast
fussed	pest	zest
ghost	placed	_____
guest	post	_____

ST /st/ Final—two syllables

abreast	Far East	post-test
adjust	farthest	pre-test
against	flautist	pronounced
almost	florist	protest
amidst	forecast	request
arrest	forest	resist
artist	French toast	richest
assist	furthest	ripest
August	gatepost	robust
Baptist	greatest	safest
bed rest	gymnast	sandblast
biggest	half-mast	sand-cast
breakfast	harvest	sawdust
broadcast	honest	sheerest
chemist	inquest	shrillest
choicest	insist	signpost
combust	invest	sleekest
compost	Key West	slickest
conquest	largest	slowest
consist	locust	slyest
contest	longest	smallest
contrast	loosest	smartest
cutest	loudest	smoothest
cyclist	low-cost	Southeast
deepest	lyrist	Southwest
defrost	Midwest	steadfast
dentist	milepost	strongest
detest	modest	stylist
digest	nearest	subsist
driest	neatest	suggest
druggist	newest	tempest
earnest	newscast	thinnest
eldest	nicest	toothpaste
embossed	Northeast	tourist
enlist	Northwest	trimmest
ernest	oldest	truest
exhaust	outpost	typist
exist	poorest	unjust

unrest	widest	_____
upmost	youngest	_____
utmost	_____	_____

ST /st/ Final—three syllables

activist	luckiest	scientist
amethyst	Middle East	silliest
analyst	monarchist	skinniest
atheist	narrowest	smelliest
bassoonist	naughtiest	soggiest
classicist	novelist	soloist
daintiest	optimist	specialist
dramatist	organist	stockiest
fuzziest	overcast	theorist
happiest	parcel post	therapist
hornet's nest	pessimist	thriftiest
hungriest	pharmacist	tidiest
idealist	physicist	trombonist
immodest	pianist	unbalanced
interest	prettiest	unnoticed
journalist	quietist	uppermost
kindliest	rebroadcast	vocalist
littlest	roomiest	wealthiest
loveliest	satirist	_____

ST /st/ Final—four syllables

antagonist	naturalist	rhinologist
apologist	nonconformist	unhappiest
autonomist	orthodontist	urologist
biologist	otologist	ventriloquist
economist	pathologist	violinist
enthusiast	philanthropist	_____
geologist	psychiatrist	_____
iconoclast	psychologist	_____

ST /st/ Final—five syllables

audiologist	entomologist	ornithologist
audiometrist	etymologist	_____
cardiologist	ophthalmologist	_____

TS /ts/ Medial—two syllables

batsman	outside	ritzy
Betsy	outsing	schizo
Datsun	outsit	schizoid
gutsy	outsize	schnitzel
itself	outsold	Scotsman
jet set	outsole	Scottsville
jetsam	Patsy	sitz bath
Matson	pit saw	Watson
Mezzo	pizza	yachtsman
Nazi	pretzel	_____
outsell	quartzlike	_____
outset	quetzal	_____

TS /ts/ Medial—three syllables

Fitzgerald	outsider	ritziest
gutsiness	pit sample	_____
outselling	ritzier	_____

TS /ts/ Medial—four syllables

outsettlement	pizzicato	_____
pizzeria	schizophrenic	_____

TS /ts/ Final—one syllable

ants	cuts	gents
aunts	dates	gnats
baits	debts	goats
bats	eats	grates
bites	fates	greets
bits	fights	grits
blitz	fits	guts
blots	Fitz	hoots
boats	flats	huts
boots	fleets	jets
cats	flits	kites
cheats	floats	knits
chutes	flutes	knots
cleats	fruits	let's
crates	gates	lights

loots	quits	slats
lots	quotes	slits
lutes	rates	slots
mates	rats	spits
mats	rights	splits
meats	roots	sports
meets	rots	spots
mites	routes	spouts
mitts	routs	states
mutes	ruts	threats
nets	scouts	tights
nights	Scouts	toots
notes	seats	totes
nuts	sets	vats
oats	sheets	votes
pants	shoots	waits
pats	shorts	wants
pets	sights	weights
pits	sites	wits
plates	sits	writes
pleats	skates	yachts
pots	skits	_____
putts	slates	_____

TS /ts/ Final—two syllables

acquits	cutlets	footlights
admits	debates	footnotes
ballots	defeats	forfeits
biscuits	denotes	garnets
bonnets	dictates	giants
brackets	diets	Giants
buckets	digits	giblets
cadets	doughnuts	Girl Scouts
carrots	duets	goblets
cold cuts	eaglets	hatchets
comets	edits	ice boats
commits	emits	ice skates
commutes	equates	ignites
cornets	faucets	inlets

insights	pirates	rotates
invites	pivots	rowboats
jackets	planets	sailboats
jackpots	playmates	salutes
kumquats	pockets	secrets
lifeboats	poets	senates
limits	polecats	skillets
locates	portraits	slingshots
lockets	primates	snapshots
lookouts	profits	sockets
magnets	promotes	speedboats
mallets	pullets	spirits
markets	pulpits	spotlights
mascots	puppets	steamboats
merits	quintets	tablets
midgets	rabbits	targets
minutes	rackets	termites
muskets	raincoats	thickets
muskrats	rebates	tickets
narrates	receipts	tidbits
nuggets	recites	tomcats
omits	recruits	tugboats
orbits	red-hots	two-bits
outfits	regrets	unites
outwits	repeats	units
pamphlets	retreats	visits
parrots	ringlets	wallets
peanuts	riots	whaleboats
pellets	rivets	whole notes
permits	robots	_____
pheasants	rockets	_____
pilots	roommates	_____

TS /ts/ Final—three syllables

copyrights	irritates	nominates
dominates	isolates	ocelots
elevates	kilowatts	omelets
estimates	minuets	opposites
irrigates	motorboats	overcoats

parachutes	radiates	skyrockets
parakeets	regulates	statuettes
parasites	roller skates	tolerates
patriots	satellites	violets
penetrates	separates	_____
powerboats	shelled walnuts	_____
prohibits	silhouettes	_____

TS /ts/ Final—four syllables

initiates	Massachusetts	participates
marionettes	originates	_____

SW /sw/ Initial—one syllable

suave	swat	swine
suede	swatch	swing
suite	sway	swipe
swab	swear	swipes
swag	sweat	swirl
swale	Swede	swish
swam	sweep	Swiss
swamp	sweet	switch
swan	swell	swoon
swank	swept	swoop
swap	swerve	swore
sward	swift	sworn
swarm	swig	_____
swash	swim	_____

SW /sw/ Initial—two syllables

swallow	sweat pants	sweeten
swallows	sweat shirt	sweetheart
swami	sweat suit	sweet pea
swampland	Sweden	sweet tooth
swampy	Swedish	swelling
swan dive	sweeper	swelter
swanky	sweeping	swifter
swap shop	sweepstakes	swim fins
sweater	sweetbread	swim mask
sweat gland	sweet corn	swimmer

swimming	swinging	swivel
swimsuit	Swiss cheese	swollen
swindle	switchback	_____
swindled	switchboard	_____
swinger	switchbox	_____

SW /sw/ Initial—three syllables

swallowtail	sweltering	swine fever
swastika	swift-footed	swinging bridge
sweet and sour	swimming hole	swinging door
sweetening	swimming pool	Switzerland

RST /rst/ Final—one syllables

burst	hurst	thirst
cursed	Hurst	worst
first	nursed	_____
forced	pierced	_____

RST /rst/ Final—two syllables

airburst	endorsed	rehearsed
cloudburst	enforced	reversed
coerced	imbursed	sunburst
dispersed	immersed	unversed
divorced	outburst	_____

RTS /rts/ Final—one syllable

arts	forts	skirts
blurts	hearts	sorts
carts	parts	sports
charts	ports	spurts
courts	quarts	squirts
darts	shirts	warts
flirts	shorts	_____

RTS /rts/ Final—two syllables

airports	deserts	exports
alerts	desserts	imports
concerts	distorts	inserts
departs	experts	inverts

passports	seaports	_____
reports	supports	_____
resorts	transports	_____
reverts	_____	_____

SER /sɚ/ Medial—three syllables

glossary	sponsorship	_____
grocery	Switzerland	_____
nursery	ulcerate	_____

SER /sɚ/ Medial—four syllables

accessory	rhinoceros	_____
nursery man	_____	_____
nursery school	_____	_____

SER /sɚ/ Final—two syllables

bracer	lacer	slicer
chaser	leaser	splicer
closer	lesser	tracer
creaser	nicer	ulcer
crosser	pacer	_____
dicer	piercer	_____
dresser	placer	_____
grocer	presser	_____
guesser	racer	_____
kisser	saucer	_____

SER /sɚ/ Final—three syllables

aggressor	horse racer	reducer
assessor	officer	successor
compressor	oppressor	transgressor
conducer	possessor	_____
embosser	producer	_____
enticer	professor	_____
eraser	progressor	_____

SER /sɚ/ Final—four syllables

| dog sled racer | predecessor | _____ |
| interlacer | reproducer | _____ |

NSER /nsɚ/ Final—two syllables

answer	denser	Spencer
cancer	fencer	sponsor
Cancer	glancer	tensor
censor	lancer	_____
chancer	prancer	_____
dancer	spencer	_____

NSER /nsɚ/ Final—three syllables

advancer	dispenser	extensor
announcer	enhancer	romancer
condenser	entrancer	_____

STER /stɚ/ Medial—three syllables

asterisk	masterpiece	yesterday
castor oil	mastery	_____
history	oyster crab	_____
mastering	westerly	_____

STER /stɚ/ Medial—four syllables

master-at-arms	preposterous	upholstery
masterfully	sister-in-law	_____
prehistory	southeasterly	_____

STER /stɚ/ Final—two syllables

aster	Foster	roadster
blister	hamster	roaster
booster	holster	rooster
Buster	lobster	roster
caster	luster	sister
Chester	master	spinster
cluster	mister	tester
coaster	monster	thruster
Custer	muster	toaster
duster	oyster	twister
Easter	pastor	Webster
faster	pester	youngster
fluster	plaster	_____
foster	poster	_____

STER /stɚ/ Final—three syllables

adjuster	minister	taskmaster
ancestor	postmaster	toastmaster
bandmaster	register	upholster
canister	resister	Worcester
disaster	scoutmaster	_____
forecaster	semester	_____
gangbuster	shipmaster	_____
Grand Master	sinister	_____
half-sister	Sylvester	_____

STER /stɚ/ Final—four syllables

administer	prime minister	_____
flabbergaster	quartermaster	_____
Gila monster	roller coaster	_____

SKR /skr/ Initial—one syllable

scram	screen	scrub
scrap	screw	scrunch
scrape	scribe	_____
scratch	scrimp	_____
scrawl	script	_____
scream	scroll	_____
screech	Scrooge	_____

SKR /skr/ Initial—two syllables

scraggly	screening	scrub nurse
scramble	screenplay	scrumptious
scrambled	screentest	scruple
scrapbook	screwball	_____
scraper	scribble	_____
scrapper	scribbled	_____
scratchy	scrimmage	_____
scrawny	scripture	_____

SKR /skr/ Initial—three syllables

screen writer	scrutinize	_____
screwdriver	scrutiny	_____
scrupulous	_____	_____

SKR /skr/ Medial—two syllables

ascribe	ice cream	subscribe
ascribed	inscribe	subscribed
corkscrew	muskrat	subscript
describe	postscript	transcribe
described	prescribe	transcribed
discreet	prescribed	_____
escrow	silkscreen	_____

SKR /skr/ Medial—three syllables

description	inscription	subscription
descriptive	manuscript	_____
ice-cream man	prescription	_____
ice-cream truck	skyscraper	_____

SKS /sks/ Final—one syllable

asks	disks	risks
basks	flasks	tasks
casks	husks	tusks
desks	masks	_____

SKW /skw/ Initial—one syllable

squab	squawk	squint
squad	squeak	squire
squall	squeal	squirm
square	squeeze	squirt
squash	squelch	squish
squat	squib	_____
squaw	squid	

SKW /skw/ Initial—two syllables

squabble	square dance	square mile
squabbling	square deal	square off
squad car	square feet	square root
squadron	square foot	squarest
squalid	square inch	square yard
squally	squarely	squashy
squalor	square knot	squatted
squander	square meal	squatter

484 • SKW /skw/ Initial—three syllables

squatting	squeezer	squirrel
squatty	squeezing	squirt gun
squeaky	squelcher	squishy
squeamish	squiggle	_____
squeegee	squirmy	_____

SKW /skw/ Initial—three syllables

square away	square rigger	squeezable
square inches	square shooter	_____
square meters	squashiest	_____

SPL /spl/ Initial—one syllable

splash	splice	splits
splat	spliced	splotch
splay	splint	splurge
spleen	split	_____

SPL /spl/ Initial—two syllables

splashdown	splendor	split shift
splash guard	splicer	splitting
splatter	splicing	splutter
splendid	splinter	_____

SPL /spl/ Initial—three syllables

splintery	split level	_____
split entrance	split second	_____
split entry	_____	_____

SPR /spr/ Initial—one syllable

sprain	spree	sprout
sprang	sprig	spruce
sprawl	spring	sprung
spray	sprint	spry
spread	sprite	_____

SPR /spr/ Initial—two syllables

spraddle	spreader	Springfield
sprayer	spreadsheet	springing
spray gun	springboard	springtime

sprinkle	sprinkling	_____
sprinkler	sprocket	_____

SPR /spr/ Medial—two syllables

bedspread	hot springs	Rock Springs
hair spray	Hot Springs	_____
handspring	offspring	_____

SPR /spr/ Medial—three syllables

Brussels sprouts	shopping spree	Union Springs
ocean spray	Silver Spring	_____

STR /str/ Initial—one syllable

straight	strength	stroke
strain	stress	strokes
strained	stressed	stroll
strait	stretch	strolled
strand	stretched	strong
strange	strict	strove
strap	stride	struck
strapped	strike	strum
straw	string	strung
stray	strip	strut
strayed	stripe	_____
streak	stripped	_____
stream	strive	_____
street	strobe	_____

STR /str/ Initial—two syllables

straggle	stretching	stringy
stranger	stretch-out	stripping
strapping	stretchy	striving
streaking	stricken	strobe lamp
streamer	strident	stroller
streamline	strike out	strolling
streetcar	strike zone	strongbox
strengthen	string beans	stronghold
stressing	stringent	strongly
stretcher	stringing	structure

strudel	strutting	_____
struggle	strychnine	_____
strumming	_____	_____

STR /str/ Initial—three syllables

straightforward	strawberry	structural
strait jacket	strenuous	_____
strategy	string quartet	_____
stratosphere	stroboscope	_____

STR /str/ Initial—four syllables

streptococcus	stringed instruments	_____
streptomycin	_____	_____

STR /str/ Medial—two syllables

abstract	distress	ostrich
airstrip	downstream	pastry
astray	frustrate	restrain
astride	gold stream	restrict
backstroke	high-strung	rostrum
bloodstream	instruct	seamstress
bowstring	minstrel	shoestring
breaststroke	mistreat	side street
constrict	mistress	sidestroke
construct	monstrous	upstream
destroy	nostril	vestry
distract	obstruct	_____

STR /str/ Medial—three syllables

Astrodome	destructive	orchestra
astronaut	distraction	reconstruct
Australia	distribute	restraining
Austria	doll stroller	restricting
chemistry	Gaza Strip	restriction
comic strip	illustrate	Sunset Strip
construction	industry	tapestry
demonstrate	instruction	_____
destroyer	instructor	_____
destruction	instrument	_____

STR /str/ Medial—four syllables

apostrophe	catastrophe	instrumental
astrology	catastrophic	orchestra pit
astronomer	demonstration	pedestrian
astronomy	distribution	reconstruction
baby stroller	illustration	string orchestra
band instruments	industrial	_____
candy striper	industrious	_____

STR /str/ Medial—five syllables

administration	boa constrictor	_____
astronomical	instrumentalist	_____

STS /sts/ Final—one syllable

beasts	hosts	roosts
blasts	lasts	tastes
boasts	lists	tests
casts	mists	thrusts
dusts	nests	toasts
feasts	pastes	twists
fists	pests	vests
frosts	posts	wastes
ghosts	priests	wrists
guests	quests	yeasts
gusts	rests	_____
hoists	roasts	_____

STS /sts/ Final—two syllables

adjusts	defrosts	gate posts
arrests	dentists	harvests
artists	detests	insists
assists	digests	invests
Baptists	druggists	locusts
broadcasts	enlists	mainmasts
chemists	exhausts	Marxists
conquests	exists	miscasts
consists	florists	newscasts
contests	forecasts	outposts
contrasts	forests	post-tests

pre-tests	sandblasts	tourists
protests	sand casts	typists
requests	stylists	_____
resists	toothpastes	_____

LTS /lts/ Final—one syllable

belts	melts	tilts
bolts	molts	vaults
colts	pelts	welts
faults	quilts	wilts
jolts	salts	_____
kilts	silts	_____
malts	stilts	_____

LTS /lts/ Final—two syllables

adults	pole vaults	_____
consults	revolts	_____
insults	scat belts	_____

MPS /mps/ Final—one syllable

amps	glimpse	romps
blimps	imps	shrimps
bumps	jumps	skimps
champs	lamps	slumps
chumps	limps	stamps
clamps	lumps	stumps
clumps	mumps	thumps
cramps	primps	tramps
crimps	pumps	trumps
dumps	ramps	_____

SH

Pronounced: /ʃ/

Spelled: sh, ce, ch, ci, psh, s, sch, sci, se, si, ss, ssi, su, ti

SH /ʃ/ Initial—one syllable

chaise	shears	shoe
chef	sheath	shone
Cher	sheaves	shook
chic	shed	shoot
shack	she'd	shop
shad	sheen	shopped
shade	sheep	shore
shaft	sheer	shorn
shag	sheered	short
shake	sheet	shot
shale	sheik	should
shall	shelf	shout
shalt	shell	shove
sham	she'll	show
shame	shelve	showed
Shane	she's	shown
shank	shield	shucks
shan't	shift	shun
shape	shim	shunt
share	shin	shush
shared	shine	shut
shares	shined	shy
shark	ship	sure
sharp	shipped	_____
shave	shirk	_____
shaw	shirt	_____
shawl	shoal	_____
shay	shoat	_____
she	shock	_____
sheaf	shocked	_____
shear	shod	_____

[489]

SH /ʃ/ Initial—two syllables

chagrin	shameless	Sherlock
chalet	shammy	Sherman
chamois	shampoo	Sherry
chapeau	shamrock	Sherwood
charade	Shanghai	Sheryl
Charlene	Shannon	Shetland
Charlotte	shanty	shilling
chartreuse	shape-up	shimmer
chateau	shaping	shimmy
chauffer	sharing	shinbone
chenille	Sharon	shindig
Cheri	sharpen	shiner
Cheryl	sharper	shingles
chevron	sharp-set	shin guard
Chevy	shatter	shining
Cheyenne	shattered	shiny
chiffon	shaving	shipboard
chignon	Shawnees	shipload
Chinook	shearing	shipmate
shabby	Sheba	shipment
shackle	shedding	shipping
shaded	sheepdog	shipwreck
shade tree	sheepish	shipyard
shading	sheepskin	shirker
shadow	sheeting	Shirley
shadowed	sheetrock	shirtwaist
shady	Sheffield	shiver
shaggy	Sheldon	shocking
shag rug	shellac	shock wave
shaker	Shelley	shoddy
Shakespeare	shellfish	shoebrush
shaking	shellproof	shoehorn
shaky	shelter	shoelace
shallow	sheltered	shoeshine
shallows	shepherd	shoeshop
shamble	sherbet	shoestring
shamefaced	Sherese	shoji
shameful	sheriff	shopper

shopping
shopworn
shoreline
Shoreview
shoreward
shortage
shortbread
shortcake
shortcut
shorten
shorthand
shorthorn
shortly
shortstop
short-term
short wave

shorty
shotput
shoulder
shovel
showboat
showcase
showdown
shower
showered
showing
showman
showroom
showy
shudder
shuffle
shutdown

shut-in
shutoff
shutout
shutter
shuttle
Shylock
shyly
shyster
sugar
_____
_____
_____
_____
_____
_____
_____

SH /ʃ/ Initial—three syllables

chandelier
chaperone
charlotte russe
Charlottesville
Charlottetown
Chicago
chivalry
shadowbox
shadowy
shampooing
shantytown
sharpener
sharpening
sharp-witted
shatterproof
shaving brush
shaving cream
shaving soap
sheepherder
sheet metal
sheet music

shelled pecans
shelled walnuts
Sheridan
shipbuilder
shipmaster
ship-to-shore
shivering
shoemaker
shooting star
shopkeeper
shopping bag
shopping cart
shopping mall
shore patrol
shortening
short-handed
short order
short-sighted
short story
shot-putter
shoulder bag

shuffleboard
shutterbug
shuttle bus
sugarbush
sugar cane
sugar-coat
sugar-cured
sugarhouse
sugar loaf
sugar pine
sugar plum
sugary
_____
_____
_____
_____
_____
_____
_____
_____

SH /ʃ/ Initial—four syllables

shaving lather	Shetland pony	sugaring off
Shenandoah	shopping center	sugar maple
Sherwood Forest	sugarberry	_____
Shetland Islands	sugar daddy	_____

SH /ʃ/ Medial—two syllables

action	fishes	midship
anxious	fishing	mission
ashamed	flashback	moonshine
ashes	flash bulb	motion
ashore	flash card	musher
auction	flashcube	mushing
backsheesh	flash flood	Nashville
bashful	flashing	nation
bishop	flashlight	nightshade
bloodshot	flushing	nightshirt
bushcs	fractions	notion
bushy	freshman	nutshell
cashbook	friction	ocean
cashier	function	offshoot
cashmere	gashes	offshore
caution	glacier	option
cautious	gracious	outshine
clamshell	gusher	outshoot
cocksure	handshake	pawnshop
conscience	hardship	pension
conscious	horseshoe	pressure
courtship	inshore	pushcart
crankshaft	insure	pushing
cushion	kosher	push-ups
dashboard	lasher	quotient
dashing	lotion	ration
diction	luscious	ricksha
dish cloth	machine	roughshod
dishes	makeshift	rusher
dishful	mansion	rushes
fashion	masher	rushing
fiction	mention	sanction

seashore
section
shipshape
shoeshine
shoeshop
smashing
snapshot
snowshoe
social
soft-shell
special
stanchion
station
steamship

suction
sunshine
tension
thrasher
thresher
tissue
traction
unsure
usher
washboard
washbowl
washcloth
washday
washer

washing
washout
washstand
washtub
Welshman
windshield
wishbone
wishes
wishful
woodshed
workshop
worship
_____
_____

SH /ʃ/ Medial—three syllables

absorption
addition
admission
adoption
affection
ambition
assumption
attention
attraction
audition
Ayesha
beanshooter
beautician
beauty shop
blood pressure
Britisher
British Isles
bus station
carnation
clinician
cockleshell
collection
commission

compassion
completion
complexion
compulsion
condition
conduction
confession
conjunction
connection
constriction
construction
contraption
convention
conviction
correction
creation
crustacean
deception
description
destruction
detection
devotion
dictation

dimension
direction
distinction
distraction
donation
elation
emotion
eruption
essential
exception
exertion
extinction
extraction
eyelashes
financial
fire station
fisherman
fishermen
fishery
fishing hole
fishing pole
fishing rod
formation

foundation	parachute	selection
frustration	partition	sensation
furnishing	pay station	solution
gas station	penmanship	space station
goldfish bowl	pensioner	spear fishing
high pressure	perfection	starvation
horseshoer	permission	subscription
impression	physician	sufficient
infection	pincushion	suspicion
infraction	plantation	technician
initial	polishing	temptation
initialed	position	toothbrushes
injection	possession	tortoise shell
inscription	potential	tradition
inspection	prescription	train station
instruction	pressuring	transaction
insurance	prevention	transcription
intention	procession	transition
kingfisher	production	translation
lavishness	profession	trash masher
location	progression	unshaken
low pressure	promotion	unshaven
luxury	protection	vacation
migration	publisher	vibration
musician	punishment	vivacious
narration	quotation	vocation
national	ramshackle	washable
New Hampshire	reaction	Washington
nonchalant	reception	way station
nourishes	reduction	wishing well
nourishment	reflection	_____
nutrition	regression	_____
nutritious	rejection	_____
objection	relation	_____
official	restriction	_____
omission	ricochet	_____
oppression	salt shaker	_____
oration	salvation	_____
ovation	secretion	_____

SH /ʃ/ Medial—four syllables

acceptation	derivation	intuition
accomplishment	designation	invitation
adding machine	desperation	irritation
admiration	destination	isolation
adoration	dictionary	lifeguard station
affirmation	dietician	limitation
aggravation	disposition	locomotion
amputation	domination	malformation
application	education	malnutrition
artificial	elevation	maturation
aspiration	establishment	mediation
aviation	estimation	meditation
beneficial	exclamation	moderation
cash register	exhalation	navigation
celebration	expectation	negotiate
combination	explanation	nomination
commendation	exploration	obligation
compensation	exportation	observation
competition	generation	occupation
complication	genuflection	operation
composition	graduation	opposition
comprehension	habitation	orthodontia
concentration	hesitation	persecution
condensation	illustration	perspiration
confidential	imitation	police station
congregation	inauspicious	politician
conservation	inclination	population
constitution	indication	preparation
consultation	inflammation	presentation
contribution	information	preservation
conversation	inhalation	proclamation
corporation	initialize	proficiency
cultivation	insatiable	publication
declaration	inspiration	radiation
dedication	institution	rationalize
definition	insulation	recitation
delegation	intermission	recognition
demonstration	introduction	recollection

reconstruction
registration
regulation
relaxation
repetition
reproduction
reputation
reservation
resignation
resolution
respiration
restoration
retardation

revolution
sanitation
satisfaction
separation
situation
social worker
speech clinician
station wagon
stationary
stimulation
substitution
superstition
termination

toleration
transportation
vaccination
variation
vegetation
ventilation
weather station
_____
_____
_____
_____
_____
_____

SH /ʃ/ Medial—five syllables

abbreviation
acceleration
accommodation
administration
amplification
approximation
articulation
asphyxiation
association
certification
classification
colonization
communication
congratulations
consideration
continuation
cooperation
coordination

deceleration
determination
discrimination
dissatisfaction
elaboration
elimination
evaporation
exaggeration
examination
humiliation
imagination
incineration
initiation
interpretation
investigation
manipulation
mathematician
modification

multiplication
nationality
organization
participation
preoccupation
procrastination
pronunciation
recommendation
refrigeration
representation
sophistication
_____
_____
_____
_____
_____
_____
_____

SH /ʃ/ Medial—six syllables

decolonization
disarticulation
disorganization
misinterpretation

mispronunciation
misrepresentation
postexamination
precommunication

rehabilitation
uncoordination
_____
_____

SH /ʃ/ Final—one syllable

ash	gnash	slash
bash	gosh	slosh
blush	gush	slush
brash	hash	smash
brush	hush	splash
bush	Josh	squash
cache	Kush	squish
cash	lash	swash
clash	leash	swish
crash	lush	thrash
crush	mash	thresh
dash	mesh	thrush
dish	mush	Tish
fish	Nash	trash
flash	plush	Trish
flesh	push	wash
flush	rash	Welsh
fresh	rush	wish
gash	sash	_____

SH /ʃ/ Final—two syllables

abash	cherish	foolish
afresh	childish	furbish
anguish	clothes brush	furnish
backlash	codfish	galosh
backwash	crawfish	garish
banish	Danish	garnish
blackfish	dervish	goldfish
blackish	elfish	gooseflesh
blandish	English	goulash
blemish	enmesh	grayish
bluefish	eyelash	greenish
blueish	eyewash	hairbrush
British	famish	hogwash
bulrush	finish	inrush
burnish	Finnish	Irish
car wash	flatfish	kibosh
catfish	flourish	lavish

modish
mouthwash
mustache
nail brush
nourish
paintbrush
parish
perish
pinkish
polish
Polish
potash
publish
punish
radish
reddish
refresh
relish

rosebush
rubbish
sagebrush
Scottish
scrub brush
selfish
sheepish
shellfish
shoebrush
skirmish
skittish
sluggish
snobbish
Spanish
Standish
starfish
stylish
sunfish

Swedish
tarnish
ticklish
toothbrush
unlash
unleash
vanquish
varnish
Wabash
whiplash
whitefish
whitewash
whitish
wood thrush
Yiddish
_____
_____
_____

SH /ʃ/ Final—three syllables

accomplish
admonish
astonish
babyish
demolish
diminish
distinguish
embellish

establish
extinguish
horseradish
licorice
McIntosh
Old English
outlandish
relinquish

replenish
Scotch-Irish
steeplebush
succotash
underbrush
unselfish
yellowish
_____

SH /ʃ/ Final—four syllables

bayberry bush
cranberry bush
mulberry bush

raspberry bush
satellite dish
strawberry bush

undernourish
_____
_____

SHL /ʃl/ Final—two syllables

bushel
crucial
facial
glacial

marshal
partial
racial
social

spatial
special
_____
_____

SHL /ʃl/ Final—three syllables

commercial	impartial	potential
essential	initial	provincial
financial	judicial	torrential
fire marshal	official	_____

SHL /ʃl/ Final—four syllables

antisocial	differential	prejudicial
artificial	influential	presidential
beneficial	nonessential	residential
consequential	preferential	_____

SHR /ʃr/ Initial—one syllable

shrank	shrill	shrub
shred	shrimp	shrug
shrew	shrine	shrugged
shrewd	shrines	shrugs
shrews	shrink	shrunk
shriek	shrive	_____
shrift	shroud	_____
shrike	shrove	_____

SHR /ʃr/ Initial—two syllables

shredded	shrimper	shrubby
Shreveport	Shriners	shrugging
shrewdly	shrinkage	shrunken
shrewdness	shrinking	_____
shrewish	shrivel	_____
shrillest	shriveled	_____
shrimp boat	shriven	_____

SHR /ʃr/ Initial—three syllables

shriveling	_____	_____
shrubbery	_____	_____

SHR /ʃr/ Medial—two syllables

enshrine	preshrink	washrag
mushroom	preshrunk	washroom
preshred	unshred	_____

SHER /ʃɚ/ Medial—three syllables

fisherman	fishery	_____
fishermen	pressuring	_____

SHER /ʃɚ/ Final—two syllables

crusher	masher	thrasher
glacier	plusher	thresher
gusher	pressure	usher
kosher	rusher	washer
lasher	squasher	_____

SHER /ʃɚ/ Final—three syllables

blood pressure	kingfisher	publisher
Britisher	low-pressure	trash masher
high-pressure	New Hampshire	_____

RSH /rʃ/ Medial—two syllables

airship	marshal	portion
earshot	martial	warship
Marsha	partial	worship

RSH /rʃ/ Medial—three syllables

censorship	martial arts	partnership
commercial	martial law	pastorship
contortion	membership	proportion
distortion	overshade	scholarship
fire marshal	overshine	sponsorship
foreshadow	overshoes	undershirt
leadership	overshoot	undershot
Marshal Sea	overshot	undershrub
marshmallow	ownership	watershed

RSH /rʃ/ Medial—four syllables

antique airship	overshadow	treasurership
chancellorship	thundershower	undersheriff
Marshall Islands	torsionally	_____

RSH /rʃ/ Final—one syllable

harsh	kirsch	marsh

T

Pronounced: /t/
Spelled: t, ed, ght, th, tt, tw

T /t/ Initial—one syllable

tab	tart	tick
Tab	task	ticked
tabs	taste	tide
tack	taught	tie
tact	taunt	tiff
Tad	taut	tight
Taft	tax	tights
tag	tea	till
tagged	teach	tilt
tail	teak	Tim
tailed	teal	time
tails	team	timed
take	tear	tin
tale	tears	tip
talk	tease	tipped
talked	Ted	tips
tall	tee	tire
tame	teen	Tish
tamed	teeth	to
tan	teethe	toad
tang	tell	toast
tank	ten	Todd
tanned	tend	toe
tap	tense	toil
tape	tent	toll
taped	tenth	Tom
tapes	term	tomb
tapped	tern	ton
taps	test	tone
tar	thyme	toned

tongue	tough	tune
too	tour	tuned
took	tow	tunes
tool	towed	turf
tooth	town	Turk
top	toy	turn
tops	tub	turned
torch	tube	tusk
tore	tuck	two
toss	tucked	type
tossed	tucks	typed
tot	tug	_____
touch	tugged	_____

T /t/ Initial—two syllables

tabby	takeout	tap dance
table	taking	tape deck
tabled	talcum	taper
tablet	talent	taping
taboo	tallow	tapping
tackle	tally	tardy
tacky	tambour	target
taco	tamer	tariff
tactful	tamest	tarnish
tadpole	taming	tartan
taffy	Tammy	tarter
tagging	tamper	Tarzan
tailback	tandem	task force
tail coat	tangent	tassel
tail end	tangle	taste buds
tailor	tango	tasted
tailored	tank car	tasteful
tailpiece	tanker	tasting
tailpipe	tankful	tasty
tailspin	tankship	tattered
Taiwan	tank truck	tattle
takedown	tanner	tattler
taken	tanning	tattoo
takeoff	tantrum	Taurus

taxi	termite	tonic
tax rate	terrace	tonight
tax stamp	terry	tonsil
Taylor	Terry	toolbox
tea bag	Texas	toolhouse
teacher	textbook	toothbrush
teaching	texture	toothpaste
teacup	Thomas	toothpick
teahouse	Tibet	topaz
tea-leaf	ticket	topic
teammate	tiger	topline
teamster	tightrope	topnotch
Teamsters	tightwad	topping
teamwork	timber	topple
teapot	timecard	topsoil
tearful	timely	torrent
tearing	time-out	tortoise
tea shop	Tina	torture
teaspoon	tingle	toss-up
technique	tinsel	total
Teddy	tiny	totem
Teena	tiptoe	tour guide
teenage	tired	tourist
teeny	tissue	towel
teepee	tizzy	tower
teeter	toadstool	towline
teller	toaster	town clerk
telling	Toby	town hall
temper	today	townhouse
tempest	toddle	township
temple	toddler	T-shirt
tempo	toilet	Tuesday
tenant	token	tugboat
tender	tollbooth	tulip
tendon	toll bridge	tumbler
tennis	toll call	tumor
tension	toll road	tuna
tepid	Tommy	tundra
Terence	tom-tom	tunic

tunnel	turtle	two-way
turban	Tuscan	tycoon
turkey	tussle	Tyler
turnip	tutor	typhoon
turnoff	two bits	typist
turnpike	two-fold	_____
turqouise	two-piece	_____
turret	two-some	_____

T /t/ Initial—three syllables

tablecloth	taxpayer	terrier
tablespoon	teaberry	terrific
tabulate	teachable	testament
Tahiti	teacher's aide	testify
Tahitian	tea garden	test pilot
takcovcr	teakettle	tetherball
talented	tea party	Theresa
talent scout	teaspoonful	tidal wave
talent show	technical	Timothy
talkative	teddy bear	Titanic
tallyho	teenager	Tobias
tallysheet	Tel Aviv	toboggan
tamale	telecast	together
tamarind	telegram	Tomasa
tambourine	telegraph	tomato
tameable	telephone	tomorrow
tamper-proof	telescope	tornado
tangerine	Teletype	tortilla
tangible	televise	tournament
tantalize	tempera	tuition
tantamount	temptation	turpentine
tape player	tenderloin	turtledove
tapestry	tennis ball	two-cycle
tarpaulin	tennis court	two-sided
tarter sauce	tennis shoes	two-whcclcr
tattletale	Tennyson	tympanist
taxable	tentacle	typewriter
taxicab	tentative	typical
taxiway	terminal	_____

T /t/ Initial—four syllables

tabernacle	taxidermy	testimony
table tennis	taxonomy	Texas City
tachometer	teeter-totter	Texas Rangers
talcum powder	telephone book	Texas longhorn
tanning center	telephone booth	timidity
tape recorder	telephone pole	topography
tape recording	television	typographic
tapioca	temperature	_____
tax deduction	territory	_____

T /t/ Initial—five syllables

technicality	_____	_____
tuberculosis	_____	_____
typographical	_____	_____

T /t/ Medial—two syllables

atom	brighter	cutting
attend	Britain	data
attic	British	dating
baited	butane	daughter
baton	butter	detail
batted	button	deter
batter	cater	detour
batting	chatted	ditty
battle	chatter	duty
beater	cheated	eaten
beauty	cheater	eating
better	cheetah	Eaton
Betty	cited	eighteen
biting	city	eighty
bitten	clatter	Eton
bitter	clutter	Etta
blotter	coated	fatal
boating	cottage	fatten
booted	cotton	fatter
booting	crater	fighter
boot-up	critter	fitted
booty	cutter	fitting

fittings	knitted	nutty
flatten	knitting	otter
flatter	knotted	Otto
flitted	later	outtalk
floated	Latin	patent
floater	latter	patted
floating	lattice	patter
flutter	letter	pattern
footage	lettuce	Patti
freighter	lighter	Patty
fritter	liter	petal
getting	litter	Peter
glitter	loiter	pewter
grater	looted	photos
greater	lotto	pitied
greeted	low tide	pitter
greetings	matted	pity
gritted	matter	platter
guitar	meeting	plotted
gutters	metal	plotter
Haiti	meter	potter
hatter	mighty	pouting
heated	mitten	pretty
heater	motel	putter
heighten	motor	putty
high tide	motto	quitter
high time	mutter	quota
hitter	mutton	quoted
hooted	naughty	quoter
hotel	neater	rated
hotter	netted	rating
jetties	netting	rattle
jetting	nighttime	Rita
jetty	nineteen	rooted
jitter	ninety	rotate
jitters	Nita	rotor
jotted	notate	rotten
kitten	noted	routed
kitty	notice	satin

Saturn	splatter	Toto
scatter	splitting	tutor
scouting	spotted	utter
seated	spotter	vital
setter	sputter	voted
setting	squatter	voter
shatter	stated	waiter
shooting	stutter	water
shutter	suited	wattage
sighted	sweater	wetting
sitter	sweating	whiter
sitting	sweeten	witty
sit-up	sweeter	writer
skater	sweetie	write-up
skating	tighter	written
sleeting	title	yachting
smatter	tooted	_____
smitten	total	_____
spatter	totem	_____

T /t/ Medial—three syllables

acquitted	boutonniere	demoted
admitted	bus safety	denoted
Aletta	butterfly	devoted
Anita	butterscotch	dictator
anteater	buttonhole	diluted
atom bomb	catering	disputed
attitude	chain letter	editor
auditor	Charlottetown	elated
autobahn	Chinatown	entitle
baritone	city hall	equator
Baton Rouge	city lot	excited
battalion	computed	fairy tale
Bay City	computer	farsighted
beautiful	cottage cheese	Fayetteville
beauty shop	creator	fire safety
Benita	data base	flotilla
bike safety	data disk	flutter kick
botany	delighted	forgotten

fresh-water	notify	spectator
gas meter	omitted	spotting scope
Gettysburg	outwitted	stuttering
globe trotter	permitted	talkative
Globe Trotters	photograph	theater
gratify	photo lab	tidewater
heated pool	potato	tomato
heating pad	predator	totem pole
hospital	promoter	transistor
hot water	putting green	translator
ice water	quick-witted	typesetter
indebted	quieter	typewriter
invited	rattlesnake	typewritten
inviting	recital	unbeaten
janitor	regretted	united
jitterbug	reheated	United
Juanita	related	uniting
Jupiter	remittance	unity
latitude	repeated	unsuited
lettering	rotary	uprooted
limited	rotation	visitor
litterbug	safety belt	vitamin
littering	saltwater	voting booth
Little League	saluted	waterbed
located	saluting	water bug
locater	Saturday	white water
monitor	senator	woodcutter
narrator	shortsighted	_____
nearsighted	shot-putter	_____
newsletter	skywriting	_____
noticing	sonata	_____

T /t/ Medial—four syllables

agitator	baby-sitter	commentator
alligator	beauty salon	competitor
alma mater	boating safety	cultivator
altimeter	calculator	decorator
aviator	centimeter	diameter
baby rattle	climbing safety	dormitory

driving safety
duplicator
educator
elevator
escalator
excavator
flying safety
generator
incubator
kilometer
legislator
liberator
litter barrel
moderator

navigator
nominator
numerator
operator
parking meter
peanut butter
percolator
perimeter
potato chips
radiator
riding safety
safety glasses
safety helmet
speedometer

thermometer
underwriter
United States
vegetables
ventilator
video tape
violator
vitamin C
walking safety
water safety
_____
_____
_____
_____

T /t/ Medial—five syllables

anatomical
denominator
deteriorate
hippopotamus

hot water bottle
hot water heater
potato salad
refrigerator

Sagittarius
saltwater taffy
_____
_____

T /t/ Final—one syllable

at
ate
bait
bat
beat
beet
bet
bit
bite
blight
bloat
blot
boat
boot
bought
bout
brat

Brett
bright
brought
brute
but
byte
cat
caught
chat
cheat
Chet
chit
chute
cleat
clot
clout
coat

coot
cot
crate
cut
cute
date
·dot
doubt
drought
Dwight
eat
eight
fat
fate
feat
feet
fight

fit	jut	Pat
flat	jute	peat
fleet	Kate	pet
flight	Kit	Pete
flit	kite	pit
float	knight	plat
flout	knit	plate
flute	knot	pleat
foot	kraut	plight
fought	late	plot
frat	let	pout
fraught	light	Pratt
freight	lit	put
fret	loot	putt
fright	lot	quit
fruit	lute	quite
gait	mat	quote
gate	Mat	rat
get	mate	rate
gloat	meat	Rhet
gnat	meet	right
goat	met	rite
got	might	root
gout	mite	rot
grate	moat	rote
great	mute	rout
greet	mutt	route
grit	naught	rut
gut	neat	sat
hat	net	scat
heat	newt	scoot
height	night	Scott
hit	not	scout
hoot	note	seat
hot	nut	set
hut	oat	sheet
it	ought	shoat
jet	out	shot
jot	pat	shout

shut	sprite	trite
sight	sprout	trot
sit	squat	trout
skate	state	tut
skeet	stout	tweet
skit	straight	vat
slat	strait	vet
slate	street	vote
sleet	strut	wait
slight	suit	watt
slit	suite	weight
slot	swat	wet
smit	sweat	what
smite	sweet	wheat
snoot	taught	Whit
snout	taut	white
soot	that	wit
sought	thought	writ
spat	throat	write
spit	tight	wrote
spite	toot	wrought
splat	tot	yacht
split	tote	yet
spot	trait	_____
spout	treat	_____

T /t/ Final—two syllables

about	Bridget	Collette
acute	budget	combat
afloat	burned-out	commute
air freight	cadet	compete
Annette	camp-out	complete
athlete	cassette	compute
await	Charlotte	conceit
basket	checkmate	concrete
bike route	civet	corvette
bonnet	classmate	create
Boy Scout	clean-cut	DeWitt
bracelet	closet	dead weight

debate	granite	outvote
deceit	grapefruit	parrot
defeat	grass hut	peanut
deflate	green light	playmate
delete	habit	pocket
deplete	helmet	poet
devote	helpmate	pollute
devout	high hat	profit
discreet	hip boot	promote
diskette	houseboat	prorate
dispute	ice-skate	quartet
donate	inflate	quiet
doormat	instate	quintet
doughnut	irate	rabbit
downright	jacket	racket
dragnet	jackpot	racquet
droplet	Jeannette	rebate
dropout	King Tut	receipt
duet	knockout	red light
dugout	kumquat	regret
Dutch treat	lifeboat	relate
edit	locate	remote
elite	locket	repeat
enroute	lookout	reset
equate	lowfat	restate
estate	Main Street	rivet
exit	mandate	robot
faucet	market	rocket
fire hat	merit	rotate
fish bait	migrate	rowboat
flashlight	minute	sailboat
footnote	misquote	salute
forget	moonlight	shipmate
forgot	Nanette	showboat
format	narratc	snowboot
fresh fruit	negate	speedboat
gambit	nugget	spreadsheet
gazette	offset	square knot
Gillett	outshoot	stoplight

sunlight	typeset	watch out
sunset	unfit	webbed feet
tablet	unit	whole-wheat
tailgate	unite	without
throughout	uproot	Yvette
Tibet	upset	_____
toilet	vacate	_____
tomcat	wallet	_____
top hat	walnut	_____

T /t/ Final—three syllables

absolute	complicate	hesitate
acclimate	cookie sheet	hibernate
accurate	copyright	hockey skate
acrobat	coronet	imitate
adequate	county seat	implicate
advocate	cowboy boot	incomplete
aeronaut	decorate	institute
agitate	dehydrate	irritate
alphabet	delegate	isolate
antidote	delicate	laundromat
apricot	democrat	legislate
arrowroot	desolate	Margaret
astronaut	destitute	May basket
attribute	deviate	moderate
bassinet	diplomat	motivate
billy goat	dissipate	motorboat
bluebonnet	dynamite	navigate
cabinet	educate	nominate
calculate	elevate	nonprofit
Camelot	execute	obligate
celebrate	featherweight	obstinate
chariot	fishing net	omelet
chocolate	gadabout	one-way street
circulate	gold nugget	operate
clarinet	granny knot	overboot
clothes basket	halibut	overcoat
coconut	Harriet	overeat
compensate	heavyweight	overrate

overshoot
overstate
overwrite
paperweight
parachute
parakeet
parking lot
patriot
persecute
pilot boat
populate
prosecute
radiate
rainbow trout
recreate
regulate
reinstate

renovate
reunite
riverboat
roller skate
sauerkraut
scuttlebutt
separate
silver plate
simulate
situate
solar heat
Soviet
speculate
stimulate
stock market
substitute
terminate

thereabout
thermostat
tourniquet
underset
undershot
vaccinate
vegetate
ventilate
violate
violet
wastebasket
watertight
whereabout
_____
_____
_____
_____

T /t/ Final—four syllables

accelerate
accentuate
accumulate
anticipate
approximate
aristocrat
asphyxiate
associate
certificate

cooperate
coordinate
decelerate
Easter basket
forget-me-not
immaculate
incriminate
interrogate
invalidate

officiate
originate
refrigerate
regenerate
shopping basket
supermarket
unfortunate
_____
_____

FT /ft/ Medial—two syllables

after
chieftain
Clifton
driftwood
fifteen
fifteenth
fifty
half time
left field

left hand
lifter
lift-off
lift truck
lofty
nifty
rafter
ruffed grouse
sifter

softball
soft drink
softness
software
softwood
thriftless
thrift store
thrifty
_____

FT /ft/ Medial—three syllables

afterglow	afterwards	soft-shell crab
afterlife	afterworld	thereafter
aftermath	after-years	thriftier
aftermost	hereafter	thriftiest
afternoon	leftovers	thriftily
aftertaste	shoplifter	_____
afterthought	soft-hearted	_____

FT /ft/ Final—one syllable

aft	laughed	soft
cleft	left	swift
craft	lift	Taft
croft	loft	theft
daft	oft	thrift
deft	raft	tuft
draft	rift	waft
drift	roofed	weft
gift	ruffed	_____
goofed	shaft	_____
graft	shift	_____
heft	shrift	_____
huffed	sift	_____

FT /ft/ Final—two syllables

adrift	hayloft	spacecraft
aircraft	ingraft	spendthrift
airlift	life raft	uncuffed
aloft	makeshift	uplift
crankshaft	night shift	witchcraft
day shift	ski lift	woodcraft
gearshift	skin graft	_____
handcraft	snowdrift	_____

FT /ft/ Final—three syllables

birthday gift	leisure craft	water craft
Christmas gift	overdraft	_____
handicraft	pleasure craft	_____
leather craft	rubber raft	_____

KT /kt/ Medial—two syllables

active	lecturn	tractor
cactus	necktie	vector
Choctaw	octane	victim
doctor	octave	victor
doctrine	pectin	Victor
factor	practice	_____
Hector	spectant	_____

KT /kt/ Medial—three syllables

activate	director	nocturnal
actively	doctoral	objected
affected	effective	objective
affective	elective	obstructing
attracted	elector	octagon
attractive	electron	October
bisected	erector	octopus
character	exacting	pact-maker
conducting	exactly	perspective
conductor	factitious	practical
connecting	factory	prospective
connector	hectagon	prospector
deducted	impacted	reactor
destructive	inactive	selective
detective	infected	spectator
dictaphone	inflicting	transacting
dictation	instructor	_____
dictator	neglected	_____

KT /kt/ Medial—four syllables

activity	destructible	respectable
bacteria	directory	retractable
benefactor	objectable	Victoria
deductible	predictable	_____

KT /kt/ Final—one syllable

act	blocked	cooked
backed	booked	cracked
biked	checked	docked

ducked	picked	strict
duct	poked	tacked
fact	raked	tact
faked	reeked	talked
hiked	rocked	ticked
joked	sacked	tracked
kicked	sect	tract
knocked	shocked	tricked
leaked	sneaked	trucked
liked	soaked	tucked
locked	spooked	walked
looked	squeaked	wrecked
packed	stacked	_____
pact	staked	_____
peaked	stocked	_____

KT /kt/ Final—two syllables

abduct	deflect	inflict
abstract	deject	inject
affect	depict	insect
afflict	detect	inspect
aspect	detract	instruct
attacked	direct	intact
attract	dissect	neglect
barebacked	distract	object
bisect	district	obstruct
collect	effect	perfect
compact	eject	predict
conduct	elect	prefect
conflict	enact	product
connect	erect	project
constrict	evict	prospect
construct	evoked	protect
contact	exact	protract
contract	expect	react
convict	extract	reflect
correct	impact	reject
deduct	induct	respect
defect	infect	restrict

retract	subtract	_____
select	suspect	_____
subject	transact	_____

KT /kt/ Final—three syllables

architect	intellect	subcontract
cataract	interject	viaduct
derelict	intersect	_____
dialect	misdirect	_____
disconnect	overact	_____
disinfect	recollect	_____
incorrect	reelect	_____
indirect	self-respect	_____

TL /tl/ Medial—two syllables

atlas	outlet	potluck
butler	outline	settler
lightly	outlook	_____
outlaw	potlatch	_____

TL /tl/ Medial—three syllables

anciently	outlining	quietly
Atlanta	outlying	sedately
Atlantic	perfectly	_____
irately	politely	_____

TL /tl/ Final—three syllables

belittle	parental	skeletal
capital	pedestal	subtitle
entitle	rose beetle	_____
immortal	segmental	_____

TL /tl/ Final—four syllables

accidental	incidental	tittle tattle
congenital	monumental	_____
continental	noncommittal	_____
elemental	oriental	_____
fundamental	sentimental	_____
horizontal	thermos bottle	_____

LT /lt/ Medial—two syllables

alter	halter	smelter
alto	hilltop	voltage
Colton	Hilton	Walter
cultist	melted	welter
delta	molten	yuletide
falter	poultry	___
faultless	quilting	___
filter	salted	___
guilty	shelter	___

LT /lt/ Medial—three syllables

alternate	malted milk	royalty
altitude	multiple	saltshaker
Central Time	multiply	specialty
cultism	multitude	voltmeter
cultivate	novelty	welterweight
dial tone	penalty	___
faultfinding	resulting	___
loyalty	revolted	___

LT /lt/ Medial—four syllables

altimeter	difficulty	___
altogether	multiplier	___
cultivator	seat belt safety	___

LT /lt/ Final—one syllable

belt	jolt	smelt
bolt	kilt	spilt
built	knelt	stilt
colt	lilt	tilt
dealt	malt	vault
dwelt	melt	volt
fault	molt	Walt
felt	pelt	welt
guilt	quilt	wilt
halt	salt	Wilt
hilt	shalt	___
jilt	silt	___

LT /lt/ Final—two syllables

adult	default	result
asphalt	exalt	revolt
bank vault	exult	rock salt
black belt	fan belt	seat belt
blue belt	farm belt	tumult
cobalt	insult	white belt
consult	pole vault	_____
Corn Belt	Renault	_____

LT /lt/ Final—three syllables

difficult	patchwork quilt	thunderbolt
garlic salt	Roosevelt	_____
leather belt	somersault	_____

NT /nt/ Medial—two syllables

ante	entrance	painter
antler	entry	painting
banter	fainted	pantry
cantor	frantic	plaintiff
center	frontal	plaintive
centered	gentle	planter
central	granted	planting
chanting	grantor	pointer
contempt	hinted	pointing
contend	hunter	pontiff
content	hunting	printed
contest	huntress	printer
context	into	printing
contort	junta	punted
contour	mantle	quaintly
country	mental	rental
county	mentor	rented
dainty	minted	saintly
dental	Monty	Santa
dented	nineteen	scented
dentist	ninety	shanty
Denton	onto	slanted
enter	painted	splinter

squinted	Trenton	wanton
squinter	vantage	winter
syntax	vented	_____
tantrum	vintage	_____
tinted	wanted	_____

NT /nt/ Medial—three syllables

advantage	fantasy	re-enter
Antarctic	gigantic	repentant
Atlantic	imprinted	repented
attentive	incentive	repenting
carpenter	indented	resented
centerpiece	interact	resentful
Centerville	intercede	resentment
Central Park	intercept	romantic
Central Time	intercom	Santa Claus
consented	interest	Santa Cruz
container	interface	Santa Fe
contented	interfere	self-centered
contention	interfold	seventeen
contentment	intersect	seventy
contestant	interval	storm center
continent	interview	tentative
continue	invented	tormentor
counterfeit	inventor	transplanting
enchanted	Kentucky	wintergreen
encounter	Kon Tiki	wintertime
enterprise	misprinted	_____
entertain	parental	_____
eventful	presenting	_____

NT /nt/ Medial—four syllables

accidental	contaminate	conventional
adventurer	contemplating	departmental
antagonist	continental	differential
antagonize	contingency	disadvantage
antecedent	continual	egocentric
cantilever	continuous	governmental
commentary	continuum	horizontal

instrumental	pigmentation	trans-Atlantic
integrity	presentation	transcendental
interesting	radiant heat	uneventful
intermission	radiantly	unprevented
intersection	regimental	unrepentant
intimidate	representant	Valentine's Day
monumental	rudimental	ventriloquist
oriental	sacramental	yellow bunting
ornamental	sentimental	_____
pedimental	supplemental	_____

NT /nt/ Medial—five syllables

antibiotic	experiential	representation
contaminated	intermediate	supplementary
contemporary	international	temperamental
differentiate	involuntary	testamentary
disinterested	orientation	_____
documentary	parliamentary	_____
elementary	Protestantism	_____

NT /nt/ Final—one syllable

ant	grant	print
aunt	Grant	punt
bent	grunt	quaint
blunt	haunt	quint
brunt	hint	rant
bunt	hunt	rent
can't	jaunt	runt
cent	lent	saint
chant	lint	scant
count	meant	scent
dent	mint	sent
don't	mount	shunt
faint	paint	slant
feint	pant	spent
flint	pent	sprint
front	pint	squint
gaunt	plant	stunt
gent	point	taunt

tent	want	_____
tint	went	_____
vent	won't	_____

NT /nt/ Final—two syllables

absent	For Rent	potent
accent	frequent	preprint
account	gallant	present
affront	garment	prevent
agent	hydrant	prudent
ailment	imprint	quadrant
amount	indent	quotient
anoint	infant	rampant
appoint	instant	recent
ascent	intent	recount
aslant	invent	remnant
basement	judgment	resent
Belmont	merchant	rodent
blueprint	moment	sea front
brilliant	movement	segment
buoyant	newsprint	sergeant
cement	oil paint	serpent
client	ointment	servant
cogent	pageant	shipment
cold front	parchment	silent
comment	parent	spearmint
consent	patent	stagnant
constant	patient	standpoint
content	pavement	statement
descent	payment	strident
discount	peasant	stringent
distant	pennant	student
eggplant	percent	talent
enchant	pheasant	tenant
entente	pigment	torrent
event	pinpoint	transient
extent	placement	transplant
ferment	pleasant	treatment
foment	poignant	urgent

vacant   _____   _____

valiant   _____   _____

Vermont   _____   _____

vibrant   _____   _____

NT /nt/ Final—three syllables

abundant	document	operant
accident	dominant	opponent
accountant	efficient	orient
adjacent	elephant	ornament
adornment	elopement	palpitant
advancement	emigrant	parliament
affluent	encroachment	peppermint
allotment	enjoyment	permanent
amazement	enrollment	persistent
amendment	filament	petulant
amusement	ignorant	precedent
announcement	immigrant	president
apartment	implement	prominent
apparent	improvement	Protestant
appointment	impudent	punishment
arrangement	incident	radiant
atonement	indignant	recurrent
commencement	inherent	refreshment
compartment	innocent	regiment
competent	insolvent	relevant
compliment	installment	reluctant
component	instrument	represent
consonant	investment	requirement
contentment	lenient	resentment
continent	lieutenant	resident
convenient	ligament	resistant
decedent	malignant	respondent
dependent	management	restaurant
descendant	measurement	retirement
detergent	monument	reverent
different	nourishment	ruminant
diligent	nutrient	sediment
dissonant	occupant	sentiment

subjacent
subsequent
succulent
sufficient
supplement
sycophant

tenement
testament
tolerant
tournament
variant
vigilant

violent
wonderment

_____
_____
_____
_____

NT /nt/ Final—four syllables

accomplishment
adolescent
advertisement
apportionment
astonishment
determinant
entertainment
environment
equivalent
establishment
expedient
experiment
extravagant

independent
indifferent
ingredient
intelligent
intolerant
iridescent
magnificent
noncombatant
obedient
participant
precipitant
predicament
predominant

preponderant
presentiment
reinforcement
significant
single parent
subservient
superjacent
temperament
understatement
vice-president

_____
_____
_____

NT /nt/ Final—five syllables

insignificant
interdependent
superintendent

_____
_____
_____

_____
_____
_____

PT /pt/ Final—one syllable

chapped
chipped
chopped
clapped
clipped
crept
dipped
dripped
dropped
flapped
flipped

flopped
griped
gripped
heaped
hoped
hopped
kept
lapped
leaped
mapped
mopped

napped
nipped
peeped
piped
plopped
popped
propped
rapped
reaped
ripped
roped

scooped	snapped	tripped
scoped	snipped	typed
scraped	stepped	wept
scrapped	stopped	wiped
script	strapped	wrapped
seeped	swapped	yipped
shipped	swooped	zapped
shopped	taped	zipped
sipped	tapped	_____
skipped	tipped	_____
slept	topped	_____
slipped	trapped	_____

PT /pt/ Final—two syllables

abrupt	corrupt	gossiped
accept	disrupt	postscript
adapt	Egypt	precept
adept	erupt	subscript
adopt	escaped	unwrapped
bankrupt	except	_____
concept	galloped	_____

PT /pt/ Final—three syllables

intercept	_____	_____
non-adept	_____	_____

TS /ts/ Medial—two syllables

batsman	outside	ritzy
Betsy	outsing	schizo
Datsun	outsit	schizoid
gutsy	outsize	schnitzel
itself	outsold	Scotsman
jet set	outsole	Scottsville
jetsam	Patsy	sitz bath
Matson	pit saw	Watson
Mezzo	pizza	yachtsman
Nazi	pretzel	_____
outsell	quartzlike	_____
outset	quetzal	_____

TS /ts/ Medial—three syllables

Fitzgerald	outsider	ritziest
gutsiness	pit sample	_____
outselling	ritzier	_____

TS /ts/ Medial—four syllables

outsettlement	pizzicato	_____
pizzeria	schizophrenic	_____

TS /ts/ Final—one syllable

ants	gates	nuts
aunts	gents	oats
baits	gnats	pants
bats	goats	pats
bites	grates	pets
bits	greets	pits
blitz	grits	plates
blots	guts	pleats
boats	hoots	pots
boots	huts	putts
cats	jets	quits
cheats	kites	quotes
chutes	knits	rates
cleats	knots	rats
crates	let's	rights
cuts	lights	roots
dates	loots	rots
debts	lots	routes
eats	lutes	routs
fates	mates	ruts
fights	mats	scouts
fits	meats	Scouts
Fitz	meets	seats
flats	mites	sets
fleets	mitts	sheets
flits	mutes	shoots
floats	nets	shorts
flutes	nights	sights
fruits	notes	sites

sits	sports	votes
skates	spots	waits
skits	spouts	wants
slates	states	weights
slats	threats	wits
slits	tights	writes
slots	toots	yachts
spits	totes	_____
splits	vats	_____

TS /ts/ Final—two syllables

acquits	footlights	merits
admits	footnotes	midgets
ballots	forfeits	minutes
biscuits	garnets	muskets
bonnets	giants	muskrats
brackets	Giants	narrates
buckets	giblets	nuggets
cadets	Girl Scouts	omits
carrots	goblets	orbits
cold cuts	hatchets	outfits
comets	ice boats	outwits
commits	ice skates	pamphlets
commutes	ignites	parrots
cornets	inlets	peanuts
cutlets	insights	pellets
debates	invites	permits
defeats	jackets	pheasants
denotes	jackpots	pilots
dictates	kumquats	pirates
diets	lifeboats	pivots
digits	limits	planets
doughnuts	locates	playmates
duets	lockets	pockets
eaglets	lookouts	poets
edits	magnets	polecats
emits	mallets	portraits
equates	markets	primates
faucets	mascots	profits

promotes	robots	termites
pullets	rockets	thickets
pulpits	roommates	tickets
puppets	rotates	tidbits
quintets	rowboats	tomcats
rabbits	sailboats	tugboats
rackets	salutes	two-bits
raincoats	secrets	unites
rebates	senates	units
receipts	skillets	visits
recites	slingshots	wallets
recruits	snapshots	whaleboats
red-hots	sockets	whole notes
regrets	speedboats	_____
repeats	spirits	_____
retreats	spotlights	_____
ringlets	steamboats	_____
riots	tablets	_____
rivets	targets	_____

TS /ts/ Final—three syllables

copyrights	opposites	separates
dominates	overcoats	shelled walnuts
elevates	parachutes	silhouettes
estimates	parakeets	skyrockets
irrigates	parasites	statuettes
irritates	patriots	tolerates
isolates	penetrates	violets
kilowatts	powerboats	_____
minuets	prohibits	_____
motorboats	radiates	_____
nominates	regulates	_____
ocelots	roller skates	_____
omelets	satellites	_____

TS /ts/ Final—four syllables

initiates	originates	_____
marionettes	participates	_____
Massachusetts	_____	_____

ST /st/ Initial—one syllable

stack	steak	stood
stacked	steam	stool
staff	steed	stoop
stag	steel	stop
stage	steep	stopped
staged	steer	store
stain	stem	stored
stair	stemmed	stork
stairs	step	storm
stake	stepped	stout
staked	stern	stove
stale	stew	stow
stalk	stick	stub
stall	stiff	stubbed
stalled	still	stud
stamp	stilt	stuff
stamped	sting	stump
stand	stink	stun
star	stir	stung
starch	stirred	stunk
stare	stitch	stunned
stared	stock	stunt
start	stocks	sty
state	stoke	style
states	stole	_____
stave	stomp	_____
stay	stone	_____

ST /st/ Initial—two syllables

stable	Stanford	static
stagecoach	Stanley	station
stagger	stanza	statue
staircase	staple	steadfast
stallage	starboard	stcady
stallion	starfish	steamboat
stammer	starling	steamer
stampede	statement	steamship
standard	statesman	steeple

steerage	Stone Age	stuck-up
steel wool	stoneware	student
sterling	stonework	studied
Steven	stoplight	study
steward	stop-off	stuffing
Stewart	stoppage	stuffy
sticky	stopper	stumble
stifle	stopping	stunning
stinger	stopwatch	sturdy
stingray	storage	sturgeon
stirrup	storehouse	stutter
stock car	storeroom	stylish
stocker	stories	stylist
Stockholm	stormy	stylize
stocking	story	stylus
stockroom	stovepipe	stymied
stocky	stowage	_____
stockyard	stubble	_____
stolen	stubborn	_____
stomach	stubby	_____

ST /st/ Initial—three syllables

stadium	sterilize	storybook
stalactite	stethoscope	stowaway
stalagmite	stimulate	studio
stateswoman	stimulus	studious
statistics	stock exchange	study group
steam engine	stock market	study hall
steam shovel	stomach ache	stumbling block
stepbrother	stonecutter	stupendous
stepfather	stopover	stuttering
stepladder	storm cellar	_____
stepmother	storm center	_____
stepping stone	storm warning	_____
stereo	storm window	_____

ST /st/ Initial—four syllables

stationary	station master	_____
stationery	station wagon	_____

ST /st/ Medial—two syllables

abstain	footstep	misty
bandstand	footstool	mostly
beefsteak	frostbite	mustang
breastbone	frosting	nasty
bus stop	ghastly	North Star
cast iron	ghost town	pastel
castoff	grandstand	pastels
Chester	grindstone	pastime
chestnut	hailstone	pastor
chopsticks	hailstorm	pester
coastal	hasty	piston
Coast Guard	haystack	postage
coastline	head start	postal
constant	headstone	postcard
costume	homestead	posted
crystal	hostage	posting
Crystal	hostel	postman
custom	hostess	postmark
destine	hostile	postpaid
distal	housetop	postpone
distance	Houston	postscript
distant	iced tea	question
distaste	install	restless
distend	instance	rhinestone
distill	instant	rustic
distinct	instead	rusty
distort	instep	Rusty
disturb	instinct	sandstorm
drugstore	justice	shoe store
drumstick	keystone	shortstop
dustcloth	lasting	smokestack
Easter	limestone	substance
eastern	lipstick	sustain
eastward	livestock	sweepstakes
Einstein	milestone	tasty
estate	mistake	test tube
Estelle	mister	toadstool
Ester	mistook	tombstone

tungsten western wristband
turnstile West Point yardstick
two-step westward _____
vista withstand _____
waistband withstood _____

ST /st/ Medial—three syllables

accustom fiesta post office
adjustment gas station predestine
armistice gymnastics Protestant
artistic high-stepping questioner
asbestos historic question mark
assistance hockey stick questionnaire
assistant honesty resistance
astonish injustice sarcastic
bus station installment shooting star
bystander instantly siesta
candlestick institute southeastern
castanets intestine space station
castaway investment substandard
consistent justify substantial
constitute Lone Star State substation
contestant long distance substitute
crop duster majestic summer stock
custody majesty superstar
customer mastodon sustenance
destiny mistaken testament
destitute northwestern testify
devastate Northwestern thermostat
distasteful obstacle tossed salad
distemper outstanding tostada
distiller pasteurize train station
distinction pedestal understand
distinguish persistent understood
establish photostat vestibule
estimate pogo stick youth hostel
existence postage stamp _____
fantastic postmaster _____
festival postmistress _____

ST /st/ Medial—four syllables

consistency	institution	realistic
constituent	interesting	relay station
constitution	investigate	solar system
Costa Rica	misunderstand	superstition
custodian	misunderstood	T.V. station
customary	optimistic	testimony
establishment	pessimistic	unaccustomed
grocery store	posterior	understanding
historian	questionable	United States
hysterical	readjustment	_____

ST /st/ Medial—five syllables

constituency	predestination	_____
investigative	unquestionable	_____
postmeridian	_____	_____

ST /st/ Final—one syllable

baste	feast	missed
beast	fist	mist
best	frost	moist
blast	fussed	most
blest	ghost	must
boast	guest	nest
boost	gust	passed
bussed	haste	past
bust	hoist	paste
cast	host	pest
chest	iced	placed
coast	jest	post
cost	just	pressed
crest	last	priest
crossed	least	quest
crust	lest	raced
dressed	list	rest
dust	lost	roast
east	mast	roost
faced	messed	rust
fast	midst	taste

test	vest	wrest
thrust	voiced	wrist
toast	waist	yeast
twist	waste	zest
vast	west	_____
versed	wist	_____

ST /st/ Final—two syllables

abreast	earnest	lyrist
adjust	eldest	Midwest
against	embossed	milepost
almost	enlist	modest
amidst	ernest	nearest
arrest	exhaust	neatest
artist	exist	newest
assist	Far East	newscast
August	farthest	nicest
Baptist	flautist	Northeast
bed rest	florist	Northwest
biggest	forecast	oldest
breakfast	forest	outpost
broadcast	French toast	poorest
chemist	furthest	post-test
choicest	gatepost	pre-test
combust	greatest	pronounced
compost	gymnast	protest
conquest	half-mast	request
consist	harvest	resist
contest	honest	richest
contrast	inquest	ripest
cutest	insist	robust
cyclist	invest	safest
deepest	Key West	sandblast
defrost	largest	sand-cast
dentist	locust	sawdust
detest	longest	sheerest
digest	loosest	shrillest
driest	loudest	signpost
druggist	low-cost	sleekest

slickest	stylist	unjust
slowest	subsist	unrest
slyest	suggest	upmost
smallest	tempest	utmost
smartest	thinnest	widest
smoothest	toothpaste	youngest
Southeast	tourist	_____
Southwest	trimmest	_____
steadfast	truest	_____
strongest	typist	_____

ST /st/ Final—three syllables

activist	Middle East	skinniest
amethyst	monarchist	smelliest
analyst	narrowest	soggiest
atheist	naughtiest	soloist
bassoonist	novelist	specialist
classicist	optimist	stockiest
daintiest	organist	theorist
dramatist	overcast	therapist
fuzziest	parcel post	thriftiest
happiest	pessimist	tidiest
hornet's nest	pharmacist	trombonist
hungriest	physicist	unbalanced
idealist	pianist	unnoticed
immodest	prettiest	uppermost
interest	quietist	vocalist
journalist	rebroadcast	wealthiest
kindliest	roomiest	_____
littlest	satirist	_____
loveliest	scientist	_____
luckiest	silliest	_____

ST /st/ Final—four syllables

antagonist	enthusiast	orthodontist
apologist	geologist	otologist
autonomist	iconoclast	pathologist
biologist	naturalist	philanthropist
economist	nonconformist	psychiatrist

psychologist	urologist	_____
rhinologist	ventriloquist	_____
unhappiest	violinist	_____

ST /st/ Final—five syllables

audiologist	entomologist	ornithologist
audiometrist	etymologist	_____
cardiologist	ophthalmologist	_____

TR /tr/ Initial—one syllable

trace	treats	trot
traced	tree	troth
track	trek	trough
tracked	trench	trounce
tract	trend	trout
trade	Trent	trow
trades	tress	Troy
trail	tribe	truce
trailed	trice	truck
trails	trick	trucked
train	tried	trudge
trained	tries	true
trait	trill	trump
tram	trim	trumped
tramp	trimmed	trunk
tramped	trip	trunks
trance	tripe	truss
trap	tripped	trust
trapped	Trish	truth
trash	trite	truths
trawl	trod	try
tray	troll	_____
tread	troop	_____
treat	troops	_____

TR /tr/ Initial—two syllables

tracing	trackless	tractor
tracker	track meet	Tracy
tracking	traction	trademark

trade name	transplant	tribute
tradesman	transport	trickle
trade wind	transpose	trickster
trading	transverse	tricky
traduce	trapdoor	trident
traffic	trapeze	trifle
tragic	trapper	trifler
trailer	trapping	trifling
trainee	trappings	trigger
trainer	trash can	trillion
training	travel	trimmer
trainman	traveled	trimming
traitor	traverse	trimmings
tramcar	trawler	trinket
tramline	treadle	trio
trammel	treadmill	triple
tramper	treason	triplet
trample	treasure	triplex
trampler	treating	tripod
trampling	treatment	tripping
tramway	treaty	triumph
tranquil	treble	trivet
transact	tree house	trodden
transcend	trekking	Trojan
transcribe	trellis	trolley
transcript	tremble	trombone
transept	trembling	trooper
transfer	tremor	troopship
transfix	trenchant	trophy
transform	trencher	tropic
transfuse	Trenton	trotter
transgress	trespass	trotting
transient	trestle	trouble
transit	triad	troubled
translate	trial	troubling
transmit	tribal	troublous
transmute	tribesman	trouncing
transom	tribesmen	trousers
transpire	tribune	trousseau

trowel
truant
trucking
truckle
truckled
truck route
truck stop
Trudy

truffle
truly
Truman
trumpet
trundle
trustee
trustees
trustful

trusting
trusty
truthful
trying
tryout

_____
_____
_____

TR /tr/ Initial—three syllables

traceable
trachea
trackable
tractable
trade union
trading post
tradition
traducement
traducer
tragedy
tragical
trailblazer
trailer camp
trailer court
trailer park
train station
trainable
training aid
training school
traitorous
trammeling
trampoline
tranquilest
tranquilize
transaction
transcendent
transcribing
transcription
transference

transferring
transfigured
transformer
transfusion
transgression
transgressor
transition
transitive
translation
translator
translucent
transmission
transmitter
transonic
transparent
transpolar
trapezoid
traveler
treacherous
treasure chest
treasure house
treasure hunt
treasure map
treasurer
treasury
tremendous
tremulous
trespassing
triangle

triathlon
tribunal
trickery
tricolor
tricycle
trilogy
Trinidad
trinity
triplicate
triumphal
triumphant
trivial
tropical
troubadour
troublesome
truculence
truculent
truism
trumpery
trumpeter
trundle bed
trustworthy
truthfulness

_____
_____
_____
_____
_____

TR /tr/ Initial—four syllables

tracking station	transcendental	transportation
traditional	transferable	treasonable
tragedian	transferential	trepidation
tragedienne	transforamtion	triangular
tragically	transitional	tribulation
trajectory	transitory	tributary
tranquility	transmigration	triennial
tranquilizer	transmutation	triplicating
trans-Andean	transparency	triumphal arch
transatlantic	transplantation	_____

TR /tr/ Initial—five syllables

tracheotomy	transcontinental	trigonometry
traditionally	transfiguration	triviality
transcendentalist	triangulation	_____

TR /tr/ Medial—two syllables

actress	horse trail	race track
attract	intrigue	retract
betray	matrix	retreat
central	matron	retrieve
citrus	mattress	round trip
contract	metric	sentry
control	neutral	ski trail
country	neutron	spectrum
detract	nitrate	subtract
detrain	pantry	sultry
Detroit	partridge	tantrum
doctrine	Patrick	tightrope
dog track	patrol	untried
entrance	patrolled	untrue
entry	patron	untruth
extra	pine tree	waitress
extract	portrait	_____
extreme	portray	_____
field trip	poultry	_____
firetrap	protract	_____
fire truck	protrude	

TR /tr/ Medial—three syllables

attraction
attractive
Australia
Beatrice
Central Park
concentrate
contraction
contradict
contrary
country club
countryside
detraction
detriment
electric
electron
extremely
infantry
inside track
intricate
introduce
maple tree
matriarch

metrical
metronome
nitrogen
nutrient
nutrition
nutritious
orchestra
outrageous
patriarch
Patricia
patriot
Patriots
patrolman
penetrate
petrify
poetry
postmistress
protractor
railroad track
rainbow trout
reentry
retraction

retrenchment
retrieval
retriever
retrieving
retrograde
retrogress
retrospect
ski patrol
spectroscope
state trooper
subcontract
subtraction
subtropics
untruthful
victrola
_____
_____
_____
_____
_____
_____
_____

TR /tr/ Medial—four syllables

catastrophe
concentration
contribution
control tower
controversy
electrical
electrician
electronics
entrepreneur
extravagance
extravagant
geometry
illustrated
introduction

matriarchy
matriculate
matrimony
metric system
metropolis
no trespassing
paratrooper
patriotic
patrolwoman
pedestrian
petrified wood
petroleum
remote control
retribution

retroactive
retroflexion
retrogression
retroversion
St. Patrick's Day
subtropical
ultrasonic
unobtrusive
ventriloquist
_____
_____
_____
_____

TR /tr/ Medial—five syllables

electricity	pediatrician	_____
metropolitan	_____	_____

RT /rt/ Medial—two syllables

artful	mortal	shorten
artist	mortar	shorthand
barter	Myrtle	shorthorn
Bertram	partake	shortly
Burton	parted	shortstop
Carter	parting	shortwave
carton	partly	Shorty
cartoon	partner	smarter
cartridge	partridge	smartly
cartwheel	part-time	sorting
certain	party	sport car
charter	pertain	sporting
Cortez	portage	sportive
courthouse	Portage	sportsman
courtyard	porter	sporty
curtain	Porter	squirting
Curtis	porthole	started
dirty	Portland	starter
fertile	portrait	startle
forty	portray	thirteen
fourteen	quarter	thirteenth
garter	quartet	thirty
Gertrude	quart jar	tortoise
hearty	quarto	turtle
martin	shortage	vertex
Martin	shortcake	warthog
Marty	short-changed	wiretap
martyr	short-cut	_____

RT /rt/ Medial—three syllables

advertise	artichoke	assortment
Alberta	article	bartering
aorta	artifact	cartilage
apartment	artisan	certainty

certified
certify
chartering
compartment
courtesy
departed
department
deportment
fertilize
fortieth
fortify
garter snake
Gilberta
headquarters
heartbroken
heartily
immortal
importance
important
liberty

light-hearted
particle
partition
partnership
portable
property
quarterback
report card
reporter
reporting
Roberta
Roquefort cheese
short circuit
shortening
short-handed
short-sighted
short story
soft-hearted
sportsmanlike
sportsmanship

sportswoman
sportswriter
summertime
support group
support staff
thirtieth
tortilla
turtledove
vertebra
vertebral
vertical
vertigo

_____
_____
_____
_____
_____
_____
_____

RT /rt/ Medial—four syllables

advertisement
articulate
artificial
certificate
certified check
certified mail
comfortable
convertible
departable
fertility
invertebrate
Liberty Bell

participate
participle
particular
porterhouse steak
portfolio
property tax
Puerto Rico
refertilize
reportedly
self-imparting
short division
short-handedness

short-sightedness
smart-alecky
unfortified
unimportant
unsportsmanlike
well-fortified
well-supported

_____
_____
_____
_____

RT /rt/ Medial—five syllables

false advertising
opportunity
past participle

pertinacity
quarterly report
uncomfortable

_____
_____
_____

RT /rt/ Final—one syllable

art	heart	sort
Bart	hurt	sport
Bert	Kurt	spurt
blurt	mart	squirt
cart	part	start
carte	pert	tart
chart	port	thwart
court	quart	wart
Curt	quirt	_____
dart	shirt	_____
dirt	short	_____
flirt	skirt	_____
fort	smart	_____
girt	snort	_____

RT /rt/ Final—two syllables

advert	evert	resort
airport	exert	revert
Albert	expert	Robert
alert	export	seaport
apart	extort	Shreveport
assert	filbert	sportshirt
athwart	Gilbert	stalwart
avert	go-cart	subvert
comfort	Head Start	support
concert	Herbert	sweatshirt
convert	Hubert	sweetheart
Delbert	impart	transport
depart	import	transvert
deport	inert	T-shirt
desert	insert	unhurt
dessert	invert	yogurt
distort	Lambert	_____
divert	outsmart	_____
dress shirt	oxcart	_____
effort	passport	_____
Elbert	pushcart	_____
escort	report	_____

RT /rt/ Final—three syllables

a la carte	introvert	shopping cart
counterpart	liverwort	tennis court
davenport	martial art	trailer court
disconcert	miniskirt	undershirt
extrovert	preconcert	_____
hula skirt	retrovert	_____

TW /tw/ Initial—one syllable

twang	twice	twinge
tweak	twig	twinned
tweed	twigged	twirl
tweet	twill	twist
tweeze	twilled	twitch
twelfth	twin	_____
twelve	twine	_____
twerp	twined	_____

TW /tw/ Initial—two syllables

twangle	twilight	twirler
twangy	twin bed	twister
tweedle	twinborn	twisting
tweedy	Twin Falls	twitch grass
tweezers	twinkle	twitter
twenty	twinkling	_____
twiddle	twin sheet	_____

TW /tw/ Initial—three syllables

twentieth	twilight sleep	twinflower
twenty-five	twinberry	twisted pine
twenty-one	Twin Cities	_____
twenty yards	twin-engine	_____

TY /tj/ Medial—two syllables

courtyard	light-year	_____
front yard	_____	_____

TY /tj/ Medial—four syllables

credit union	meticulous	_____

RCHT /rtʃt/ Final—one syllable

arched	perched	starched
marched	scorched	_____
parched	searched	_____

RKT /rkt/ Final—one syllable

arcked	jerked	sparked
barked	marked	worked
irked	parked	_____

RKT /rkt/ Final—two syllables

embarked	uncorked	_____
postmarked	unmarked	_____
remarked	unworked	_____

LTS /lts/ Final—one syllable

belts	melts	tilts
bolts	molts	vaults
colts	pelts	welts
faults	quilts	wilts
jolts	salts	_____
kilts	silts	_____
malts	stilts	_____

LTS /lts/ Final—two syllables

adults	pole vaults	_____
consults	revolts	_____
insults	seat belts	_____

RST /rst/ Final—one syllables

burst	hurst	thirst
cursed	Hurst	worst
first	nursed	_____
forced	pierced	_____

RST /rst/ Final—two syllables

airburst	dispersed	enforced
cloudburst	divorced	imbursed
coerced	endorsed	immersed

outburst	sunburst	_____
rehearsed	unversed	_____
reversed	_____	_____

RTS /rts/ Final—one syllable

arts	hearts	sports
blurts	parts	spurts
carts	ports	squirts
charts	quarts	warts
courts	shirts	_____
darts	shorts	_____
flirts	skirts	_____
forts	sorts	_____

RTS /rts/ Final—two syllables

airports	exports	seaports
alerts	imports	supports
concerts	inserts	transports
departs	inverts	_____
deserts	passports	_____
desserts	reports	_____
distorts	resorts	_____
experts	reverts	_____

STR /str/ Initial—one syllable

straight	strength	stroke
strain	stress	strokes
strained	stressed	stroll
strait	stretch	strolled
strand	stretched	strong
strange	strict	strove
strap	stride	struck
strapped	strike	strum
straw	string	strung
stray	strip	strut
strayed	stripe	_____
streak	stripped	_____
stream	strive	_____
street	strobe	_____

STR /str/ Initial—two syllables

straggle	stretchy	stroller
stranger	stricken	strolling
strapping	strident	strongbox
streaking	strike out	stronghold
streamer	strike zone	strongly
streamline	string beans	structure
streetcar	stringent	strudel
strengthen	stringing	struggle
stressing	stringy	strumming
stretcher	stripping	strutting
stretching	striving	strychnine
stretch-out	strobe lamp	_____

STR /str/ Initial—three syllables

straightforward	strawberry	structural
strait jacket	strenuous	_____
strategy	string quartet	_____
stratosphere	stroboscope	_____

STR /str/ Initial—four syllables

streptococcus	_____	_____
streptomycin	_____	_____
stringed instruments	_____	_____

STR /str/ Medial—two syllables

abstract	downstream	restrain
airstrip	frustrate	restrict
astray	gold stream	rostrum
astride	high-strung	seamstress
backstroke	instruct	shoestring
bloodstream	minstrel	side street
bowstring	mistreat	sidestroke
breaststroke	mistress	upstream
constrict	monstrous	vestry
construct	nostril	_____
destroy	obstruct	_____
distract	ostrich	_____
distress	pastry	_____

STR /str/ Medial—three syllables

Astrodome
astronaut
Australia
Austria
chemistry
comic strip
construction
demonstrate
destroyer
destruction

destructive
distraction
distribute
doll stroller
Gaza Strip
illustrate
industry
instruction
instructor
instrument

orchestra
reconstruct
restraining
restricting
restriction
Sunset Strip
tapestry

_____

_____

_____

STR /str/ Medial—four syllables

apostrophe
astrology
astronomer
astronomy
baby stroller
band instruments
candy striper

catastrophe
catastrophic
demonstration
distribution
illustration
industrial
industrious

instrumental
orchestra pit
pedestrian
reconstruction
string orchestra

_____

_____

STR /str/ Medial—five syllables

administration
astronomical

boa constrictor
instrumentalist

_____

_____

STS /sts/ Final—one syllable

beasts
blasts
boasts
casts
dusts
feasts
fists
frosts
ghosts
guests
gusts
hoists
hosts

lasts
lists
mists
nests
pastes
pests
posts
priests
quests
rests
roasts
roosts
tastes

tests
thrusts
toasts
twists
vests
wastes
wrists
yeasts

_____

_____

_____

_____

_____

STS /sts/ Final—two syllables

adjusts	enlists	post-tests
arrests	exhausts	pre-tests
artists	exists	protests
assists	florists	requests
Baptists	forecasts	resists
broadcasts	forests	sandblasts
chemists	gate posts	sand casts
conquests	harvests	stylists
consists	insists	toothpastes
contests	invests	tourists
contrasts	locusts	typists
defrosts	mainmasts	_____
dentists	Marxists	_____
detests	miscasts	_____
digests	newscasts	_____
druggists	outposts	_____

TER /tɚ/ Medial—three syllables

aftermath	interest	smattering
afterward	interfere	splintery
alternate	interpret	utterance
artery	intersect	utterly
attorney	interval	uttermost
buttercup	interview	veteran
butterfly	lateral	water bed
butterscotch	lettergram	waterbird
counterfeit	letterhead	water bug
determine	lettering	watercress
enterprise	loitering	waterfall
entertain	lottery	waterfowl
eternal	motorboat	waterfront
external	motorhome	water hole
factory	nectarine	waterline
interact	outer space	waterlogged
interblend	pottery	watermark
intercede	quarterback	water plant
intercept	quarterly	waterproof
intercom	shutterbug	water rat

watertight waterworks _____

waterway   yesterday   _____

waterwheel _____ _____

TER /tɚ/ Medial—four syllables

alternative	intersection	watering place
directory	literature	water lily
eternity	motorcycle	watermelon
externalize	predetermine	water polo
illiterate	quartermaster	water skiing
interesting	quartersection	_____
intermission	watercolor	_____

TER /tɚ/ Medial—five syllables

disinterested	literarily	water buffalo
distributorship	uninterrupted	_____
intermediate	unutterable	_____
international	veterinary	_____

TER /tɚ/ Final—two syllables

batter	fighter	loiter
beater	flatter	matter
better	floater	meter
bitter	flutter	motor
bloater	freighter	mutter
blotter	fritter	neater
brighter	glitter	otter
butter	grater	patter
canter	greater	pewter
chatter	gutter	platter
cheater	heater	plotter
clatter	hitter	potter
clutter	hotter	putter
crater	later	quitter
critter	latter	quoter
cutter	letter	rotor
daughter	lighter	scatter
eater	liter	setter
fatter	litter	shatter

shutter	squatter	waiter
sitter	stutter	water
skater	sweater	whiter
slaughter	tighter	writer
smatter	traitor	_____
spatter	tutor	_____
splatter	twitter	_____
spotter	utter	_____
sputter	voter	_____

TER /tɚ/ Final—three syllables

anteater	janitor	storm center
auditor	Jupiter	theater
beanshooter	locater	tidewater
chain letter	monitor	transistor
computer	narrator	translator
creator	newsletter	typesetter
dictator	predator	typewriter
editor	promoter	visitor
equator	saltwater	wood cutter
fire fighter	Senator	_____
gas meter	shot-putter	_____
globe trotter	spectator	_____
high water	stonecutter	_____

TER /tɚ/ Final—four syllables

agitator	duplicator	numerator
alligator	educator	operator
alma mater	elevator	parking meter
altimeter	escalator	peanut butter
aviator	excavator	percolator
calculator	generator	perimeter
centimeter	incubator	radiator
commentator	kilometer	thermometer
competitor	legislator	_____
cultivator	liberator	_____
decorator	moderator	_____
demonstrator	navigator	_____
diameter	nominator	

TER /tɚ/ Final—five syllables

accelerator	anemometer
amphitheater	denominator

STER /stɚ/ Medial—three syllables

asterisk	mastery
castor oil	oyster crab
history	westerly
mastering	yesterday
masterpiece	

STER /stɚ/ Medial—four syllables

master-at-arms	sister-in-law
masterfully	southeasterly
prehistory	upholstery
preposterous	

STER /stɚ/ Final—two syllables

aster	hamster	rooster
blister	holster	roster
booster	lobster	sister
Buster	luster	spinster
caster	master	tester
Chester	mister	thruster
cluster	monster	toaster
coaster	muster	twister
Custer	oyster	Webster
duster	pastor	youngster
Easter	pester	
faster	plaster	
fluster	poster	
foster	roadster	
Foster	roaster	

STER /stɚ/ Final—three syllables

adjuster	disaster	half-sister
ancestor	forecaster	minister
bandmaster	gangbuster	postmaster
canister	Grand Master	register

resister	Sylvester	_____
scoutmaster	taskmaster	_____
semester	toastmaster	_____
shipmaster	upholster	_____
sinister	Worcester	_____

STER /stɚ/ Final—four syllables

administer	prime minister	_____
flabbergaster	quartermaster	_____
Gila monster	roller coaster	_____

TH

Pronounced: /ð/
Spelled: th, the

TH /ð/ Initial—one syllable

than	thence	thine
that	there	this
that's	there's	those
the	these	thou
thee	they	though
their	they'd	thus
their's	they'll	thy
them	they're	_____
then	they've	_____

TH /ð/ Initial—two syllables

The Hague	therein	thusly
themselves	thereof	thyself
thenceforth	thereon	_____
thereby	thereto	_____
therefore	therewith	_____

TH /ð/ Initial—three syllables

that-away	thereafter	thereupon
thereabout	thereunder	_____

TH /ð/ Medial—two syllables

although	clothing	heather
bather	dither	Heather
bathing	either	lather
bother	father	leather
breather	fathom	loathful
breathing	feather	loathing
brethren	gather	loathsome
brother	heathen	mother

neither
other
others
rather
rhythm
rhythmic
rhythms
seething
slither
smither
smoother
smoothest

smoothly
smoothness
smother
soothing
southern
teething
tether
thither
tithing
unscathed
weather
weathered

whether
whither
withdraw
withdrawn
withdrew
wither
withstand
worthy
zither
_____
_____
_____

TH /ð/ Medial—three syllables

another
bathing cap
bathing suit
bellwether
bothersome
brotherhood
brotherly
fairweather
fatherhood
fatherland
fatherly
Father's Day
Father Time
featherbed
featherbone
featherbrain
featherhead
featherstitch
featherveined
featherweight
feathery
fine weather
gathering
godfather
godmother

grandfather
grandmother
half brother
hitherto
housemother
ingather
leathercraft
leatherette
leatherneck
leather work
motherhood
motherland
motherless
motherly
Mother's Day
Netherlands
nonetheless
otherwise
pinfeather
rhythm band
smithereens
southerly
southerner
southernmost
stepbrother

stepfather
stepmother
sunbathing
Sutherland
tetherball
together
unfathomed
ungathered
weatherboard
weather-bound
weathercock
Weatherford
weatherglass
weatherman
weather map
weatherproof
weatherstrip
weather-wise
weatherworn
_____
_____
_____
_____
_____

TH /ð/ Medial—four syllables

altogether	leather worker	togetherness
brother-in-law	mother-in-law	weatherbeaten
chicken feathers	Mother's Day card	weather radar
eagle feather	Netherlander	weather report
father-in-law	outer clothing	weather signal
Father's Day card	patent leather	weather station
ingathering	shaving lather	weather woman
leather jacket	stormy weather	_____

TH /ð/ Final—one syllable

bathe	scathe	swathe
blithe	scythe	teethe
breathe	seethe	tithe
clothe	sheathe	wreathe
lathe	smooth	writhe
loathe	soothe	_____

TH /ð/ Final—two syllables

enwreathe	unclothe	unswathe
sun bathe	unsheathe	_____

THD /ðd/ Final—one syllable

bathed	seethed	teethed
breathed	sheathed	tithed
clothed	smoothed	writhed
loathed	soothed	_____
scathed	swathed	_____

RTH /rð/ Medial—two syllables

farther	further	swarthy
farthest	norther	worthy
farthing	northern	_____

RTH /rð/ Medial—three syllables

airworthy	northerly	northernmost
blameworthy	Northern Cross	noteworthy
farthermost	northern lights	seaworthy
furthermore	Northerner	swarthier

thankworthy	worthiest	_____
trustworthy	worthily	_____
unworthy	worthiness	_____
worthier	Worthington	_____

RTH /rð/ Medial—four syllables

nevertheless	_____	_____
unseaworthy	_____	_____
unworthiness	_____	_____

THZ /ðz/ Final—one syllable

bathes	smoothes	wreathes
breathes	soothes	writhes
loathes	teethes	_____
seethes	tithes	_____

TH

Pronounced: /θ/
Spelled: th

TH /θ/ Initial—one syllable

Thad	Thier	thorned
thane	thigh	thorns
thank	thin	Thorpe
thanked	thing	thought
thanks	things	thoughts
thatch	think	thud
thatched	thinned	thug
thaw	third	thumb
thawed	thirst	thumbs
Thebes	thong	thump
theft	thongs	thumped
theme	Thor	_____
thick	thorn	_____

TH /θ/ Initial—two syllables

thankful	thick-skinned	thither
thankless	thighbone	thorax
thank-you	thimble	Thoreau
Thatcher	thinker	Thornton
Thea	thinking	thorny
Theda	thinner	thorough
Thelma	thinnest	thoughtful
theme song	thinning	thoughtless
thermal	thin-skinned	thought-out
thesis	third base	thousand
theta	third class	thumbnail
thicken	Third World	thumbscrew
thicket	thirteen	thumbtack
thickness	thirty	thumping
thickset	thistle	thunder

thundered	thymus	_____
Thursday	thyroid	_____
Thurston	_____	_____

TH /θ/ Initial—three syllables

Thackeray	thickener	thoroughfare
thankfulness	thickening	thoroughly
thanksgiver	thimbleful	thoroughness
thanksgiving	thinkable	Thousand Oaks
thank-you card	thinking cap	thunderbird
thank-you note	third baseman	thunderbolt
theater	third party	thunderclap
theistic	thirty-eight	thundercloud
thematic	thirty-five	thunderhead
Theodore	thirty-four	thundering
theorem	thirty-nine	thunderous
theorize	thirty-one	thunderstorm
theory	thirty-seven	thunderstruck
therapist	thirty-six	thundery
therapy	thirty-three	Thuringer
thermostat	thirty-two	_____
thesaurus	thistledown	_____
Thespian	thoroughbred	_____

TH /θ/ Initial—four syllables

Thanksgiving Day	theoretic	threateningly
theatrical	therapeutic	thundershower
Theodora	thermometer	_____
theology	thermostatic	_____

TH /θ/ Initial—five syllables

theologian	thermodynamic	_____
theosophical	_____	_____

TH /θ/ Medial—two syllables

Athens	bathhouse	bathtub
athlete	bathmat	Bathurst
author	bath oil	Bethune
Bethel	bath salts	breathless

buckthorn
Cathay
diphthong
Ethan
Ethel
ether
ethics
ethnic
ethos
ethyl
faithful
fifth grade
frothy
Gothic
Hawthorne
Kathleen
Kathy
lethal
Luther
Mathis
Matthew
methane
method
methyl
misthink
mothball
mothy
mouthful
mouth guard

mouthless
mouthpiece
mouthwash
naphtha
Nathan
nothing
outthink
pathway
pithy
playthings
python
rethink
Reuther
rosethorns
Rothchild
Ruth Ann
ruthful
Ruthie
ruthless
sixth grade
Smithfield
something
South Bend
South Bridge
Southdown
southeast
southland
southpaw
Southport

South Seas
southward
southwest
toothache
toothbrush
toothful
toothless
toothpaste
toothpick
toothsome
truthful
truthless
withdraw
withdrew
withheld
withhold
within
without
withstand
youthful
zither
_____
_____
_____
_____
_____
_____
_____
_____

TH /θ/ Medial—three syllables

aesthetic
Agatha
amethyst
anything
apathy
atheist
Athena
athletic

authentic
authorize
authorized
authorship
batholith
bath towel
bath water
bathyscaphe

bathysphere
Bethany
Bethesda
Bethlehem
biathlon
breath-taking
cathedral
coauthor

decathlon
Dorothy
empathy
ethical
everything
faithfully
faithfulness
faithlessness
Hathaway
Ithaca
Jonathan
Katherine
Klamath Falls
lethargic
lethargy
lithograph
Lutheran
Mammoth Cave
marathon
math homework
methodic
Methodist

methylene
moth-eaten
mythical
Nathaniel
nothingness
Othello
paint thinner
pathetic
pathfinder
pentathlon
prosthesis
Rathskeller
ruthlessly
ruthlessness
sagathy
southeaster
southeastward
stethoscope
sympathize
sympathized
sympathy
thirty-third

Timothy
tooth decay
tooth fairy
tooth powder
triathlon
two-thirty
wherewithal
youth football
youthfully
youthfulness
youth hockey
youth hostel
youth soccer
_____
_____
_____
_____
_____
_____
_____
_____
_____

TH /θ/ Medial—four syllables

anathema
anesthetic
anesthetist
antipathy
apathetic
arithmetic
atheism
athletic club
authority
bathometer
bathymetry
calisthenics
Catholic Church
diathermy
Dorothea

ethereal
ethnology
group therapy
hypothesis
hypothesize
hypothetic
isothermal
lithographer
lithographic
mathematics
mythologist
mythology
pathologist
pathology
play therapy

South Africa
South China Sea
South Dakota
South Korea
South Pacific
South Vietnam
sympathetic
sympathizer
sympathizing
sympathy card
_____
_____
_____
_____
_____

TH /θ/ Medial—five syllables

amphitheater	Elizabethan	South America
anesthesia	Ethiopia	South Carolina
authenticity	hydrotherapy	_____
Catholicism	psychotherapy	_____

TH /θ/ Final—one syllable

bath	heath	sloth
Beth	Keith	smith
Blythe	kith	Smith
booth	lath	south
both	length	swath
breath	math	teeth
broth	moth	tooth
cloth	mouth	troth
couth	myth	truth
death	oath	warmth
depth	path	with
doth	pith	wrath
drouth	quoth	wreath
faith	Roth	youth
Faith	Ruth	_____
froth	Seth	_____
growth	sheath	_____
hath	sleuth	_____

TH /θ/ Final—two syllables

Ardith	Dartmouth	forthwith
Babe Ruth	Deep South	goldsmith
bear with	dishcloth	Griffith
beneath	dog tooth	half-truth
bequeath	Duluth	headcloth
betroth	dustcloth	hot bath
bike path	Edith	ingrowth
birdbath	eyetooth	Judith
blacksmith	flight path	Kenneth
broadcloth	floorcloth	locksmith
by-path	forsooth	Macbeth
cheesecloth	Fort Smith	mammoth

oilcloth

outgrowth

phone booth

Plymouth

Portsmouth

Sabbath

sailcloth

sand cloth

steam bath

sun bath

sweet tooth

tollbooth

uncouth

untruth

upgrowth

zenith

_____

_____

_____

_____

_____

TH /θ/ Final—three syllables

aftermath

arrowsmith

baby's-breath

baby teeth

baby tooth

bridal path

bubble bath

chicken broth

coppersmith

cottonmouth

eightieth

fiftieth

flannelmouth

fortieth

ironsmith

Meredith

monolith

Nazareth

neolith

ninetieth

overgrowth

silversmith

sixtieth

tablecloth

thirtieth

tigermoth

Turkish bath

twentieth

undergrowth

underneath

voting booth

whirlpool bath

wisdom teeth

wisdom tooth

_____

_____

_____

_____

_____

TH /θ/ Final—four syllables

Elizabeth

seventieth

telephone booth

DTH /dθ/ Final—one syllable

breadth

width

DTH /dθ/ Final—two syllables

bandwidth

hairbreadth

hundredth

thousandth

DTH /dθ/ Final—three syllables

one hundredth

two thousandth

LTH /lθ/ Medial—two syllables

filthy	stealthy	_____
healthful	Waltham	_____
healthy	wealthy	_____

LTH /lθ/ Medial—three syllables

filthiest	unhealthy	_____
stealthiness	wealthier	_____
unhealthful	wealthiest	_____

LTH /lθ/ Final—one syllable

filth	stealth	wealth
health	tilth	_____

NTH /nθ/ Medial—two syllables

anthem	enthused	panther
anther	menthol	unthink
enthuse	monthly	_____

NTH /nθ/ Medial—three syllables

Anthony	synthesize	unthoughtful
Cynthia	synthetic	_____
Samantha	unthankful	_____
synthesis	unthinking	_____

NTH /nθ/ Medial—four syllables

anthology	enthusiast	pyracantha
Corinthian	mentholated	_____
Corinthians	parenthesis	_____

NTH /nθ/ Final—one syllable

month	plinth	_____
ninth	tenth	_____

NTH /nθ/ Final—two syllables

billionth	fifteenth	seventh
Corinth	fourteenth	sixteenth
dozenth	millionth	thirteenth
eighteenth	nineteenth	_____

NTH /nθ/ Final—three syllables

amaranth	hyacinth	seventeenth
eleventh	labyrinth	_____

NGTH /ŋθ/ Medial—two syllables

lengthen	lengthwise	strengthen
lengthways	lengthy	_____

NGTH /ŋθ/ Final—one syllable

length	_____	_____
strength	_____	_____

NGTH /ŋθ/ Final—two syllables

full-length	wave-length	_____
half-length	whole-length	_____

THR /θr/ Initial—one syllable

thrall	thrill	throng
thrash	thrilled	through
thread	thrills	throve
threads	thrive	throw
threat	thrived	thrown
three	throat	thrum
thresh	throb	thrummed
threw	throbbed	thrush
thrice	throne	thrust
thrift	throned	_____

THR /θr/ Initial—two syllables

thralldom	threaten	thrift shop
thrasher	threefold	thrift store
thrashing	threepence	thrifty
threadbare	three-ply	thriller
threaded	threescore	thrilling
threader	threesome	thriver
threading	threesquare	thriving
threadlike	thresher	throaty
thread mark	threshold	throbbing
thready	thriftless	thrombus

throttle	throw in	_____
throttling	throwing	_____
throughout	throw rug	_____
through street	thrumming	_____
throwback	thrusting	_____
thrower	thruway	_____

THR /θr/ Initial—three syllables

threatening	thresher shark	thrombosis
three-bagger	thriftier	throwaway
three-base hit	thriftiest	_____
three-decker	thriftily	_____
three-quarters	throatier	_____
three-wheeler	throatiest	_____

THR /θr/ Initial—four syllables

threateningly	threshing machine	_____
three-legged race	throat microphone	_____
three-ring circus	_____	_____

THR /θr/ Medial—two syllables

anthrax	Guthrie	unthrone
bathrobe	heartthrob	walk-through
bathroom	Jethro	Winthrop
cutthroat	look-through	wood thrush
drive-through	outthrew	_____
enthrall	outthrow	_____
enthrone	spendthrift	_____
free throw	unthread	_____

THR /θr/ Medial—three syllables

anthracite	brown thrasher	overthrow
anthropoid	flamethrower	Plymouth Rock
arthritic	follow-through	unthreaded
arthritis	hermit thrush	_____

THR /θr/ Medial—four syllables

erythrocyte	misanthropic	_____
javelin throw	philanthropist	_____

RTH /rθ/ Medial—two syllables

Arthur	earthquake	North Shore
Bertha	earthward	North Slope
birthday	earthworm	North Star
birthmark	earthy	northward
birthplace	forethought	northwest
birthrate	forthright	Swarthmore
birthright	forthwith	Swarthout
Carthage	fourth grade	unearthed
Eartha	hearthstone	worthless
earthborn	Martha	worthwhile
earthbound	Northcutt	_____
earthen	northeast	_____
earthling	northland	_____
earthly	North Pole	_____
earthnut	Northport	_____

RTH /rθ/ Medial—three syllables

afterthought	MacArthur	overthrow
arthritic	northeastern	Parthenon
arthritis	northeastward	Port Arthur
birthday card	Northampton	unearthing
earthenware	northwestern	unearthly
earth science	Northwestern	_____
earthshaking	orthodox	_____
forthcoming	orthoscope	_____

RTH /rθ/ Medial—four syllables

birthday party	North Dakota	orthopedic
earth satellite	orthodontics	orthopedics
Happy Birthday	orthodontist	unearthliness
Martha's Vineyard	orthogenic	_____
merthiolate	orthographic	_____
North Africa	orthography	_____

RTH /rθ/ Medial—five syllables

North America	orthochromatic	orthogenetic
North American	orthodontia	orthographical
North Carolina	orthogenesis	_____

RTH /rθ/ Final—one syllable

berth	fourth	worth
birth	girth	_____
dearth	hearth	_____
earth	mirth	_____
firth	north	_____
forth	swarth	_____

RTH /rθ/ Final—two syllables

childbirth	rebirth	_____
Ellsworth	thenceforth	_____
Emsworth	unearth	_____
Fort Worth	Wadsworth	_____
henceforth	Wentworth	_____
Kenworth	Woolworth	_____

V

Pronounced: /v/
Spelled: v, vv, f, ph

V /v/ Initial—one syllable

vague	veil	vim
Vail	vein	Vince
vain	vend	vine
Val	vent	vise
vale	verb	vogue
valve	verge	voice
vamp	Vern	voiced
van	verse	void
Van	versed	voile
Vance	verve	volt
vane	vest	vote
vase	vet	vouch
vast	vex	vow
vat	Vi	vowed
Vaughn	Vic	_____
vault	vice	_____
veal	vie	_____
veer	vile	_____

V /v/ Initial—two syllables

vacant	valise	vanguard
vacate	valley	vanish
vaccine	valor	van line
vacuum	value	vanquish
vagrant	valued	vapor
vagus	vamoose	varied
valance	vampire	varmint
valet	Vanda	varnish
valiant	Van Dyke	vary
valid	Van Gogh	vassal

[570]

vaudeville	Vernon	vintage
Veda	version	viper
Velma	versus	Virgil
velour	vessel	Virgo
velum	Vesta	virtue
velvet	vestal	virus
vendor	vestige	visa
vendue	vestry	visage
veneer	veto	vision
vengeance	via	visit
Venice	vial	visor
venom	viand	vista
venous	vibrate	vital
ventage	vicar	viva
venture	Vichy	vivid
venue	vicious	vocal
Venus	Vicky	voiceless
Vera	victim	volley
verbal	Victor	volume
verbose	Vida	vortex
verdant	vigil	voucher
Verde	vigor	vowel
Verdi	Viking	voyage
verdict	villa	Vulgate
Verlene	village	vulture
vermeil	villain	vying
vermin	Vincent	_____
Vermont	vineyard	_____

V /v/ Initial—three syllables

vacancy	validate	variance
vacation	Valley Forge	variant
vaccinate	valueless	varicose
vacillate	valuer	various
vagabond	Van Buren	varsity
vagrancy	Vancouver	vascular
Valeda	vanilla	Vatican
valentine	vanity	vegetate
Valerie	vaporize	vehement

vehicle	veteran	visible
velation	viaduct	visited
vendetta	vibration	visiting
venerate	vicarage	visitor
venetian	vice versa	visual
venison	vichyssoise	vitally
venomous	victory	vitamin
ventilate	video	vivacious
ventricle	Vienna	Vivian
veracious	Vietnam	vocalize
Vera Cruz	vigilant	vocation
veranda	vilify	volatile
verbatim	villager	volcanic
verbiage	vindicate	volcano
verify	vindictive	volition
verity	vinegar	volleyball
Vero Beach	viola	voluble
Vcrona	Viola	volunteer
versatile	violate	voyager
versify	violent	Voyager
vertebra	violet	vulcanize
vertebrate	Violet	_____
vertical	violin	_____
vertigo	Virginia	_____
vesical	virulent	_____
vestryman	viscera	_____

V /v/ Initial—four syllables

vaccination	variegated	veritable
vacillating	variety	vermiculate
vacuity	vasomotor	vernacular
Valencia	vegetable	Veronica
Valentine's Day	vegetation	Vesuvius
validity	vehemently	vicarious
valuablc	velocity	vice-president
vaporizer	venerable	vicinity
Varanasi	ventilation	vicissitude
variable	veracity	Victoria
variation	verbalizing	Victorian

victorious
video game
video tape
Vietnamese
vindictively

violinist
virologist
virtuoso
viscosity
visionary

visitation
voluminous
voluntary
vulnerable

_____

V /v/ Initial—five syllables

vaporization
vasodilator
vegetarian
verification
verisimilar
veterinary

vicariously
video cassette
vindicatory
visceromotor
vital statistics
vitrification

vocabulary
vocationally
vociferously
volatility

_____

_____

V /v/ Initial—six syllables

valedictorian
variability
vasodilatation

veterinarian
video recorder
vulnerability

_____

_____

_____

V /v/ Medial—two syllables

advance
advent
adverb
adverse
advice
advise
advised
anvil
Ava
avail
avenge
averse
avert
avid
avoid
avow
beaver
bevel
bevy

bivalve
bovine
bravo
canvas
cavern
cavort
Chavez
chevron
Chevy
civet
civic
civil
cleaver
Cleveland
clever
cloven
clover
Clovis
convent

converge
converse
convert
convex
convey
convict
convince
convoy
convulse
cover
covered
covet
covey
cravat
craven
crevice
David
Davis
Davy

Denver	favor	Levi
device	fever	levy
devil	flavor	lively
devise	gavel	liver
devoid	given	livid
devolve	giver	living
devote	giving	louver
devour	govern	lover
devout	grapevine	loving
diva	gravel	movement
divan	gravy	mover
diver	Grover	movers
diverge	haven	moving
divert	haven't	naval
divide	having	navy
divine	havoc	never
divorce	heaven	novel
divot	heavy	novice
dovecote	Hoover	oval
dovetail	hovel	over
drive-in	hover	pivot
drivel	invent	prevail
driver	inverse	prevent
driveway	invert	private
eavesdrop	invest	proverb
envied	invite	provide
envoy	invoice	provoke
envy	invoke	quaver
Eva	involve	quiver
evade	Ivan	ravel
even	ivy	raven
evening	java	ravine
event	Java	reveal
ever	Kiva	revenge
every	lava	reverse
evict	lavish	revert
evil	leaving	revise
evoke	level	revive
evolve	lever	revolt

revolve	seventh	waiver
rival	sever	waver
river	severe	weaver
rivet	shaving	weaving
rover	shiver	weever
Rover	shrivel	weevil
savage	sliver	woven
saver	Stephen	_____
saving	Stevie	_____
savvy	swivel	_____
seven	travel	_____

V /v/ Medial—three syllables

aboveboard	carnivore	covering
advantage	cavalcade	covetous
adventure	cavalier	crossover
advertise	cavalry	daredevil
advisement	caviar	davenport
adviser	cavity	deliver
advocate	Cherryvale	depriving
aggravate	Cherryville	devastate
all over	chivalry	develop
au revoir	circumvent	deviate
avalanche	civilian	deviled eggs
avarice	civilize	devilfish
avenue	clairvoyance	devilish
average	clavicle	devilment
aversion	connivance	devious
bedcover	convention	devotion
bedevil	convergence	disavow
bereavement	convergent	discover
beverage	conversion	disfavor
Beverly	conveyance	divergent
boulevard	conveyer	diversion
bravado	convolute	dividend
bravery	convulsion	division
brevity	convulsive	divisor
caravan	covenant	driveable
carnival	coverage	elevate

eleventh	Hoover Dam	misgiving
endeavor	hovering	moreover
enliven	however	movable
envelope	Hudsonville	navigate
environ	improvement	nevermore
envision	improver	Nile River
evangel	improving	novelty
evasion	improvise	November
Evelyn	improvised	obvious
everglade	innovate	Oliver
everyday	intervene	olivine
everyone	introvert	ovation
everything	invalid	oven door
everywhere	inveigle	ovenware
evident	invention	overact
excavate	inventive	overalls
favoring	inventor	overawe
favorite	invested	overblown
favorless	investment	overboard
Fayetteville	ivory	overcall
feverish	Ivy League	overcame
fevery	ivy vine	overcast
flavedo	Jacksonville	overcoat
flavorful	javelin	overdo
flavoring	jovial	overdone
flavorous	lavender	overdoor
flavorsome	lavishly	overdue
flavory	layover	overflow
forever	leftover	overgrow
forgiven	leftovers	overhand
frivolous	leverage	overhaul
Geneva	levitate	overhear
Genevieve	lime flavor	overheard
governance	livable	overjoy
governess	liverwurst	overjoyed
government	lovable	overlap
governor	maneuver	overlay
hay fever	maverick	overlook
high-level	medieval	overnight

overpass
override
overrun
overseas
oversee
oversight
overtake
overtime
overture
overweight
overwhelm
overwork
overwrite
palaver
Passover
pavilion
Peace River
persevere
pet haven
popover
poverty
prevalence
prevention
previous
privacy
privation
privilege
provender
providence
provider
providing
Provincetown
provincial

proving ground
provision
provoking
quavering
quivering
ravenous
receiver
recover
Red River
rendezvous
renovate
retriever
revenue
reverence
reverent
reverie
reversal
revision
revulsion
Rhine River
Rhone River
rivalry
rivulet
Roosevelt
saliva
Salt River
samovar
savings bond
savory
scavenger
screwdriver
seventy
several

skin diver
skin diving
souvenir
sovereign
soviet
Soviet
spring fever
stopover
subdivide
subversive
Sunnyvale
Thanksgiving
traveler
travelogue
travertine
trivial
truck driver
turnover
uncover
universe
Vancouver
vivacious
vividly
vividness
whatever
whenever
wherever
whichever
whoever
whomever
whyever

_____
_____

V /v/ Medial—four syllables

abbreviate
activator
advantageous
adversary

adversity
advertisement
advertising
advisable

alleviate
ambivalence
ambivalent
available

aviary
aviation
avionics
avocado
avocation
avoirdupois
Bavaria
Bavarian
beverages
Beverly Hills
Bolivia
Bolivian
captivity
carnivorous
charivari
controversial
controversy
conventional
conversation
convertible
convivial
convocation
covered wagon
cultivation
cultivator
delivery
derivation
derivative
devaluate
development
deviation
devitalize
disadvantage
discovery
diversify
diversity
divinity
divisible
driving safety

elevation
enviable
environment
equivalent
equivocate
evacuate
evaluate
evangelic
evangelist
evaporate
eventual
everlasting
everybody
evidently
evolution
favorable
impoverish
inadvertent
innovation
interwoven
intravenous
inventory
invertebrate
investigate
invidious
invigorate
invincible
invisible
invitation
irreverence
jovially
longevity
mint flavoring
misadventure
nativity
nevertheless
oblivion
Olivia
orange flavor

overbearing
overpower
poison ivy
positively
prevaricate
receivership
recovery
redeliver
renovation
revelation
reversible
revolution
scuba diver
scuba diving
severity
sovereignty
taxi driver
television
unavailing
universal
unsavory
vivisection
whatsoever
whensoever
Yukon River

_____
_____
_____
_____
_____
_____
_____
_____
_____
_____
_____
_____
_____

V /v/ Medial—five syllables

anniversary	inevitably	revolutionize
apple turnover	invariable	Soviet Russia
benevolently	involuntary	Soviet Union
civilization	irreverently	unequivocal
devaluation	observatory	university
governmentally	prevocational	_____
individual	recovery room	_____
inevitable	relativity	_____

V /v/ Medial—six syllables

availability	eventuality	special delivery
conversationally	involuntarily	unequivocally
developmentally	observationally	_____
environmentally	revolutionary	_____

V /v/ Final—one syllable

Bev	groove	save
brave	grove	shave
cave	halve	shove
chive	have	sieve
cleave	heave	sleeve
clove	hive	Steve
cove	I've	stove
crave	jive	strive
Dave	Jove	suave
dive	knave	they've
dove	lave	thrive
drive	leave	trove
drove	live	waive
Ev	love	wave
eve	mauve	weave
Eve	move	we've
five	nave	wove
gave	of	you've
give	pave	_____
glove	prove	_____
grave	rave	_____
grieve	rove	_____

V /v/ Final—two syllables

above	disk drive	relive
achieve	disprove	remove
alive	enclave	reprieve
approve	endive	reprove
archive	festive	retrieve
arrive	forgave	revive
beehive	forgive	shock wave
behave	foxglove	short wave
behoove	ground wave	sky wave
believe	heat wave	skydive
bereave	high dive	sound wave
captive	improve	survive
cold wave	mangrove	votive
concave	missive	_____
conceive	motive	_____
conclave	naive	_____
connive	native	_____
contrive	nose-dive	_____
cursive	olive	_____
deceive	Olive	_____
deprave	outlive	_____
deprive	passive	_____
derive	relieve	_____

V /v/ Final—three syllables

adaptive	Genevieve	sensitive
Christmas Eve	impressive	talkative
convulsive	Mammoth Cave	tentative
curative	microwave	tidal wave
decisive	misbehave	transitive
destructive	negative	_____
devisive	New Year's Eve	_____
effective	nutritive	_____
effusive	obsessive	_____
elusive	offensive	_____
expensive	positive	_____
formative	primitive	_____
fugitive	relative	

LV /lv/ Medial—two syllables

Alva	salvaged	velvet
Alvin	salvo	_____
Calvin	shelving	_____
Cleveland	silver	_____
culvert	solvent	_____
salvage	solving	_____

LV /lv/ Medial—three syllables

Alvina	quicksilver	solvable
dissolving	resolving	Sylvia
evolvement	revolving	velveteen
galvanic	salvation	velvety
galvanize	silver fox	wolverine
insolvent	silver-plate	_____
involvement	silversmith	_____
involving	silverware	_____
pulverize	silvery	_____

LV /lv/ Final—one syllable

delve	solve	_____
salve	twelve	_____
shelve	valve	_____

LV /lv/ Final—two syllables

absolve	evolve	_____
bivalve	involve	_____
devolve	resolve	_____
dissolve	revolve	_____

LVD /lvd/ Final—one syllable

delved	_____	_____
shelved	_____	_____
solved	_____	_____

LVD /lvd/ Final—two syllables

absolved	involved	unsolved
dissolved	resolved	_____
evolved	revolved	_____

LVZ /lvz/ Final—one syllable

delves	shelves	wolves
elves	solves	_____
selves	valves	_____

LVZ /lvz/ Final—two syllables

dissolves	resolves	_____
evolves	revolves	_____
involves	themselves	_____
ourselves	yourselves	_____

RV /rv/ Medial—two syllables

carver	Kerrville	serving
carving	larva	starving
carvings	marvel	survey
corvette	Marvin	survive
dervish	Mervin	swerving
fervid	nervous	_____
fervor	perverse	_____
Harvard	scurvey	_____
harvest	servant	_____
Harvey	server	_____
Irving	service	_____

RV /rv/ Medial—three syllables

Centerville	preserver	surveyor
conserver	preserving	survival
conserving	reserving	surviving
deserver	reservoir	survivor
deserving	self-service	survivors
enervate	serviceman	unnerving
fervently	servicemen	Waterville
marveling	services	wood carving
marvelous	servicing	_____
Minerva	servitude	_____
observance	starvation	_____
observant	supervise	_____
observer	survey crew	_____
observing	surveying	_____

RV /rv/ Medial—four syllables

conservation	observation	soapstone carvings
conservative	perseverence	subservient
conservator	preservation	survey party
effervescent	reservation	survival kit
enervated	reservations	survivorship
enervation	serviceable	topsy-turvy
intervention	service station	_____
life preserver	servicewoman	_____
nervous system	servicewomen	_____

RV /rv/ Final—one syllable

carve	serve	verve
curve	starve	_____
nerve	swerve	_____

RV /rv/ Final—two syllables

conserve	observe	self-serve
deserve	preserve	_____
hors d'oeuvre	reserve	_____

RVD /rvd/ Final—one syllable

carved	starved	_____
curved	swerved	_____
served	_____	_____

RVD /rvd/ Final—two syllables

deserved	reserved	_____
observed	unnerved	_____
preserved	_____	_____

RVZ /rvz/ Final—one syllable

carves	scarves	turves
dwarves	serves	wharves
nerves	starves	_____

RVZ /rvz/ Final—two syllables

conserves	observes	_____
deserves	preserves	_____

VER /vɚ/ **Medial—three syllables**

advertise	overcome	overtime
average	overdo	overture
beverage	overdraft	overweight
Beverly	overdue	overwhelm
bravery	overflow	overwork
conversion	overgrow	overwrite
coverage	overhand	poverty
covering	overhaul	reverence
diversion	overhead	reverent
evergreen	overhear	several
favorite	overjoy	Silver Age
flavoring	overlap	silverware
Hoover Dam	overlook	silvery
ivory	overnight	slavery
leverage	overpass	subversive
liverwurst	overrun	thievery
overalls	overseas	wolverine
overboard	overshoe	_____
overcast	oversight	_____
overcoat	overtake	_____

VER /vɚ/ **Medial—four syllables**

Beverly Hills	diversity	recovery
controversy	favorable	universal
conversation	invertebrate	_____
covered wagon	nevertheless	_____
delivery	overpower	_____
discovery	receivership	_____

VER /vɚ/ **Final—two syllables**

beaver	ever	lever
cleaver	favor	liver
clever	fever	louver
clover	flavor	lover
cover	giver	mover
Denver	Grover	never
diver	Hoover	over
driver	hover	plover

quaver	sever	_____
quiver	shiver	_____
river	sliver	_____
rover	waiver	_____
Rover	waver	_____
savor	weaver	_____

VER /vɚ/ Final—three syllables

deliver	recover	whoever
discover	retriever	whomever
endeavor	Rhone River	whyever
forever	screwdriver	_____
hay fever	skin diver	_____
however	stopover	_____
leftover	turn over	_____
maneuver	uncover	_____
moreover	Vancouver	_____
Passover	whatever	_____
preserver	whenever	_____
quicksilver	wherever	_____
receiver	whichever	_____

VER /vɚ/ Final—four syllables

life preserver	whatsoever	_____
redeliver	whensoever	_____
scuba diver	whosoever	_____

VY /vj/ Medial—two syllables

graveyard	_____	_____
_____	_____	_____

VY /vj/ Medial—three syllables

behavior	_____	_____
_____	_____	_____

VZ /vz/ Medial—two syllables

dove's nest	_____	_____
eavesdrop	_____	_____
thieves' den	_____	_____

VZ /vz/ Final—one syllable

beeves	groves	salves
calves	halves	saves
caves	hives	shaves
chives	hooves	shoves
cloves	jives	sieves
coves	knaves	sleeves
craves	knives	thrives
dives	leaves	waves
doves	lives	weaves
drives	loaves	wives
eaves	loves	_____
fives	moves	_____
gives	paves	_____
gloves	peeves	_____
graves	proves	_____
grieves	raves	_____
grooves	roves	_____

W

Pronounced: /w/
Spelled: w, o, u, hu, ju

W /w/ Initial—one syllable

once	wash	weights
one	washed	weird
wad	wasp	well
wade	waste	Welsh
Wade	watch	were
waft	watched	west
wag	wave	wet
wage	waved	wick
wagged	waves	wide
waif	wax	wife
wail	way	wig
waist	Wayne	wild
wait	we	will
waive	we'd	Will
wake	we'll	willed
walk	we're	wilt
walked	we've	Wilt
wall	weak	win
Walt	wealth	wince
waltz	wean	wind
wan	wear	wing
wand	weave	winged
want	web	wings
ward	wed	wink
Ward	wee	wipe
ware	weeds	wire
warm	week	wise
warn	weep	wish
warned	weigh	wisp
was	weight	wit

witch	wood	worm
with	woods	worn
woe	wool	worse
wok	word	worth
woke	words	would
wolf	wore	wound
won	work	wow
won't	worked	_____
woo	world	_____

W /w/ Initial—two syllables

Juanna	Walker	washbowl
Juarez	walk-in	washcloth
one-time	walking	washed-out
one-track	walkout	washed-up
oncsclf	walk-through	washer
Ouija	Wallace	washing
Wabash	wallet	washrag
wabble	Wallis	washroom
wabbly	wallop	wasteful
Waco	Wall Street	wasteland
waddle	Wally	wasting
wading	walnut	watchdog
wafer	walrus	watch guard
waffle	Walter	watchman
wager	Wanda	watch out
wagging	wander	watchword
waggle	wanly	water
wagon	wanting	wattage
waistline	warbler	wattled
waited	wardrobe	waving
waiter	warehouse	wavy
waiting	warmed-up	waxing
waitress	warm-ups	wayside
waken	Warner	wayside
wake-up	warning	weakness
Waldo	warrant	wealthy
Waldon	Warren	weaning
walker	Warsaw	wearing

weary
weasel
weather
weathered
weaver
webbing
Webster
wedding
wedlock
Wednesday
weedy
weekday
weekend
weekly
weeping
weepy
weevil
Weighbridge
weigh-in
weighted
welcome
Welden
welfare
well-done
well-groomed
well-known
well-off
Wendy
West Point
Westport
wetter
wettest
wicker
wide-screen
widespread
widow
wiener
wiggle
wiggly

wigwam
Wilbur
Wilda
wild boar
wildcat
wildfire
wildlife
Wild West
Wilhelm
Willard
willful
William
Willie
willies
willing
Willis
willow
Wilma
Wilson
Wilton
wind-bells
windbreak
windburn
winded
winding
windlass
windmill
window
windpipe
windproof
windshield
windsock
windstorm
wingspread
winter
wireless
wiring
wisdom
wishbone

wishful
wishing
witchcraft
withdraw
withdrawn
withdrew
withers
within
without
witness
witty
wizard
wizened
wobble
wolf cub
wolf pack
woman
women
wonder
woodchuck
wood duck
wooden
Woodrow
woodshed
wordbook
wording
wordless
wordy
workbench
workbook
worker
working
work load
workout
workroom
workshop
world's fair
worn-out
worried

worry   _____   _____

worship   _____   _____

worthy   _____   _____

wounded   _____   _____

W /w/ Initial—three syllables

Juanita	waterproof	windjammer
onceover	water ski	window box
one-bagger	water snake	window shade
one-base hit	waterspout	window sill
one-sided	waxed paper	window-shop
wading pool	way station	Winnipeg
wage earner	wearisome	wintergreen
wagoner	weather-bound	wintertime
Wagoner	Weatherford	wire cutter
Waikiki	weatherman	wirephoto
walking stick	weather map	wire service
walkover	weathervane	Wisconsin
wallaby	wedding cake	wisdom teeth
wallpaper	wedding day	wisdom tooth
wanderer	wedding march	witch hazel
wandering	wedding ring	witness-box
wanderlust	weight lifting	witness stand
warm-blooded	well-mannered	wolverine
Washington	well-to-do	Woman's Club
water bed	West Berlin	wonderful
water bird	Westchester	wood-carver
water bug	westerly	wood carving
watercraft	West Indies	woodcutter
waterfall	Westminster	wooden shoes
waterfront	wide-angle	woodpecker
water hole	widower	word-of-mouth
watering	wilderness	workable
water line	wiliness	working class
water logged	Williamsburg	World Series
Waterloo	Williamstown	worrisome
watermark	willingness	Wyoming
waterpaints	willpower	_____
water plane	windbreaker	_____

W /w/ Initial—four syllables

walking safety	weatherbeaten	Winnebago
washing machine	weather bureau	wishy-washy
water closet	weather radar	withholding tax
watercolors	weather report	wonderfully
water faucet	weather signal	wooden nickel
water jacket	weather station	woolgathering
water lily	West Germany	word processor
watermelon	West Virginia	_____
water polo	will-o'-the-wisp	_____
water safety	wind instrument	_____
water skiing	window-shopping	_____

W /w/ Medial—two syllables

always	eyewink	kiwi
await	freeway	landward
awake	gangway	leeward
award	gateway	leeway
aware	goodwill	lifework
away	green wax	lightweight
awoke	greenwood	midway
beadwork	ground wave	midweek
beeswax	guesswork	Midwest
bewail	halfway	mouthwash
beware	hallway	network
bewitch	handwork	new wave
blue wax	hardware	northwest
Bowen	haywire	one-way
bow-wow	heat wave	outward
bulwark	highway	Owen
byway	homework	pathway
causeway	housework	peewee
cobweb	iceway	pow-wow
cold wave	inward	raceway
DeWitt	jaguar	railway
driveway	jaywalk	rainwear
Edward	jetway	red wax
Edwin	Jewish	reward
eyewash	Key West	rewind

reword
rework
rewound
ringworm
roadway
roadwork
rosewood
roundworm
San Juan
sand wasp
sandwich
sandworm
sandwort
schoolwork
seatwork
scawall

seaward
seaway
seaweed
Sea World
shoe wax
short wave
sidewalk
sideways
ski wax
sky wave
skyway
small world
someone
someway
sound wave
southwest

throughway
two-way
unworn
watchword
waxwing
waxwork
wayward
well-worn
werewolf
wherewith
woodwork
Woolworth
worldwide
_____
_____
_____

W /w/ Medial—three syllables

awaken
backwater
bewaring
candlewax
candlewick
castaway
Chihuahua
Chippewa
chuck wagon
Civil War
dental wax
dumbwaiter
edelweiss
expressway
eyewinker
eyewitness
fishing worms
fizz water
forty-watt
Halloween
handiwork

hardware store
Hawaii
Hawaiian
hideaway
high water
Hollywood
inwardly
ironware
ironwood
ironwork
ironworks
kilowatt
long-winded
microwave
Midwestern
midwinter
Milky Way
New Windsor
nonworker
northwestern
Number One

office work
one-way drive
one-way street
outwardly
pea weevil
pocket watch
rainwater
rewarded
rewiring
sandalwood
sandwiches
sandwich man
seaworthy
southwestern
spider web
straight-away
tidal wave
unaware
unwilling
walkaway
wash and wear

water wave	well-wisher	wishing well
waterway	welterweight	wishing well
water wings	wherewithal	woodworking
waterworks	whippoorwill	_____
weather-wise	wide-awake	_____

W /w/ Medial—four syllables

covered wagon	southwesterly	weeping willow
pussy willow	station wagon	welcome wagon
rewardable	water wagon	_____

DW /dw/ Initial—one syllable

Duane	dwell	Dwight
dwarf	dwelled	_____
Dwayne	dwelt	_____

DW /dw/ Initial—two syllables

dwarfish	dwindle	_____
dwelling	dwindling	_____

GW /gw/ Initial—one syllable

Guam	Guelph	Gwin
guan	Guinn	Gwyn
guar	Gwen	_____

GW /gw/ Initial—two syllables

guaco	guanine	Gwenda
guana	guano	_____
guanay	guava	_____

GW /gw/ Initial—three syllables

guacharo	Guayama	Guinevere
guanaco	guayule	Gwendolyn
Guarani	Guenevere	_____

GW /gw/ Initial—four syllables

guacamole	Guadalupe	_____
Guadalcanal	Guantanamo	_____
Guadalquivir	Guatemala	_____

GW /gw/ Initial—five syllables

guacamole dip	Guadalupe Palm
Guadalajara	Guantanamo Bay

_____
_____

GW /gw/ Medial—two syllables

agua	languet	sanguine
aguar	languid	ungual
anguine	languish	unguent
anguish	lingua	unguis
anguished	lingual	wigwag
dogwood	linguist	wigwam
hogwash	penguin	_____
jaguar	pinguid	_____
language	ragweed	_____

GW /gw/ Medial—three syllables

alguazil	La Guaira	linguistics
alguicn	language arts	sign language
bilingual	language cards	tagua nut
distinguish	languages	teguexin
extinguish	languishing	unguical
iguana	languishment	_____
inguinal	linguiform	_____

GW /gw/ Medial—four syllables

Aguadilla	La Guardia	sanguineous
Agua Fria	language patterns	unguentary
extinguisher	language workbook	_____

KW /kw/ Initial—one syllable

choir	quake	queen
quack	quaked	quell
quacked	qualm	quelled
quad	quark	quench
quaff	quart	quenched
quaffed	quartz	quest
quag	quash	quick
quail	quashed	quid
quaint	quay	quill

quilt	quipped	quite
quince	quirk	quiz
quints	quirt	_____
quip	quit	_____

KW /kw/ Initial—two syllables

quadrant	quasi	quilted
quadrate	quatrain	quilting
quadrille	quaver	Quincy
quadroon	queasy	quinine
quagga	Quebec	quinsy
quagmire	Queen Anne	quintain
quaintly	quencher	quintet
Quaker	queried	quisling
quaking	query	quitclaim
qualmish	quester	quitter
quantize	question	quiver
quantum	questioned	quizzer
quarrel	quibble	quonset
quarreled	quickbread	quorum
quarry	quicken	quota
quartan	quickened	quotient
quarter	quickie	_____
quartet	quickly	_____
quartile	quicksand	_____
quarto	quickstep	_____
quartzite	quiet	_____

KW /kw/ Initial—three syllables

quadrangle	qualify	quartering
quadratic	qualities	quarter note
quadriceps	quality	quavering
quadrifid	quandary	question mark
quadrillion	quantity	questionnaire
quadruped	quarantine	quicksilver
quadruple	quarrelsome	quick-tempered
quadruplet	quarterback	quick-witted
Quakertown	quarterdeck	quiescent
qualified	quarterhorse	quietly

quintessence	quizzical	_____
quintuple	quotable	_____
quintuplet	quotation	_____
quixotic	_____	_____

KW /kw/ Initial—four syllables

quadrangular	qualitative	quinine water
quadrennial	quantifier	quinquennial
quadriplegic ·	quantitative	quotation mark
quadruplicate	quartermaster	_____
qualifier	questionable	_____

KW /kw/ Initial—five syllables

quadrilateral	quantitatively	_____
qualification	_____	_____

KW /kw/ Medial—two syllables

acquaint	catwalk	lukewarm
acquire	chickweed	milkweed
acquired	equal	misquote
acquit	equalled	request
aqua	equate	require
awkward	equip	required
backward	equipped	sequel
backwash	frequence	sequence
backwoods	frequent	sequenced
banquet	inquest	sequin
bequeath	inquire	shock wave
bequeathed	inquired	tranquil
bequest	knockwurst	unquote
bookworm	likewise	walkway
brick wall	liquid	_____
cakewalk	loquat	_____

KW /kw/ Medial—three syllables

acquaintance	acquiring	antiquate
acquainted	acquittal	aqualung
acquiesce	acquittance	aquanaut
acquiesced	acquitted	aquaplane

aquatic
aquatint
aqueduct
aqueous
aquiline
chuck wagon
chuckwalla
consequence
consequent
disquiet
equaling
equalize
equalized
equated
equating
equation
equator
equerry
equinox
equipage
equipment

equipping
equity
frequency
headquarters
hindquarter
inequal
infrequent
inquirer
inquiring
inquiry
liquefy
liquidate
liquified
loquacious
misquoted
misquoting
requirement
requiring
requisite
requital
requiter

sequential
sequoia
subsequent
tranquilize
tranquilly
unequal
unequaled
unquestioned

_____
_____
_____
_____
_____
_____
_____
_____
_____
_____
_____
_____

KW /kw/ Medial—four syllables

acquiescence
acquiescent
acquisition
acquisitive
antiquary
antiquated
antiquation
antiquity
aquamarine
aquarium
Aquarius
consequential
disqualified
disqualify
disquietude
disquisition

equality
equalizer
equalizing
equidistant
equitable
equitation
equivalence
equivalent
equivocal
equivocate
infrequented
inquisition
inquisitive
inquisitor
liquefaction
liquefying

liquidating
liquidation
liquidity
loquacity
post headquarters
requisition
tranquility
tranquilizer
unfrequented
unqualified
unquenchable
ventriloquist

_____
_____
_____
_____

KW /kw/ Medial—five syllables

antiquarian	equiangular	equivocation
disqualifying	equilateral	unequivocal
equanimity	equilibrium	unquestionable
equatorial	equivalency	_____

RW /rw/ Medial—two syllables

airways	fairway	Norway
careworn	farewell	Sherwood
carwash	fireweed	shoreward
carwax	firewood	therewith
Corwin	fireworks	_____
doorway	forward	_____
Erwin	Irwin	_____

RW /rw/ Medial—three syllables

afterword	underwaist	waterways
afterworld	underwear	waterworks
netherward	underweight	wonder-world
silverware	underwent	_____
spiderweb	underwood	_____
straightforward	underworld	_____
thenceforward	water wings	_____

RW /rw/ Medial—four syllables

underwater	_____	_____

SW /sw/ Initial—one syllable

suave	sward	swell
suede	swarm	swept
suite	swash	swerve
swab	swat	swift
swag	swatch	swig
swale	sway	swim
swam	swear	swine
swamp	sweat	swing
swan	Swede	swipe
swank	sweep	swipes
swap	sweet	swirl

swish	swore	_____
Swiss	sworn	_____
switch	_____	_____
swoon	_____	_____
swoop	_____	_____

SW /sw/ Initial—two syllables

swallow	sweeping	swindle
swallows	sweepstakes	swindled
swami	sweet corn	swinger
swampland	sweet pea	swinging
swampy	sweet tooth	Swiss cheese
swan dive	sweetbread	switchback
swanky	sweeten	switchboard
swap shop	sweetheart	switchbox
sweat gland	swelling	swivel
sweat pants	swelter	swollen
sweat shirt	swifter	_____
sweat suit	swim fins	_____
sweater	swim mask	_____
Sweden	swimmer	_____
Swedish	swimming	_____
sweeper	swimsuit	_____

SW /sw/ Initial—three syllables

swallowtail	swift-footed	swinging door
swastika	swimming hole	Switzerland
sweet and sour	swimming pool	_____
sweetening	swine fever	_____
sweltering	swinging bridge	_____

SKW /skw/ Initial—one syllable

squab	squawk	squint
squad	squeak	squire
squall	squeal	squirm
square	squeeze	squirt
squash	squelch	squish
squat	squib	_____
squaw	squid	_____

SKW /skw/ Initial—two syllables

squabble	square meal	squeegee
squabbling	square mile	squeezer
squad car	square off	squeezing
squadron	square root	squelcher
squalid	square yard	squiggle
squally	squarely	squirmy
squalor	squarest	squirrel
squander	squashy	squirt gun
square dance	squatted	squishy
square deal	squatter	_____
square feet	squatting	_____
square foot	squatty	_____
square inch	squeaky	_____
square knot	squeamish	_____

SKW /skw/ Initial—three syllables

square away	square rigger	squeezable
square inches	square shooter	_____
square meters	squashiest	_____

TW /tw/ Initial—one syllable

twang	twice	twinge
tweak	twig	twinned
tweed	twigged	twirl
tweet	twill	twist
tweeze	twilled	twitch
twelfth	twin	_____
twelve	twine	_____
twerp	twined	_____

TW /tw/ Initial—two syllables

twangle	twilight	twirler
twangy	Twin Falls	twister
tweedle	twin bed	twisting
tweedy	twin sheet	twitch grass
tweezers	twinborn	twitter
twenty	twinkle	_____
twiddle	twinkling	_____

TW /tw/ Initial—three syllables

twentieth	Twin Cities	_____
twenty yards	twin-engine	_____
twenty-five	twinberry	_____
twenty-one	twinflower	_____
twilight sleep	twisted pine	_____

WH

Pronounced: /hw/, /ʍ/, /w/
Spelled: wh

WH /wh/ Initial—one syllable

whack
whale
wharf
what
what's
wheat
wheel
wheeled
wheeze
whelk
whelm

whelp
when
whence
where
where'd
whew
whey
which
whiff
while
whim

whine
whirl
whish
whisk
whist
Whit
white
why

_____
_____
_____

WH /wh/ Initial—two syllables

whacking
whaleboat
whalebone
whaler
whammy
whapper
whate'er
whatnot
wheat cakes
wheaten
wheat germ
wheedle
wheelchair
wheeling
Wheeling
wheezing
wheezy

whereas
whereby
wherefore
wherein
whereof
whereon
wherry
whether
whetstone
whicker
whiffet
whimper
whimsy
whining
whinny
whiplash
whippet

whipping
Whipple
whirlpool
whirlwind
whirring
whiskbroom
whiskers
whisper
whistle
whistled
whistler
whistling
white belt
white bread
whitecap
whitefish
white goods

Whitehorse	white shark	whiz-bang
White House	whitewash	whizzing
whiten	whither	_____
white sale	Whitney	_____
white sauce	whittle	_____
White Sea	whittling	_____

WH /wh/ Initial—three syllables

whatever	whichever	whirlpool bath
wheelbarrow	whiffletree	whispering
whenever	whimpering	Whitaker
whereabouts	whimsical	Whitechapel
whereupon	whippoorwill	white water
wherever	whirlabout	Whitewater
wherewithal	whirligig	_____

WH /wh/ Initial—four syllables

whatsoever	whichsoever	_____
wheelbarrow race	whippersnapper	_____
whensoever	_____	_____

WH /wh/ Medial—two syllables

buckwheat	nowhere	whole wheat
cartwheel	pinwheel	worthwhile
erstwhile	somewhere	_____
meanwhile	whim-wham	_____

WH /wh/ Medial—three syllables

anywhere	free-wheeler	wagon wheel
color wheel	overwhelm	whole wheat bread
everywhere	steering wheel	_____
Ferris wheel	three-wheeler	_____
four-wheeler	two-wheeler	_____

Y

Pronounced: /j/
Spelled: eu, y, g, i, j, u, ll

Y /j/ Initial—one syllable

Jung	yea	yore
use	year	York
used	yearn	you
yacht	yeast	you'd
yak	yell	you'll
Yale	yelled	you're
yam	yelp	young
yang	yen	Young
yank	yes	your
yanks	yet	yours
yap	yew	youth
yard	yield	yowl
yarn	yip	Yule
yaw	yipe	yum
yawl	yoke	yurt
yawn	yolk	_____
ye	yon	_____

Y /j/ Initial—two syllables

Eubanks	Johann	usage
euchre	U-boat	used cars
Euclid	U-bolt	useful
Eugene	ukase	useless
Eula	Ukraine	user
Eunice	union	using
Europe	unique	usurp
Ewan	unit	Utah
ewe lamb	unite	U-turn
Ewell	Ural	yacht club
Ewing	U.S.	yachting

yachtsman
Yahoo
Yalta
yammer
Yancy
Yangtze
Yankee
Yankees
yardage
yardarm
yardbird
yard goods
yard grass
yardman
yard sale
yardstick
yarrow
yearbook
yearling
yearlong
yearly

yearning
year-round
yeasty
yelling
yellow
yelper
yeoman
yes ma'am
yes man
yeti
Yetta
Yiddish
yielding
yield sign
yippee
yodel
yodeler
Yoga
yogi
yogurt
yokel

yonder
Yonkers
Yorkshire
you-all
younger
youngest
youngster
Youngstown
yourself
youthful
yo-yo
Yuba
yucca
Yukon
yule log
yuletide
Yuma
yummy

_____
_____
_____

Y /j/ Initial—three syllables

eugenic
eulogize
eulogy
Eurasia
eureka
Eureka
eurythmics
eustachian
eutaxy
Johannes
Uganda
Ulysses
unicorn
uniform
union card
Uniondale

unionize
Union Springs
union suit
unison
united
unity
universe
Uranus
Uriah
Uruguay
U.S.A.
usable
U.S. Mail
usual
usury
utensil

Utica
utilize
uvula
yachtswoman
Yankified
yardmaster
year-end sale
yellow-dog
yellowbird
yellow rose
Yellowstone
yeomanly
yeshiva
yesterday
Yolanda
Yom Kippur

youth football	youth hockey	Yucatan
youthfully	youth hostel	_____
youthfulness	youth soccer	_____

Y /j/ Initial—four syllables

European	uranium	yellow fever
ubiquitous	urology	yellow jacket
ukelele	U.S.S.R.	Yellowstone Park
unanimous	usurious	Yosemite
unicycle	utilities	youth basketball
Union City	utility	Yukon River
united front	utopia	_____
United States	year-end clearance	_____
universal	yellow daisy	_____

Y /j/ Initial—five syllables

university	utilization	Yugoslavian
U.S. Post Office	Yugoslavia	_____

Y /j/ Medial—two syllables

Bayonne	Mayan	royal
bayou	new year	Royals
buoyant	New Year's	savior
cow yard	New York	sawyer
Doyan	oyes	Sawyer
kayak	oyez	Toya
lawyer	Paiute	yo-yo
loyal	reuse	_____
Maya	reused	_____

Y /j/ Medial—three syllables

buoyancy	New Year's Eve	royalty
coyote	no U-turn	thirty yards
Hawaiian	papaya	Tocayo
kayaking	reunion	Tom Sawyer
La Toya	reunite	tortilla
loyalty	royalist	_____
Malayan	Royal Oak	_____
New Year's Day	royalties	_____

Y /j/ Medial—four syllables

Bayou Vista	New York City	teriyaki
employer	New York Harbor	twenty-yard line
Happy New Year	papaya tree	_____
Himalaya	Royal Highness	_____
lawyer's office	sukiyaki	_____

BY /bj/ Medial—three syllables

ambulance	tabulate	_____
ambulate	tubular	_____

BY /bj/ Medial—four syllables

contributor	tabulator	_____
distributor	tribulation	_____
tabulated	tributary	_____

DY /dj/ Medial—two syllables

woodyard	_____	_____
_____	_____	_____

DY /dj/ Medial—three syllables

Scotland Yard	_____	_____
trade union	_____	_____

GY /gj/ Medial—two syllables

egg yolk	figured	_____
figure	figures	_____

GY /gj/ Medial—three syllables

figure eight	figure skate	transfigured
figure-ground	figuring	_____
figurehead	regular	_____
figure out	regulate	_____

GY /gj/ Medial—four syllables

father figure	regulating	_____
figure skating	regulation	_____
regularly	triangular	_____
regulated	_____	_____

KY /kj/ Medial—two syllables

backyard	dockyard	_____
brickyard	stockyard	_____

KY /kj/ Medial—three syllables

calculate	ocular	speculate
calculus	oculist	succulent
Hercules	porcupine	Tokyo
molecule	secular	_____

KY /kj/ Medial—four syllables

accusation	gesticulate	spectacular
articulate	lenticular	speculation
calculated	molecular	vermicular
calculator	particular	vermiculate
curriculum	ridiculous	_____
executor	security	_____

LY /lj/ Medial—two syllables

all year	Dahlia	stallion
billiards	failure	trillion
billion	Julia	valiant
bouillon	Julian	value
bullion	million	valued
coal yard	millionth	William
collier	school yard	zillion
Collier	school year	_____

LY /lj/ Medial—three syllables

alienate	Centralia	regalia
Amelia	Cornelia	valiancy
Australia	cotillion	valiantly
Australian	familial	valuate
azalea	familiar	valueless
battalion	four billion	valuing
billiard ball	magnolia	Vermillion
billionaire	medallion	Williamsburg
bouillon cube	millionaire	_____
Camellia	rebellion	_____

LY /lj/ Medial—four syllables

billiard table	salutation	_____
chameleon	valuable	_____
familiarize	valuation	_____
Julius Caesar	valuator	_____

MY /mj/ Medial—two syllables

farmyard	_____	_____

MY /mj/ Medial—three syllables

amulet	simulate	stimulus
communist	stimulant	_____
emulate	stimulate	_____

MY /mj/ Medial—four syllables

Bohemian	_____	_____
stimulation	_____	_____

NY /nj/ Medial—two syllables

banyan	Junior	señor
barnyard	Kenya	Spaniard
bunion	Kenyon	spaniel
Bunyan	lanyard	Tanya
canyon	minion	unused
Daniel	Muñoz	vineyard
genial	onion	_____
genius	Runnion	_____
junior	senior	_____

NY /nj/ Medial—three syllables

ammonia	geniuses	Paul Bunyan
annual	golden years	señora
banyan tree	Grand Canyon	sinuate
begonia	ingenious	Virginia
Black Canyon	lunula	zinnia
congenial	lunular	_____
convenience	manuscript	_____
convenient	minuet	_____
dominion	monument	_____

NY /nj/ Medial—four syllables

annual wage	Dominion Day	señorita
annually	filet mignon	triannual
biannual	gardenia	unusual
Boulder Canyon	genuinely	Virginia Beach
centennial	January	West Virginia
cocker spaniel	manufacture	_____
continual	monumental	_____

PY /pj/ Medial—two syllables

leap year	_____	_____
shipyard	_____	_____

PY /pj/ Medial—three syllables

deputize	populace	stipulate
deputy	popular	_____
impudence	populate	_____
impudent	populous	_____

PY /pj/ Medial—four syllables

manipulate	popular song	stipulation
popularize	popular vote	unpopular
popularly	population	_____

RY /rj/ Medial—three syllables

lumberyard	solar year	_____
lunar year	yesteryear	_____

RY /rj/ Medial—four syllables

labor union	_____	_____

TY /tj/ Medial—two syllables

courtyard	_____	_____
front yard	_____	_____
light-year	_____	_____

TY /tj/ Medial—four syllables

credit union	_____	_____
meticulous	_____	_____

VY /vj/ Medial—two syllables
graveyard

VY /vj/ Medial—three syllables
behavior

YER /jɚ/ Medial—three syllables
figure eight	figurine	
figurehead		

YER /jɚ/ Final—two syllables
failure	junior	savior
figure	lawyer	senior

YER /jɚ/ Final—three syllables
behavior	familiar	refigure
employer	peculiar	Tom Sawyer

YER /jɚ/ Final—four syllables
misbehavior	trial lawyer	
power failure	unfamiliar	

Y-blend in first syllable /j/ —one syllable
butte	few	Hughes
Butte	fjord	mew
cube	fuel	mule
cue	fume	muse
cued	fumes	mused
cure	fuse	pew
cured	hew	pure
cute	hue	skew
dew	huge	view
feud	Hugh	

Y-blend in first syllable /j/ —two syllables
Beaufort	bugle	Cuba
beauty	bugler	cubic
Beulah	bureau	cubit
Buford	butane	cue ball

cuing	Hugo	puree
Cupid	human	purely
cure-all	humane	purer
Curie	humid	purest
cutest	humor	skewer
cutie	humus	skewing
Dewey	mule deer	viewer
feudal	Munich	view point
furor	mural	viewy
fusion	music	_____
futile	muted	_____
future	pewter	_____
Hubert	puny	_____
hubris	pupa	_____
Hughie	pupil	_____

Y-blend in first syllable /j/ —three syllables

beauteous	cutie pie	music hall
beautician	fugitive	musician
beautified	funeral	music stand
beautiful	fuselage	muted horn
beautify	fusillade	mutual
beauty shop	Hueytown	punier
beauty sleep	Hugoton	puniest
Buchanan	humanist	purified
bureaucrat	humanize	purify
cubical	human kind	Puritan
cubic foot	humanly	purity
cubic inch	human rights	viewable
cubic mile	humidor	view finder
cubic yard	humoresque	_____
cucumber	humorist	_____
cumulate	humorous	_____
cumulus	Munich Pact	_____
cupola	muralist	_____
curative	Muriel	_____
curio	museum	_____
curious	musical	_____
cuticle	music box	_____

Y-blend in first syllable /j/ —four syllables

beauty salon	humanity	municipal
bureaucracy	human nature	munificent
bureaucratic	humidify	musical chairs
cubic measure	humidity	mutual fund
cumulative	humiliate	_____
curiously	humility	_____

Y-blend in second syllable /j/ —two syllables

abuse	excuse	reviewed
accuse	excused	reviews
accused	Fairview	secure
acute	Grandview	secured
adieu	immune	Shoreview
amuse	impure	sun-cured
amused	impute	transfuse
Bayview	infuse	transmute
Bridge View	Lakeview	tribune
Clearview	menu	tribute
commute	preview	vacuum
compute	profuse	vacuumed
confuse	rebuke	volume
confused	rebuked	volumed
confute	refuge	volumes
Danube	refuse	Zebu
debut	refused	_____
defuse	refute	_____
depute	rescue	_____
effuse	rescued	_____
emu	review	_____

Y-blend in second syllable /j/ —three syllables

accusing	Bermuda	debutant
acuate	communal	document
amputate	commuter	excusing
amputee	commuting	genuine
amusement	computer	imputed
amusing	Confucius	infusion
annual	confusion	manual

Manuel	refugee	securing
peculiar	refusing	slide viewer
previewing	refuted	transfusion
profusely	refuting	tribunal
profusion	rescuing	Van Buren
profusive	reviewing	_____
rebuking	Samuel	_____

Y-blend in second syllable /j/ —four syllables

accumulate	community	refutative
acuity	genuinely	security
acupuncture	impunity	_____
amusement park	impurity	_____
communicate	refutation	_____

Y-blend in third syllable /j/ —three syllables

attribute	Harborview	overview
barbeque	interfuse	ridicule
Blue Danube	interview	Riverview
continue	malamute	scenic view
continued	manicure	vestibule
contribute	miniscule	_____
curlicue	Mountain View	_____
execute	Oceanview	_____

Y-blend in third syllable /j/ Medial—four syllables

barbecue chips	contribution	intramural
barbecue grill	distributed	intramurals
barbecue sauce	distributing	manicurist
barbecued steak	distribution	therapeutic
continual	evacuate	_____
continuing	evacuee	_____
continuous	evaluate	_____

NKY /nkj/ Medial—two syllables

junkyard	thank you	_____

NKY /nkj/ Medial—three syllables

thank-you card	thank-you note	_____

Z

Pronounced: /z/
Spelled: z, zz, s, ss, ssc, x

Z /z/ Initial—one syllable

czar	Zek	zoom
Zach	Zeke	zoomed
zag	Zen	zooms
zagged	zest	zounds
Zane	Zeus	_____
zap	zinc	_____
zapped	zing	_____
zax	zip	_____
zeal	zipped	_____
Zeb	zone	_____
Zed	zoned	_____
zee	zoo	_____

Z /z/ Initial—two syllables

xebec	zeta	zoom lens
zagging	zigzag	zoospore
zany	zillion	zoot suit
zapping	Zion	Zorro
Zardax	zip code	Zouave
zealot	zipper	Zulu
zealous	zipping	Zurich
zebra	zippy	zygote
zebu	zircon	_____
Zelda	zither	_____
zenith	Zoe	_____
zephyr	zombie	_____
zero	zonal	_____
zeroed	zone time	_____
zeros	zoning	_____
zestful	zooming	_____

Z /z/ Initial—three syllables

czarevitch	zebra fish	zodiac
czarevna	zeppelin	zonation
czarina	zero hour	zucchini
czarism	zeroing	Zululand
xylophone	zestfully	Zuyder Zee
Zachary	zigzagging	zymosis
Zambezi	zinc oxide	_____
Zambia	zinnia	_____
Zanzibar	zirconate	_____

Z /z/ Initial—four syllables

Zacharias	zoning permit	zootomy
Zamboanga	zoographer	Zoroaster
zeroing-in	zoography	zygomatic
zinciferous	zoologist	zymology
zirconium	zoology	_____

Z /z/ Medial—two syllables

asthma	cheesecake	desert
Aztec	cheesecloth	deserve
bazaar	cheesy	design
beeswax	chisel	desire
benzene	chosen	dessert
blazer	cleanser	diesel
blizzard	closes	disease
Boise	closet	dismal
brazen	clothesline	dissolve
brazier	clothespin	dizzy
Brazil	clumsy	doesn't
breezy	cosmic	dozen
bruiser	cosmos	dozing
business	cousin	drizzle
busy	cozy	drizzly
buzzard	crazy	easel
buzzer	cruiser	easement
buzzing	daisy	easy
Caesar	Daisy	enzyme
causeway	dazzle	Ezra

fizzle	miser	reserve
flimsy	Moses	reside
frazzle	Moslem	resign
freezer	music	resist
freezing	Muslim	resolve
frenzy	muslin	resort
frizzle	muzzle	resound
frowzy	nasal	result
frozen	newsprint	resume
fuzzy	newsreel	risen
gazelle	newsstand	rises
gazette	noisy	rising
gazing	nosebleed	Rosa
geyser	nosegay	rosin
gizzard	nosy	rosy
grizzly	nozzle	scissors
guzzle	observe	season
has-been	oozing	sizzle
hasn't	Ozzie	sleazy
hazard	pansy	sneezing
hazel	pheasant	spasm
Hazel	Pisa	squeezer
hazy	plaza	stanza
houses	pleasant	Susan
housing	poison	Susie
husband	posy	Suzanne
isn't	presence	teaser
jasmine	present	teasing
Kaiser	preserve	thousand
Kansas	presume	Thursday
laser	prison	tizzy
lazy	puzzle	treason
Lisbon	quasar	trouser
Liza	quizzer	Tuesday
lizard	raisin	tweezers
loser	raising	tweezing
lousy	razor	user
mazy	reason	visit
measles	resent	visor

wasn't	wisecrack	_____
weasel	wiser	_____
Wednesday	wizard	_____

Z /z/ Medial—three syllables

accusal	Gaza Strip	raspberry
accuser	gazebo	razorback
advisor	horizon	refusal
Alonzo	horned lizard	reprisal
amazing	imprison	requisite
Amazon	inasmuch	resemble
amusing	incisor	reservoir
artisan	Louisa	resident
azalea	magazine	residue
bonanza	mezzanine	résumé
bulldozer	misery	resurrect
busily	Missouri	Roosevelt
composer	museum	rosary
cosmetic	musical	sousaphone
deep freezer	music box	Susanna
deposit	music hall	teasingly
desertion	musician	trail blazer
disaster	newspaper	trapezoid
divisor	New Zealand	usable
easier	observing	visited
easiest	opposite	visiting
easily	physician	visitor
emblazon	position	_____
exquisite	president	_____
freezing point	prisoner	_____
fusible	quizzical	_____

Z /z/ Medial—four syllables

advertising	divisible	horizontal
advisable	Eisenhower	imprisonment
appetizer	Elizabeth	influenza
atomizer	fertilizer	inquisitive
desirable	fertilizing	invisible
diesel engine	gymnasium	Kalamazoo

miserable
miserably
Montezuma
observation
observership
poison ivy

preservable
preservation
reservation
resolution
seismologist
stabilizer

supervisor
vaporizer

_____

_____

_____

_____

Z /z/ Medial—five syllables

cosmopolitan
desirableness
dramatization
Elizabethan

lapis lazuli
Louisiana
mechanization
observatory

organization
Presbyterian

_____

_____

Z /z/ Final—one syllable

as
awes
bees
blaze
blows
blues
bows
boys
braise
breeze
browse
bruise
buys
buzz
cause
cheese
choose
chose
clause
close
clothes
clues
craze
crews
cries

crows
cruise
cues
days
daze
does
doze
draws
dries
dues
ease
eyes
fez
fizz
fleas
flows
freeze
fries
froze
fuse
fuzz
gauze
gaze
glaze
glows

goes
graze
grows
guise
has
Hayes
haze
he's
hose
Hughes
is
jays
jazz
joys
Kaz
keys
knees
laws
lies
Liz
lose
maize
mews
news
noise

nose	razz	those
ones	rise	threes
ooze	rose	ties
owes	Rose	toes
Oz	rouse	toys
pause	rows	trays
paws	says	trees
peas	seas	tries
phase	sees	twos
phrase	seize	use
pies	she's	views
plays	shoes	was
please	size	ways
poise	skies	weighs
pose	skis	wheeze
praise	sneeze	whizz
prize	snooze	whose
prose	spies	wise
quiz	squeeze	_____
raise	stews	_____
rays	tease	_____
raze	these	_____

Z /z/ Final—two syllables

ablaze	baptize	comas
accuse	bases	commas
advise	because	compose
agaze	blue cheese	comprise
always	blue eyes	confuse
amaze	blue jays	cookies
amuse	blue skies	Cortez
applause	bulldoze	cream cheese
appraise	Burmese	crochets
Aries	bylaws	deep freeze
arise	byways	defies
arose	carouse	defrays
arouse	chastise	degrees
arrows	Chavez	denies
babies	Chinese	despise

disclose
disease
disguise
dispose
dress shoes
echoes
enclose
enthuse
essays
excuse
expose
fire hose
first prize
French fries
glasses
grand prize
highrise
highways
house keys
Indies
judges

ladies
Lopez
Louise
missus
misuse
Mrs.
oppose
pieces
pillows
Pisces
play shoes
primrose
propose
red rose
refuse
repose
revise
sea breeze
series
sideways
sixes

snowshoes
South Seas
stories
Suez
sunrays
sunrise
suppose
surprise
sweetpeas
Swiss cheese
tacos
third prize
track shoes
transfuse
trapeze
Valdez
whereas

_____
_____
_____
_____

Z /z/ Final—three syllables

advertise
Alcatraz
ballet shoes
bananas
baseball shoes
beautifies
besieges
challenges
cheddar cheese
compromise
corduroys
criticize
dominos
downhill skis
dramatize
Eloise

empathize
emphasize
exercise
expressways
fantasize
garden hose
harmonize
immunize
iodize
Japanese
magnetize
marshmallows
mayonnaise
mechanize
memorize
merchandise

modernize
motorize
multiplies
nasalize
nurseries
organize
overseas
paralyze
potatoes
publicize
realize
recognize
Santa Claus
Santa Cruz
second prize
standardize

stereos	tennis shoes	water skis
sunglasses	theorize	World Series
supervise	tomatoes	wrestling shoes
sympathize	tragedies	yellow rose
synthesize	unionize	_____
systemize	Vera Cruz	_____

Z /z/ Final—four syllables

alphabetize	familiarize	refineries
analyses	generalize	secretaries
antagonize	initialize	societies
apologize	internalize	_____
basketball shoes	loganberries	_____
cross-country skis	musical chairs	_____

BZ /bz/ Final—one syllable

babes	garbs	rubs
bibs	gobs	sobs
cabs	grubs	stubs
clubs	hobs	subs
cobs	hubs	swabs
crabs	jibes	tabs
cribs	jobs	throbs
cubes	knobs	tribes
cubs	labs	tubes
dabs	lobes	tubs
debs	mobs	webs
dubs	nabs	_____
fibs	probes	_____
fobs	ribs	_____
gabs	robes	_____

BZ /bz/ Final—two syllables

bathrobes	doorknobs	ice cubes
bathtubs	earlobes	sand crabs
bear cubs	flashcubes	sea crabs
book clubs	girls' clubs	spareribs
boys' clubs	golf clubs	wolf cubs
cobwebs	health clubs	_____

ZD /zd/ Final—one syllable

braised	hosed	sized
brazed	paused	sneezed
breezed	phased	teased
caused	phrased	wheezed
closed	pleased	_____
dazed	posed	_____
eased	praised	_____
gazed	raised	_____
grazed	seized	_____

DZ /dz/ Final—one syllable

adds	leads	sides
aids	lids	sleds
beads	loads	slides
bids	modes	spades
codes	needs	speeds
creeds	nodes	suds
crowds	nods	tides
dads	odds	toads
deeds	odes	trades
fades	pads	wades
fads	pleads	wads
feeds	pods	weds
floods	raids	weeds
gods	reads	woods
goods	reds	_____
grades	rides	_____
guides	rids	_____
heads	roads	_____
hides	seeds	_____
kids	shades	_____
lads	sheds	_____

LDZ /ldz/ Final—one syllable

builds	molds	yields
fields	scalds	_____
folds	scolds	_____
holds	worlds	_____

GZ /gz/ Medial—two syllables

exact	exert	exist
exalt	exhaust	exult
exam	exhort	zigzag
exempt	exile	_____

GZ /gz/ Medial—three syllables

eczema	exemption	exhibit
exacting	exertion	existence
exaction	exertive	existent
exactly	exhaustion	exotic
examine	exhaustive	exultant
example	exhaustless	_____

GZ /gz/ Medial—four syllables

exactitude	exemplify	exorbitance
exaggerate	exemptible	exorbitant
examinant	exhaustible	exordium
examinate	exhibitive	exuberance
examinee	exhibitor	exuberant
exasperate	exhilarant	exuberate
executant	exhilarate	exultancy
executive	exhortation	exultation
executrix	existential	_____
exemplary	exonerate	_____

GZ /gz/ Medial—five syllables

exaggeration	executory	exonerator
exaggerative	exercitation	exorbitancy
exaggerator	exhibitory	exotically
examinable	exhilaration	exuberancy
examination	exhilarative	_____
exasperation	exoneration	_____

GZ /gz/ Final—one syllable

bags	cogs	gags
begs	digs	hogs
bogs	dogs	hugs
bugs	eggs	jigs

jogs	pegs	togs
kegs	pigs	tugs
lags	rags	wags
legs	rigs	wigs
logs	rogues	_____
lugs	rugs	_____
mugs	sags	_____
nags	tags	_____

LZ /lz/ Medial—two syllables

bailsman	salesman	_____
fool's cap	school zone	_____
fool's gold	_____	_____

LZ /lz/ Final—one syllable

aisles	foils	nails
bails	fools	oils
bales	fouls	pails
balls	frills	peals
bells	gales	piles
Bill's	gals	pills
bills	gills	poles
boils	goals	polls
bowls	grills	pools
calls	growls	pulls
Charles	gulls	quails
chills	hails	quills
coils	halls	rails
deals	heels	reels
dills	hills	roles
dolls	holes	rolls
drills	hulls	rules
eels	jails	sails
fails	kneels	sales
falls	males	scales
feels	meals	scowls
files	miles	seals
fills	mills	sells
foals	moles	shrills

sills
skills
skulls
smells
smiles
snails
snarls
soils
soles
souls
spells
spills
spoils

spools
squalls
squeals
stalls
stools
strolls
styles
tails
tales
tells
thrills
tiles
toils

tolls
tools
walls
wells
whales
wheels
wills
wools
yells
_____
_____
_____
_____

LZ /lz/ Final—two syllables

angels
annals
ant hills
barrels
baseballs
battles
bluebells
bottles
bundles
bushels
camels
candles
capsules
carols
cattails
cradles
cymbals
dawdles
details
dwellers
eggshells
equals
females
fiddles

finals
footballs
formals
fossils
fuels
gruels
handles
hymnals
jewels
kindles
ladles
middles
needles
nettles
noodles
paddles
petals
poodles
portholes
pretzels
prevails
profiles
propels
pupils

quarrels
quetzals
rascals
rattles
rebels
recalls
refills
rentals
reptiles
retails
reveals
riddles
rivals
roll calls
saddles
sandals
sawmills
scandals
seagulls
seashells
settles
signals
Sioux Falls
skittles

snowballs	tittles	tonsils
softballs	toadstools	towels
tadpoles	toddles	windmills
tattles	toenails	_____

LZ /lz/ Final—three syllables

aerials	cardinals	generals
animals	Cardinals	principals
annuals	carnivals	projectiles
axials	carousels	rehearsals
basketballs	casseroles	rituals
bass viols	cathedrals	spectacles
Blue Angels	coveralls	syllables
bookmobiles	enamels	utensils
burials	fairy tales	volleyballs
buttonholes	festivals	_____
cannonballs	fingernails	_____

LVZ /lvz/ Final—one syllable

delves	shelves	wolves
elves	solves	_____
selves	valves	_____

LVZ /lvz/ Final—two syllables

dissolves	ourselves	themselves
evolves	resolves	yourselves
involves	revolves	_____

MZ /mz/ Medial—two syllables

doomsday	Jamestown	time zone
groomsman	thumbs down	_____
helmsman	thumbs up	_____

MZ /mz/ Final—one syllable

beams	clams	crimes
bums	climbs	crumbs
calms	comes	deems
charms	crams	dimes
chimes	creams	dims

domes	James	rooms
dooms	jams	Sam's
drams	Jim's	seems
dreams	lambs	shames
drums	limbs	stems
flames	limes	sums
foams	looms	tames
fumes	palms	teams
games	Pam's	Thames
gems	psalms	themes
gums	rams	thumbs
gyms	reams	times
hams	Reims	trams
hems	rhymes	trims
homes	rims	_____
hums	roams	_____

MZ /mz/ Final—two syllables

Adams	daydreams	windchimes
assumes	exams	_____
bedrooms	schoolrooms	_____

NZ /nz/ Medial—two syllables

benzene	frenzy	_____
Bronze Age	Kansas	_____
clansman	Wednesday	_____

NZ /nz/ Final—one syllable

bans	clowns	gains
Benz	coins	grains
bins	cones	groans
bones	crowns	jeans
bronze	Dan's	lanes
buns	deans	lawns
canes	dines	leans
cans	drains	lines
chains	fans	loans
chins	fines	manes
cleans	fins	mines

moans	queens	thins
moons	rains	tins
Nan's	shines	tones
nines	shins	tons
nouns	signs	trains
pains	skins	tunes
pans	sons	twins
pens	spans	vans
phones	spins	vines
pines	spoons	wanes
pins	stains	wins
plains	stones	zones
planes	swans	_____
plans	tans	_____
prunes	teens	_____
puns	tens	_____

NZ /nz/ Final—two syllables

balloons	machines	ravens
batons	Marines	remains
blue jeans	mountains	retains
buttons	napkins	ribbons
cake pans	nations	robins
cartoons	notions	sevens
chickens	oceans	sidelines
complains	opens	soybeans
detains	outshines	swim fins
Great Plains	pecans	trombones
hailstones	pie pans	wagons
heavens	pigeons	_____
kitchens	platoons	_____
lions	puffins	_____

NDZ /ndz/ Final—one syllable

bends	grinds	mends
binds	hands	minds
ends	kinds	ponds
finds	lands	rends
glands	lends	rinds

sands	stands	_____
sends	tends	_____
sounds	winds	_____
spends	_____	_____

NGZ /ŋz/ Final—one syllable

bangs	pangs	things
brings	pings	tongs
fangs	rings	wings
gangs	sings	wrongs
gongs	songs	_____
hangs	stings	_____
kings	swings	_____

NGZ /ŋzz/ Final—two syllables

cravings	pavings	_____
drawings	savings	_____
paintings	_____	_____

RZ /rz/ Final—one syllable

airs	fairs	lures
bars	fares	mares
bears	fears	mars
blares	fires	Mars
blurs	firs	nears
bores	flares	oars
burrs	floors	ours
cares	fours	pairs
cars	furs	pears
chairs	gears	peers
cheers	glares	piers
choirs	hares	pores
chores	hears	pours
clears	heirs	purrs
corcs	hers	rears
dares	hires	roars
doors	hours	scares
ears	jars	scars
errs	jeers	scores

scours	sours	theirs
shares	spares	tires
shears	spars	tours
shirrs	spears	wares
shores	spurs	wars
sirs	squares	wears
slurs	stairs	wires
smears	stares	years
snares	stars	yours
snores	steers	_____
soars	stirs	_____
sores	tears	_____

RZ /rz/ Final—two syllables

admires	borders	dinners
affairs	boulders	dippers
allures	boxers	divers
altars	breakers	doctors
anchors	brokers	dollars
angers	builders	downstairs
answers	burners	drawers
antlers	buzzers	dressers
appears	callers	drivers
arbors	campers	drummers
aspires	campfires	empires
Azores	captors	errors
backfires	captures	explores
badgers	carvers	farmers
barbers	cashiers	fenders
batters	casters	fielders
bazaars	catchers	figures
beavers	cedars	fillers
beggars	checkers	filters
bidders	colors	fingers
binders	compares	fixtures
bleachers	crackers	Flanders
blisters	declares	flatcars
boilers	devours	flickers
bookstores	diners	fliers

flippers	powders	sparklers
flounders	powers	speakers
flowers	quarters	squad cars
founders	rangers	tankers
fractures	razors	tweezers
glaciers	readers	umpires
guitars	refers	upstairs
ignores	rivers	vampires
indoors	rockers	velours
lathers	rollers	vespers
matures	rompers	wafers
members	roosters	_____
minors	rulers	_____
molars	rumors	_____
movers	scissors	_____
odors	seashores	_____
outdoors	showers	_____
pillars	sisters	_____
pliers	slippers	_____
poplars	slivers	_____
posters	sneakers	_____

RZ /rz/ Final—three syllables

adventures	engineers	remainders
amateurs	erasers	reporters
ancestors	fasteners	sandpipers
announcers	firecrackers	screwdrivers
anteaters	foreigners	state troopers
beginners	horse lovers	studded tires
bystanders	leftovers	teenagers
calendars	loudspeakers	unawares
campaigners	managers	volunteers
candy bars	polar bears	_____
carpenters	professors	_____
carriers	propellers	_____
diapers	receivers	_____
dinosaurs	recorders	_____
disappears	recovers	_____
discovers	registers	_____

RDZ /rdz/ Final—one syllable

bards	gourds	yards
beards	guards	_____
birds	hoards	_____
boards	lords	_____
cards	towards	_____
chords	wards	_____
cords	words	_____

RDZ /rdz/ Final—two syllables

backyards	lifeguards	Spaniards
blackbirds	lizards	surfboards
bluebirds	orchards	timecards
buzzards	postcards	vineyards
clipboards	punch cards	wizards
cupboards	rear guards	_____
discards	rewards	_____
flashcards	score cards	_____
kick boards	shepherds	_____
leewards	skateboards	_____
leopards	songbirds	_____

RLZ /rlz/ Final—one syllable

Charles	pearls	whorls
curls	purls	_____
Earl's	snarls	_____
girls	swirls	_____
gnarls	twirls	_____
hurls	whirls	_____

RVZ /rvz/ Final—one syllable

carves	serves	_____
dwarves	starves	_____
nerves	turves	_____
scarves	wharves	_____

RVZ /rvz/ Final—two syllables

conserves	observes	_____
deserves	preserves	_____

THZ /ðz/ Final—one syllable

bathes	soothes	writhes
breathes	teethes	_____
loathes	tithes	_____
seethes	truths	_____
smoothes	wreathes	_____

VZ /vz/ Medial—two syllables

dove's nest	_____	_____
eavesdrop	_____	_____
thieves' den	_____	_____

VZ /vz/ Final—one syllable

beeves	grooves	raves
calves	groves	roves
caves	halves	salves
chives	hives	saves
cloves	hooves	shaves
coves	jives	shoves
craves	knaves	sieves
dives	knives	sleeves
doves	leaves	thrives
drives	lives	waves
eaves	loaves	weaves
fives	loves	wives
gives	moves	_____
gloves	paves	_____
graves	peeves	_____
grieves	proves	_____

ZER /zɚ/ Medial—three syllables

misery	_____	_____
observing	_____	_____
reservoir	_____	_____

ZER /zɚ/ Medial—four syllables

miserable	preservation	_____
miserably	reservation	_____
observation	_____	_____

ZER /zɚ/ Final—two syllables

blazer	geyser	riser
bruiser	hawser	squeezer
buzzer	laser	user
Caesar	loser	visor
cleanser	miser	Windsor
cruiser	quizzer	_____
freezer	razor	_____

ZER /zɚ/ Final—three syllables

accuser	deep freezer	_____
adviser	divisor	_____
bulldozer	incisor	_____
composer	trailblazer	_____

ZER /zɚ/ Final—four syllables

appetizer	polarizer	_____
atomizer	stabilizer	_____
fertilizer	vaporizer	_____

ZL /zl/ Final—two syllables

chisel	frizzle	nuzzle
damsel	fusil	puzzle
dazzle	grizzle	schnozzle
diesel	guzzle	sizzle
drizzle	Hazel	weasel
easel	muzzle	_____
fizzle	nasal	_____
frazzle	nozzle	_____

ZL /zl/ Final—three syllables

appraisal	embezzle	_____
arousal	refusal	_____
disposal	witch hazel	_____

ZH

Pronounced: /ʒ/
Spelled: si, g, s, z, zi

ZH /ʒ/ Initial—one syllable
Jacques
_____   _____

ZH /ʒ/ Initial—two syllables
jabot
Jacquerie
Joinville

ZH /ʒ/ Initial—three syllables
Jacques Bonhomme	Joinvile	
Javary	Jolivet	

ZH /ʒ/ Medial—two syllables
Asia	fusion	pleasure
azure	glazier	regime
bijou	Hoosier	seizure
bourgeois	leisure	treasure
brazier	lesion	version
closure	measure	vision
crosier	Persia	
crozier	Persian	

ZH /ʒ/ Medial—three syllables
abrasion	aversion	confusion
adhesion	casual	contusion
allusion	Caucasian	conversion
ambrosia	cohesion	corrosion
amnesia	collision	decision
aphasia	collusion	delusion
artesian	composure	derision
aspersion	conclusion	diffusion

disposure
diversion
division
elision
elusion
emersion
enclosure
envision
erasion
erosion
evasion
exclusion
excursion
explosion
exposure
fantasia

incision
inclosure
inclusion
intrusion
invasion
inversion
leisurely
measurement
measuring
obtrusion
occasion
Parisian
persuasion
precision
profusion
protrusion

provision
reclusion
remeasure
revision
seclusion
subversion
transfusion
treasurer
treasury
usual
usury
visual

_____
_____
_____
_____

ZH /ʒ/ Medial—four syllables

accusation
Asiatic
casually
disillusion
measurable
measuring cup

measuring tape
pleasurable
Polynesia
subdivision
supervision
television

unusual
usually
usurious
visualize

_____

ZH /ʒ/ Final—one syllable

beige
loge

luge
rouge

_____
_____

ZH /ʒ/ Final—two syllables

barrage
collage
corsage

garage
massage
menage

mirage
prestige

_____

ZH /ʒ/ Final—three syllables

Baton Rouge
bon voyage
camouflage
concierge

decoupage
entourage
fuselage
sabotage

_____
_____
_____
_____

638 • ZHER /ʒɚ/ Final—three syllables

ZHER /ʒɚ/ Medial—three syllables

azurite	measurement	treasury
glaziery	measuring	_____
leisurely	treasurer	_____

ZHER /ʒɚ/ Medial—four syllables

measuring cup	pleasurable	_____
measuring tape	Treasure Island	_____

ZHER /ʒɚ/ Final—two syllables

closure	pleasure	_____
leisure	treasure	_____
measure	_____	_____

ZHER /ʒɚ/ Final—three syllables

composure	exposure	_____
displeasure	foreclosure	_____
enclosure	remeasure	_____